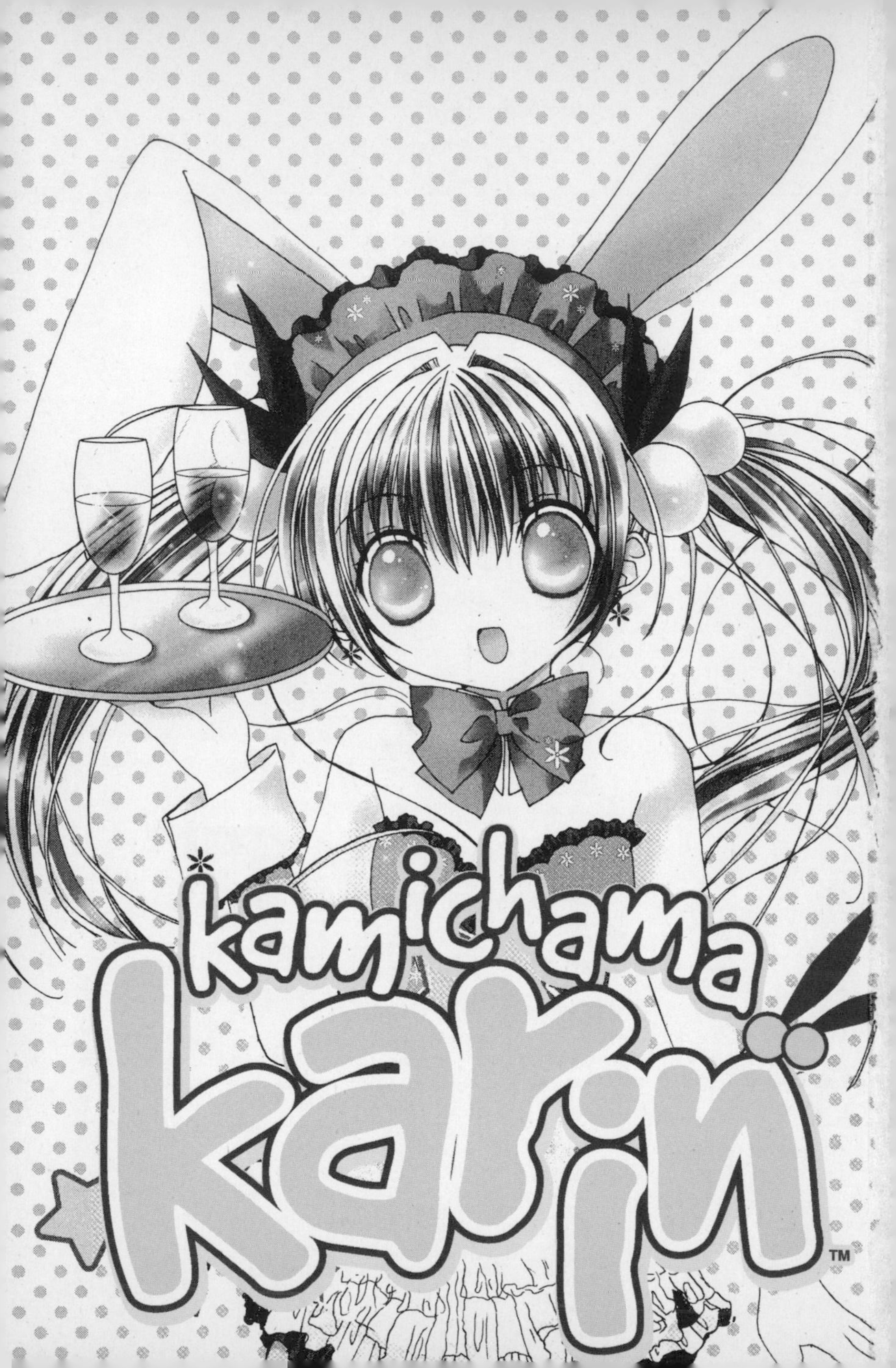
kamichama
karin™

Kamichama Karin Volume 7
Created by Koge-Donbo

Translation - Nan Rymer
English Adaptation - Lianne Sentar
Retouch and Lettering - Star Print Brokers
Production Artist - Jennifer Carbajal
Graphic Designer - James Lee

Editor - Carol Fox
Digital Imaging Manager - Chris Buford
Pre-Production Supervisor - Erika Terriquez
Art Director - Anne Marie Horne
Production Manager - Elisabeth Brizzi
Managing Editor - Vy Nguyen
VP of Production - Ron Klamert
Editor-in-Chief - Rob Tokar
Publisher - Mike Kiley
President and C.O.O. - John Parker
C.E.O. and Chief Creative Officer - Stuart Levy

A  Manga

TOKYOPOP Inc.
5900 Wilshire Blvd. Suite 2000
Los Angeles, CA 90036

E-mail: info@TOKYOPOP.com
Come visit us online at www.TOKYOPOP.com

ISBN: 978-1-59816-883-9

First TOKYOPOP printing: May 2007
10 9 8 7 6 5 4 3 2
Printed in the USA

kamichama karin™

Volume 7

Created by
Koge-Donbo

HAMBURG // LONDON // LOS ANGELES // TOKYO

Cast of Characters and Story Thus Far

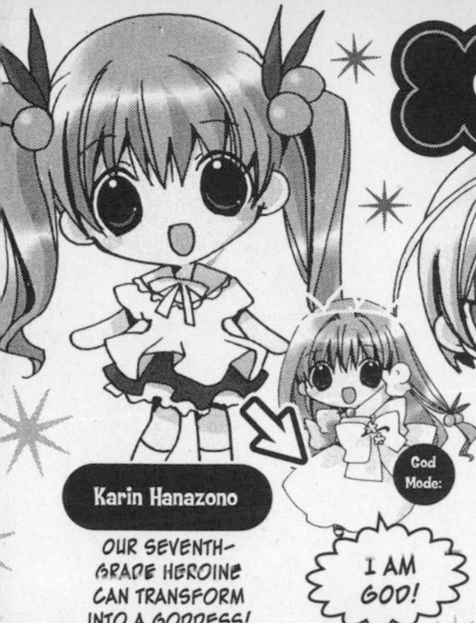
God Mode:
I AM GOD!

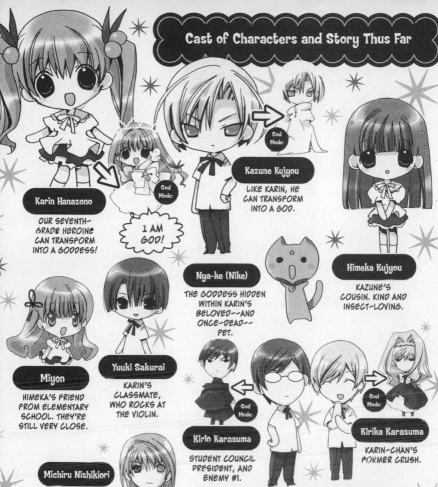

Karin Hanazono

OUR SEVENTH-GRADE HEROINE CAN TRANSFORM INTO A GODDESS!

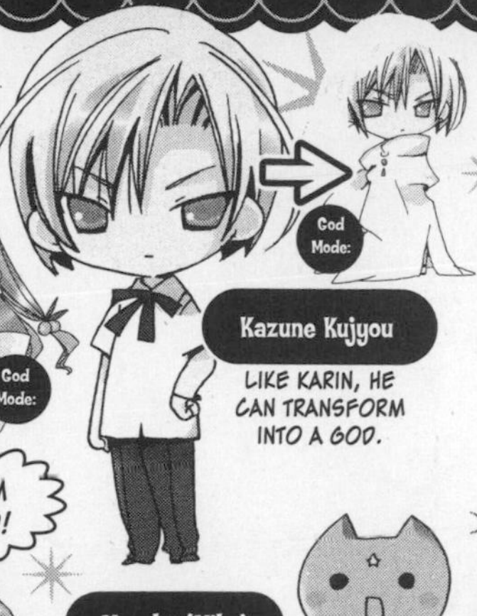
God Mode:

Kazune Kujyou

LIKE KARIN, HE CAN TRANSFORM INTO A GOD.

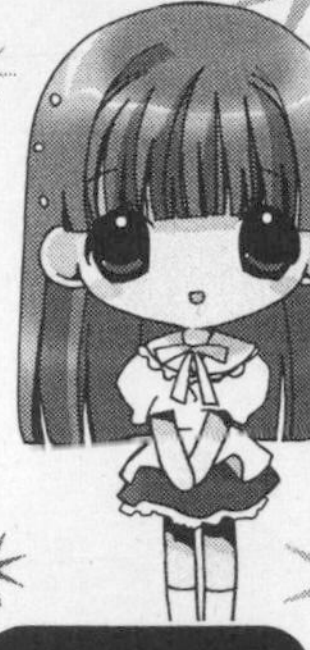

Himeka Kujyou

KAZUNE'S COUSIN. KIND AND INSECT-LOVING.

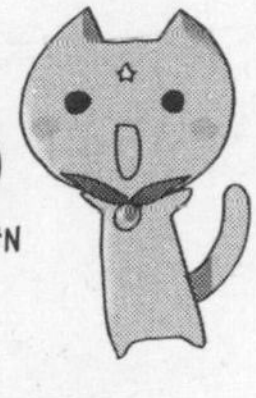

Nya-ke (Nike)

THE GODDESS HIDDEN WITHIN KARIN'S BELOVED--AND ONCE-DEAD--PET.

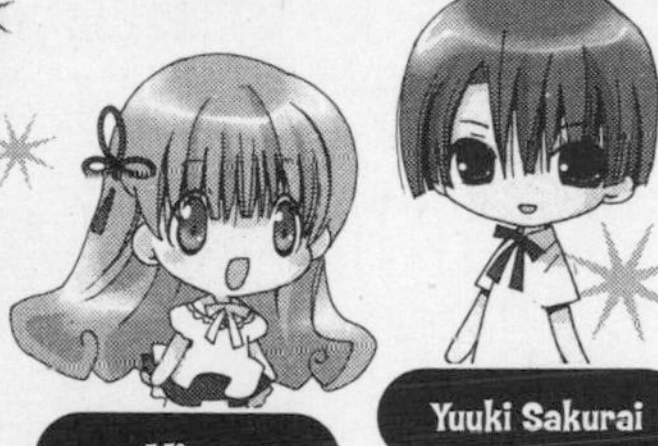

Miyon

HIMEKA'S FRIEND FROM ELEMENTARY SCHOOL. THEY'RE STILL VERY CLOSE.

Yuuki Sakurai

KARIN'S CLASSMATE, WHO ROCKS AT THE VIOLIN.

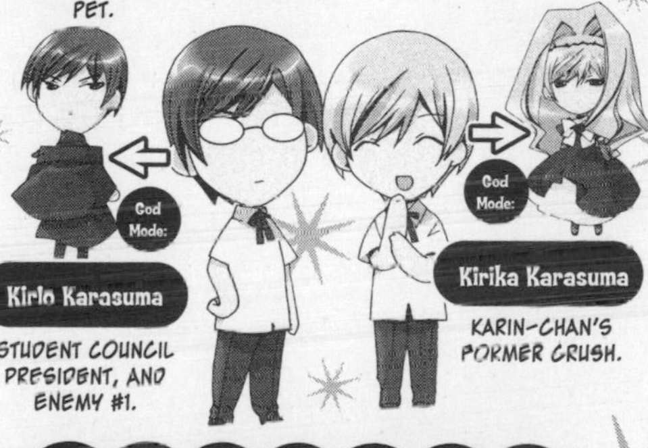
God Mode:
God Mode:

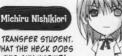

Kirio Karasuma

STUDENT COUNCIL PRESIDENT, AND ENEMY #1.

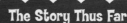

Kirika Karasuma

KARIN-CHAN'S FORMER CRUSH.

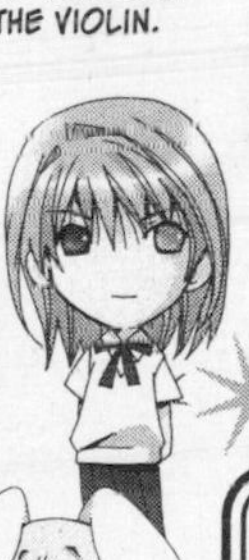

Michiru Nishikiori

A TRANSFER STUDENT. WHAT THE HECK DOES THIS GUY KNOW?!

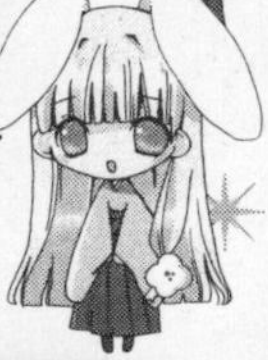

Kazusa

SHE'S INTRODUCED HERSELF TO KIRIKA, BUT WHO IS SHE REALLY?

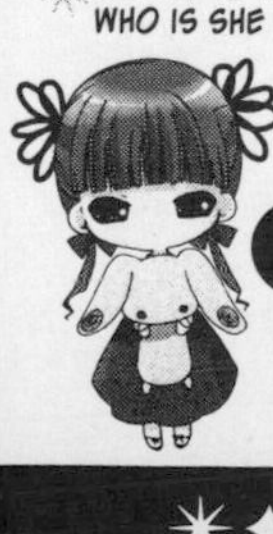

Himeka

ANOTHER HIMEKA WHO LIVES WITH KIRIO AND KIRIKA.

The Story Thus Far

KARIN HANAZONO, A TROUBLED ORPHAN GRANTED DIVINE POWERS BY A RING LEFT BY HER PARENTS, HAS FINALLY COME HEAD-TO-HEAD WITH DESTINY. HER ROMANTIC FEELINGS FOR MICHIRU AND KAZUNE--BOTH OF WHOM HAVE KISSED HER--HAVE THROWN KARIN INTO A STATE OF CONFUSION AS THE STAKES OF THE FINAL FIGHT ARE RAISED! MICHIRU IS PREPARING TO USE HIS POWERS, KAZUNE CLAIMS THAT DESTROYING THE RINGS WILL HEAL BOTH HIMEKAS, AND KARASUMA HAS TARGETED KARIN'S CLASSMATE YUUKI FOR SOME MYSTERIOUS, NEFARIOUS PLOT! AND IF ALL THAT WEREN'T ENOUGH, KAZUNE'S FAILING HEALTH CAUSED HIM TO COLLAPSE AFTER DESTROYING KARASUMA'S RING. ALONE IN THE RAIN, KARIN HAS SWORN TO SAVE HIM...

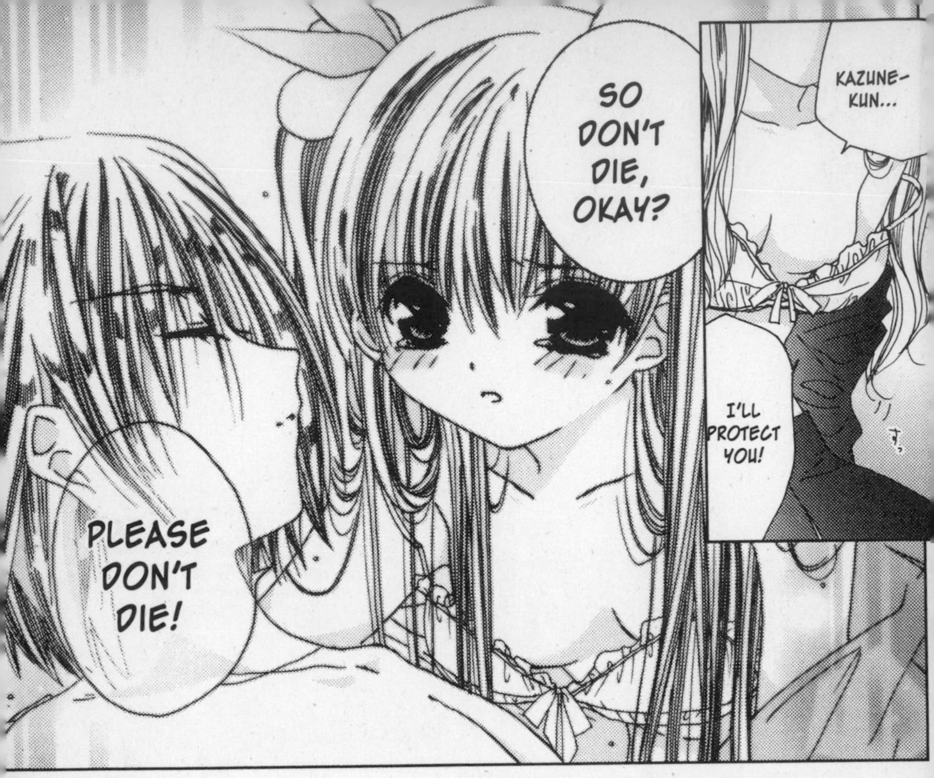
KAZUNE-KUN...
I'LL PROTECT YOU!
SO DON'T DIE, OKAY?
PLEASE DON'T DIE!

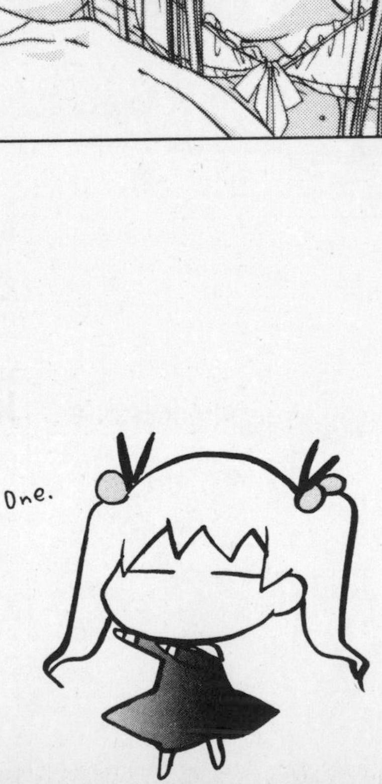
One.

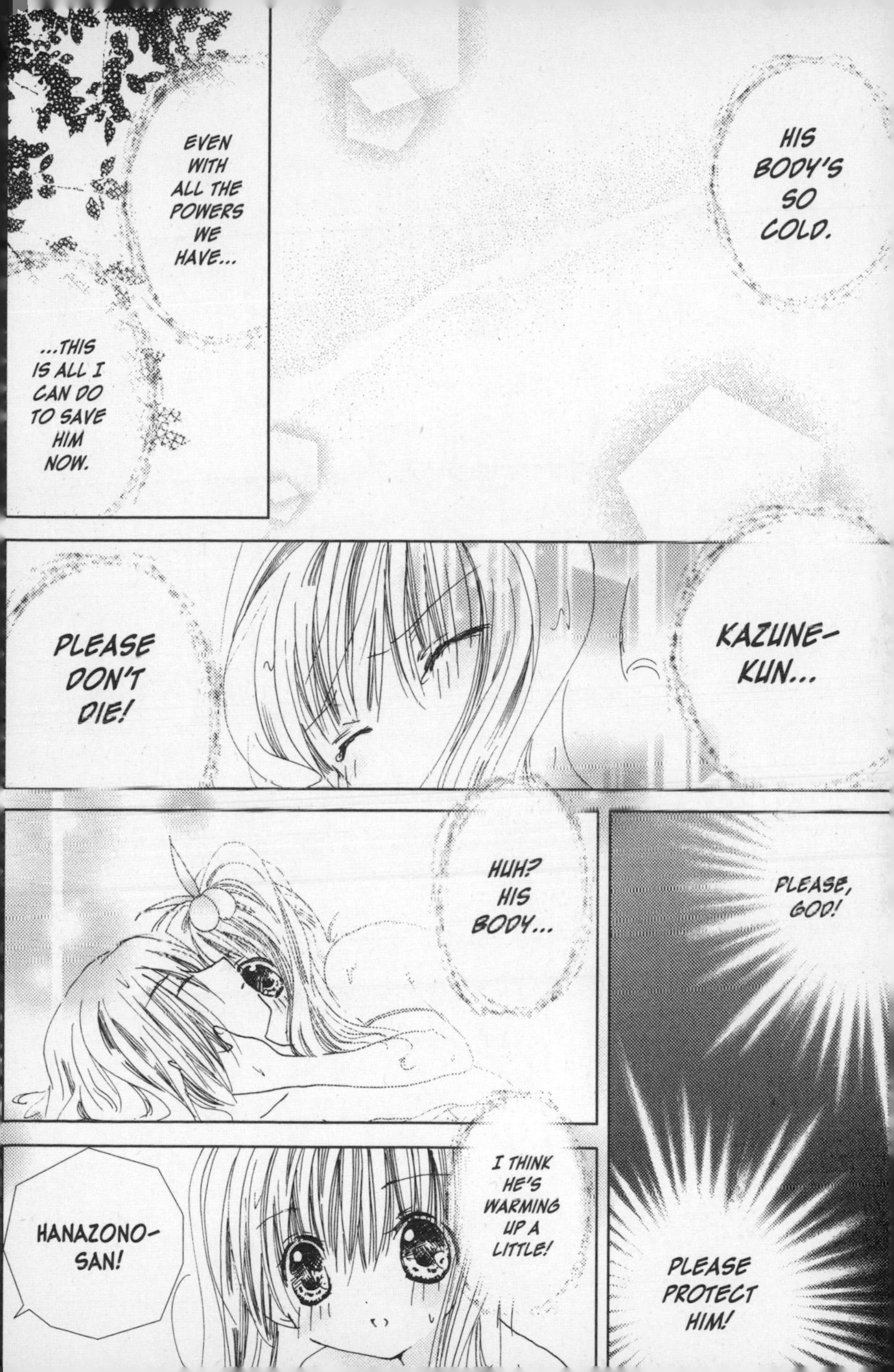
HIS BODY'S SO COLD.
EVEN WITH ALL THE POWERS WE HAVE...
...THIS IS ALL I CAN DO TO SAVE HIM NOW.
KAZUNE-KUN...
PLEASE DON'T DIE!
PLEASE, GOD!
PLEASE PROTECT HIM!
HUH? HIS BODY...
I THINK HE'S WARMING UP A LITTLE!
HANAZONO-SAN!

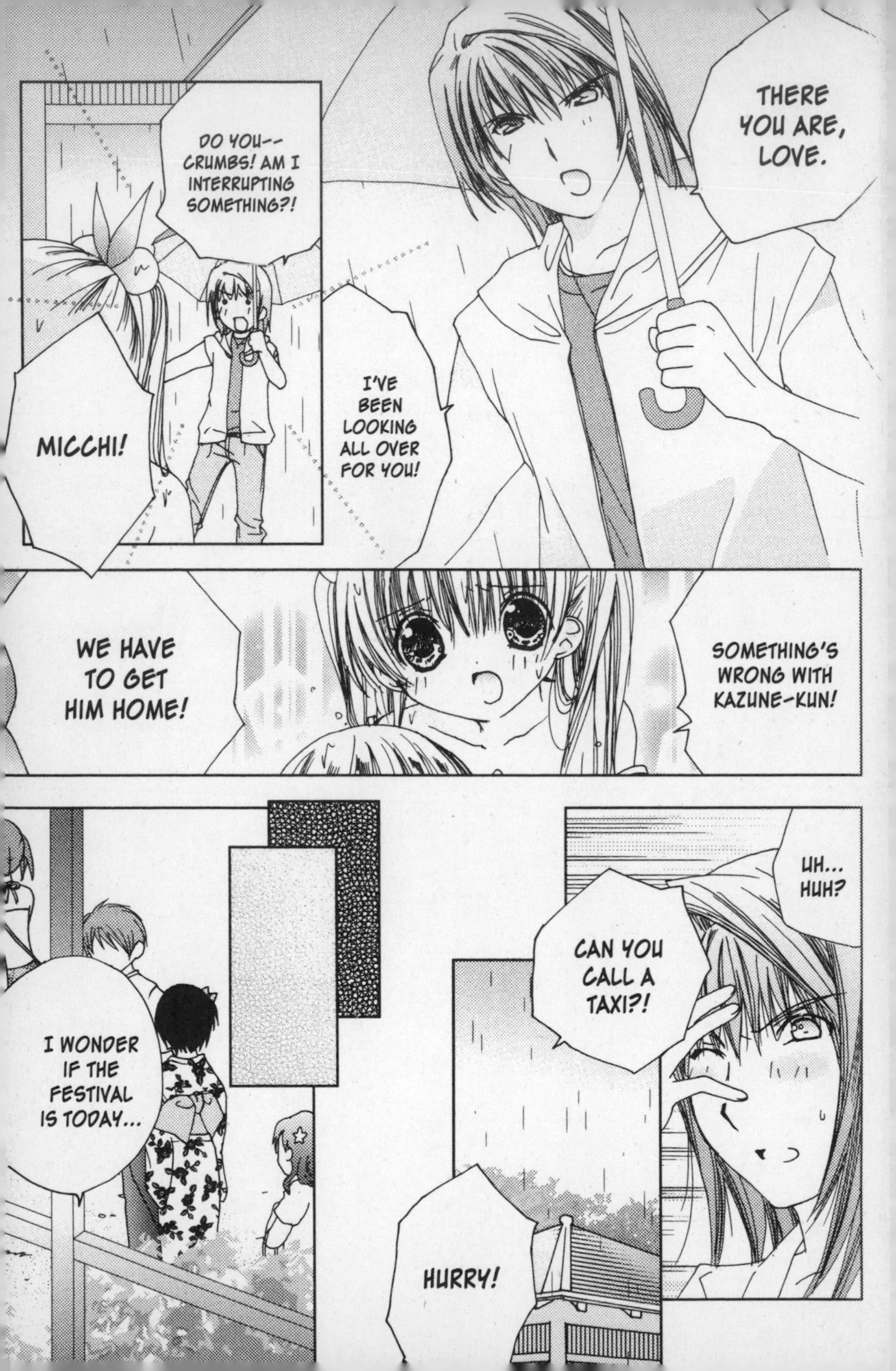
THERE YOU ARE, LOVE.
I'VE BEEN LOOKING ALL OVER FOR YOU!
DO YOU-- CRUMBS! AM I INTERRUPTING SOMETHING?!
MICCHI!
SOMETHING'S WRONG WITH KAZUNE-KUN!
WE HAVE TO GET HIM HOME!
UH... HUH?
CAN YOU CALL A TAXI?!
HURRY!
I WONDER IF THE FESTIVAL IS TODAY...

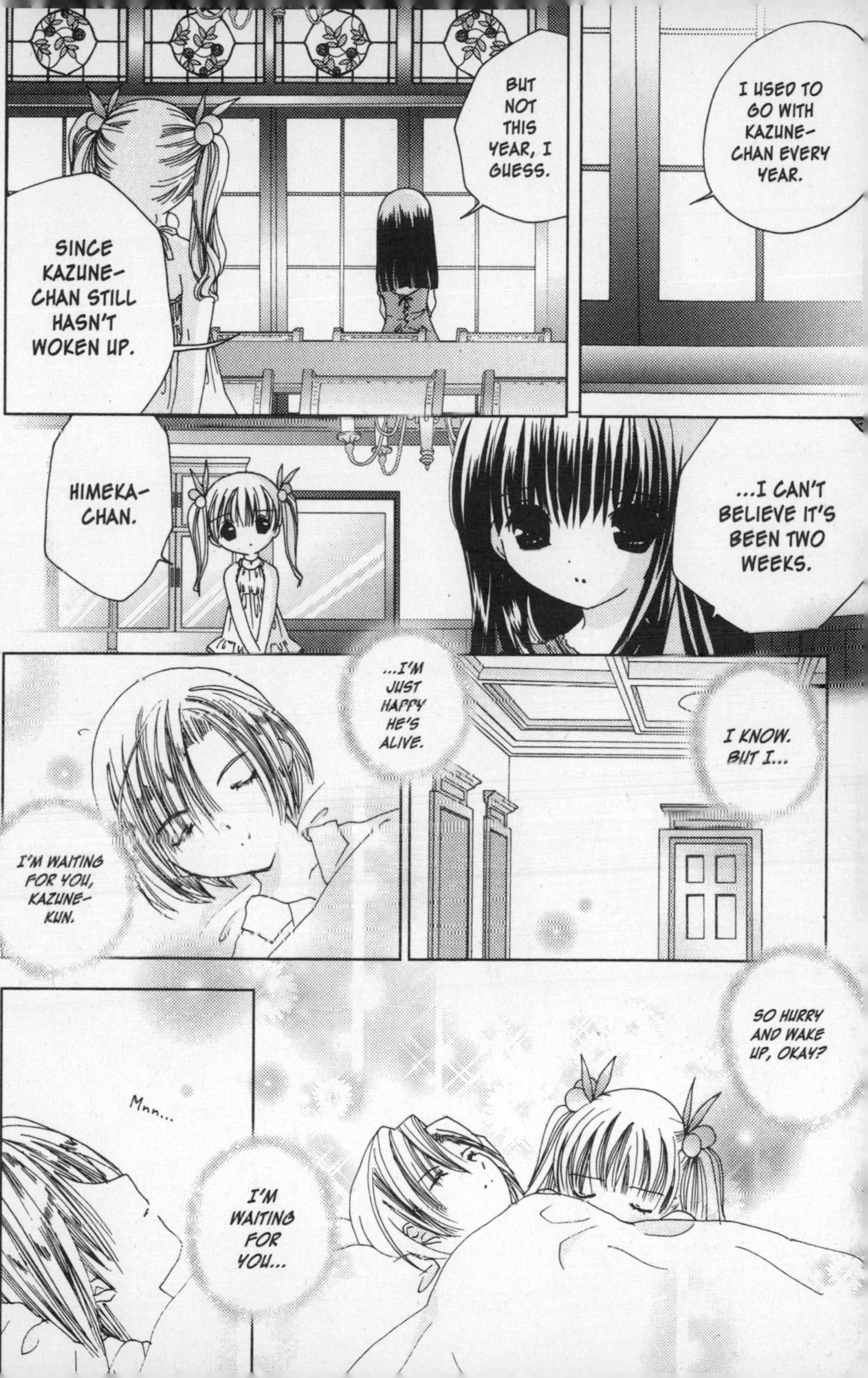
I USED TO GO WITH KAZUNE-CHAN EVERY YEAR.
BUT NOT THIS YEAR, I GUESS.
SINCE KAZUNE-CHAN STILL HASN'T WOKEN UP.
...I CAN'T BELIEVE IT'S BEEN TWO WEEKS.
HIMEKA-CHAN.
I KNOW. BUT I...
...I'M JUST HAPPY HE'S ALIVE.
I'M WAITING FOR YOU, KAZUNE-KUN.
SO HURRY AND WAKE UP, OKAY?
Mnn...
I'M WAITING FOR YOU...

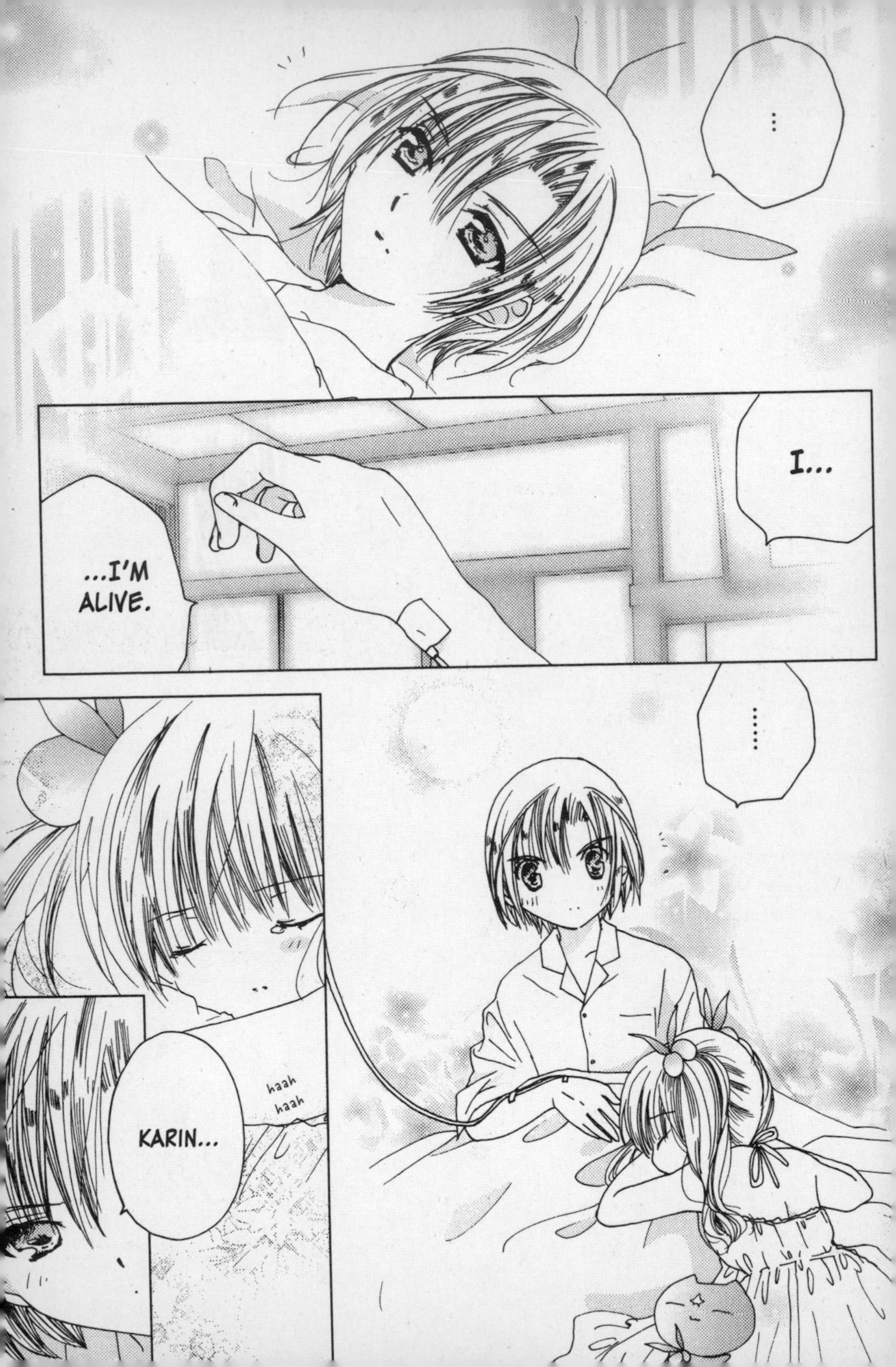
...
I...
...I'M ALIVE.
......
haah haah
KARIN...

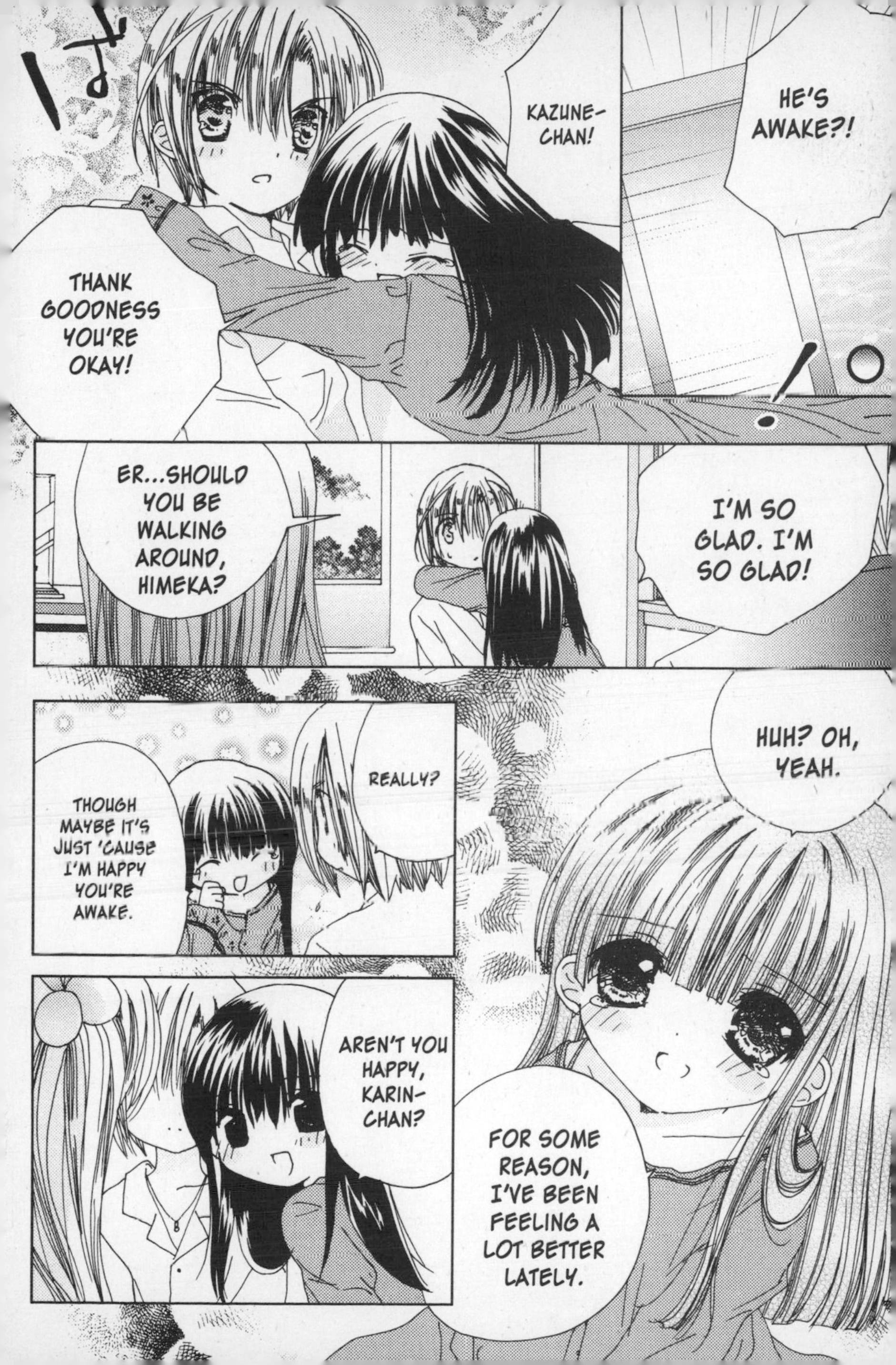
HE'S AWAKE?!
ぱ
KAZUNE-CHAN!
THANK GOODNESS YOU'RE OKAY!
I'M SO GLAD. I'M SO GLAD!
ER...SHOULD YOU BE WALKING AROUND, HIMEKA?
HUH? OH, YEAH.
FOR SOME REASON, I'VE BEEN FEELING A LOT BETTER LATELY.
REALLY?
THOUGH MAYBE IT'S JUST 'CAUSE I'M HAPPY YOU'RE AWAKE.
AREN'T YOU HAPPY, KARIN-CHAN?

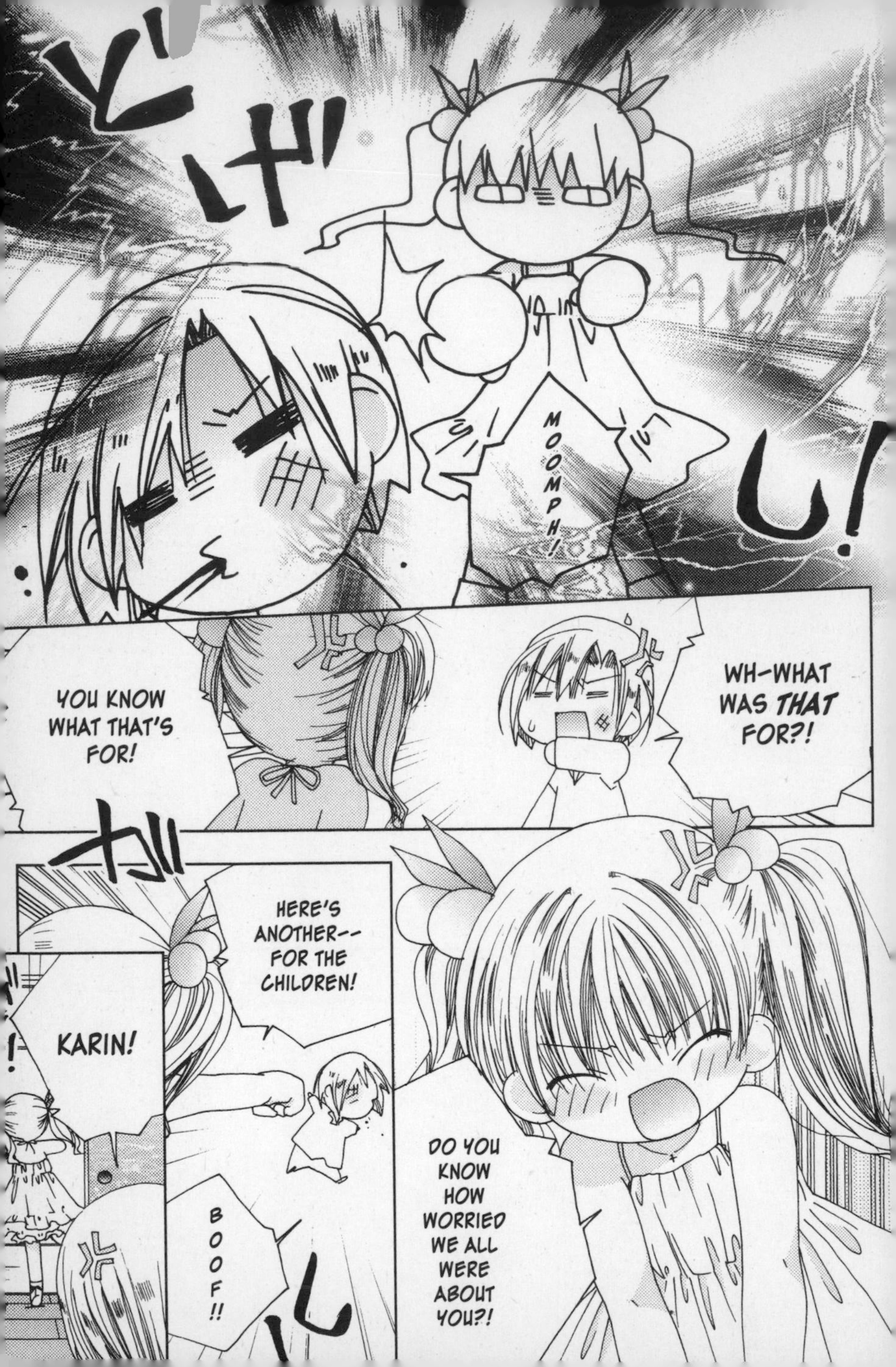
MOOMPH!
WH-WHAT WAS *THAT* FOR?!
YOU KNOW WHAT THAT'S FOR!
DO YOU KNOW HOW WORRIED WE ALL WERE ABOUT YOU?!
HERE'S ANOTHER-- FOR THE CHILDREN!
BOOF!!
KARIN!

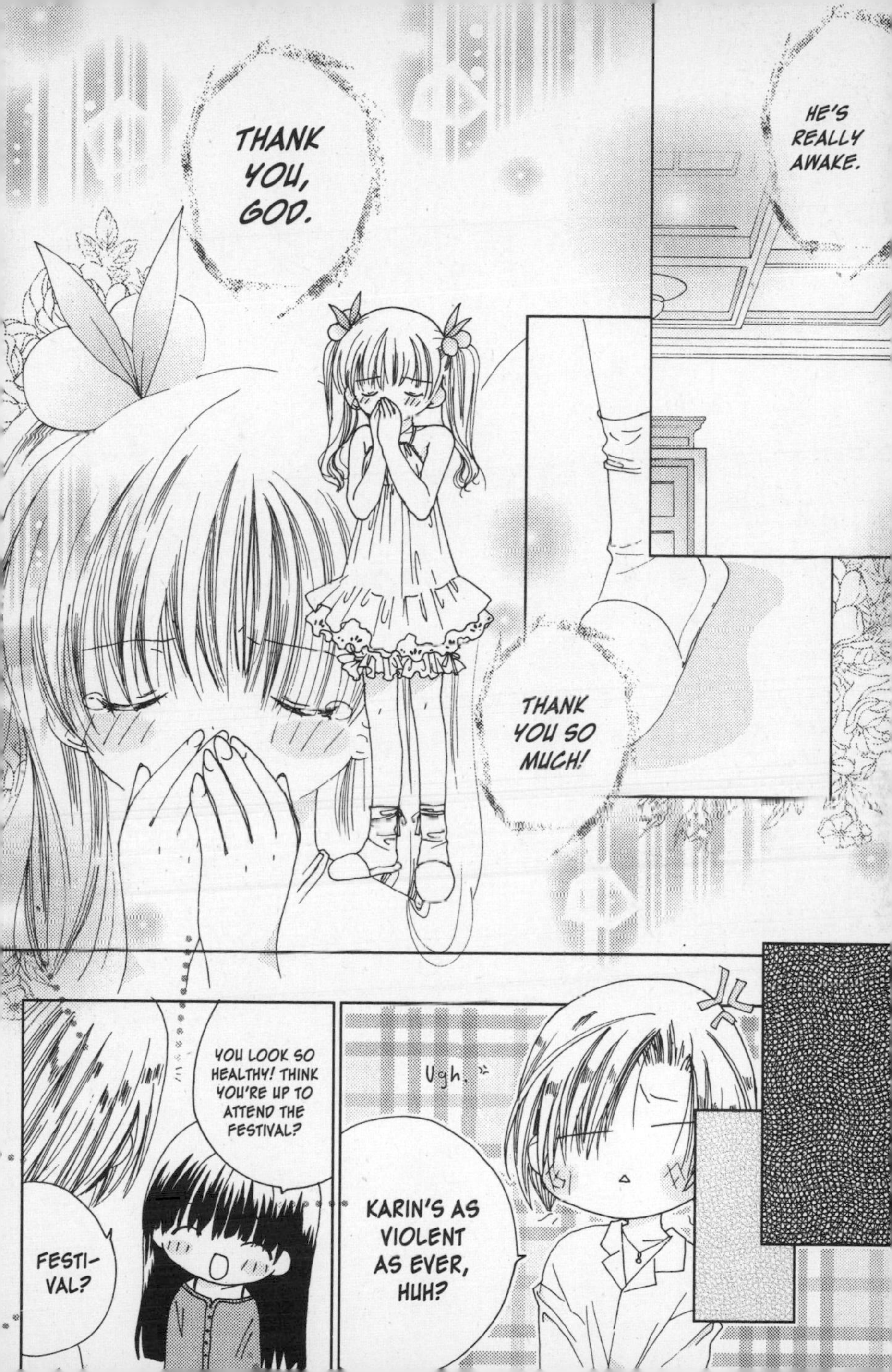
HE'S REALLY AWAKE.
THANK YOU SO MUCH!
THANK YOU, GOD.
Ugh.
KARIN'S AS VIOLENT AS EVER, HUH?
YOU LOOK SO HEALTHY! THINK YOU'RE UP TO ATTEND THE FESTIVAL?
FESTI-VAL?

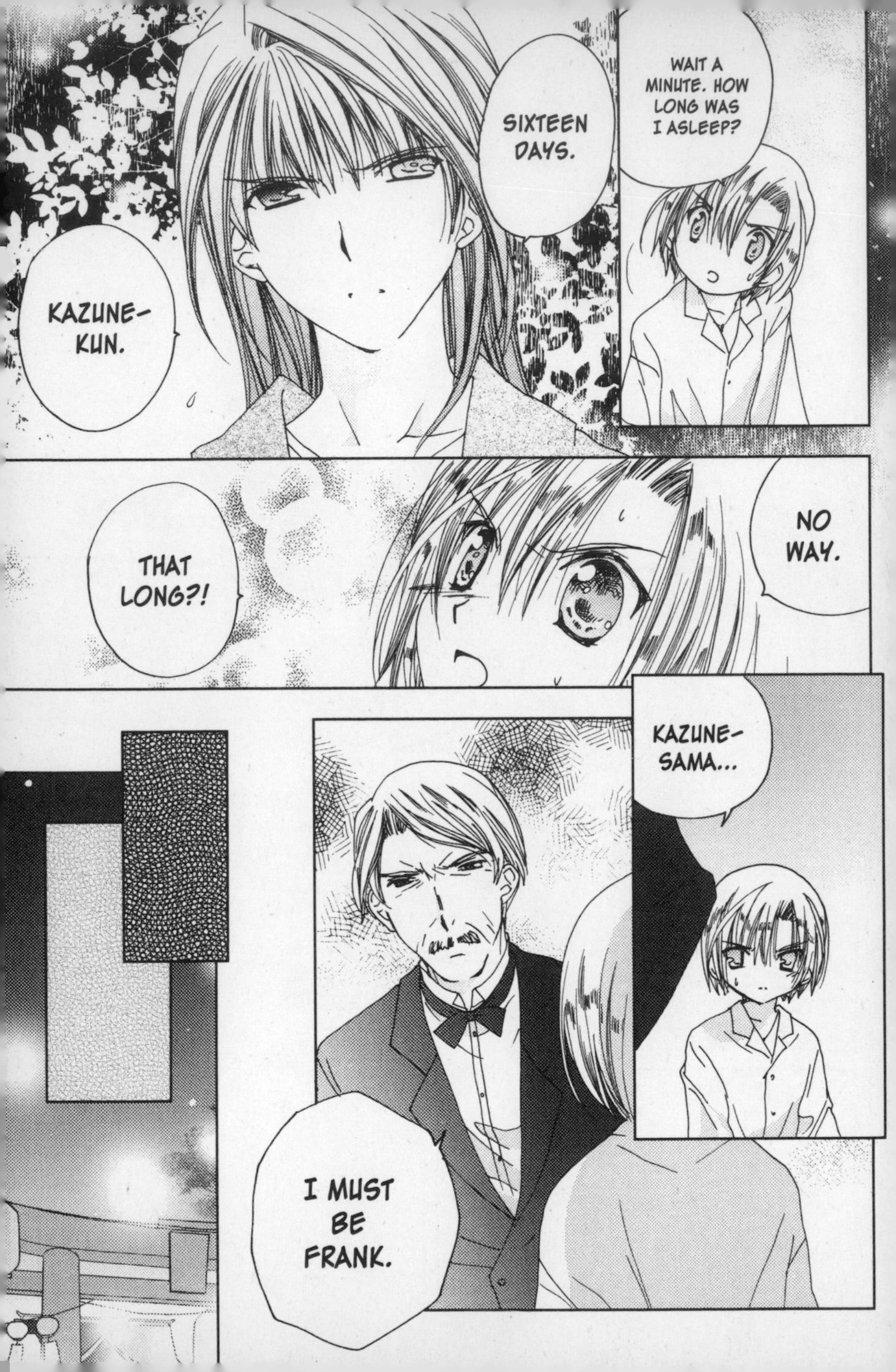
WAIT A MINUTE. HOW LONG WAS I ASLEEP?
SIXTEEN DAYS.
KAZUNE-KUN.
NO WAY.
THAT LONG?!
KAZUNE-SAMA...
I MUST BE FRANK.

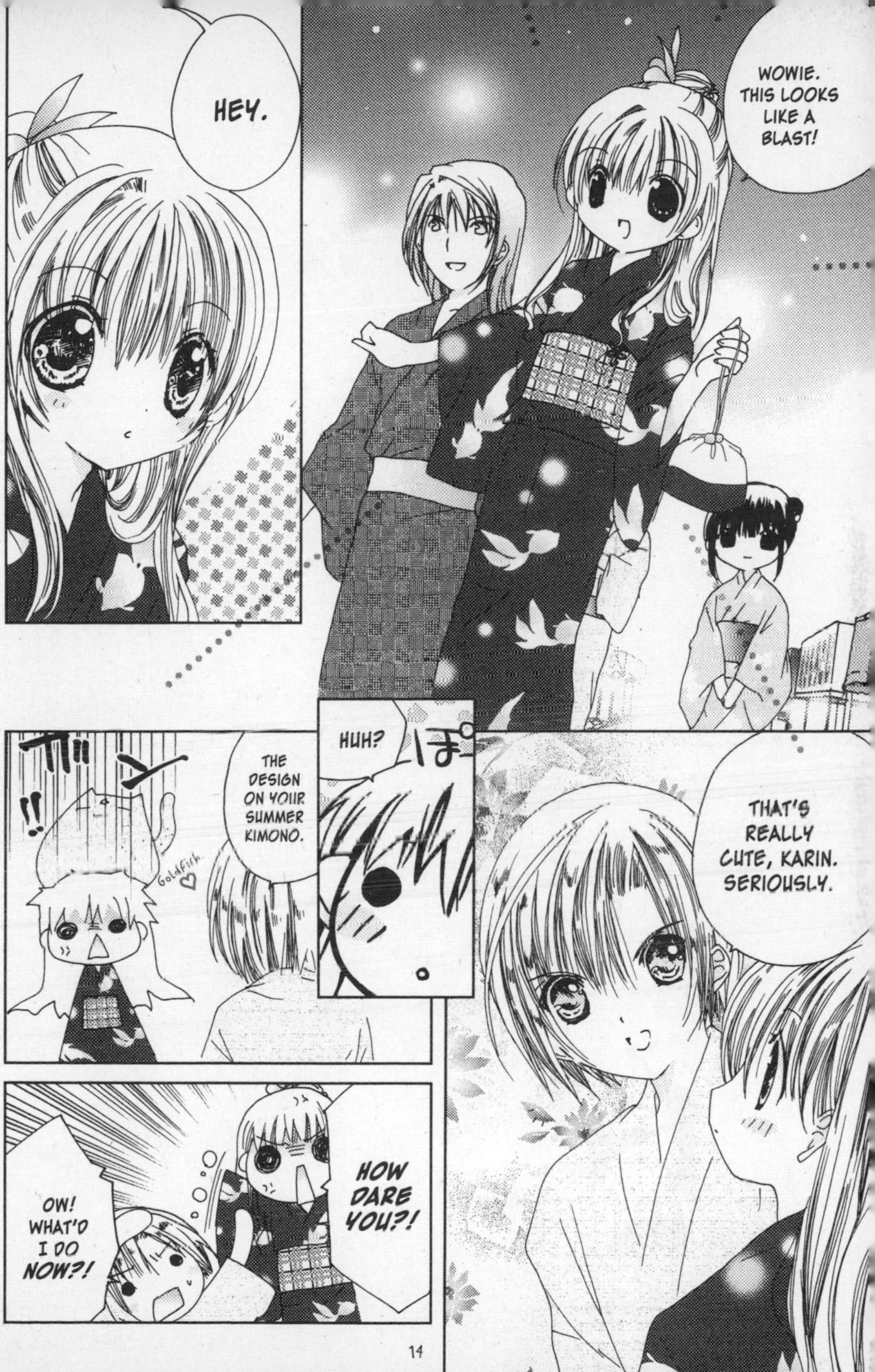
WOWIE. THIS LOOKS LIKE A BLAST!
HEY.
THAT'S REALLY CUTE, KARIN. SERIOUSLY.
HUH?
ぽ
THE DESIGN ON YOUR SUMMER KIMONO.
Goldfish ♡
HOW DARE YOU?!
OW! WHAT'D I DO NOW?!

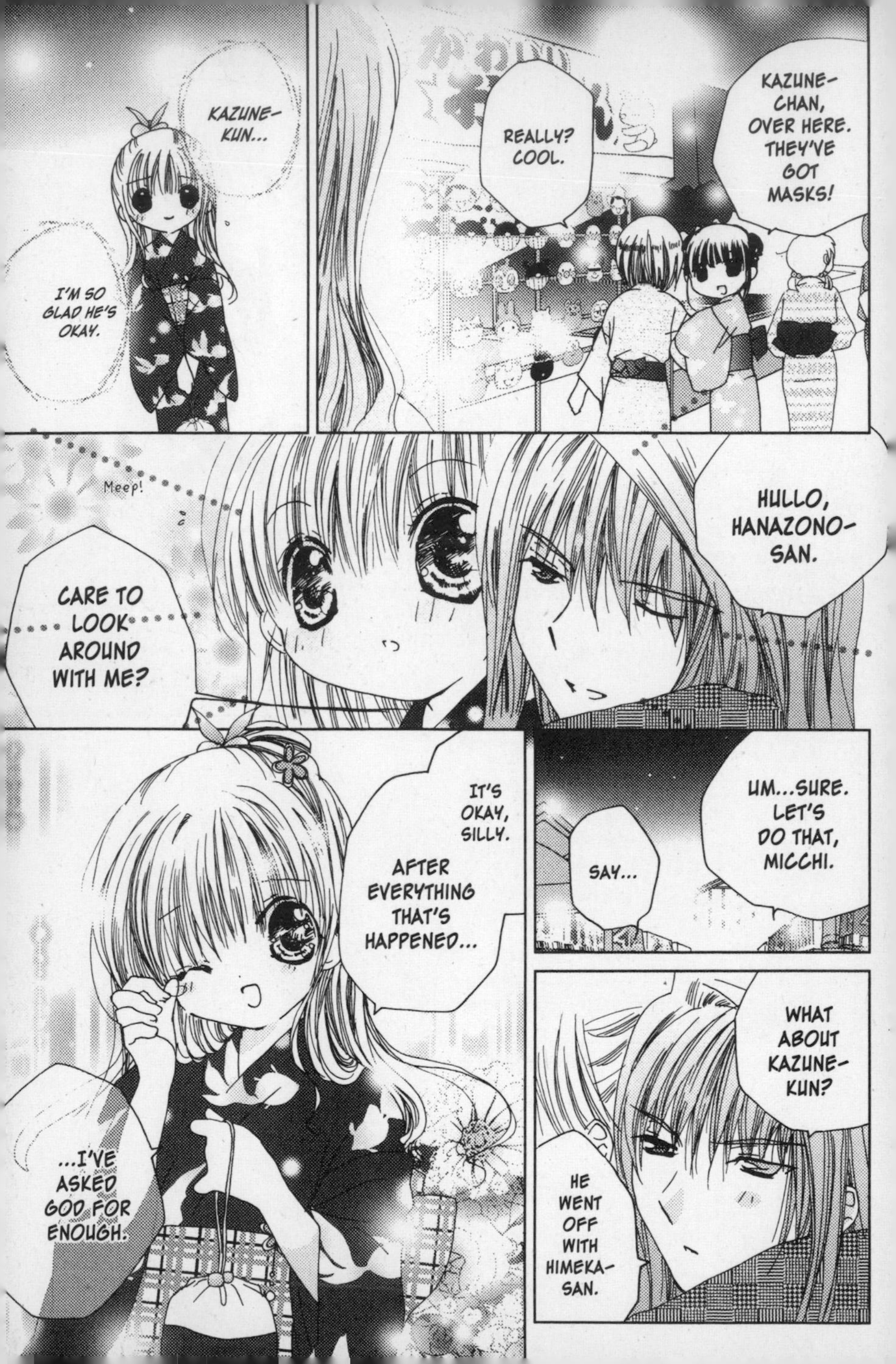
KAZUNE-CHAN, OVER HERE. THEY'VE GOT MASKS!
REALLY? COOL.
KAZUNE-KUN...
I'M SO GLAD HE'S OKAY.
HULLO, HANAZONO-SAN.
Meep!
CARE TO LOOK AROUND WITH ME?
UM...SURE. LET'S DO THAT, MICCHI.
SAY...
WHAT ABOUT KAZUNE-KUN?
HE WENT OFF WITH HIMEKA-SAN.
IT'S OKAY, SILLY.
AFTER EVERYTHING THAT'S HAPPENED...
...I'VE ASKED GOD FOR ENOUGH.

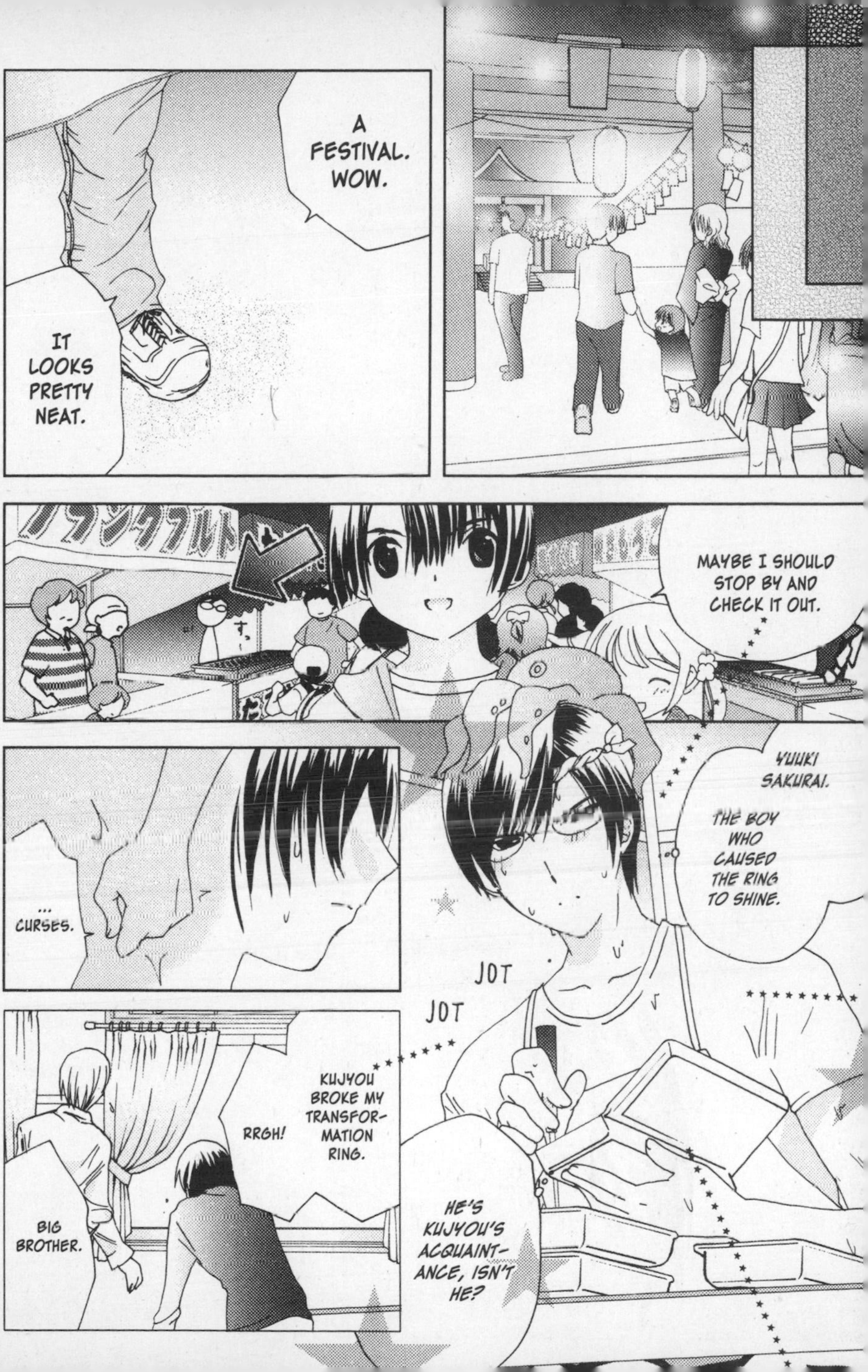
A FESTIVAL. WOW.
IT LOOKS PRETTY NEAT.
MAYBE I SHOULD STOP BY AND CHECK IT OUT.
YUUKI SAKURAI.
THE BOY WHO CAUSED THE RING TO SHINE.
JOT
JOT
HE'S KUJYOU'S ACQUAINT-ANCE, ISN'T HE?
... CURSES.
KUJYOU BROKE MY TRANSFOR-MATION RING.
RRGH!
BIG BROTHER.

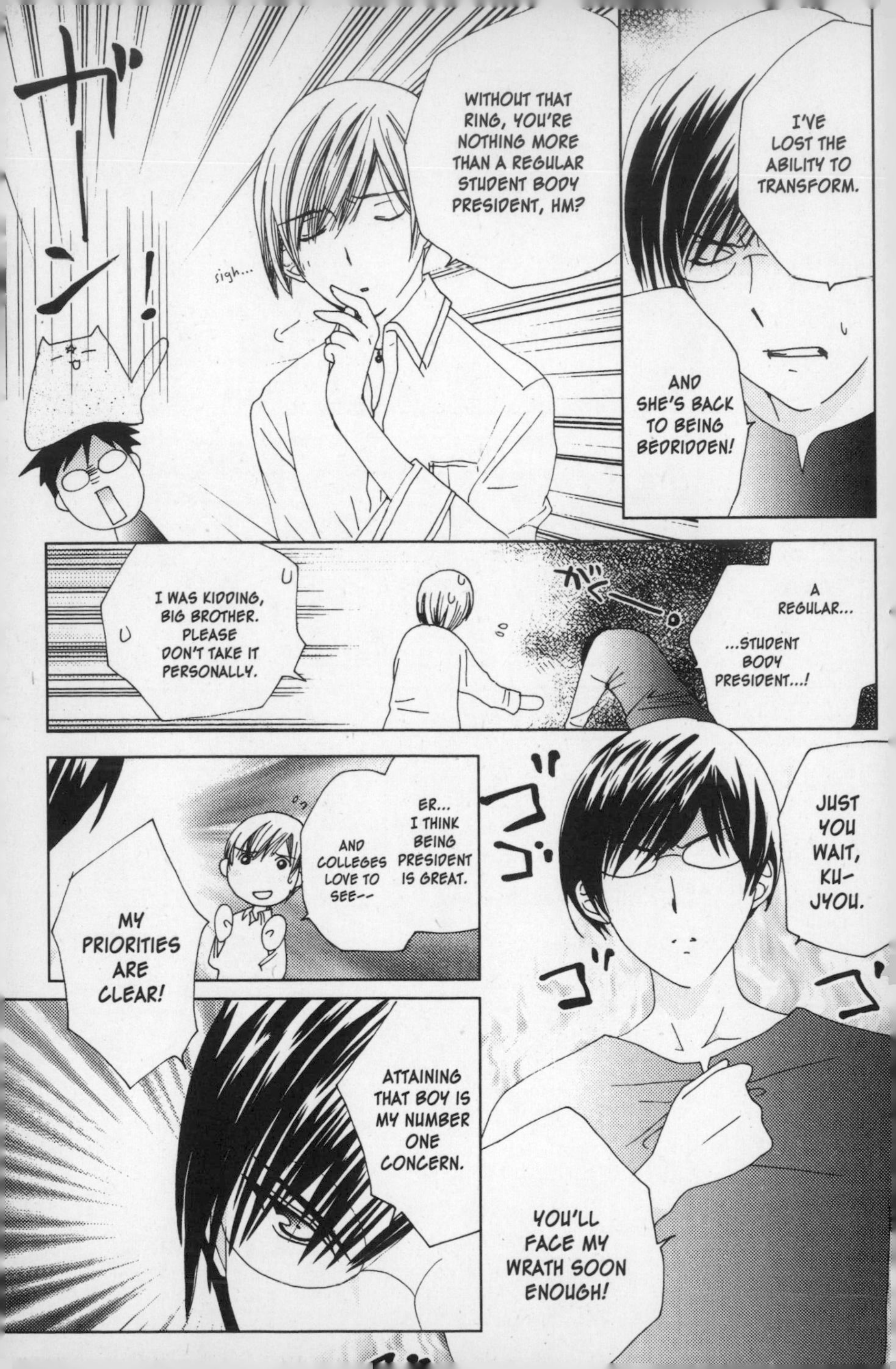
I'VE LOST THE ABILITY TO TRANSFORM.
AND SHE'S BACK TO BEING BEDRIDDEN!
WITHOUT THAT RING, YOU'RE NOTHING MORE THAN A REGULAR STUDENT BODY PRESIDENT, HM?
sigh...
ガーン!
A REGULAR...
...STUDENT BODY PRESIDENT...!
I WAS KIDDING, BIG BROTHER. PLEASE DON'T TAKE IT PERSONALLY.
JUST YOU WAIT, KU-JYOU.
YOU'LL FACE MY WRATH SOON ENOUGH!
ER... I THINK BEING PRESIDENT IS GREAT.
AND COLLEGES LOVE TO SEE--
MY PRIORITIES ARE CLEAR!
ATTAINING THAT BOY IS MY NUMBER ONE CONCERN.

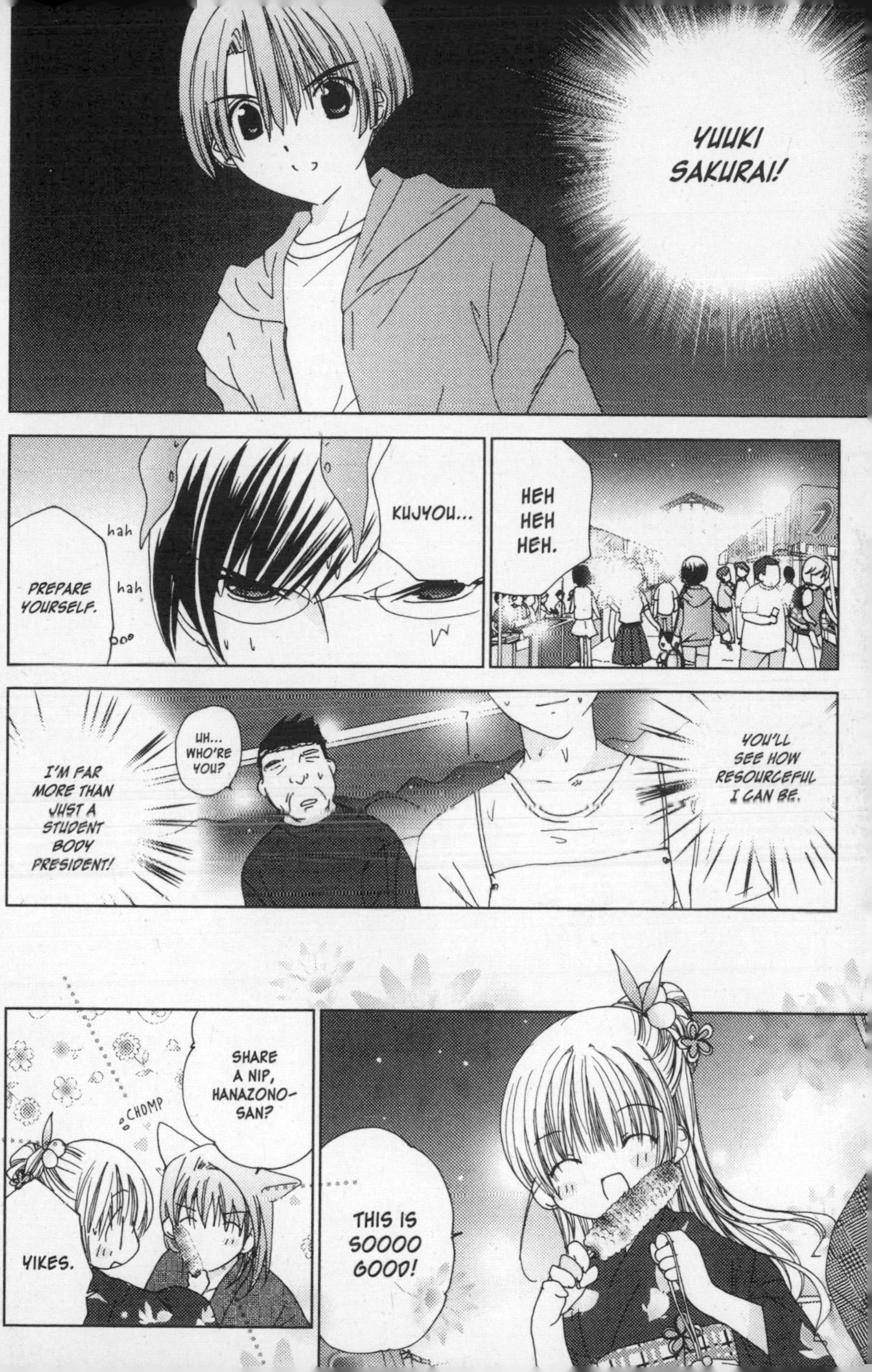
YUUKI SAKURAI!
HEH HEH HEH.
KUJYOU...
hah
hah
PREPARE YOURSELF.
YOU'LL SEE HOW RESOURCEFUL I CAN BE.
UH... WHO'RE YOU?
I'M FAR MORE THAN JUST A STUDENT BODY PRESIDENT!
THIS IS SOOOO GOOD!
SHARE A NIP, HANAZONO-SAN?
CHOMP
YIKES.

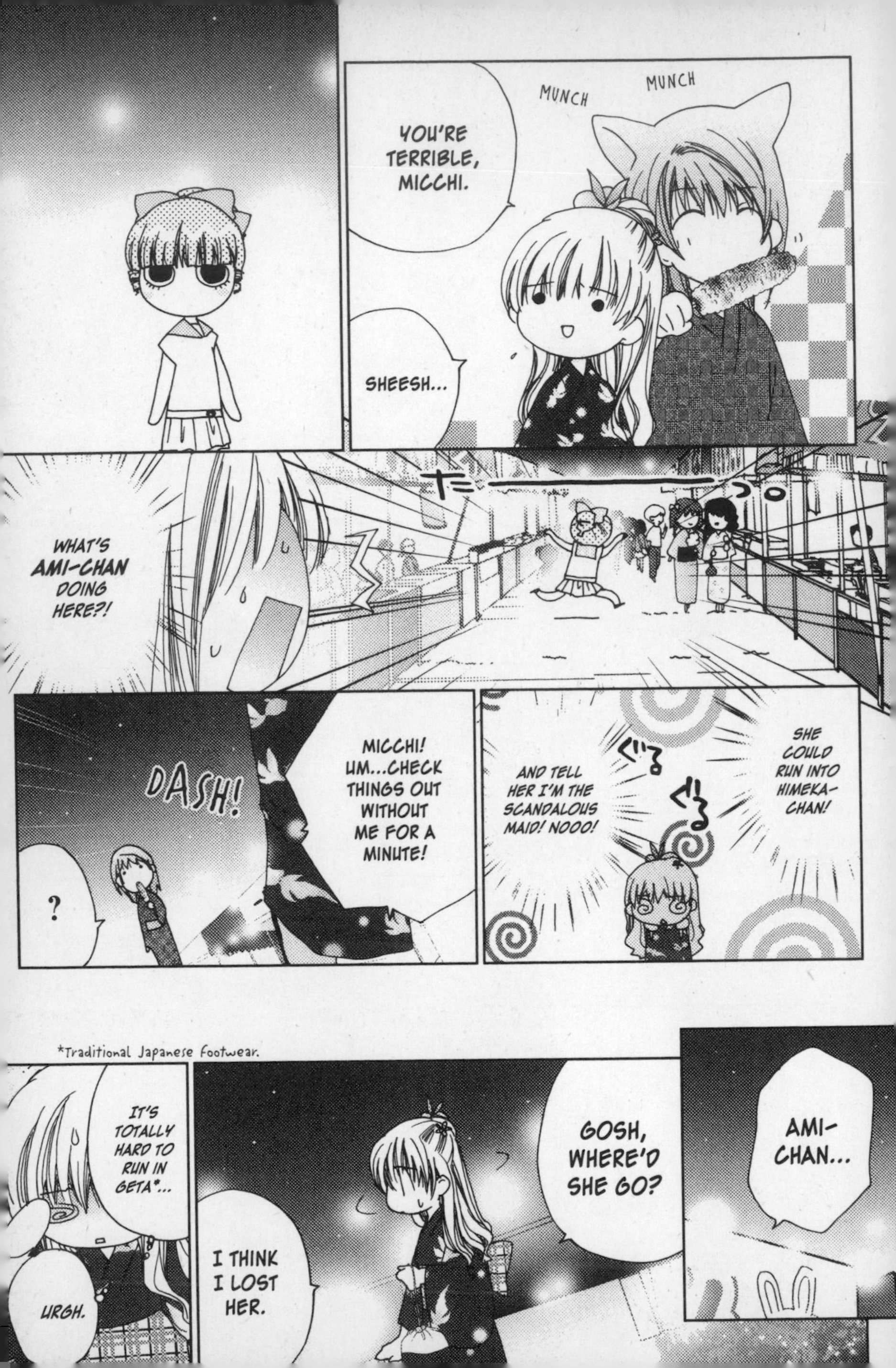
MUNCH
MUNCH
YOU'RE TERRIBLE, MICCHI.
SHEESH...
WHAT'S AMI-CHAN DOING HERE?!
SHE COULD RUN INTO HIMEKA-CHAN!
AND TELL HER I'M THE SCANDALOUS MAID! NOOO!
ぐる
ぐる
MICCHI! UM...CHECK THINGS OUT WITHOUT ME FOR A MINUTE!
DASH!
?
AMI-CHAN...
GOSH, WHERE'D SHE GO?
I THINK I LOST HER.
IT'S TOTALLY HARD TO RUN IN GETA*...
URGH.

*Traditional Japanese footwear.

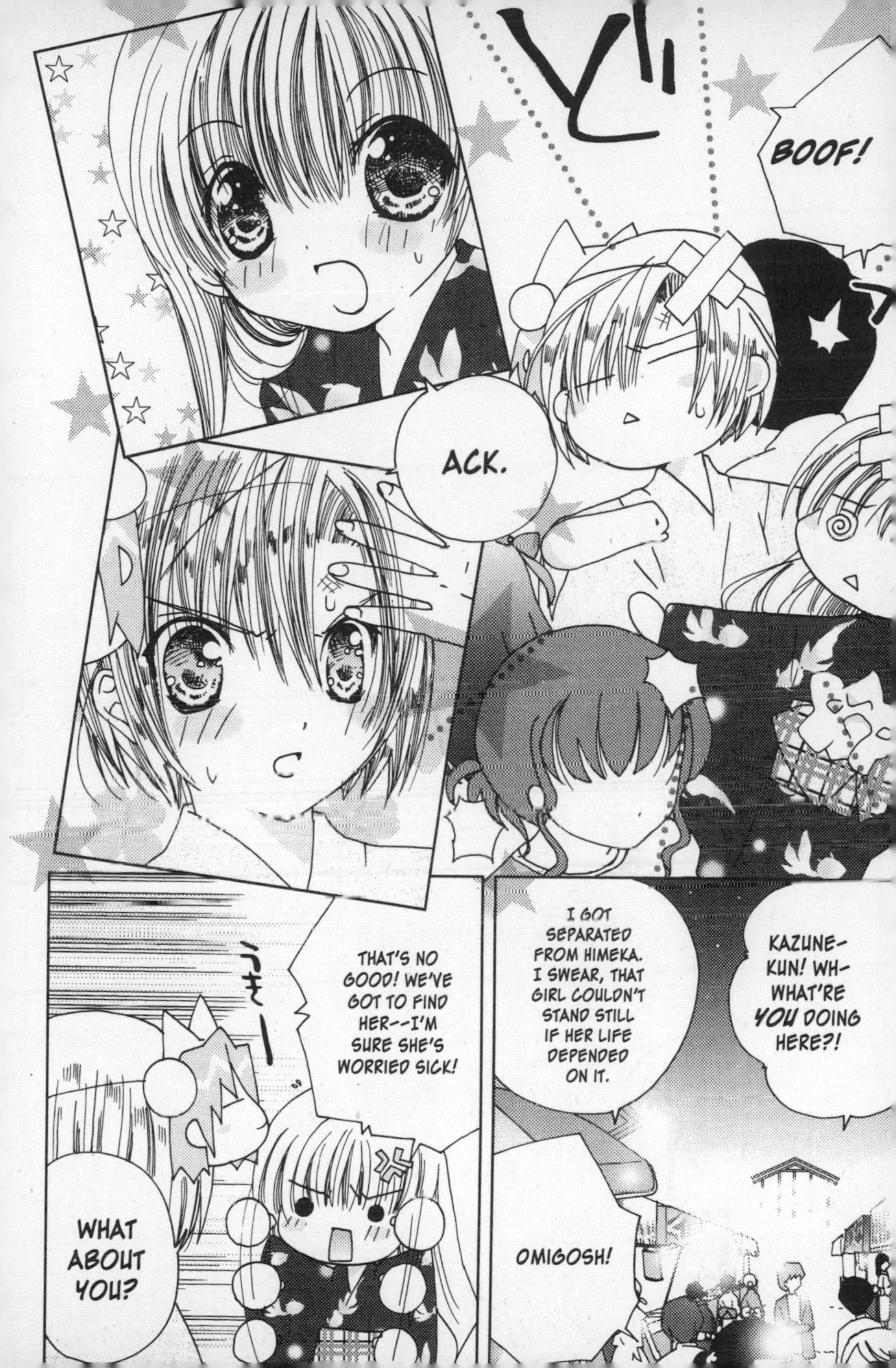
BOOF!
ACK.
KAZUNE-KUN! WH-WHAT'RE *YOU* DOING HERE?!
I GOT SEPARATED FROM HIMEKA. I SWEAR, THAT GIRL COULDN'T STAND STILL IF HER LIFE DEPENDED ON IT.
OMIGOSH!
THAT'S NO GOOD! WE'VE GOT TO FIND HER--I'M SURE SHE'S WORRIED SICK!
WHAT ABOUT YOU?

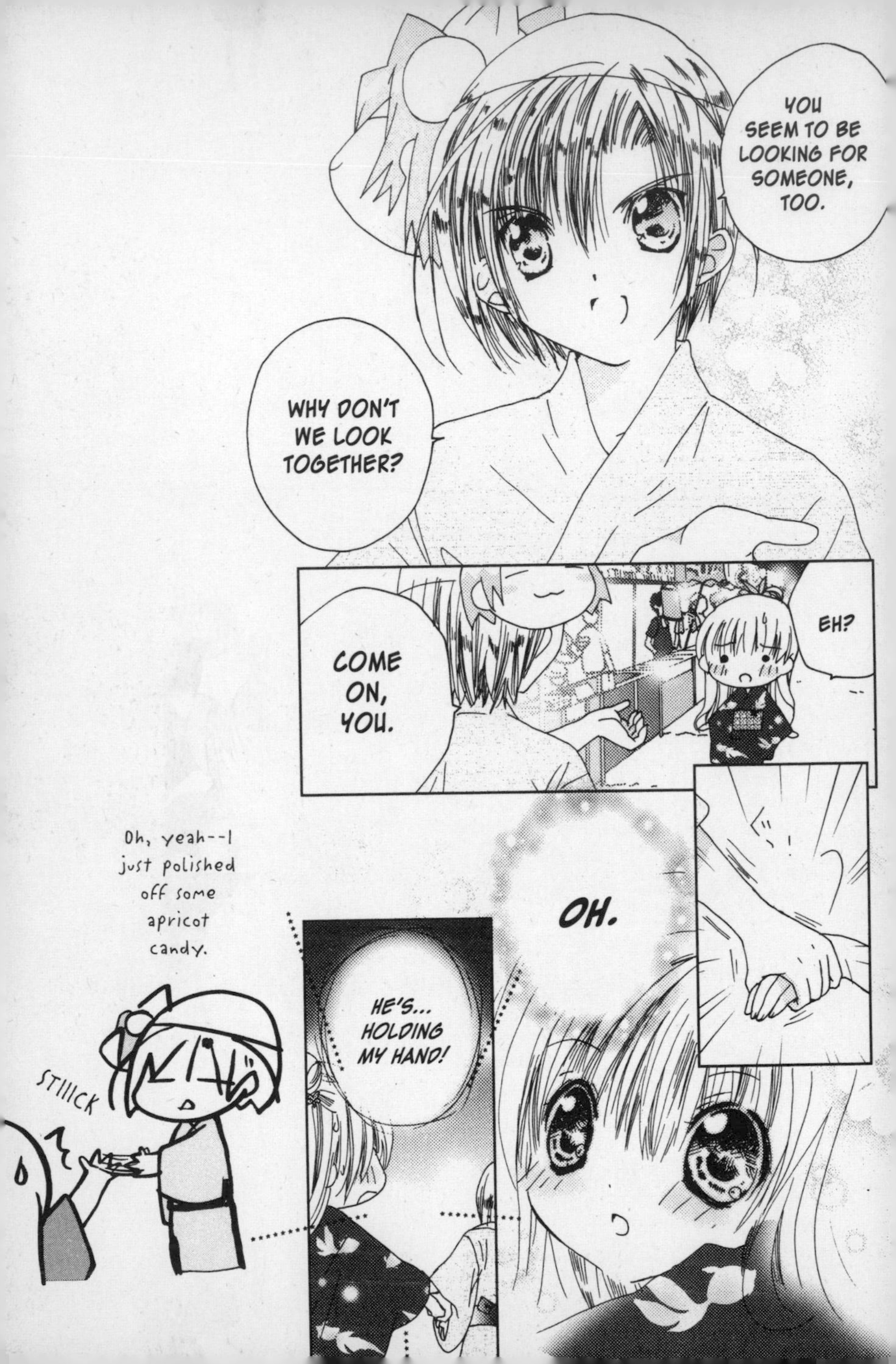
YOU SEEM TO BE LOOKING FOR SOMEONE, TOO.
WHY DON'T WE LOOK TOGETHER?
EH?
COME ON, YOU.
OH.
HE'S... HOLDING MY HAND!
Oh, yeah--I just polished off some apricot candy.
STIIICK

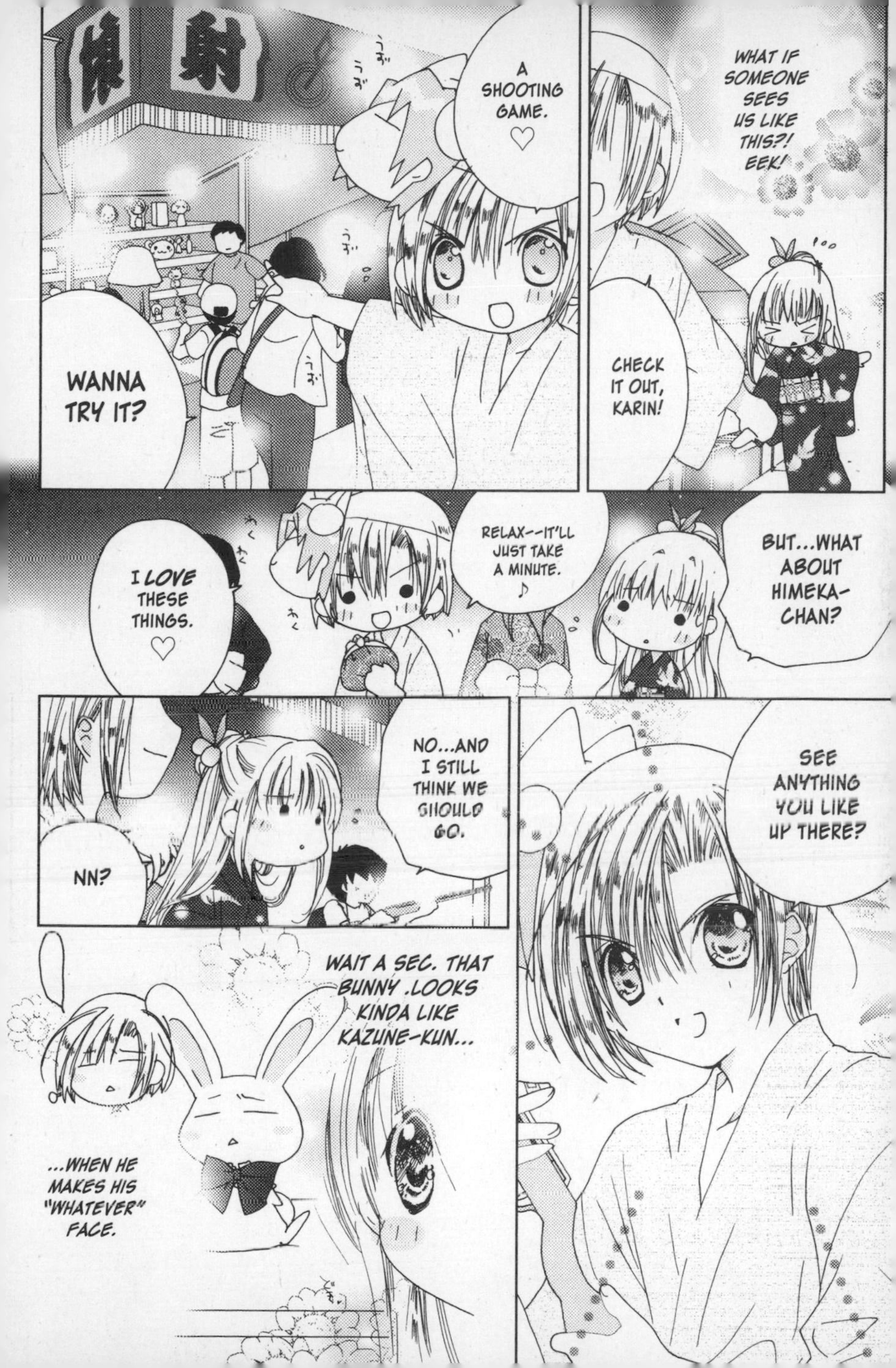
WHAT IF SOMEONE SEES US LIKE THIS?! EEK!
CHECK IT OUT, KARIN!
A SHOOTING GAME. ♡
WANNA TRY IT?
BUT...WHAT ABOUT HIMEKA-CHAN?
RELAX--IT'LL JUST TAKE A MINUTE. ♪
I LOVE THESE THINGS. ♡
SEE ANYTHING YOU LIKE UP THERE?
NO...AND I STILL THINK WE SHOULD GO.
NN?
WAIT A SEC. THAT BUNNY LOOKS KINDA LIKE KAZUNE-KUN...
...WHEN HE MAKES HIS "WHATEVER" FACE.

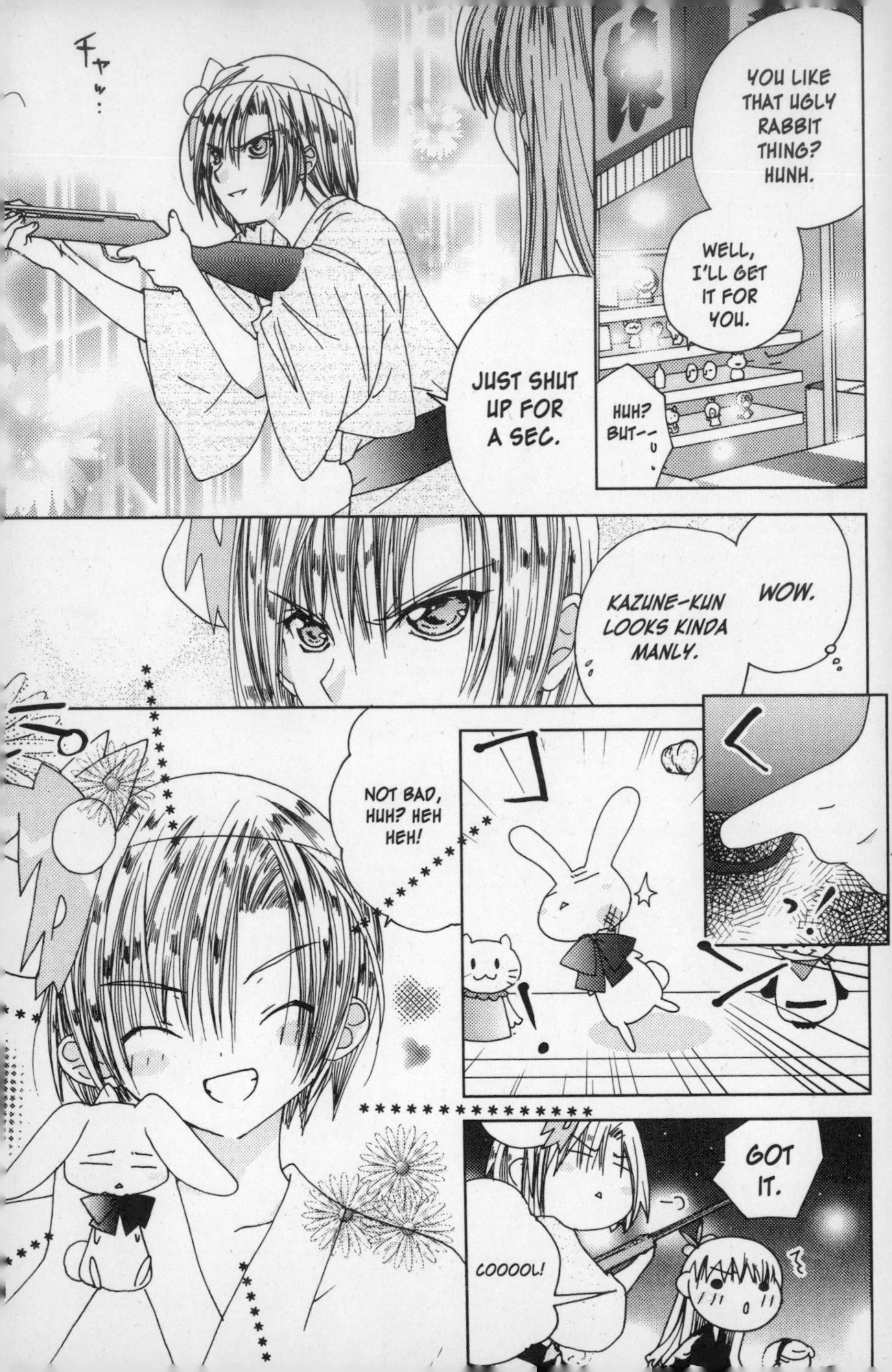
YOU LIKE THAT UGLY RABBIT THING? HUNH.
WELL, I'LL GET IT FOR YOU.
HUH? BUT--
チャッ..
JUST SHUT UP FOR A SEC.
WOW.
KAZUNE-KUN LOOKS KINDA MANLY.
NOT BAD, HUH? HEH HEH!
GOT IT.
COOOOL!

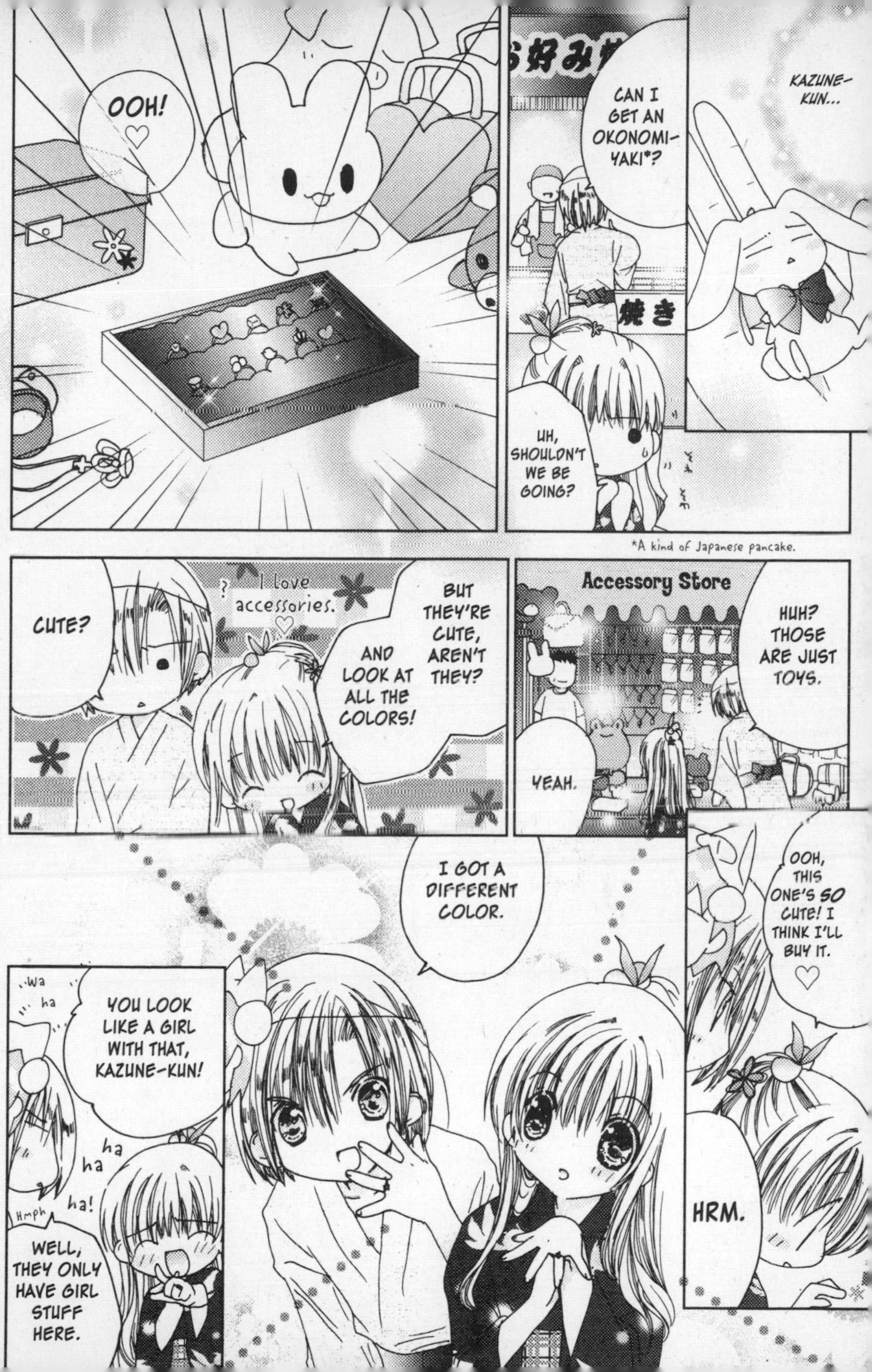
KAZUNE-KUN...
お好み
CAN I GET AN OKONOMIYAKI*?
焼き
UH, SHOULDN'T WE BE GOING?
OOH! ♡
Accessory Store
HUH? THOSE ARE JUST TOYS.
YEAH.
BUT THEY'RE CUTE, AREN'T THEY?
AND LOOK AT ALL THE COLORS!
I love accessories. ♡
CUTE?
OOH, THIS ONE'S SO CUTE! I THINK I'LL BUY IT. ♡
HRM.
I GOT A DIFFERENT COLOR.
YOU LOOK LIKE A GIRL WITH THAT, KAZUNE-KUN!
...wa ha ... ha ha ha!
Hmph
WELL, THEY ONLY HAVE GIRL STUFF HERE.

*A kind of Japanese pancake.

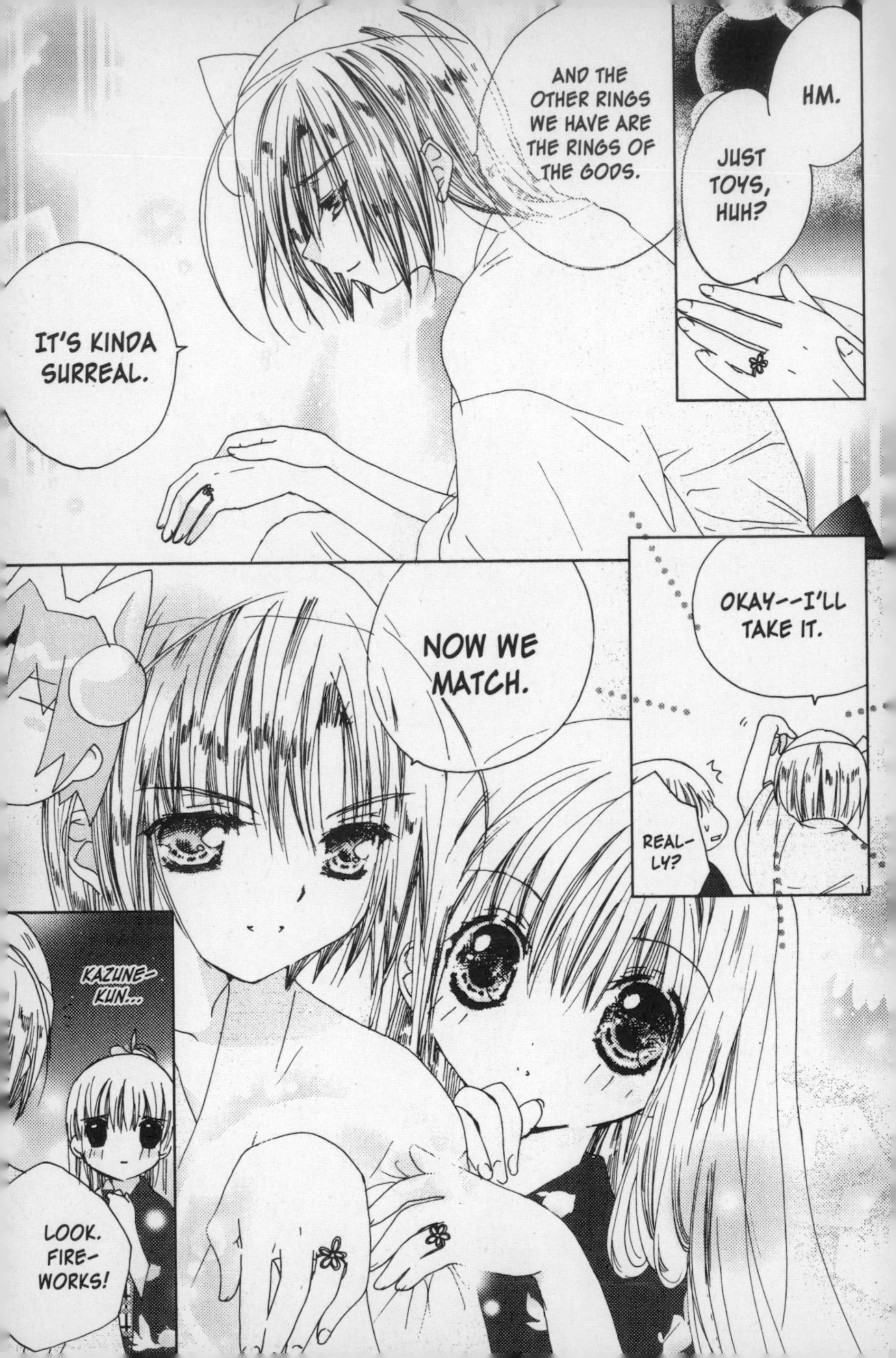
HM.
JUST TOYS, HUH?
AND THE OTHER RINGS WE HAVE ARE THE RINGS OF THE GODS.
IT'S KINDA SURREAL.
OKAY--I'LL TAKE IT.
REAL-LY?
NOW WE MATCH.
KAZUNE-KUN...
LOOK. FIRE-WORKS!

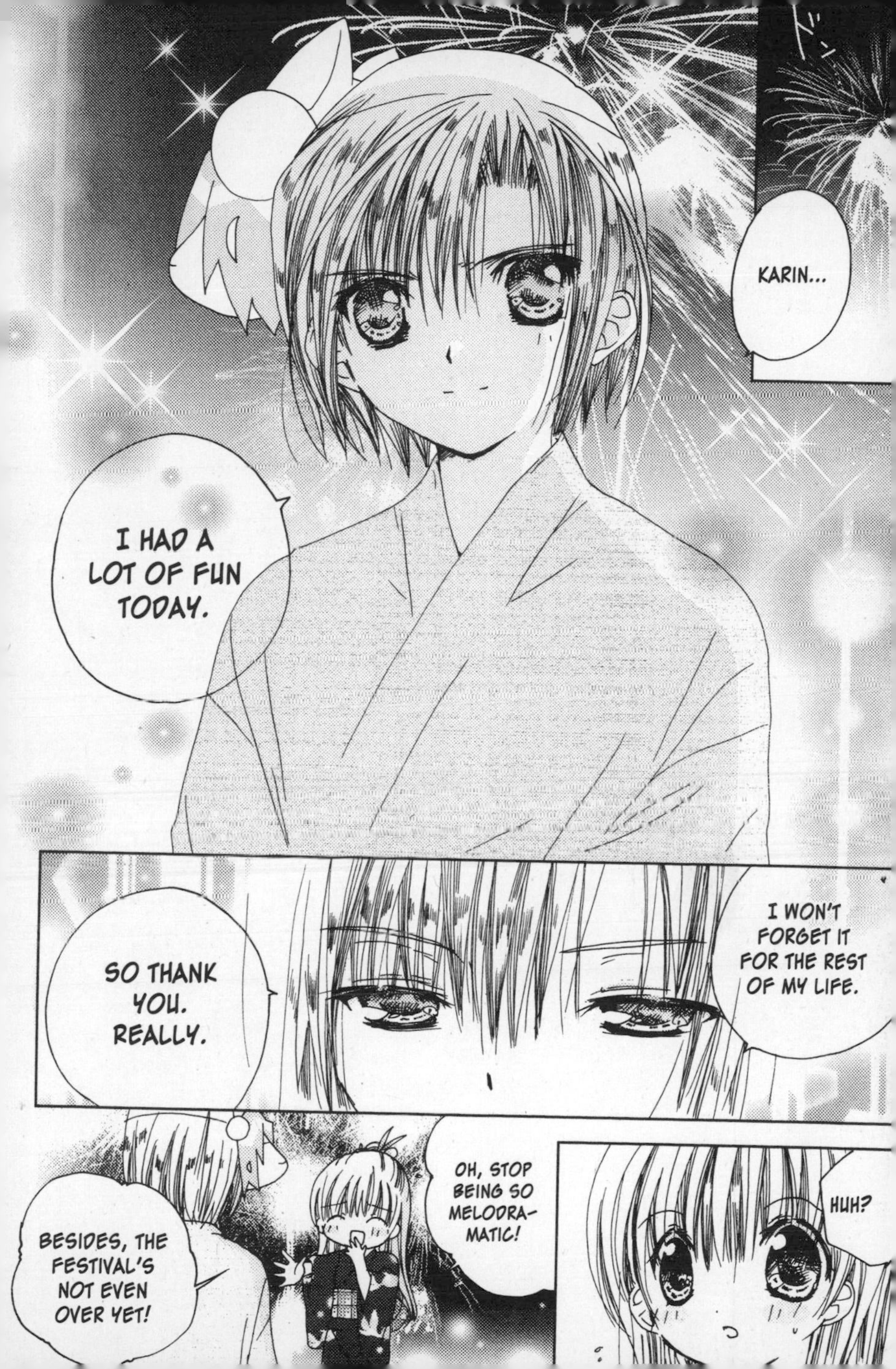
KARIN...
I HAD A LOT OF FUN TODAY.
I WON'T FORGET IT FOR THE REST OF MY LIFE.
SO THANK YOU. REALLY.
HUH?
OH, STOP BEING SO MELODRA-MATIC!
BESIDES, THE FESTIVAL'S NOT EVEN OVER YET!

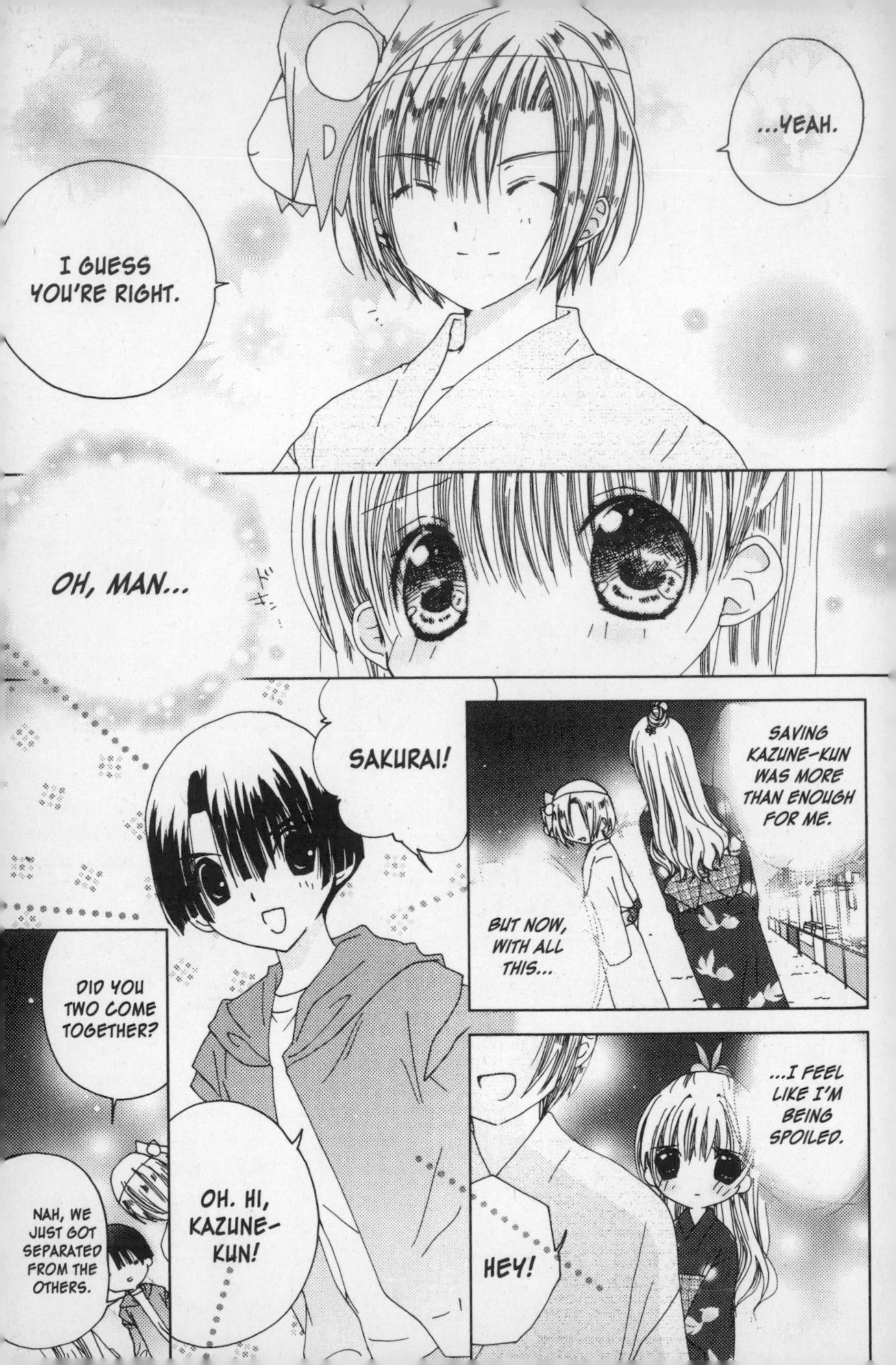
...YEAH.
I GUESS YOU'RE RIGHT.
OH, MAN...
SAVING KAZUNE-KUN WAS MORE THAN ENOUGH FOR ME.
BUT NOW, WITH ALL THIS...
...I FEEL LIKE I'M BEING SPOILED.
HEY!
SAKURAI!
OH. HI, KAZUNE-KUN!
DID YOU TWO COME TOGETHER?
NAH, WE JUST GOT SEPARATED FROM THE OTHERS.

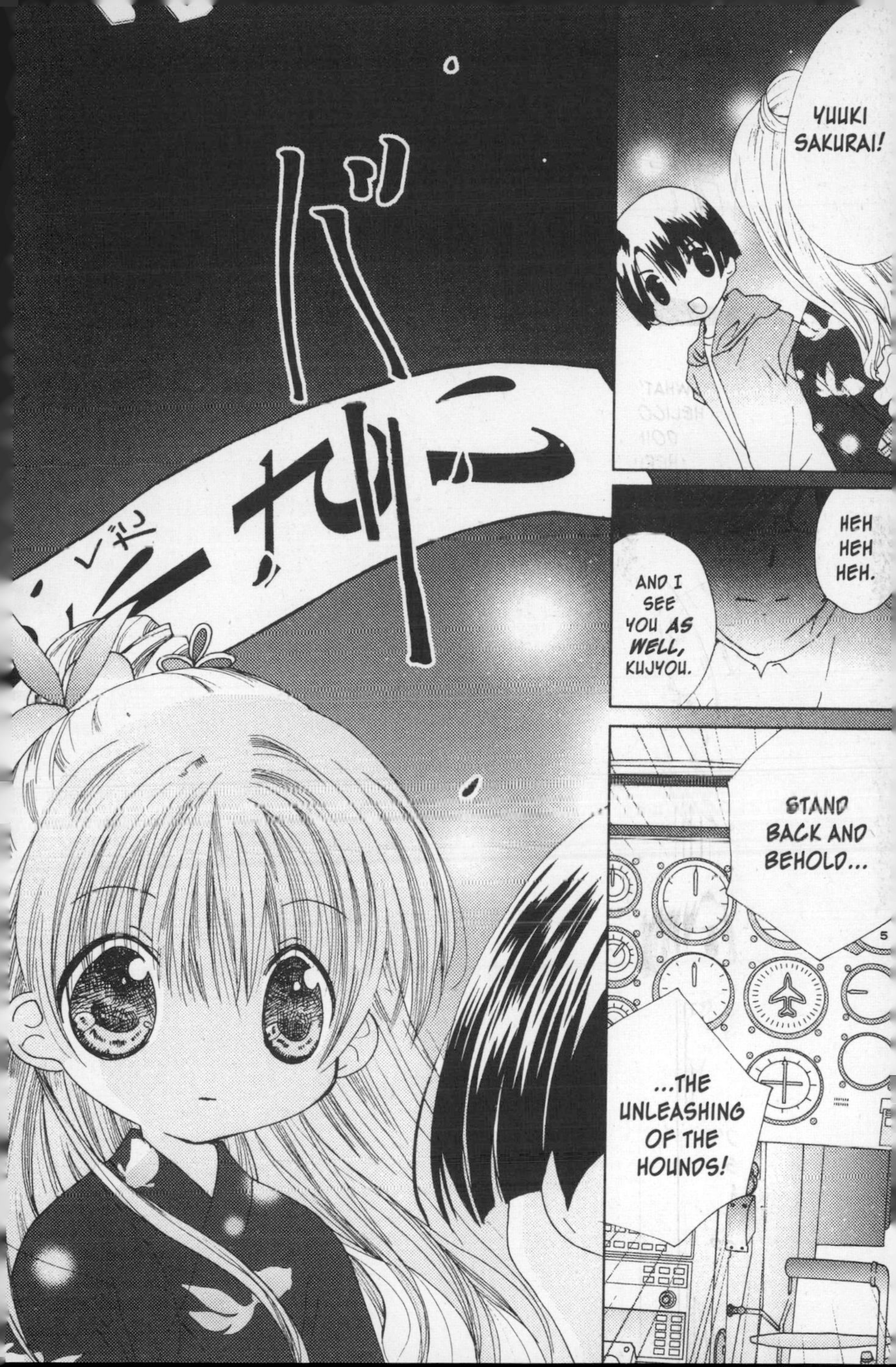
YUUKI SAKURAI!
HEH HEH HEH.
AND I SEE YOU AS WELL, KUJYOU.
STAND BACK AND BEHOLD...
...THE UNLEASHING OF THE HOUNDS!

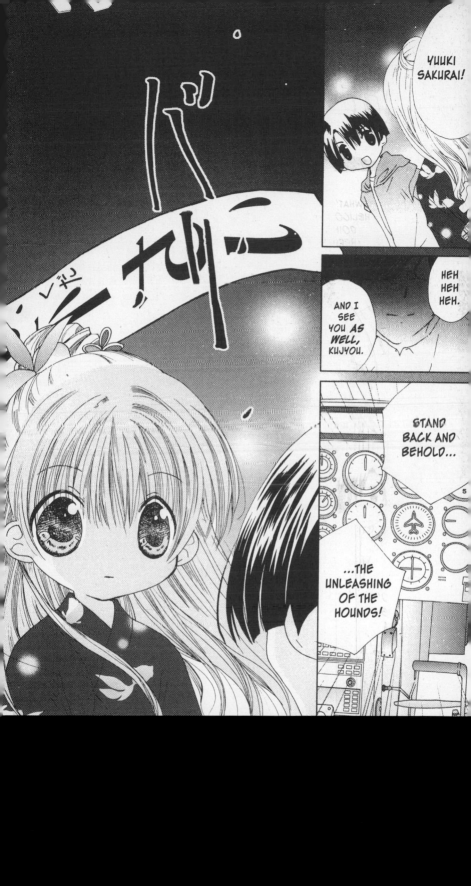

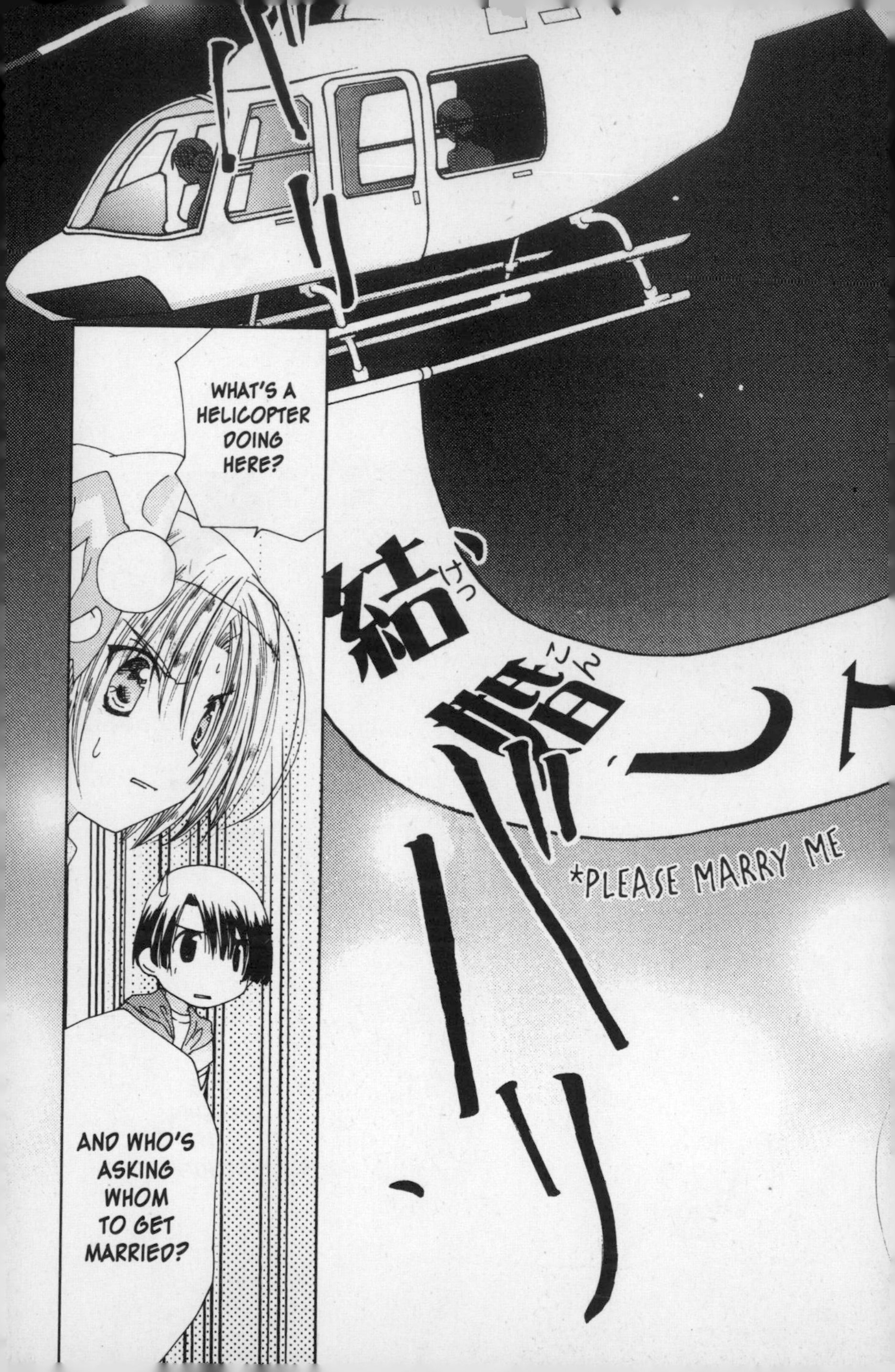
結婚
*PLEASE MARRY ME
WHAT'S A HELICOPTER DOING HERE?
AND WHO'S ASKING WHOM TO GET MARRIED?

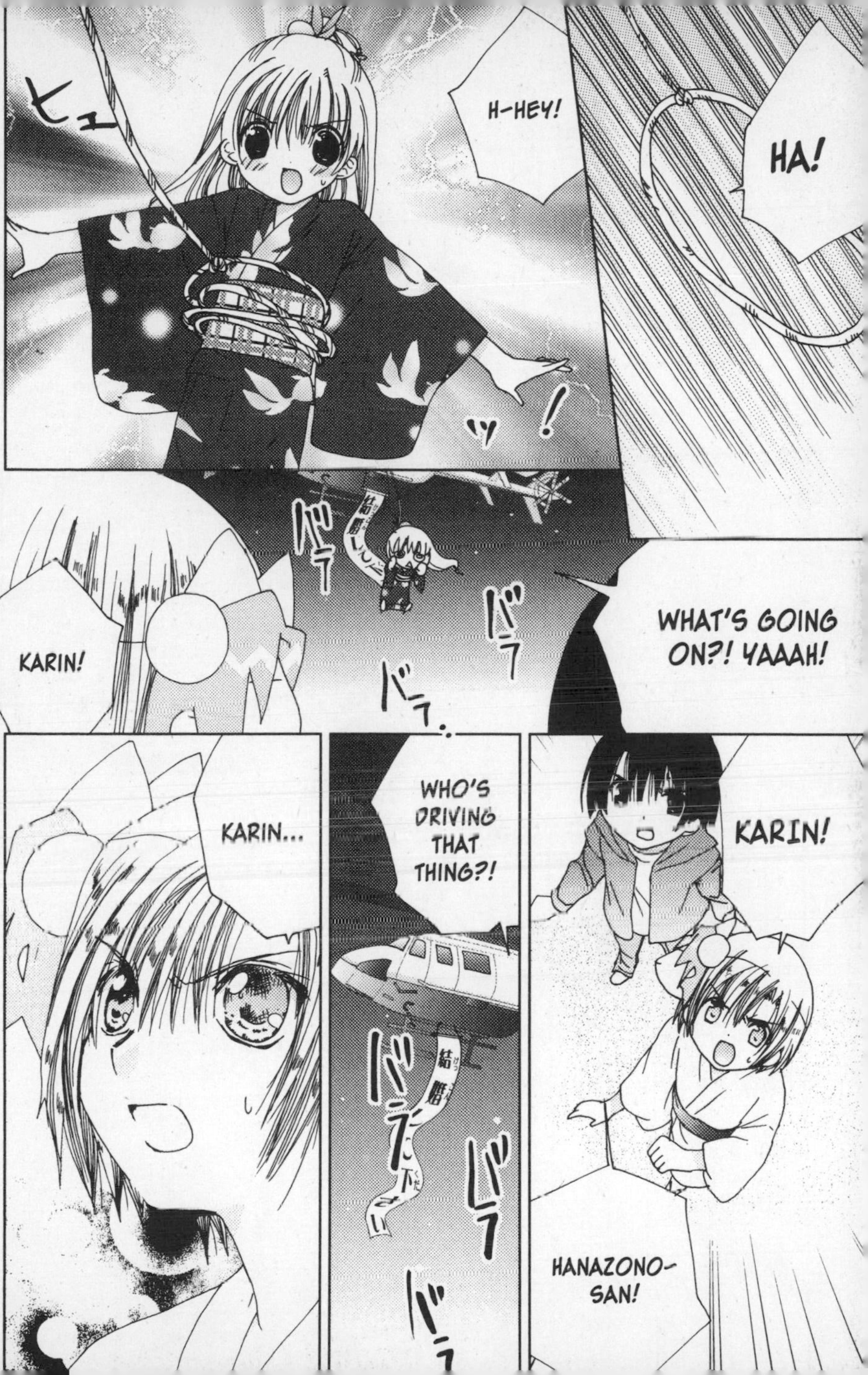
HA!
H-HEY!
ヒュ
ッ!
WHAT'S GOING ON?! YAAAH!
バラ
バラ
バラ...
KARIN!
KARIN!
HANAZONO-SAN!
WHO'S DRIVING THAT THING?!
結婚して下さい
バラ
バラ
KARIN...

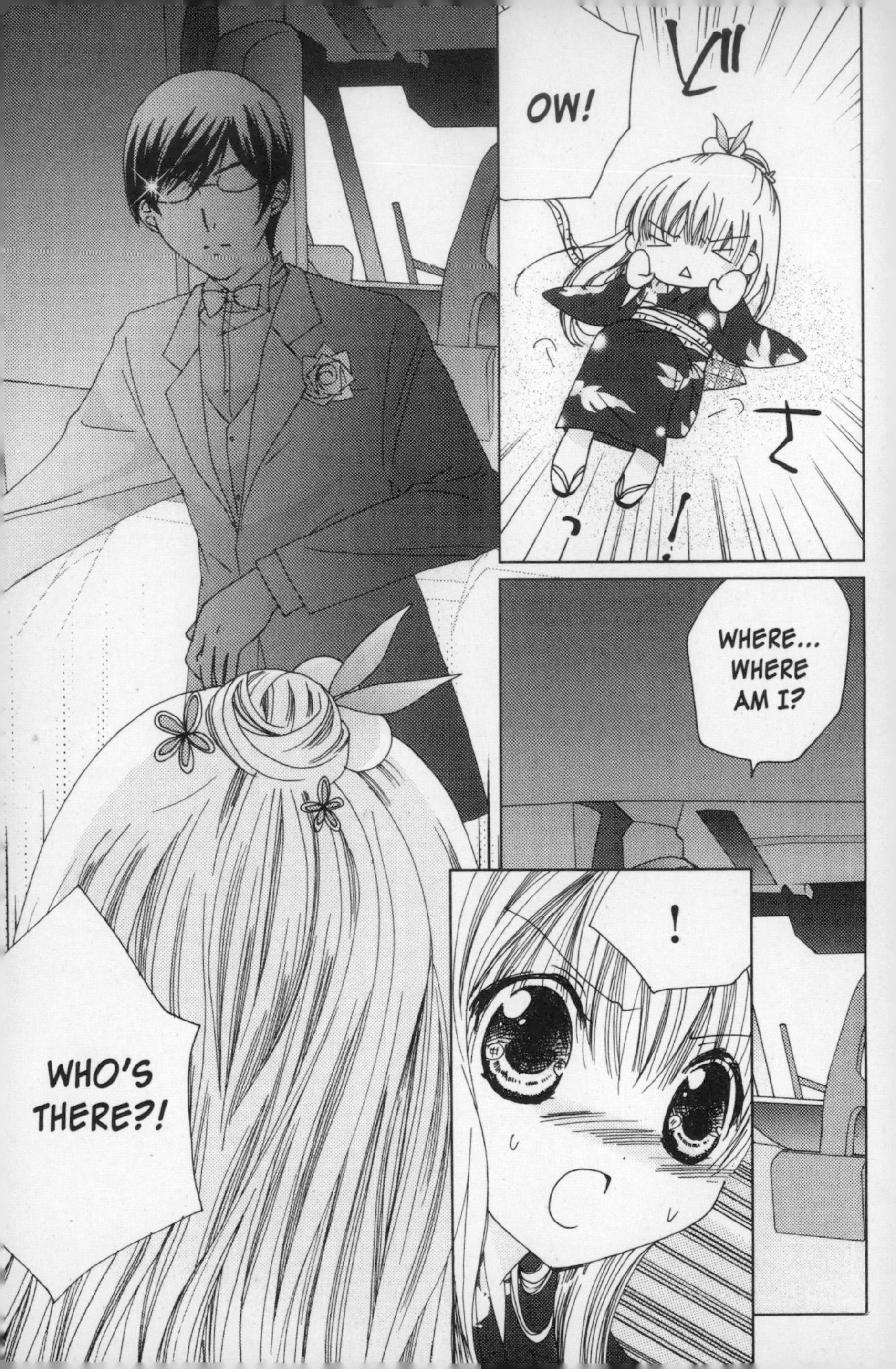
OW!
WHERE... WHERE AM I?
!
WHO'S THERE?!

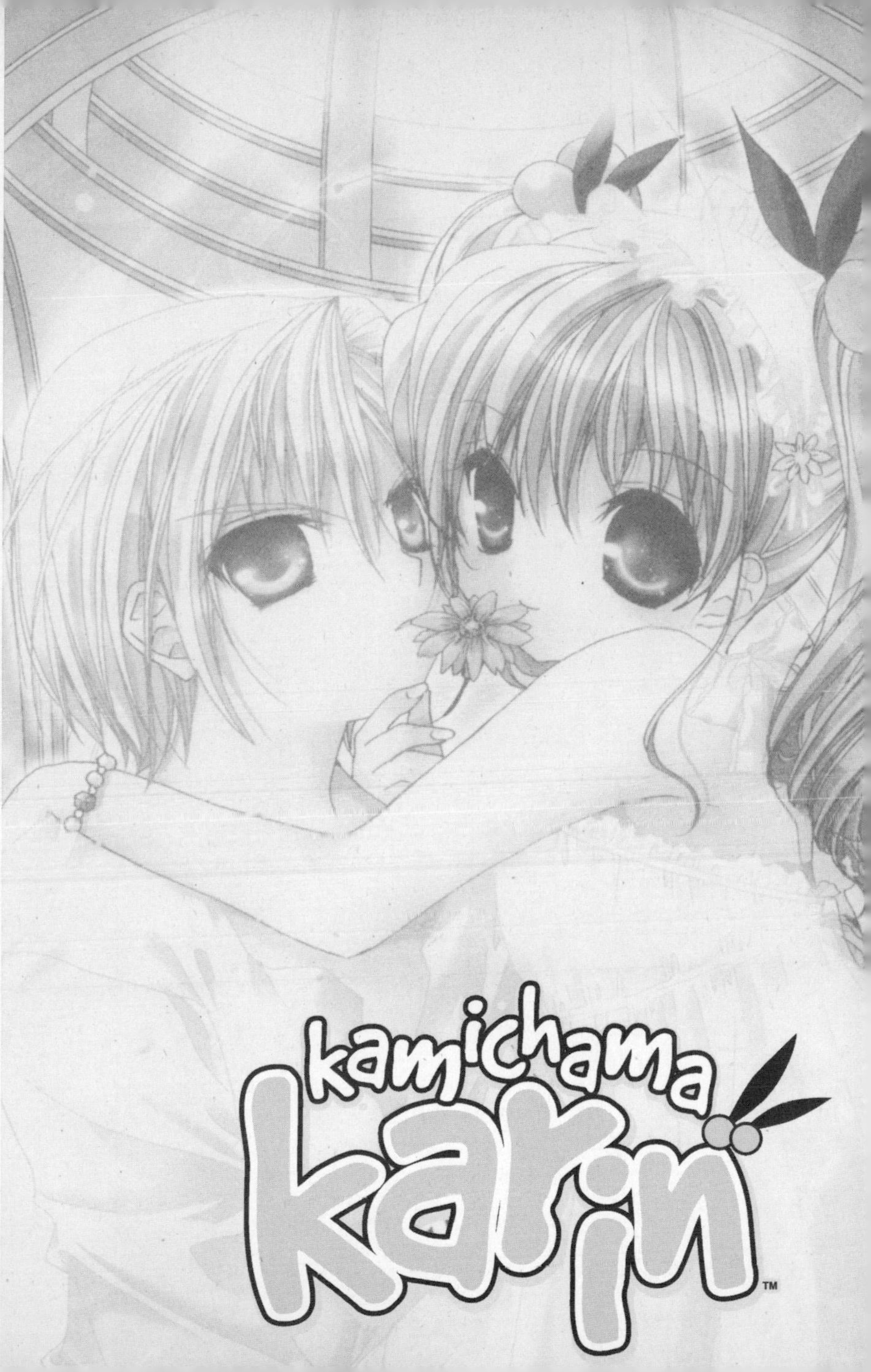
kamichama
karin™

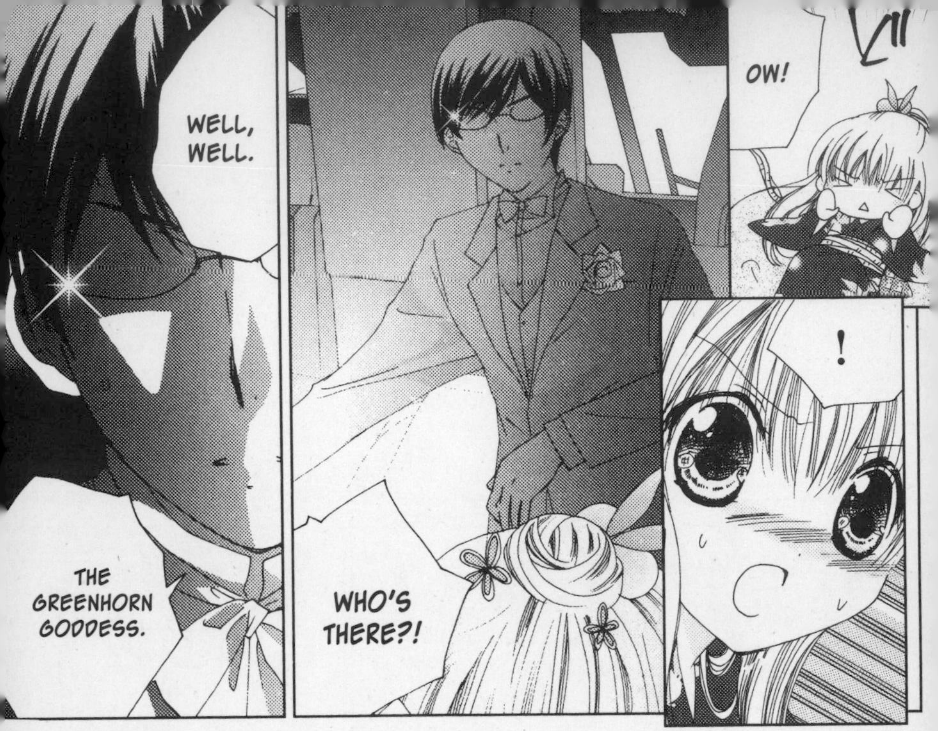
OW!
!
WHO'S THERE?!
WELL, WELL.
THE GREENHORN GODDESS.

Two.

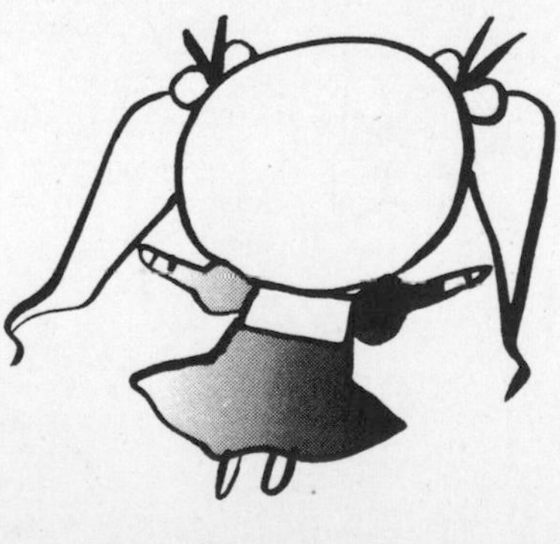

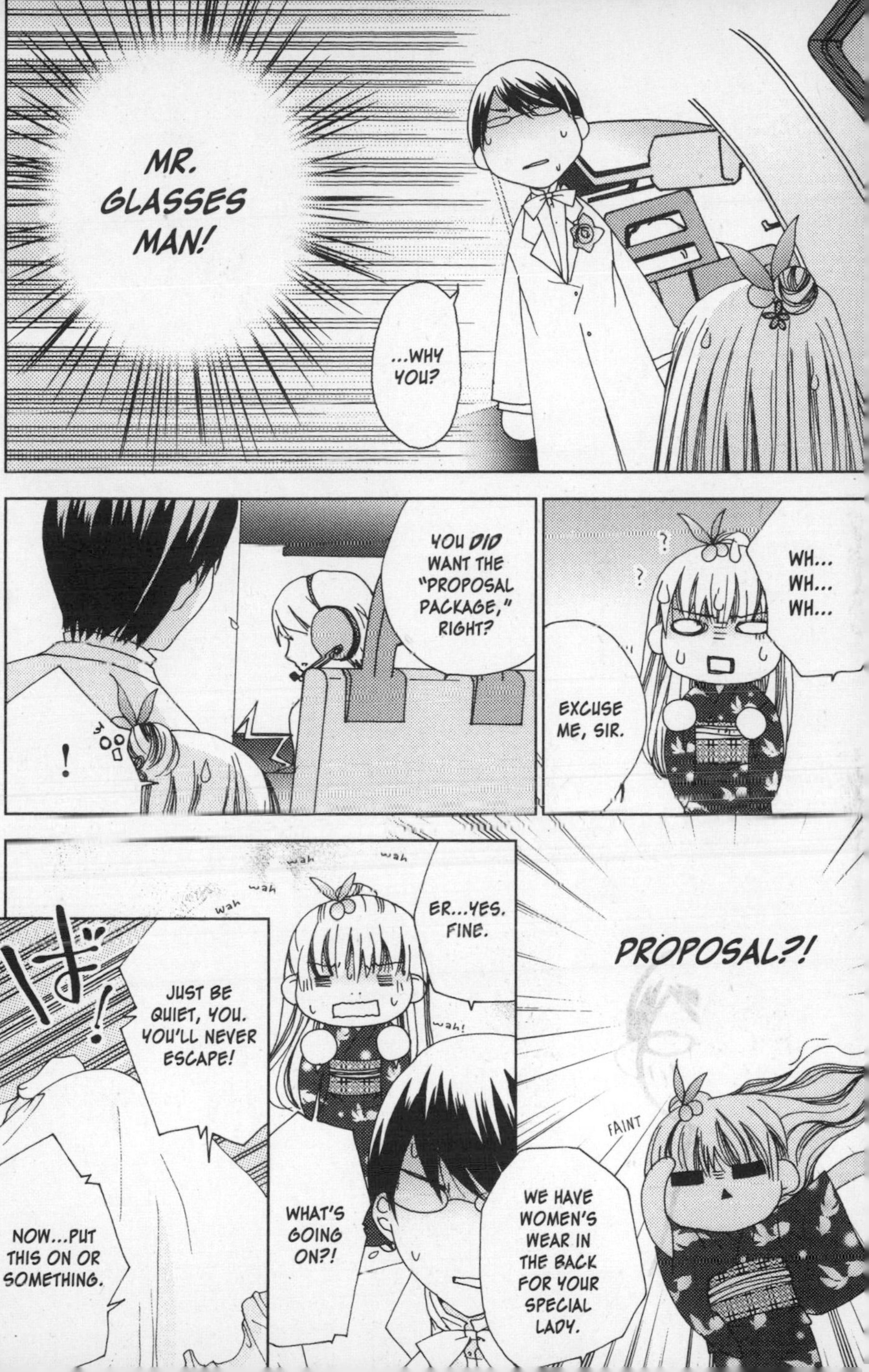
MR. GLASSES MAN!
...WHY YOU?
WH... WH... WH...
EXCUSE ME, SIR.
YOU DID WANT THE "PROPOSAL PACKAGE," RIGHT?
!
PROPOSAL?!
FAINT
WE HAVE WOMEN'S WEAR IN THE BACK FOR YOUR SPECIAL LADY.
wah wah wah wah
ER...YES. FINE.
wah!
WHAT'S GOING ON?!
JUST BE QUIET, YOU. YOU'LL NEVER ESCAPE!
NOW...PUT THIS ON OR SOMETHING.

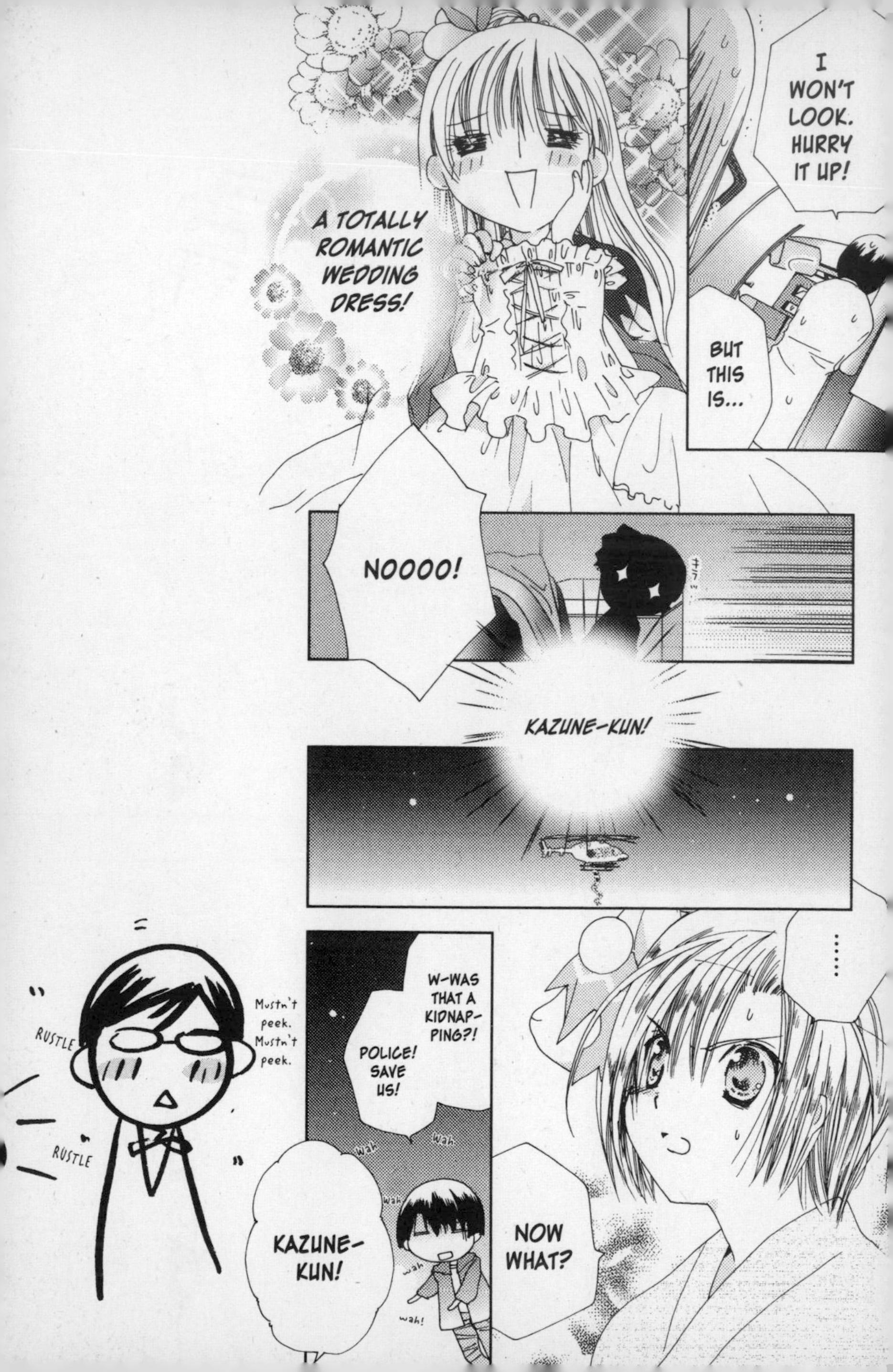
I WON'T LOOK. HURRY IT UP!
BUT THIS IS...
A TOTALLY ROMANTIC WEDDING DRESS!
NOOOO!
KAZUNE-KUN!
......
NOW WHAT?
W-WAS THAT A KIDNAPPING?!
POLICE! SAVE US!
wah
wah
wah
wah
wah!
KAZUNE-KUN!
Mustn't peek. Mustn't peek.
RUSTLE
RUSTLE

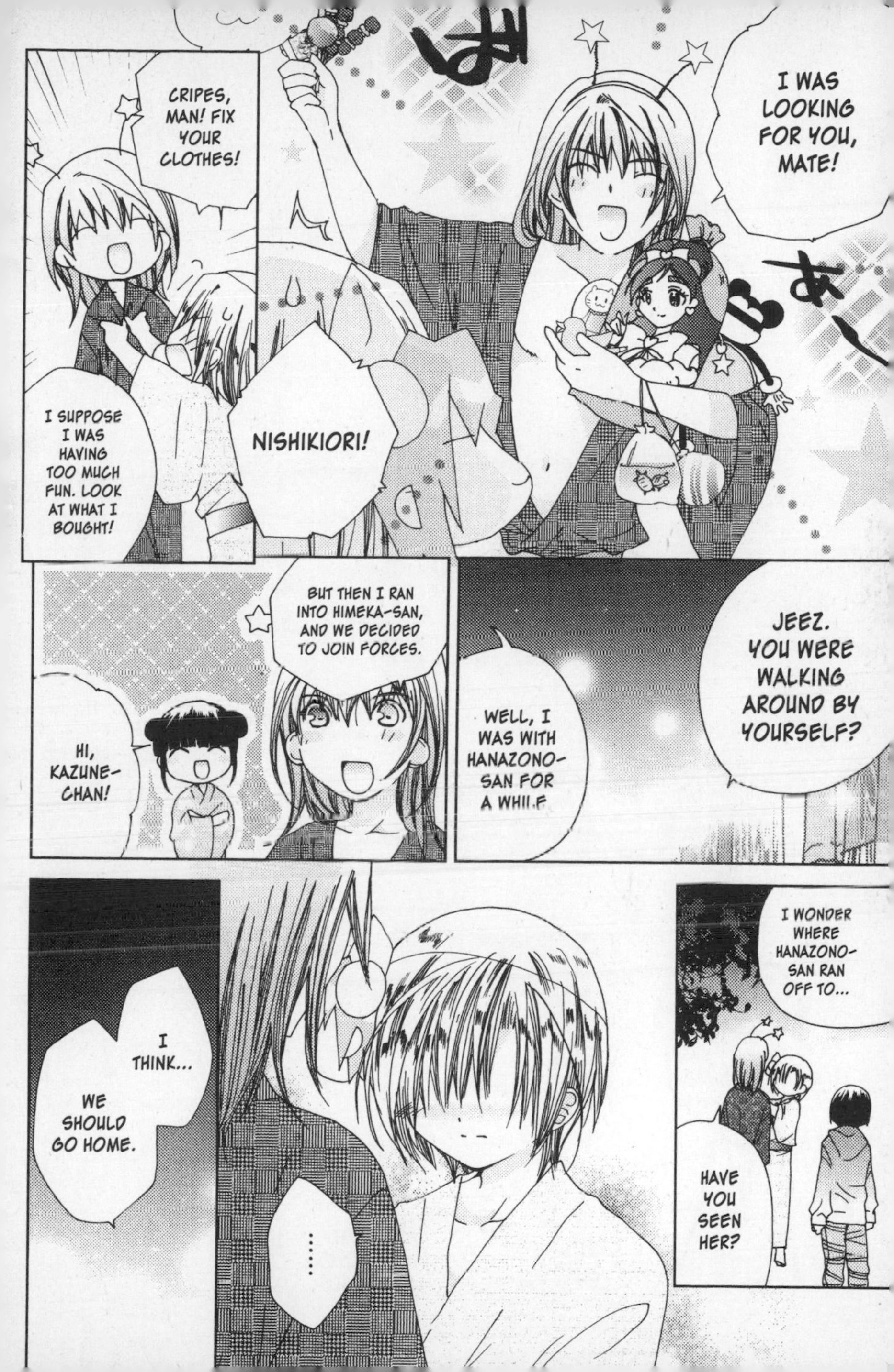

I WAS LOOKING FOR YOU, MATE!
あ〜
NISHIKIORI!
CRIPES, MAN! FIX YOUR CLOTHES!
I SUPPOSE I WAS HAVING TOO MUCH FUN. LOOK AT WHAT I BOUGHT!
JEEZ. YOU WERE WALKING AROUND BY YOURSELF?
WELL, I WAS WITH HANAZONO-SAN FOR A WHILE
BUT THEN I RAN INTO HIMEKA-SAN, AND WE DECIDED TO JOIN FORCES.
HI, KAZUNE-CHAN!
I WONDER WHERE HANAZONO-SAN RAN OFF TO...
HAVE YOU SEEN HER?
......
I THINK...
WE SHOULD GO HOME.

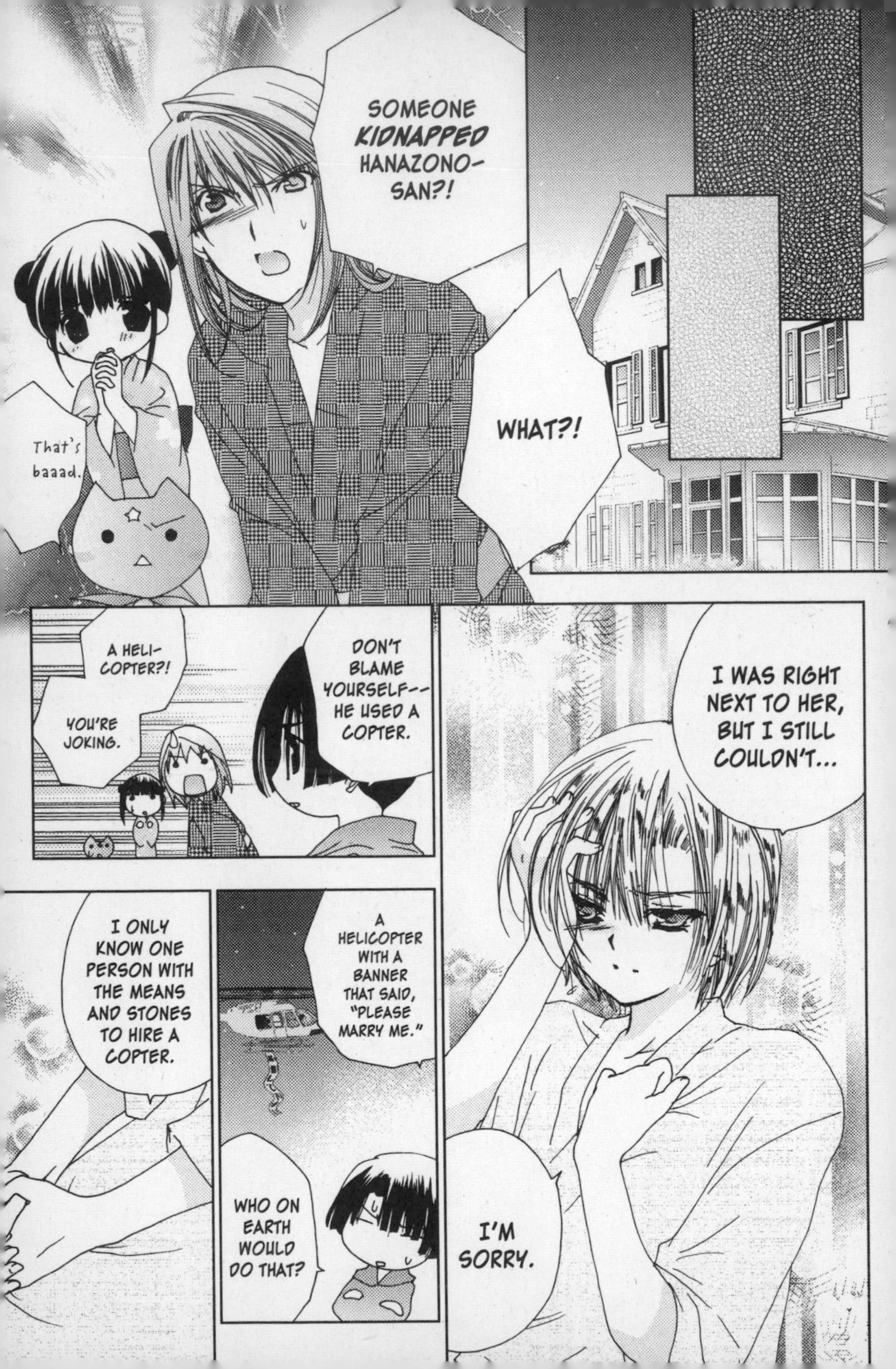
WHAT?!
SOMEONE KIDNAPPED HANAZONO-SAN?!
That's baaad.
I WAS RIGHT NEXT TO HER, BUT I STILL COULDN'T...
I'M SORRY.
DON'T BLAME YOURSELF--HE USED A COPTER.
A HELI-COPTER?!
YOU'RE JOKING.
A HELICOPTER WITH A BANNER THAT SAID, "PLEASE MARRY ME."
WHO ON EARTH WOULD DO THAT?
I ONLY KNOW ONE PERSON WITH THE MEANS AND STONES TO HIRE A COPTER.

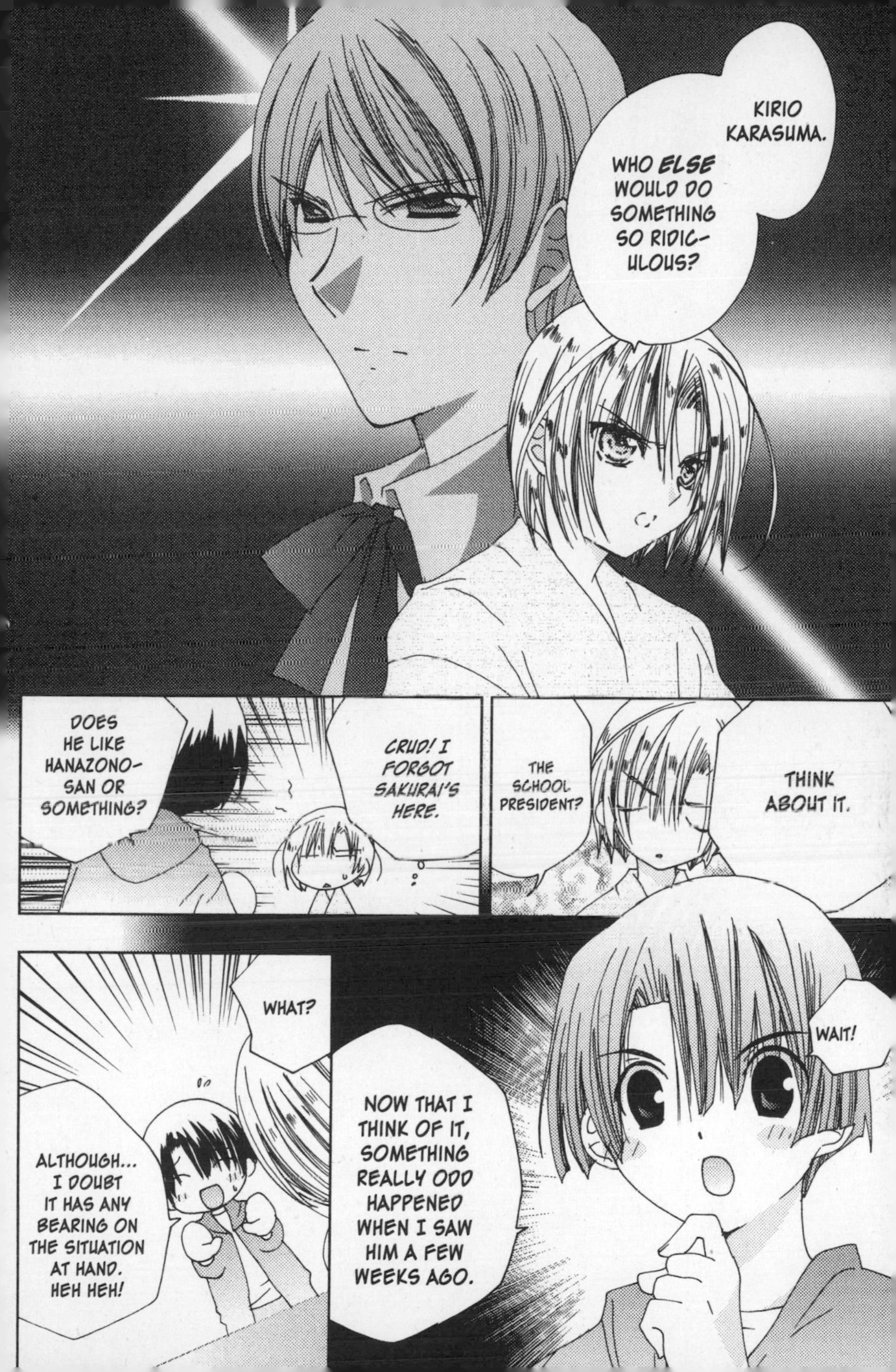
KIRIO KARASUMA.
WHO ELSE WOULD DO SOMETHING SO RIDICULOUS?
THINK ABOUT IT.
THE SCHOOL PRESIDENT?
CRUD! I FORGOT SAKURAI'S HERE.
DOES HE LIKE HANAZONO-SAN OR SOMETHING?
WAIT!
NOW THAT I THINK OF IT, SOMETHING REALLY ODD HAPPENED WHEN I SAW HIM A FEW WEEKS AGO.
WHAT?
ALTHOUGH... I DOUBT IT HAS ANY BEARING ON THE SITUATION AT HAND. HEH HEH!

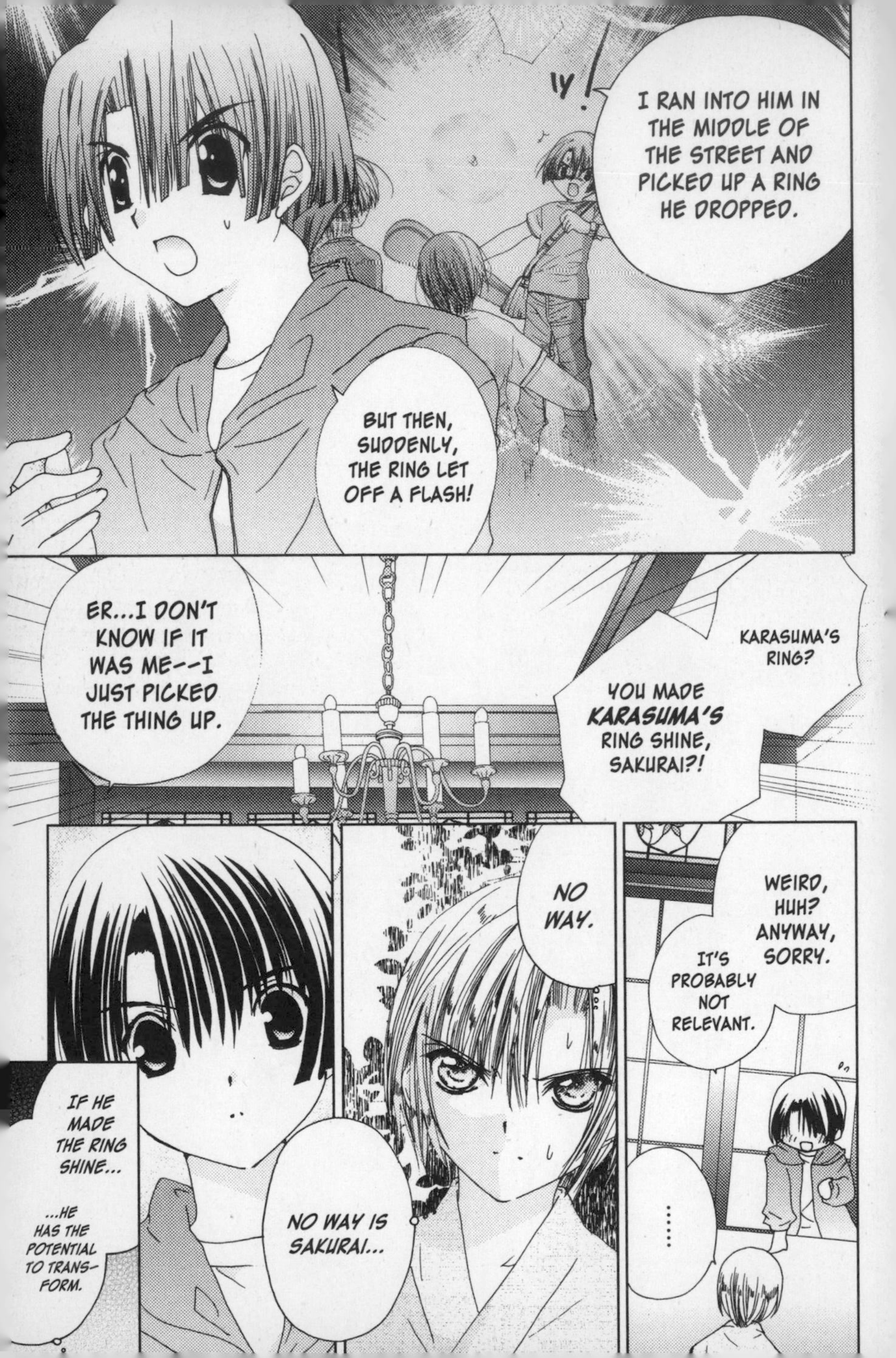
I RAN INTO HIM IN THE MIDDLE OF THE STREET AND PICKED UP A RING HE DROPPED.
BUT THEN, SUDDENLY, THE RING LET OFF A FLASH!
KARASUMA'S RING?
YOU MADE KARASUMA'S RING SHINE, SAKURAI?!
ER...I DON'T KNOW IF IT WAS ME--I JUST PICKED THE THING UP.
WEIRD, HUH? ANYWAY, SORRY.
IT'S PROBABLY NOT RELEVANT.
......
NO WAY.
NO WAY IS SAKURAI...
IF HE MADE THE RING SHINE...
...HE HAS THE POTENTIAL TO TRANSFORM.

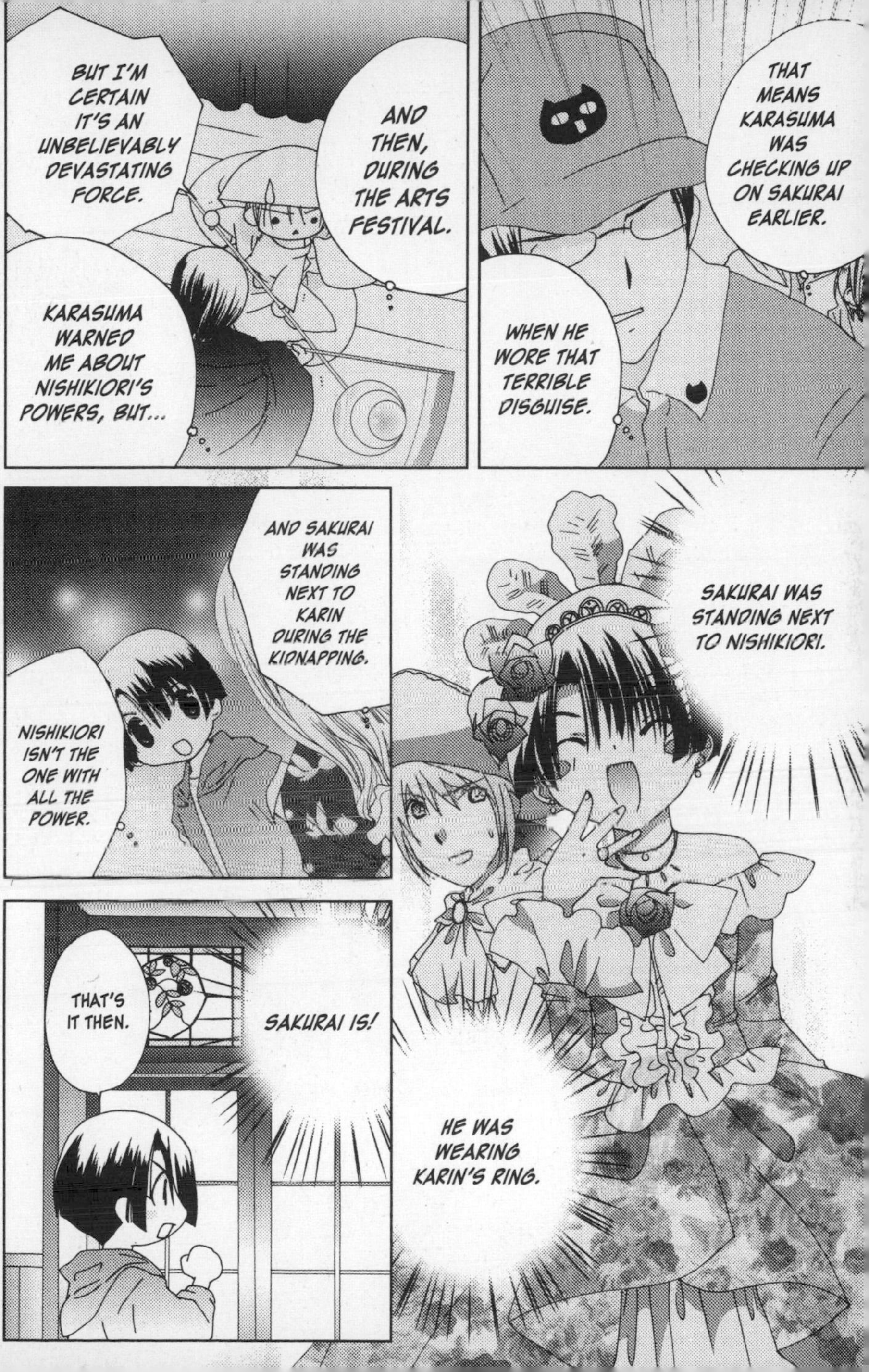
THAT MEANS KARASUMA WAS CHECKING UP ON SAKURAI EARLIER.
WHEN HE WORE THAT TERRIBLE DISGUISE.
AND THEN, DURING THE ARTS FESTIVAL.
BUT I'M CERTAIN IT'S AN UNBELIEVABLY DEVASTATING FORCE.
KARASUMA WARNED ME ABOUT NISHIKIORI'S POWERS, BUT...
SAKURAI WAS STANDING NEXT TO NISHIKIORI.
HE WAS WEARING KARIN'S RING.
AND SAKURAI WAS STANDING NEXT TO KARIN DURING THE KIDNAPPING.
NISHIKIORI ISN'T THE ONE WITH ALL THE POWER.
THAT'S IT THEN.
SAKURAI IS!

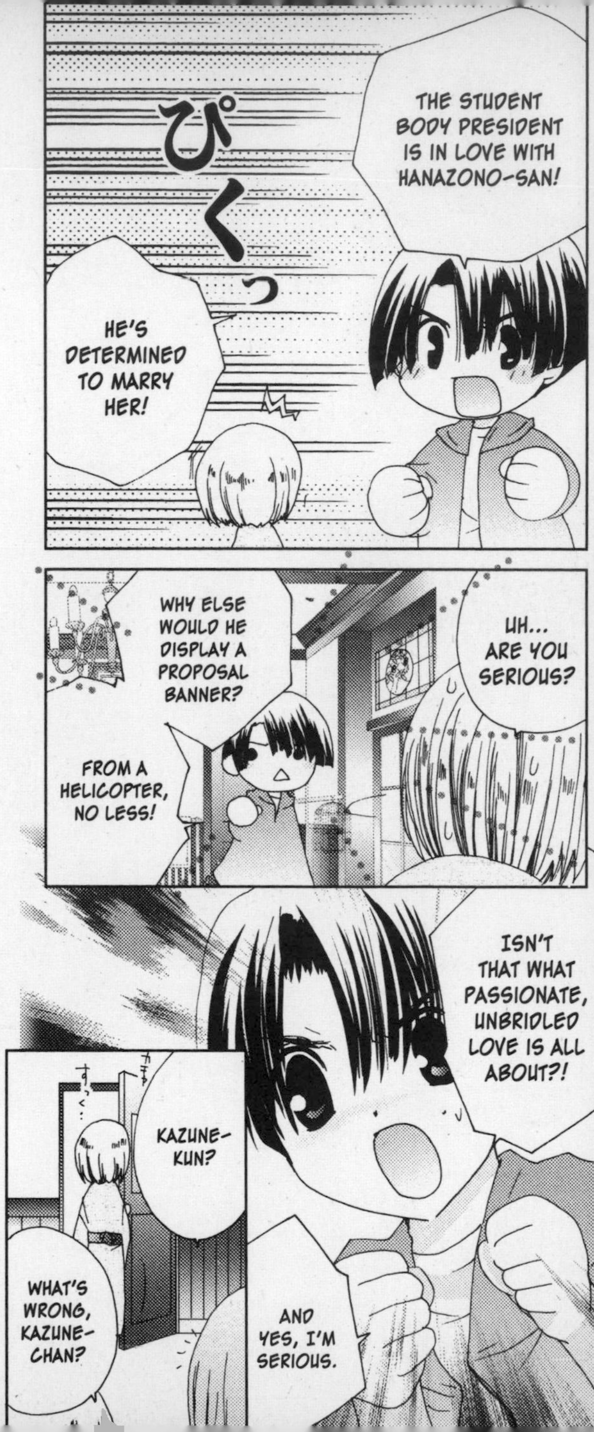
THE STUDENT BODY PRESIDENT IS IN LOVE WITH HANAZONO-SAN!
ぴくっ
HE'S DETERMINED TO MARRY HER!
UH... ARE YOU SERIOUS?
WHY ELSE WOULD HE DISPLAY A PROPOSAL BANNER?
FROM A HELICOPTER, NO LESS!
ISN'T THAT WHAT PASSIONATE, UNBRIDLED LOVE IS ALL ABOUT?!
AND YES, I'M SERIOUS.
KAZUNE-KUN?
WHAT'S WRONG, KAZUNE-CHAN?

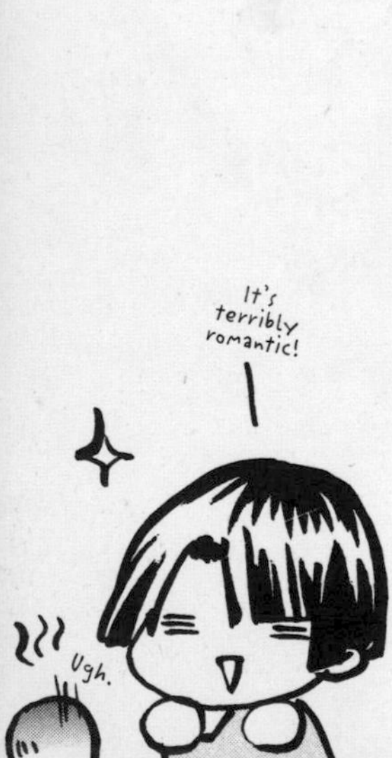
It's terribly romantic!
Ugh.

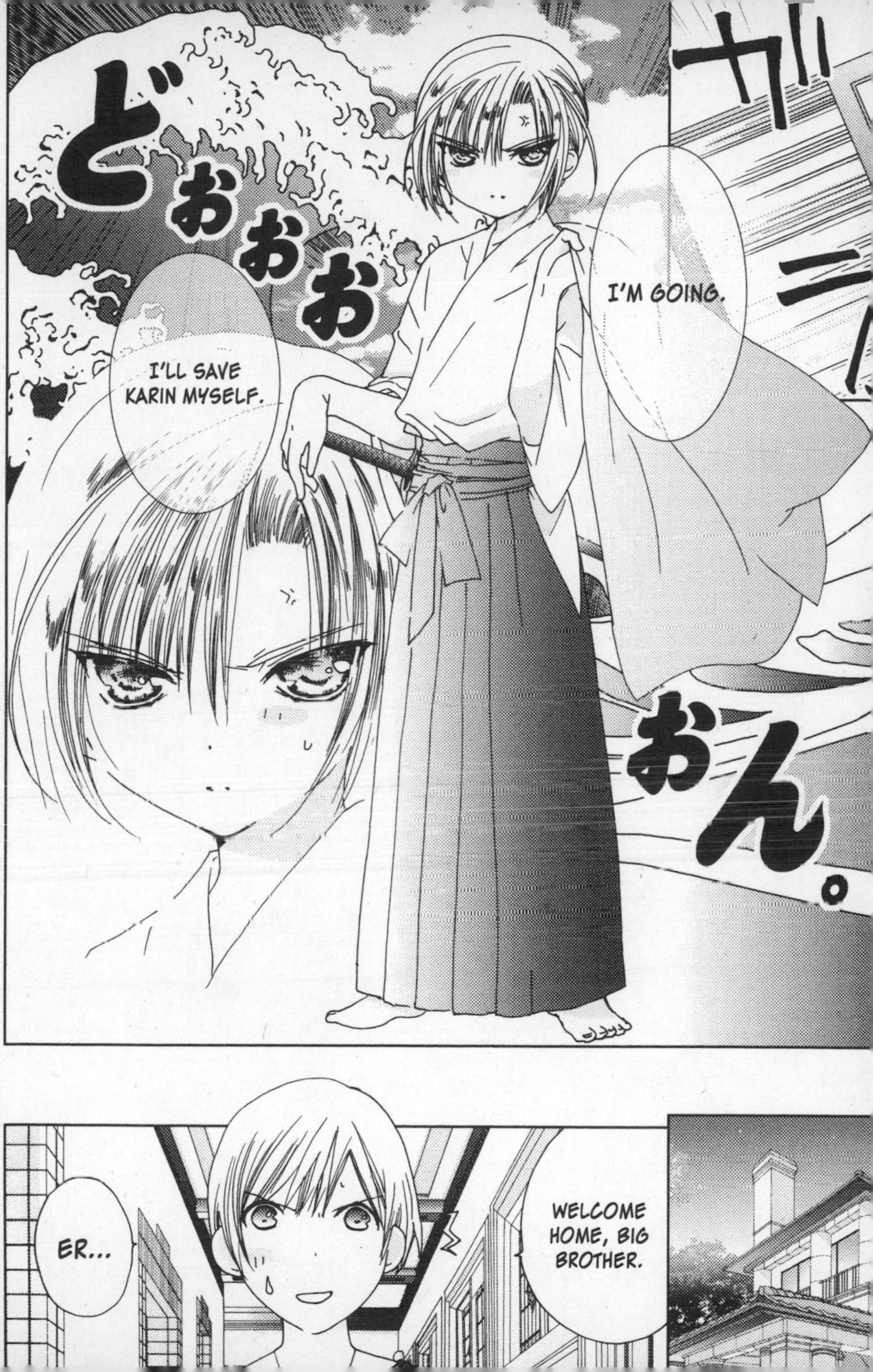
I'M GOING.
どぉぉぉ
I'LL SAVE KARIN MYSELF.
おん。
WELCOME HOME, BIG BROTHER.
ER...

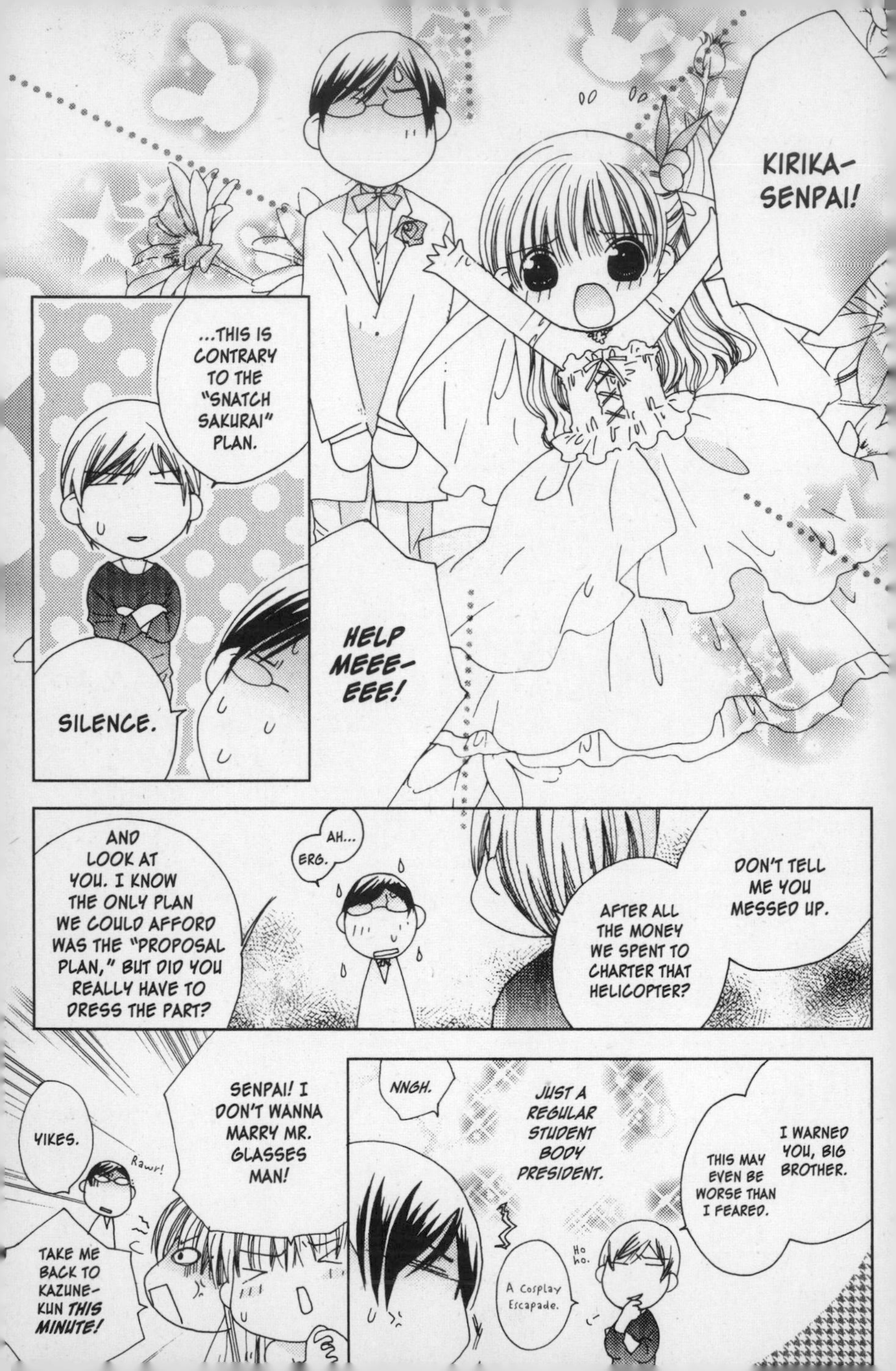
KIRIKA-SENPAI!
HELP MEEEEEE!
...THIS IS CONTRARY TO THE "SNATCH SAKURAI" PLAN.
SILENCE.
DON'T TELL ME YOU MESSED UP.
AFTER ALL THE MONEY WE SPENT TO CHARTER THAT HELICOPTER?
AH... ERG.
AND LOOK AT YOU. I KNOW THE ONLY PLAN WE COULD AFFORD WAS THE "PROPOSAL PLAN," BUT DID YOU REALLY HAVE TO DRESS THE PART?
I WARNED YOU, BIG BROTHER.
THIS MAY EVEN BE WORSE THAN I FEARED.
JUST A REGULAR STUDENT BODY PRESIDENT.
NNGH.
Ho ho.
A Cosplay Escapade.
SENPAI! I DON'T WANNA MARRY MR. GLASSES MAN!
YIKES.
Rawr!
TAKE ME BACK TO KAZUNE-KUN *THIS MINUTE!*

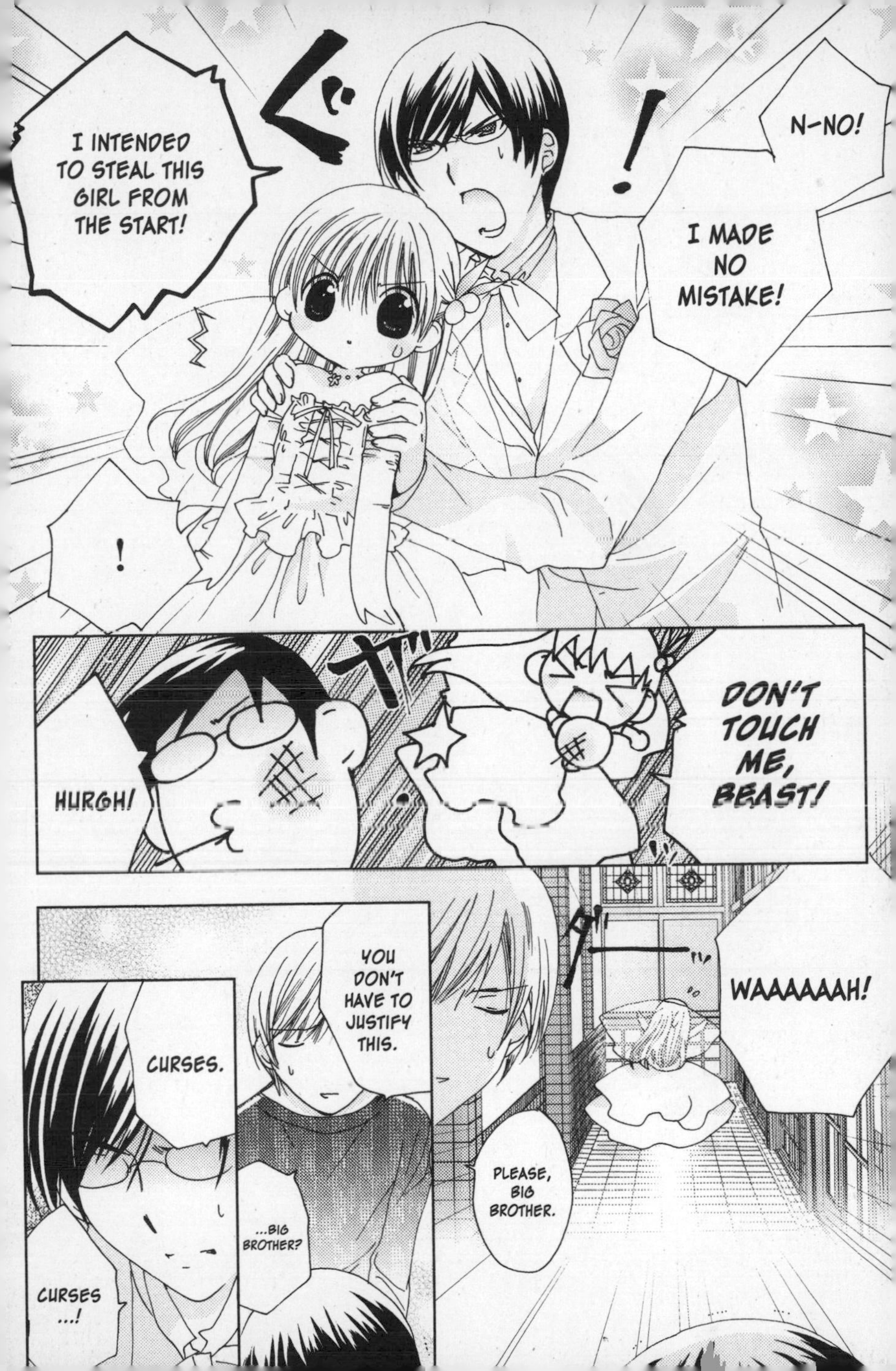

N-NO!
I MADE NO MISTAKE!
I INTENDED TO STEAL THIS GIRL FROM THE START!
!
!
DON'T TOUCH ME, BEAST!
HURGH!
WAAAAAAH!
YOU DON'T HAVE TO JUSTIFY THIS.
PLEASE, BIG BROTHER.
...BIG BROTHER?
CURSES.
CURSES ...!

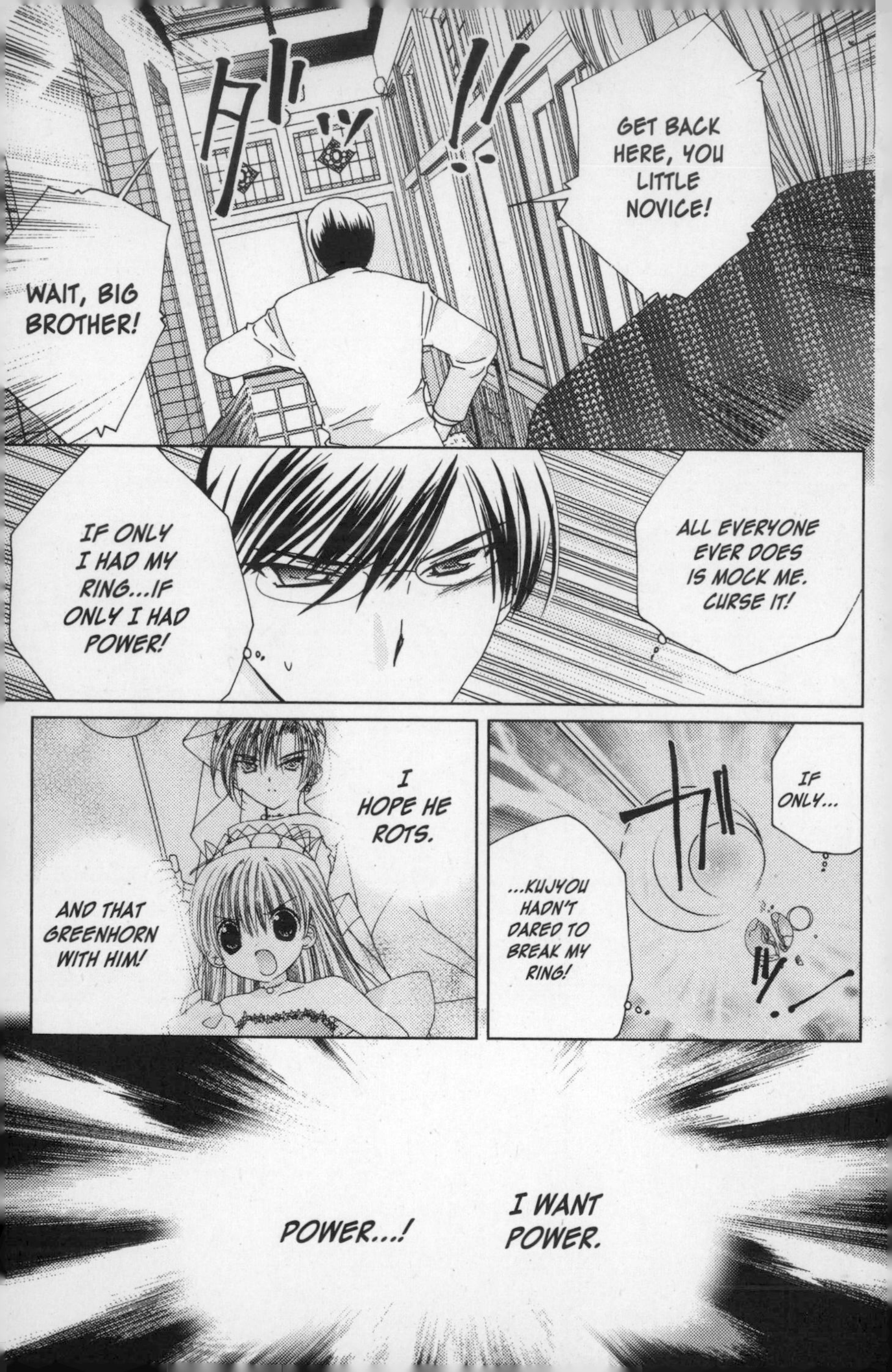
GET BACK HERE, YOU LITTLE NOVICE!
WAIT, BIG BROTHER!
ALL EVERYONE EVER DOES IS MOCK ME. CURSE IT!
IF ONLY I HAD MY RING...IF ONLY I HAD POWER!
IF ONLY...
...KUJYOU HADN'T DARED TO BREAK MY RING!
I HOPE HE ROTS.
AND THAT GREENHORN WITH HIM!
I WANT POWER.
POWER...!

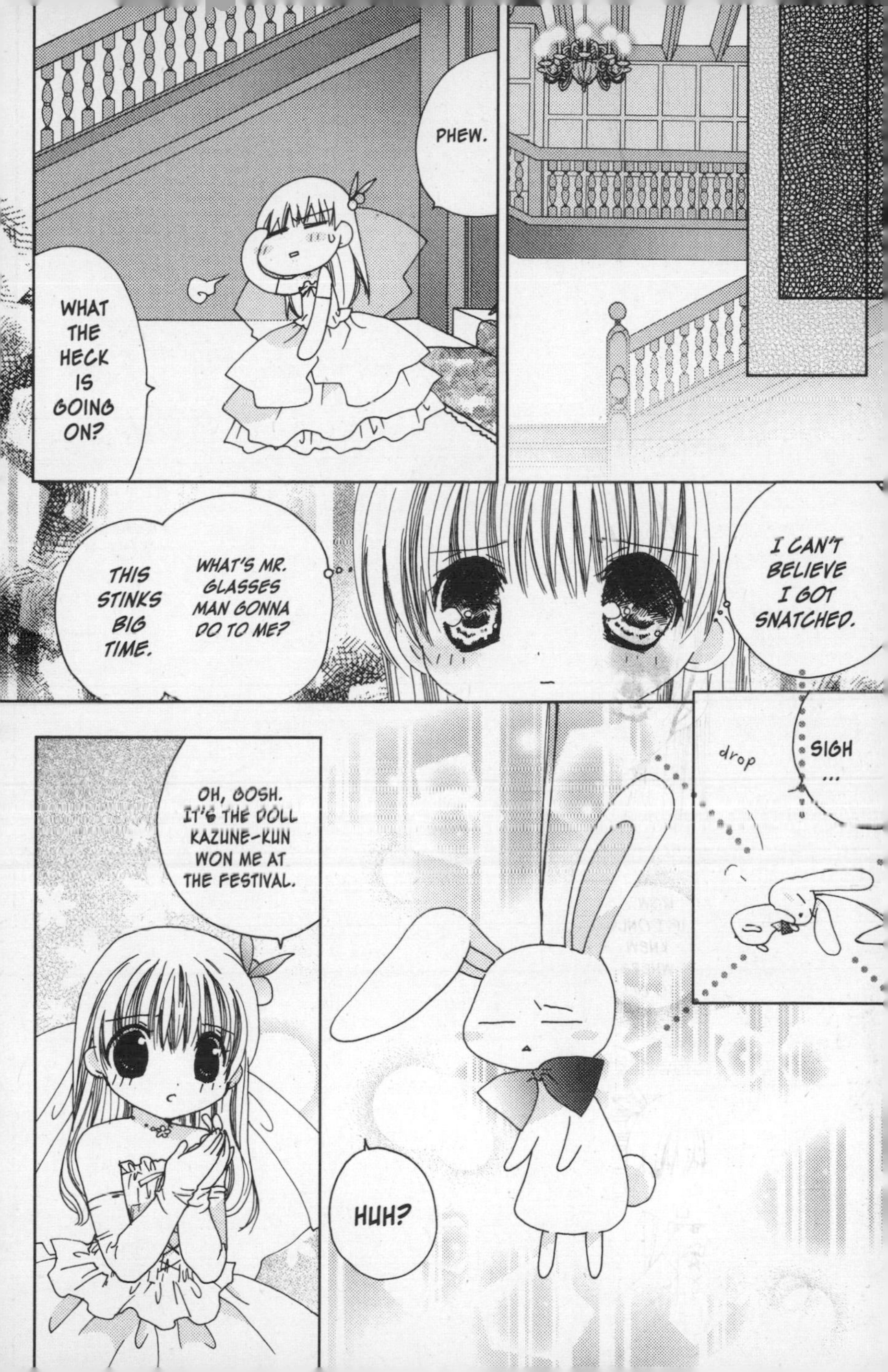
PHEW.
WHAT THE HECK IS GOING ON?
I CAN'T BELIEVE I GOT SNATCHED.
WHAT'S MR. GLASSES MAN GONNA DO TO ME?
THIS STINKS BIG TIME.
SIGH ...
drop
HUH?
OH, GOSH. IT'S THE DOLL KAZUNE-KUN WON ME AT THE FESTIVAL.

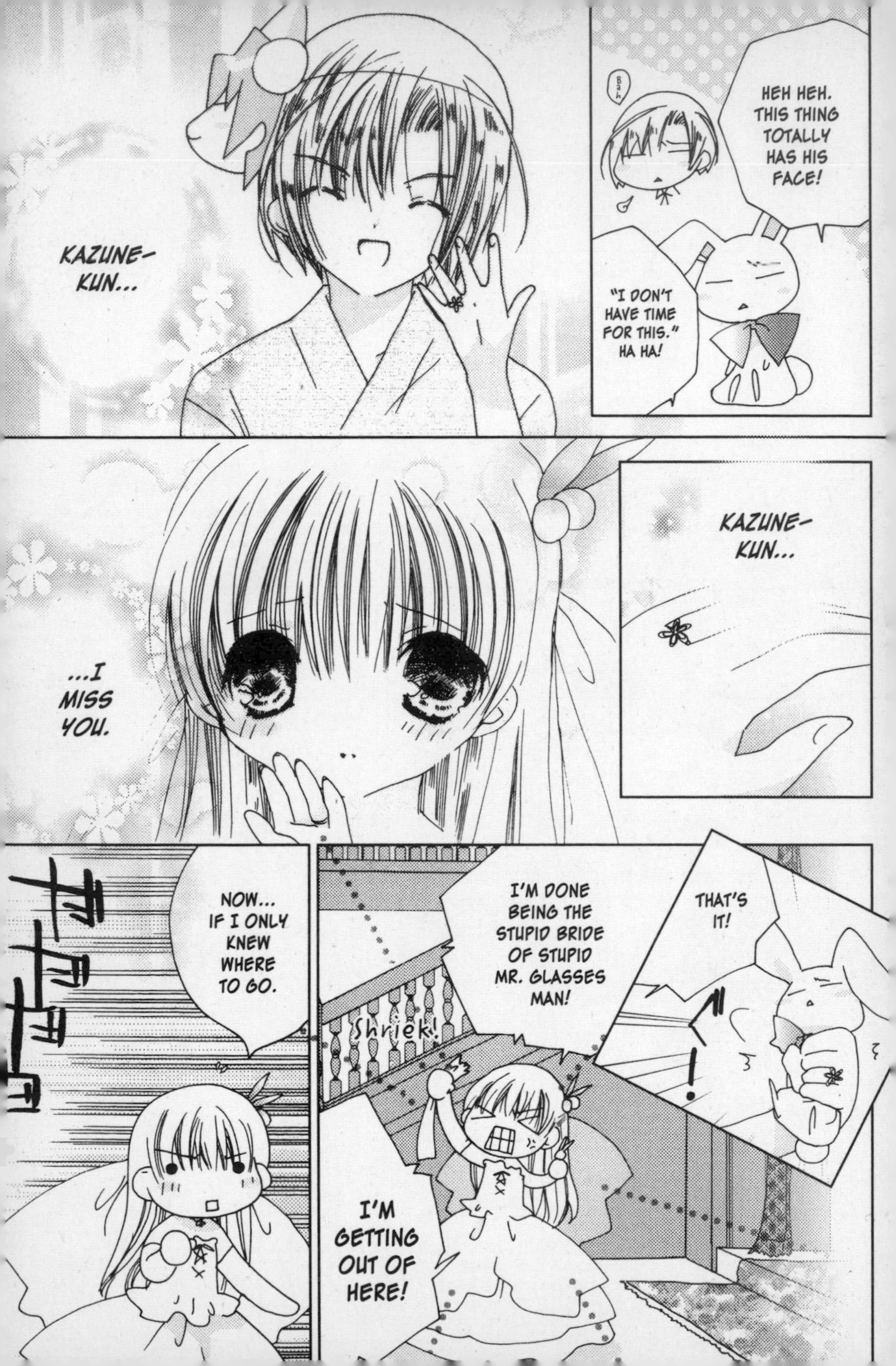
HEH HEH. THIS THING TOTALLY HAS HIS FACE!
"I DON'T HAVE TIME FOR THIS." HA HA!
KAZUNE-KUN...
KAZUNE-KUN...
...I MISS YOU.
THAT'S IT!
I'M DONE BEING THE STUPID BRIDE OF STUPID MR. GLASSES MAN!
Shriek!
I'M GETTING OUT OF HERE!
NOW... IF I ONLY KNEW WHERE TO GO.

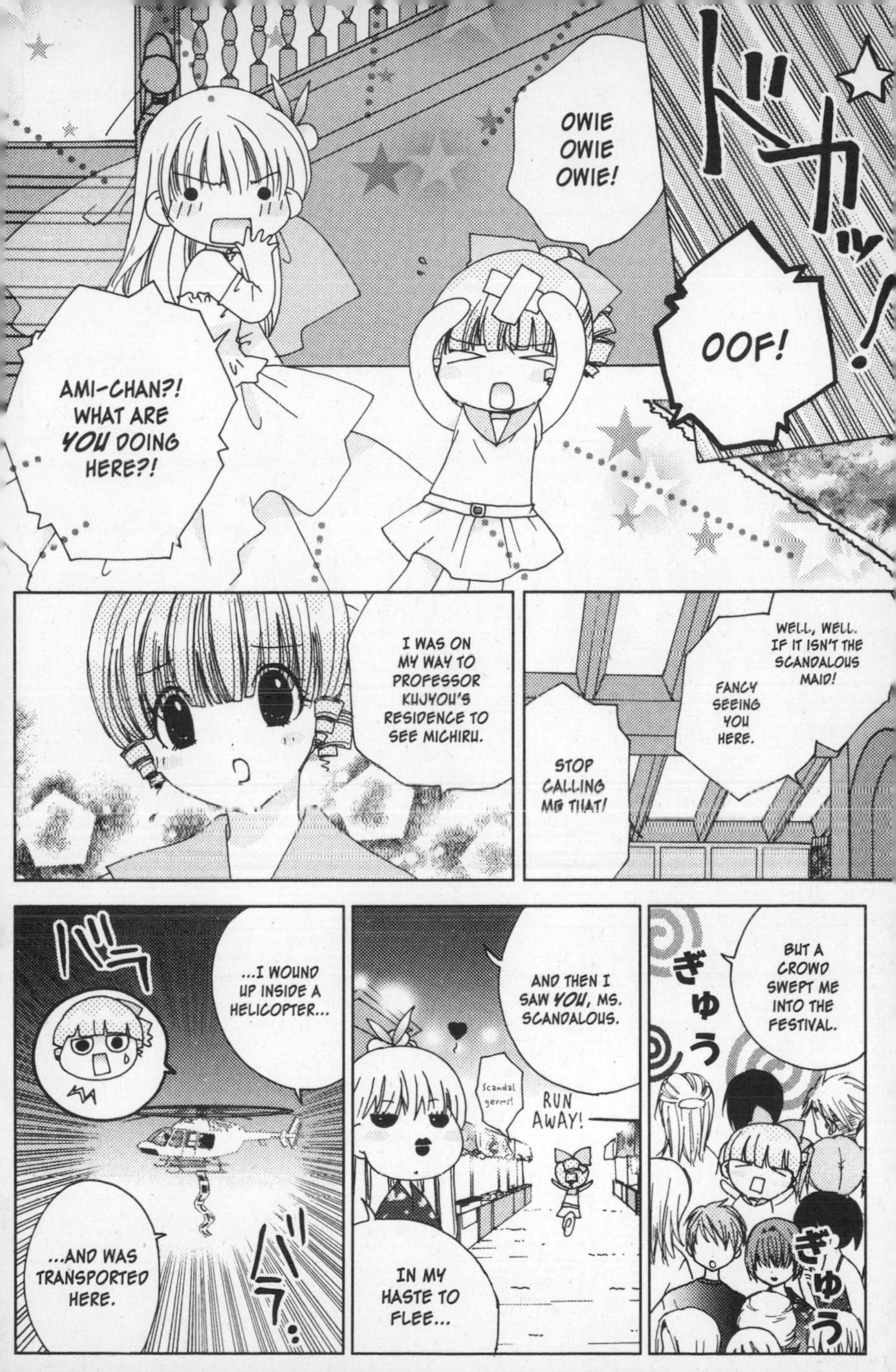

ドカッ!
OOF!
OWIE OWIE OWIE!
AMI-CHAN?! WHAT ARE YOU DOING HERE?!
WELL, WELL. IF IT ISN'T THE SCANDALOUS MAID!
FANCY SEEING YOU HERE.
STOP CALLING ME THAT!
I WAS ON MY WAY TO PROFESSOR KUJYOU'S RESIDENCE TO SEE MICHIRU.
BUT A CROWD SWEPT ME INTO THE FESTIVAL.
ぎゅう
ぎゅう
AND THEN I SAW YOU, MS. SCANDALOUS.
Scandal germs!
RUN AWAY!
IN MY HASTE TO FLEE...
...I WOUND UP INSIDE A HELICOPTER...
バラ
...AND WAS TRANSPORTED HERE.
バラ..

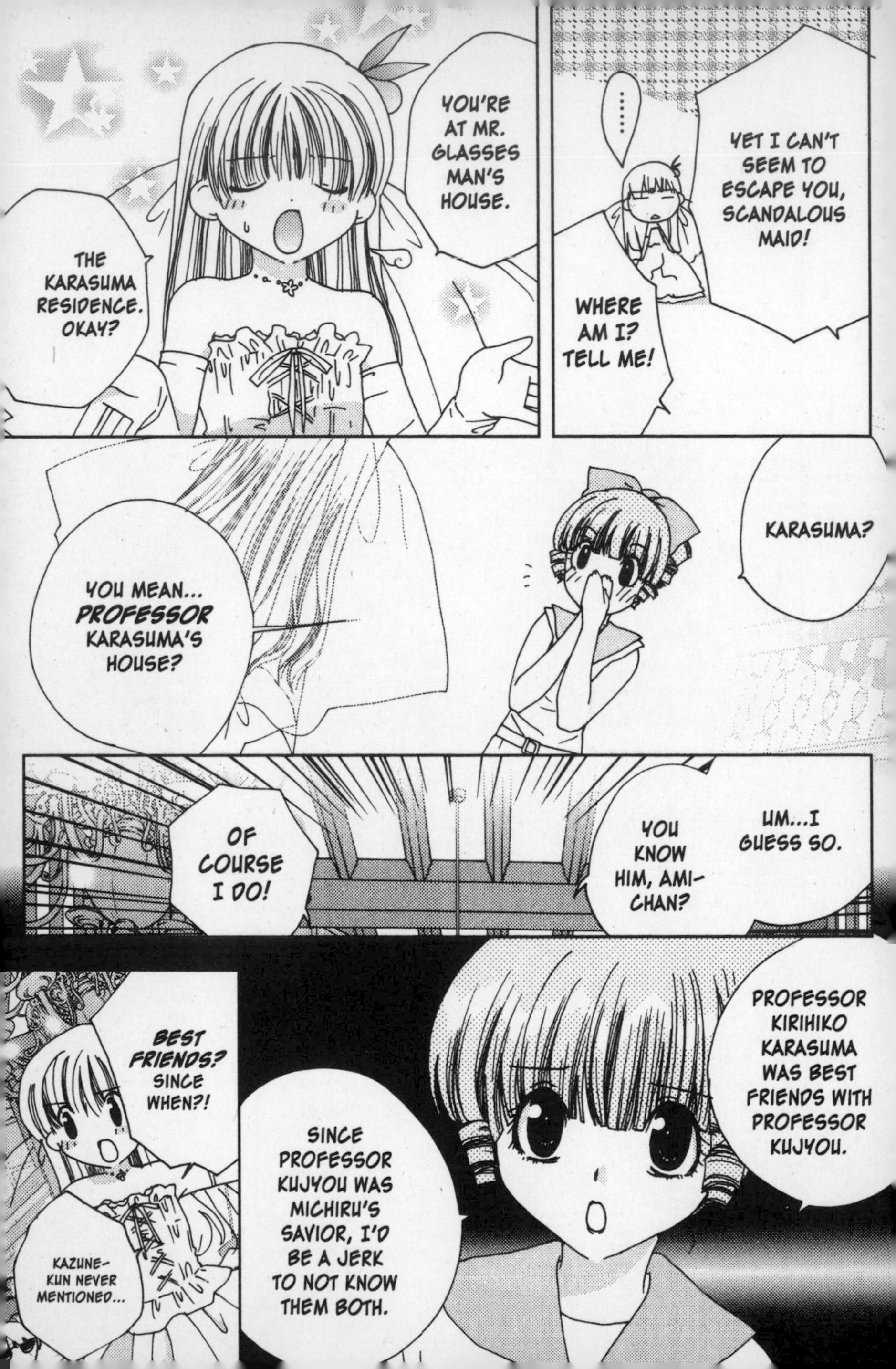
......
YET I CAN'T SEEM TO ESCAPE YOU, SCANDALOUS MAID!
WHERE AM I? TELL ME!
YOU'RE AT MR. GLASSES MAN'S HOUSE.
THE KARASUMA RESIDENCE. OKAY?
KARASUMA?
YOU MEAN... *PROFESSOR* KARASUMA'S HOUSE?
UM...I GUESS SO.
YOU KNOW HIM, AMI-CHAN?
OF COURSE I DO!
PROFESSOR KIRIHIKO KARASUMA WAS BEST FRIENDS WITH PROFESSOR KUJYOU.
SINCE PROFESSOR KUJYOU WAS MICHIRU'S SAVIOR, I'D BE A JERK TO NOT KNOW THEM BOTH.
BEST FRIENDS? SINCE WHEN?!
KAZUNE-KUN NEVER MENTIONED...

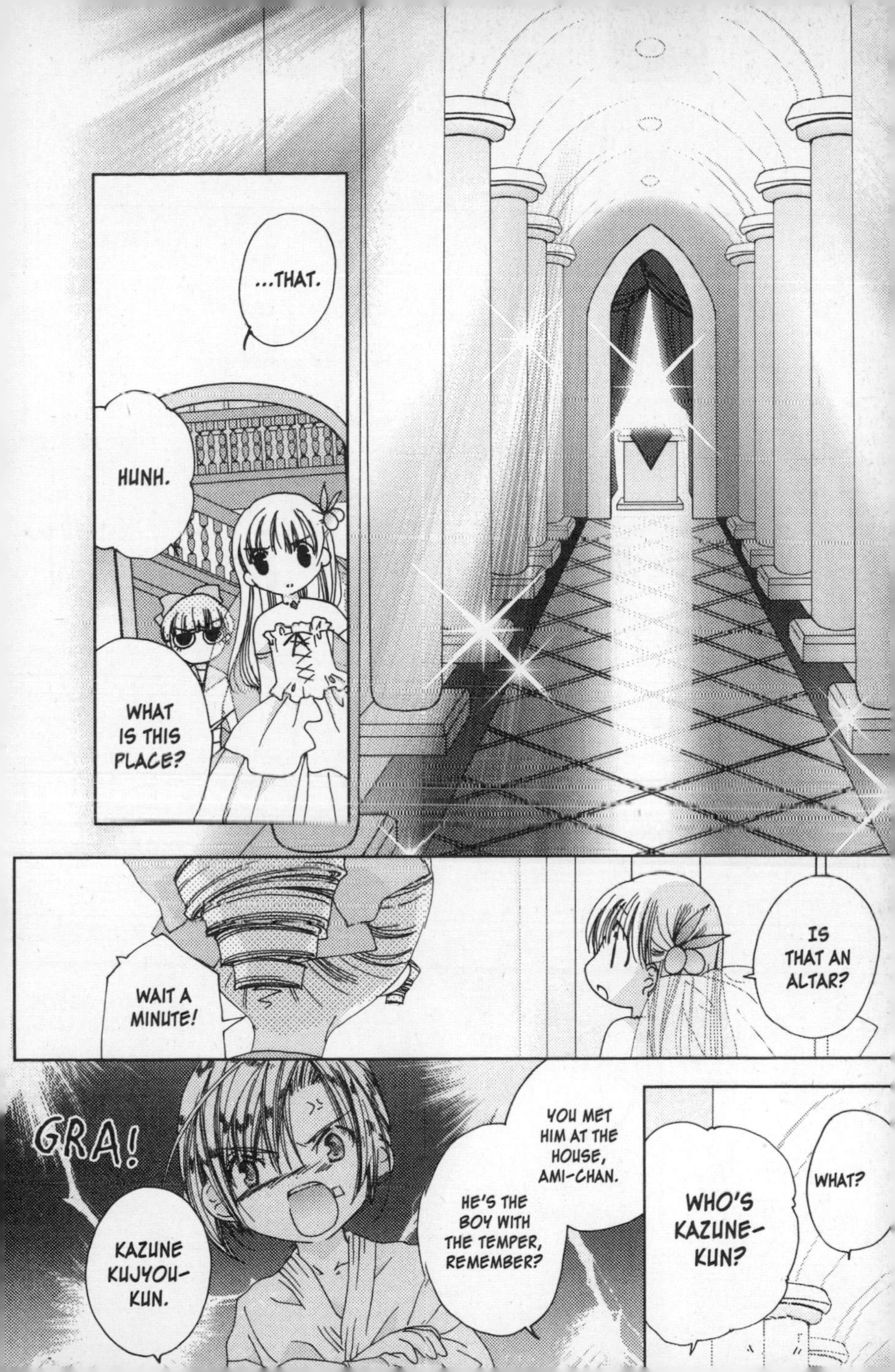
...THAT.
HUNH.
WHAT IS THIS PLACE?
IS THAT AN ALTAR?
WAIT A MINUTE!
WHAT?
WHO'S KAZUNE-KUN?
YOU MET HIM AT THE HOUSE, AMI-CHAN.
HE'S THE BOY WITH THE TEMPER, REMEMBER?
GRA!
KAZUNE KUJYOU-KUN.

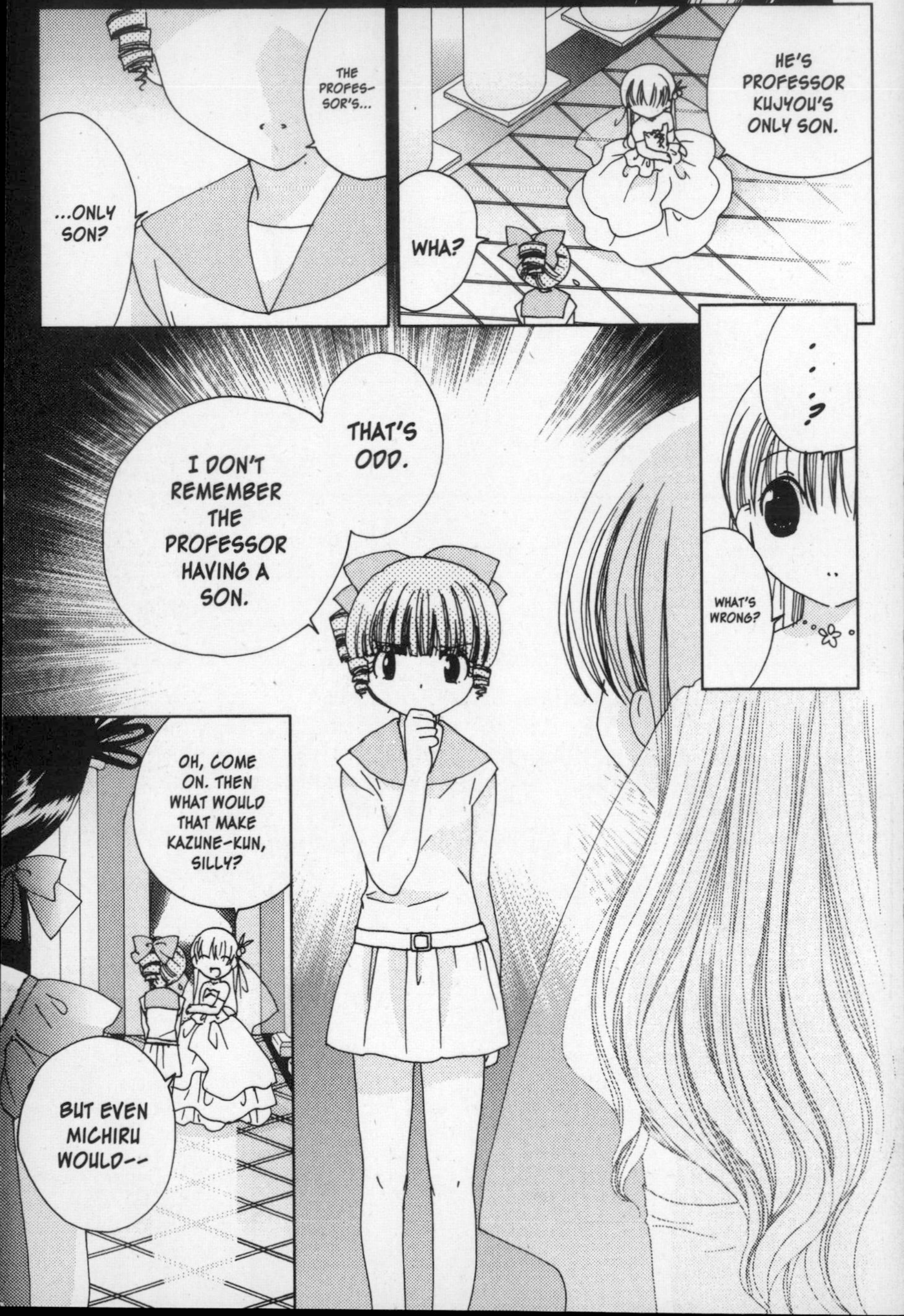

HE'S PROFESSOR KUJYOU'S ONLY SON.
WHA?
THE PROFES-SOR'S...
...ONLY SON?
...
...?
WHAT'S WRONG?
THAT'S ODD.
I DON'T REMEMBER THE PROFESSOR HAVING A SON.
OH, COME ON. THEN WHAT WOULD THAT MAKE KAZUNE-KUN, SILLY?
BUT EVEN MICHIRU WOULD--

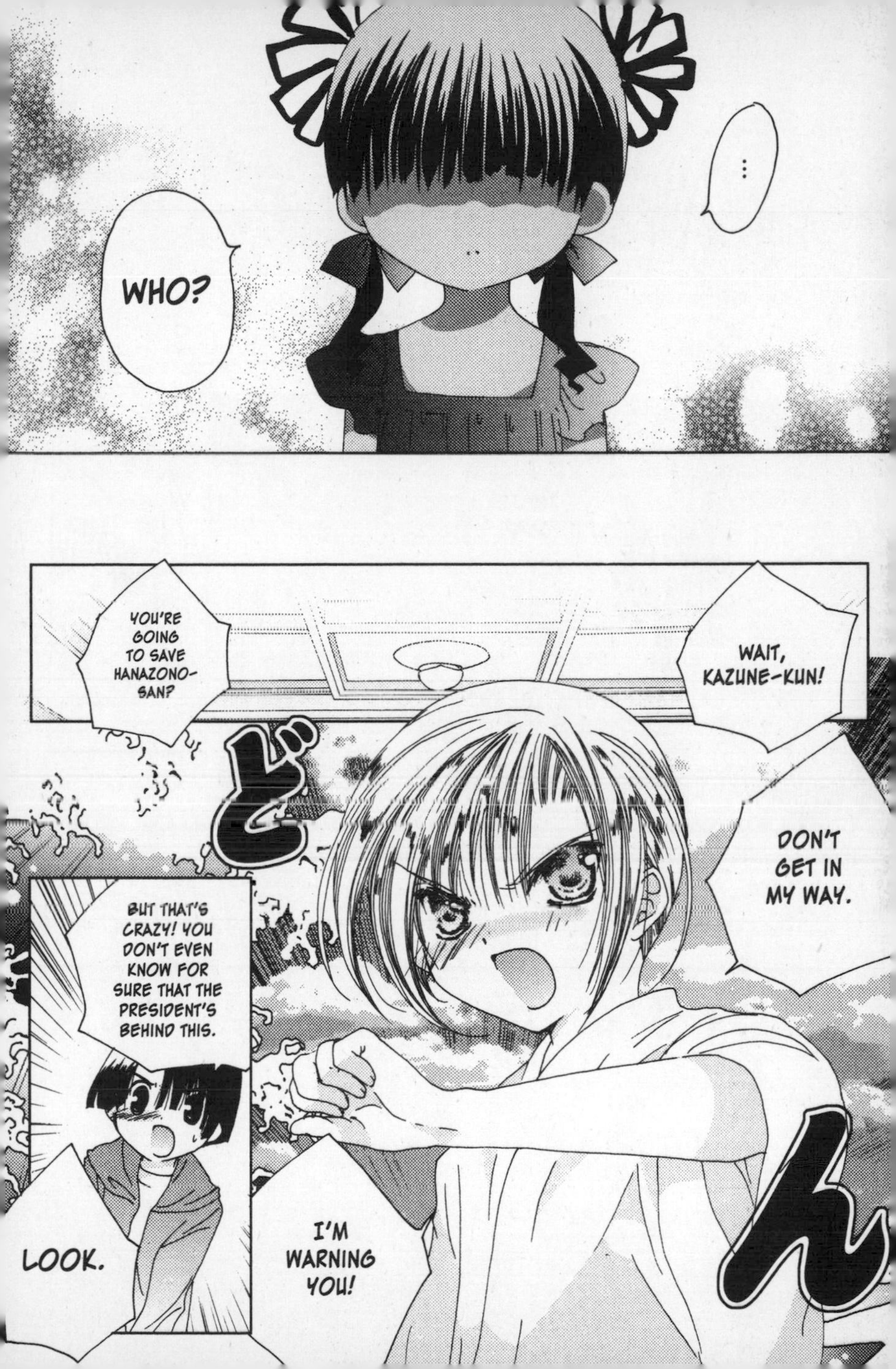
...
WHO?
WAIT, KAZUNE-KUN!
YOU'RE GOING TO SAVE HANAZONO-SAN?
ど
ん
DON'T GET IN MY WAY.
I'M WARNING YOU!
BUT THAT'S CRAZY! YOU DON'T EVEN KNOW FOR SURE THAT THE PRESIDENT'S BEHIND THIS.
LOOK.

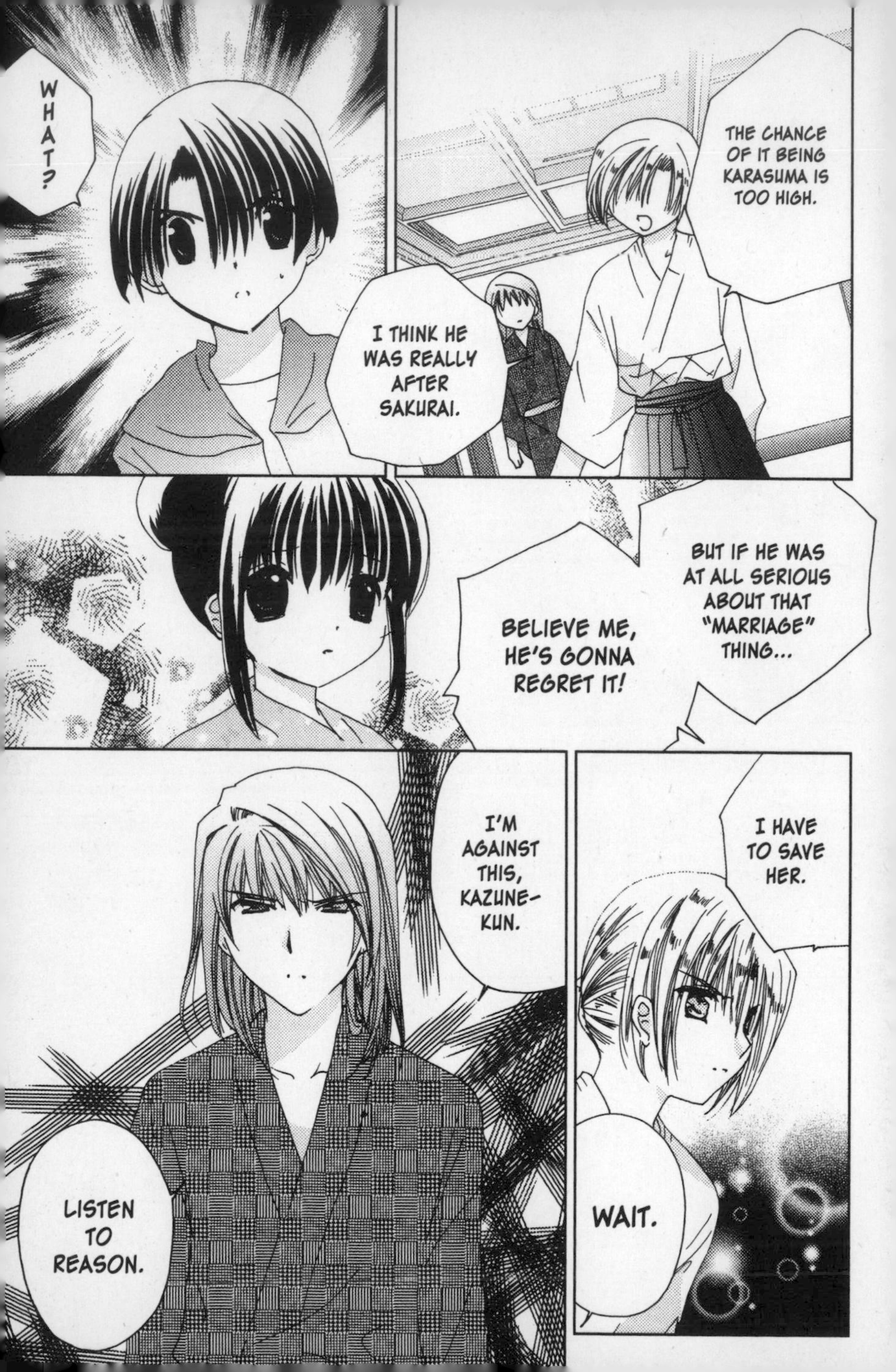
THE CHANCE OF IT BEING KARASUMA IS TOO HIGH.
I THINK HE WAS REALLY AFTER SAKURAI.
WHAT?
BUT IF HE WAS AT ALL SERIOUS ABOUT THAT "MARRIAGE" THING...
BELIEVE ME, HE'S GONNA REGRET IT!
I HAVE TO SAVE HER.
WAIT.
I'M AGAINST THIS, KAZUNE-KUN.
LISTEN TO REASON.

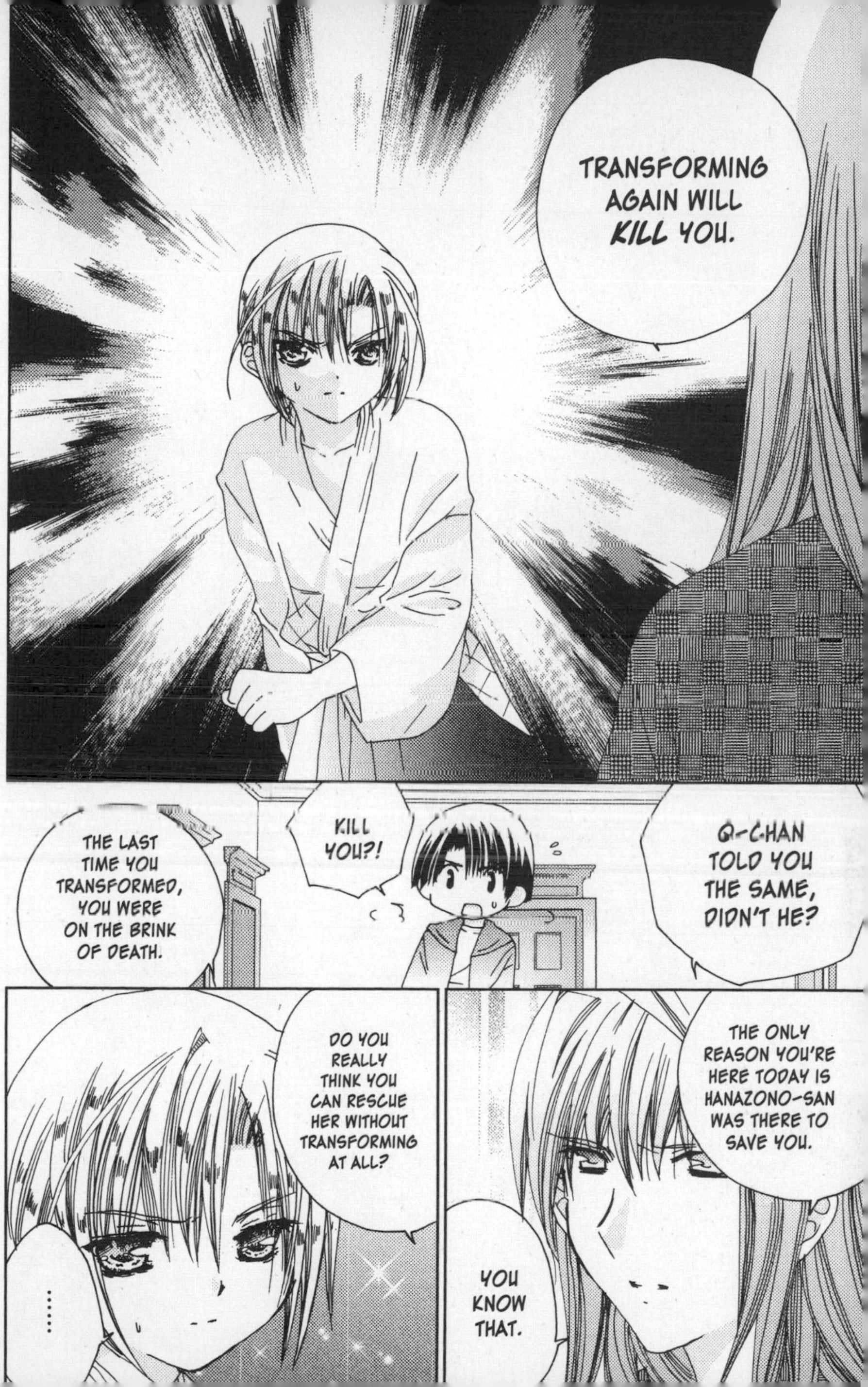
TRANSFORMING AGAIN WILL KILL YOU.
Q-CHAN TOLD YOU THE SAME, DIDN'T HE?
KILL YOU?!
THE LAST TIME YOU TRANSFORMED, YOU WERE ON THE BRINK OF DEATH.
THE ONLY REASON YOU'RE HERE TODAY IS HANAZONO-SAN WAS THERE TO SAVE YOU.
YOU KNOW THAT.
DO YOU REALLY THINK YOU CAN RESCUE HER WITHOUT TRANSFORMING AT ALL?
......

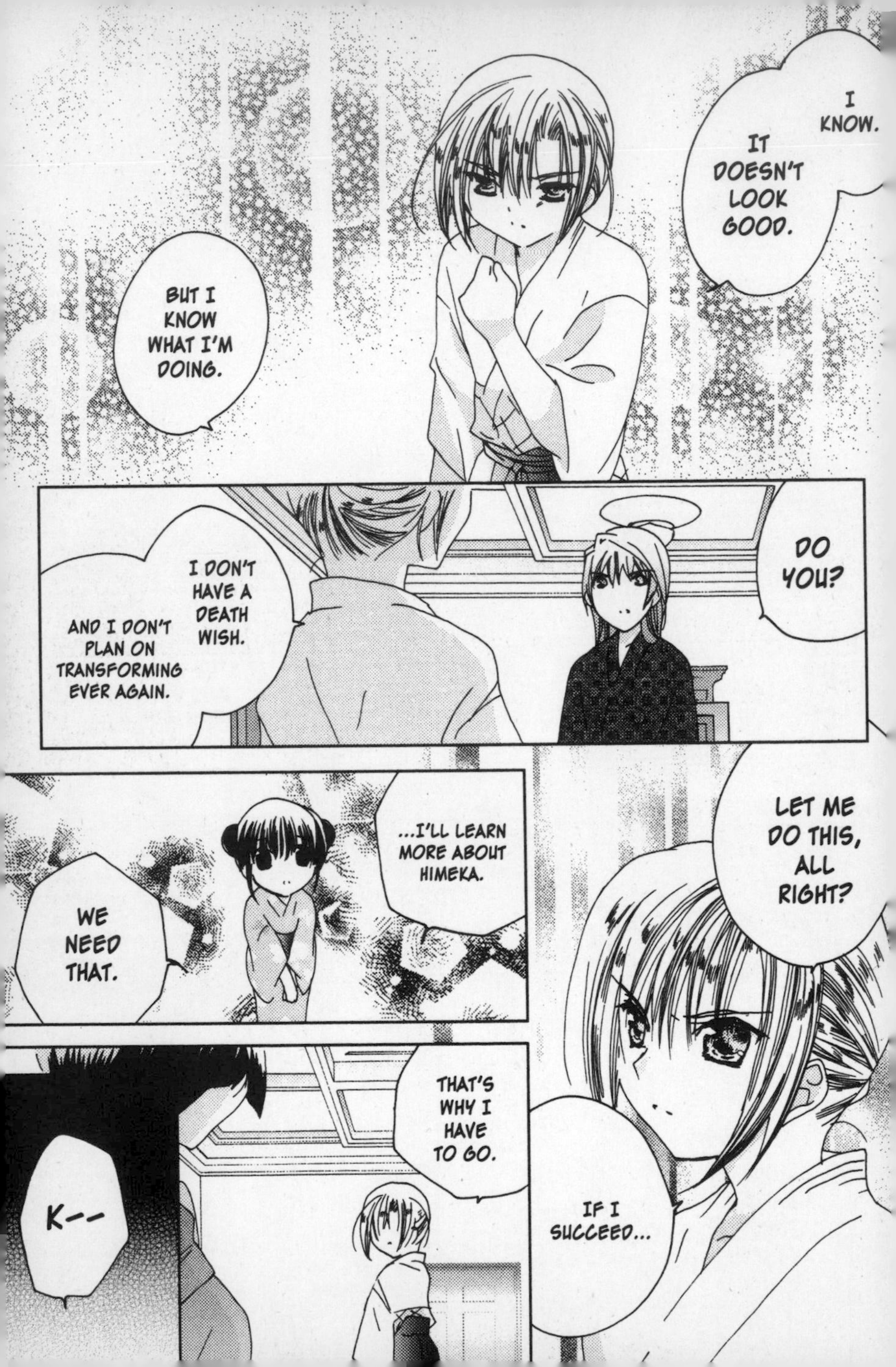

I KNOW.
IT DOESN'T LOOK GOOD.
BUT I KNOW WHAT I'M DOING.
DO YOU?
I DON'T HAVE A DEATH WISH.
AND I DON'T PLAN ON TRANSFORMING EVER AGAIN.
LET ME DO THIS, ALL RIGHT?
IF I SUCCEED...
...I'LL LEARN MORE ABOUT HIMEKA.
WE NEED THAT.
THAT'S WHY I HAVE TO GO.
K--

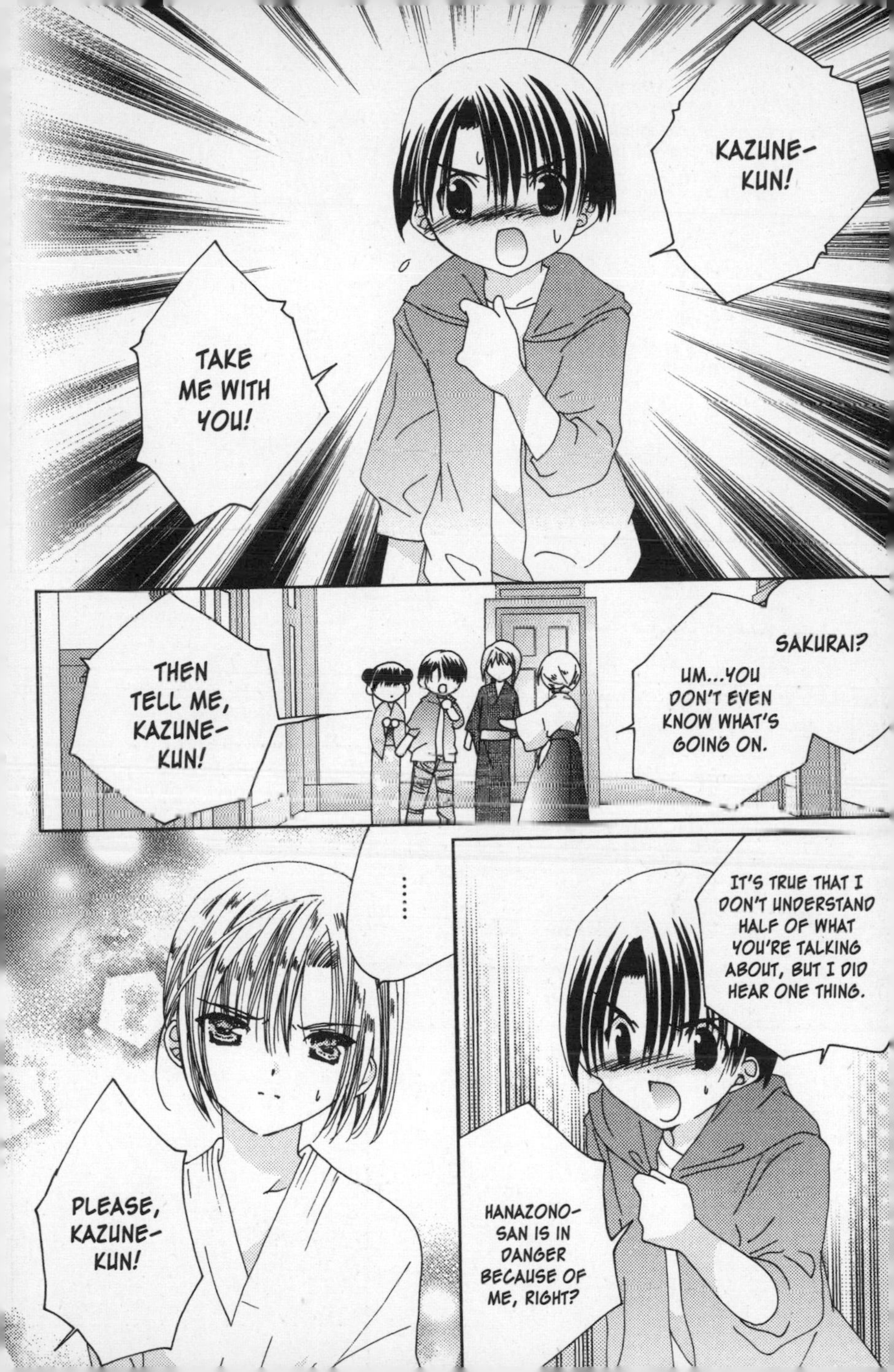
KAZUNE-KUN!
TAKE ME WITH YOU!
SAKURAI?
UM...YOU DON'T EVEN KNOW WHAT'S GOING ON.
THEN TELL ME, KAZUNE-KUN!
IT'S TRUE THAT I DON'T UNDERSTAND HALF OF WHAT YOU'RE TALKING ABOUT, BUT I DID HEAR ONE THING.
HANAZONO-SAN IS IN DANGER BECAUSE OF ME, RIGHT?
......
PLEASE, KAZUNE-KUN!

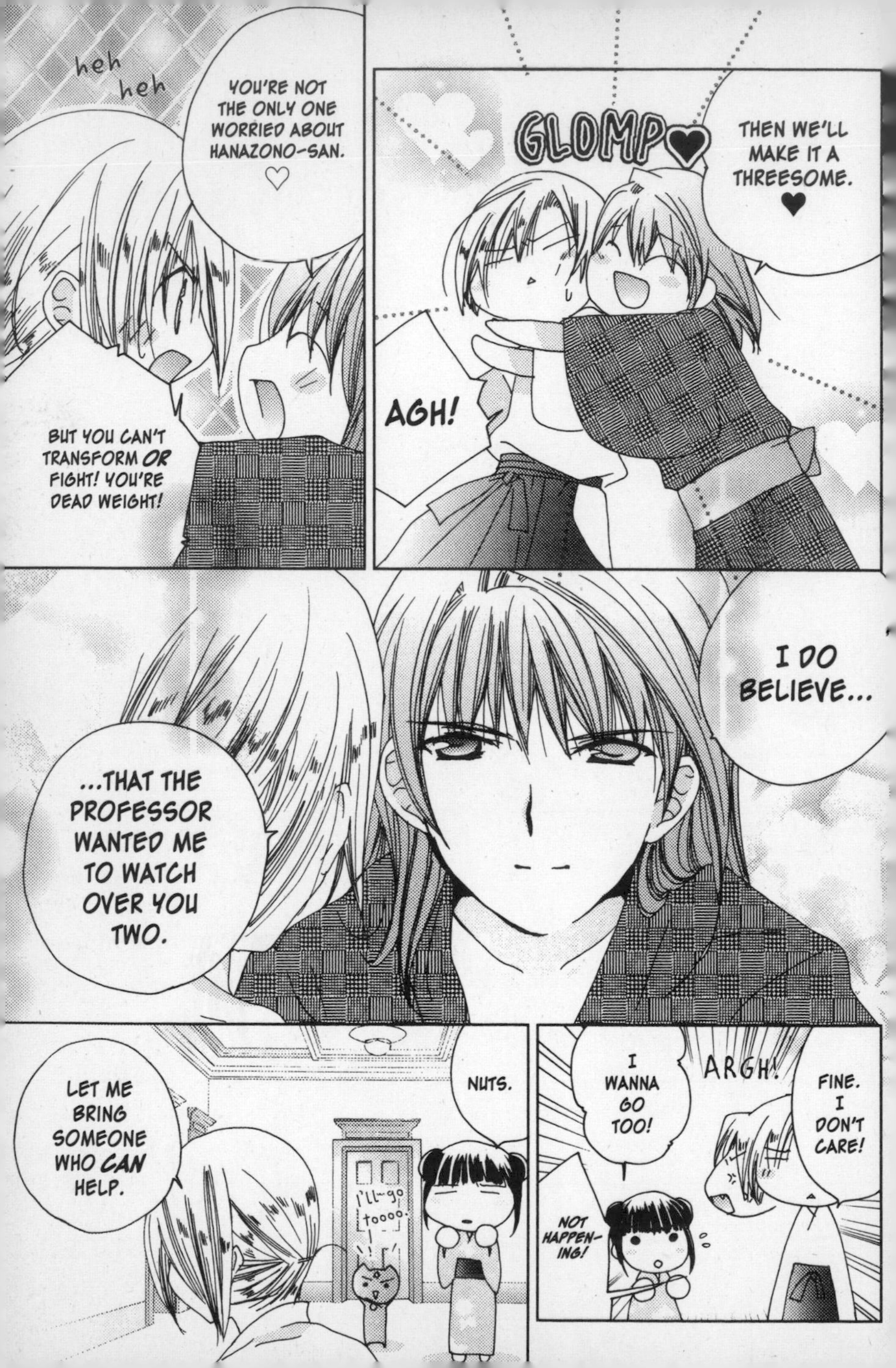
GLOMP♥
THEN WE'LL MAKE IT A THREESOME. ♥
AGH!
heh heh
YOU'RE NOT THE ONLY ONE WORRIED ABOUT HANAZONO-SAN. ♡
BUT YOU CAN'T TRANSFORM OR FIGHT! YOU'RE DEAD WEIGHT!
I DO BELIEVE...
...THAT THE PROFESSOR WANTED ME TO WATCH OVER YOU TWO.
FINE. I DON'T CARE!
ARGH!
I WANNA GO TOO!
NOT HAPPENING!
NUTS.
I'll go toooo.
LET ME BRING SOMEONE WHO CAN HELP.

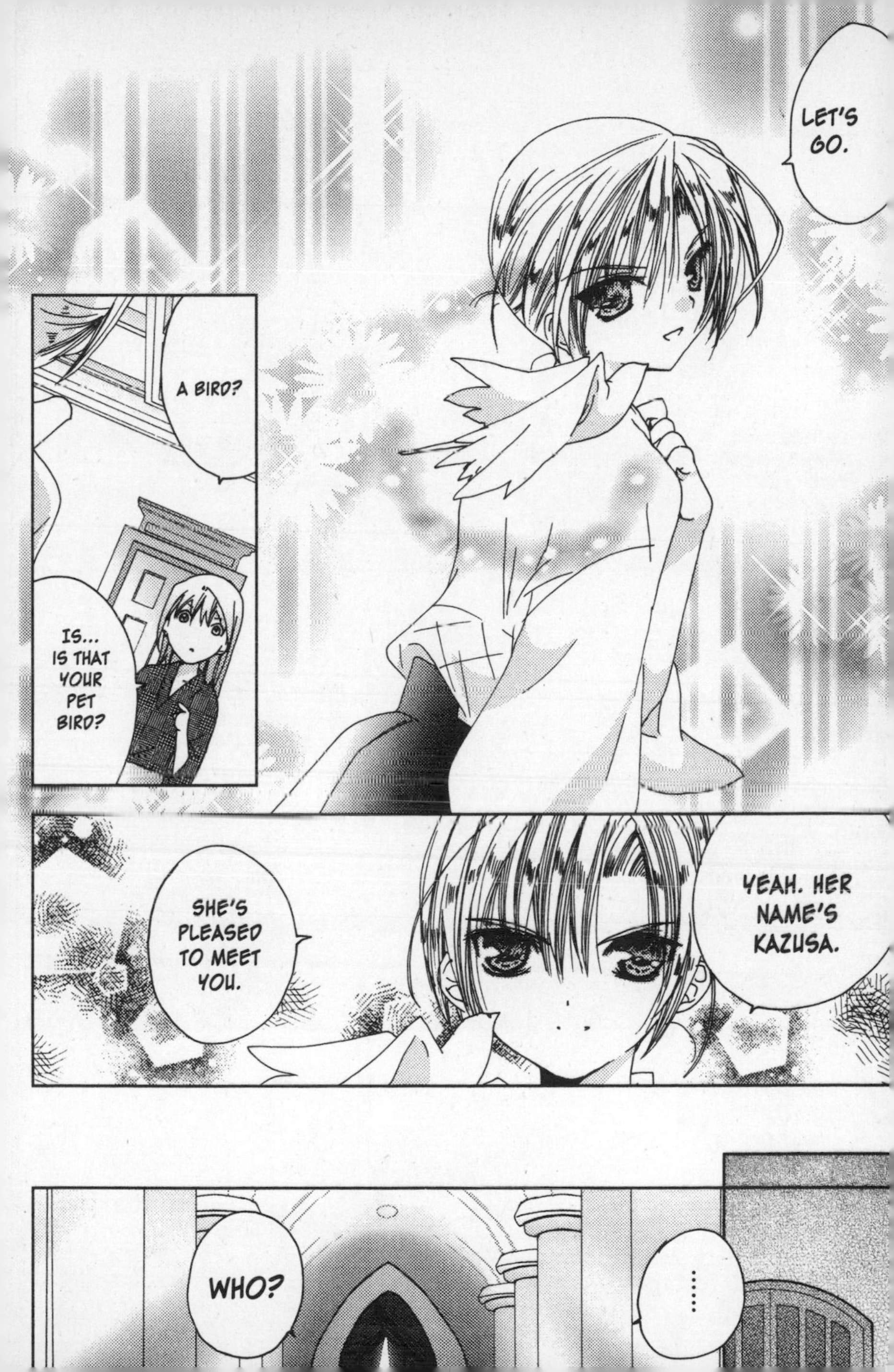
LET'S GO.
A BIRD?
IS... IS THAT YOUR PET BIRD?
YEAH. HER NAME'S KAZUSA.
SHE'S PLEASED TO MEET YOU.
......
WHO?

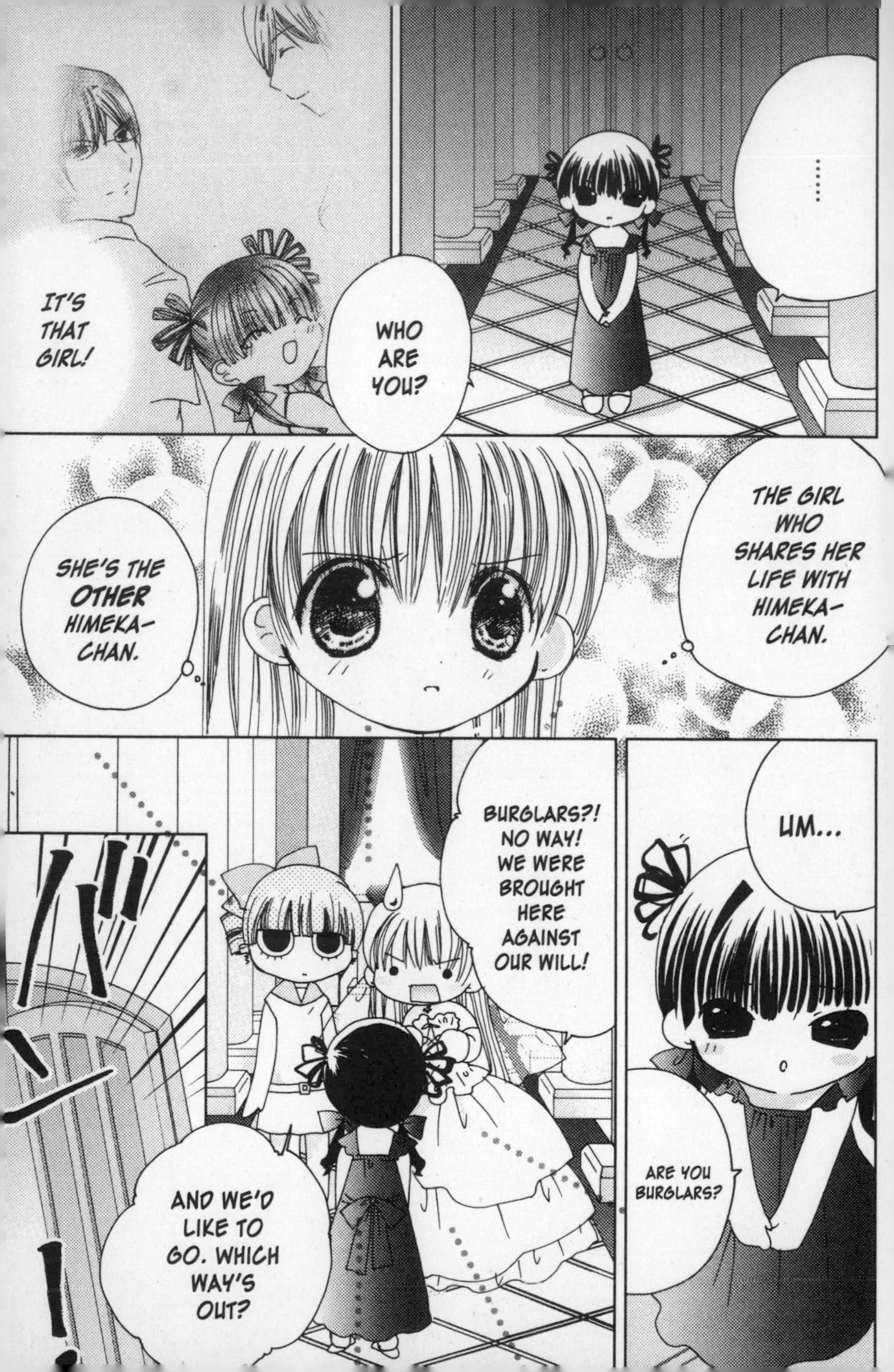
......
WHO ARE YOU?
IT'S THAT GIRL!
THE GIRL WHO SHARES HER LIFE WITH HIMEKA-CHAN.
SHE'S THE OTHER HIMEKA-CHAN.
UM...
ARE YOU BURGLARS?
BURGLARS?! NO WAY! WE WERE BROUGHT HERE AGAINST OUR WILL!
AND WE'D LIKE TO GO. WHICH WAY'S OUT?

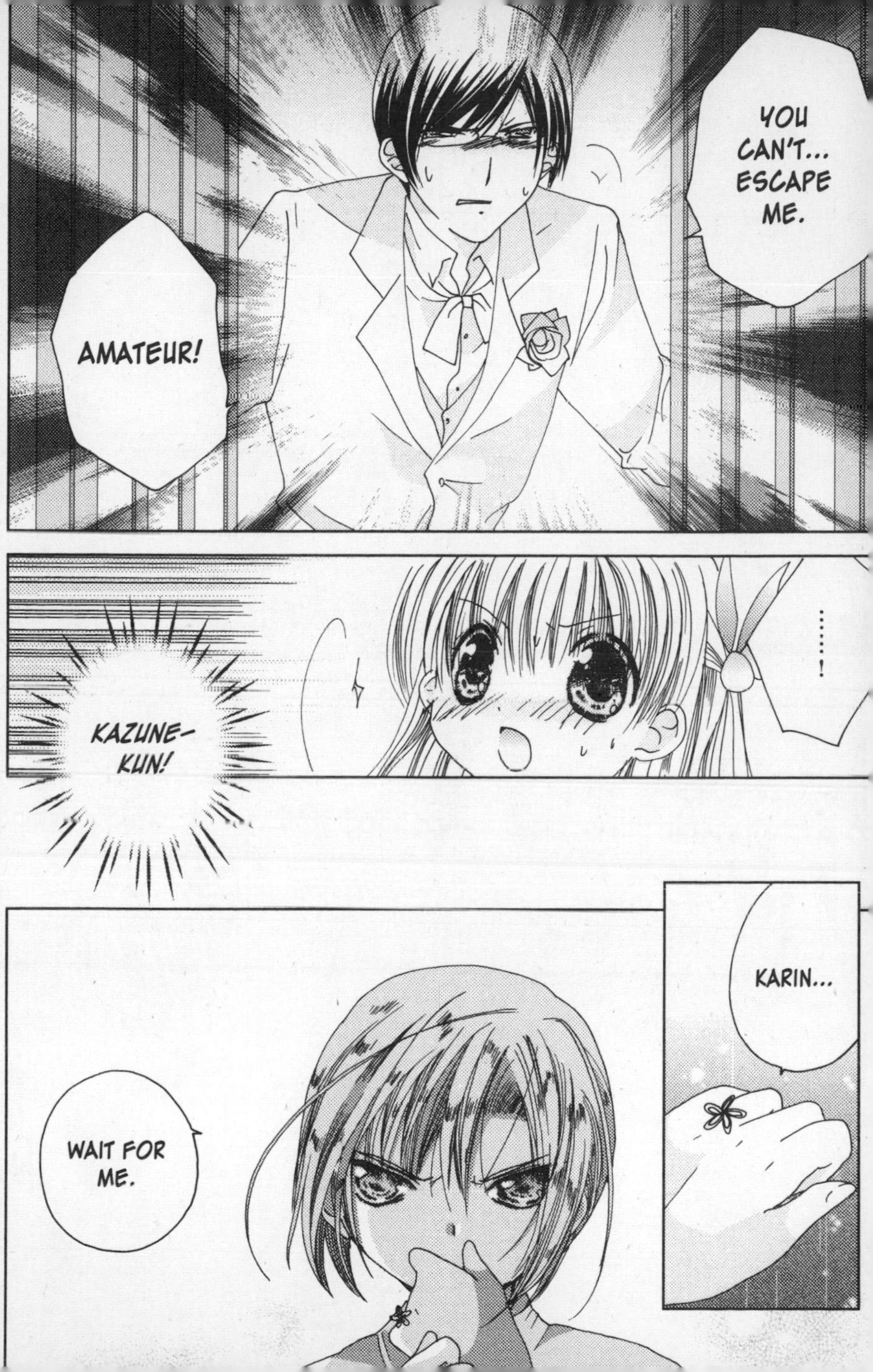
YOU CAN'T... ESCAPE ME.
AMATEUR!
......!
KAZUNE-KUN!
KARIN...
WAIT FOR ME.

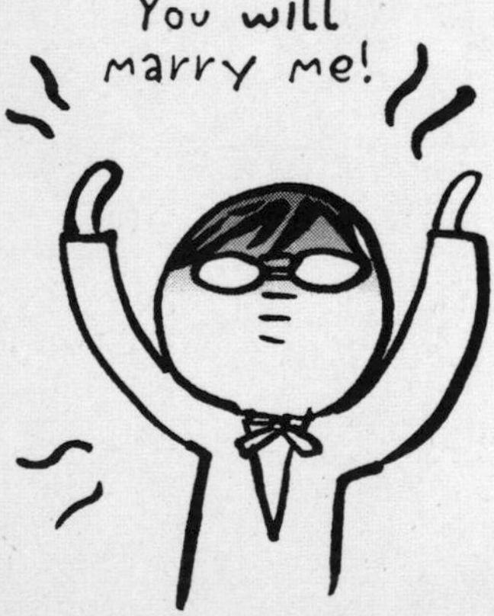
You will marry me!

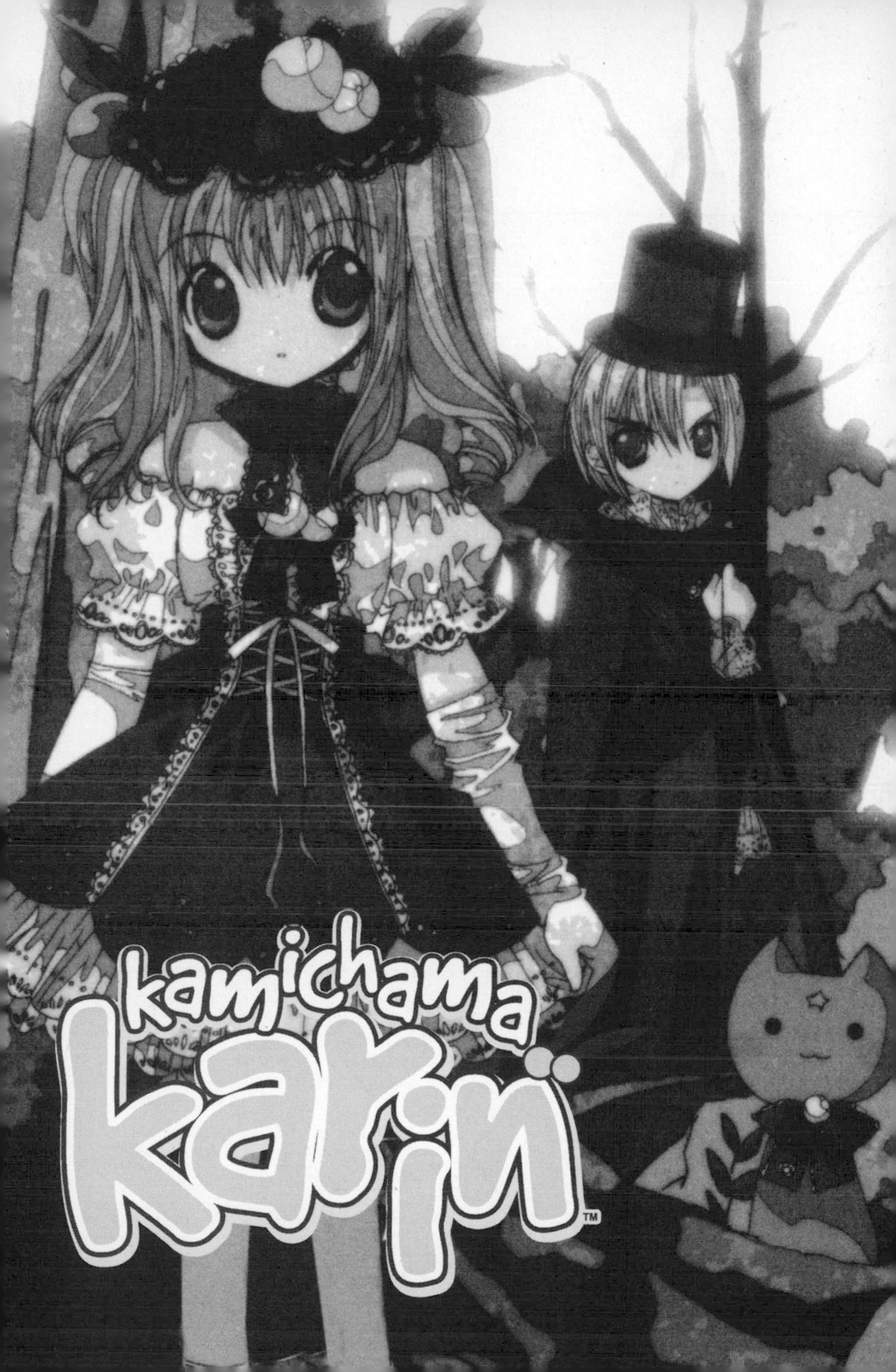
kamichama
karin™

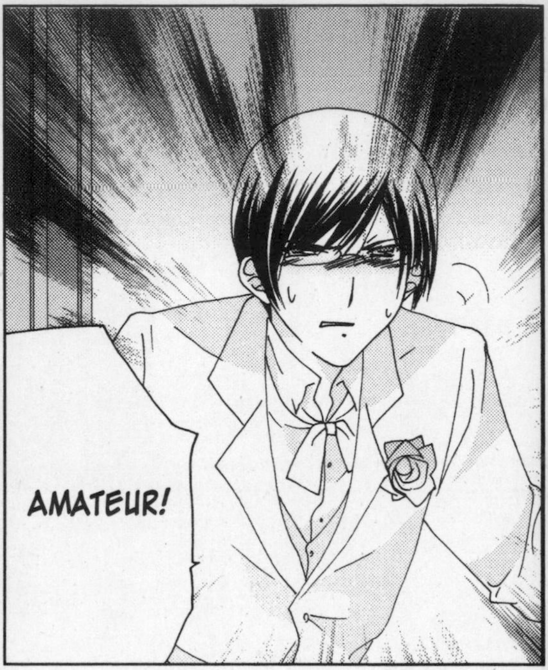
AMATEUR!

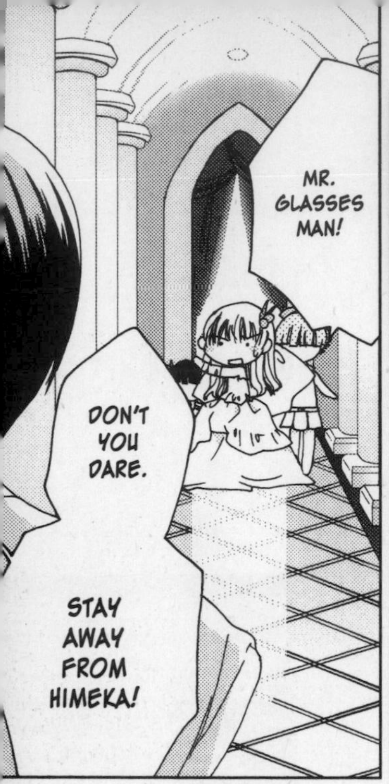
MR. GLASSES MAN!
DON'T YOU DARE.
STAY AWAY FROM HIMEKA!

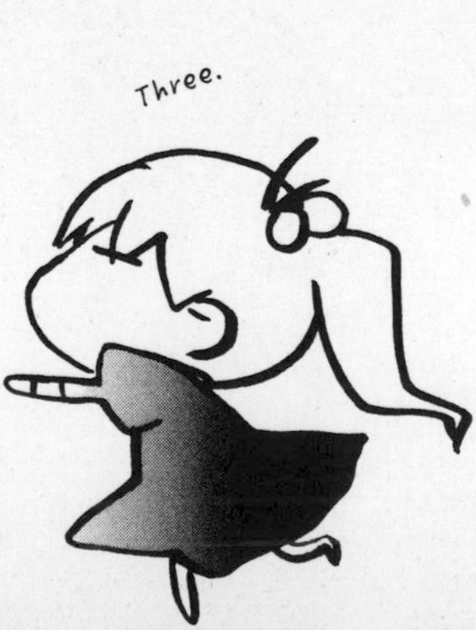
Three.

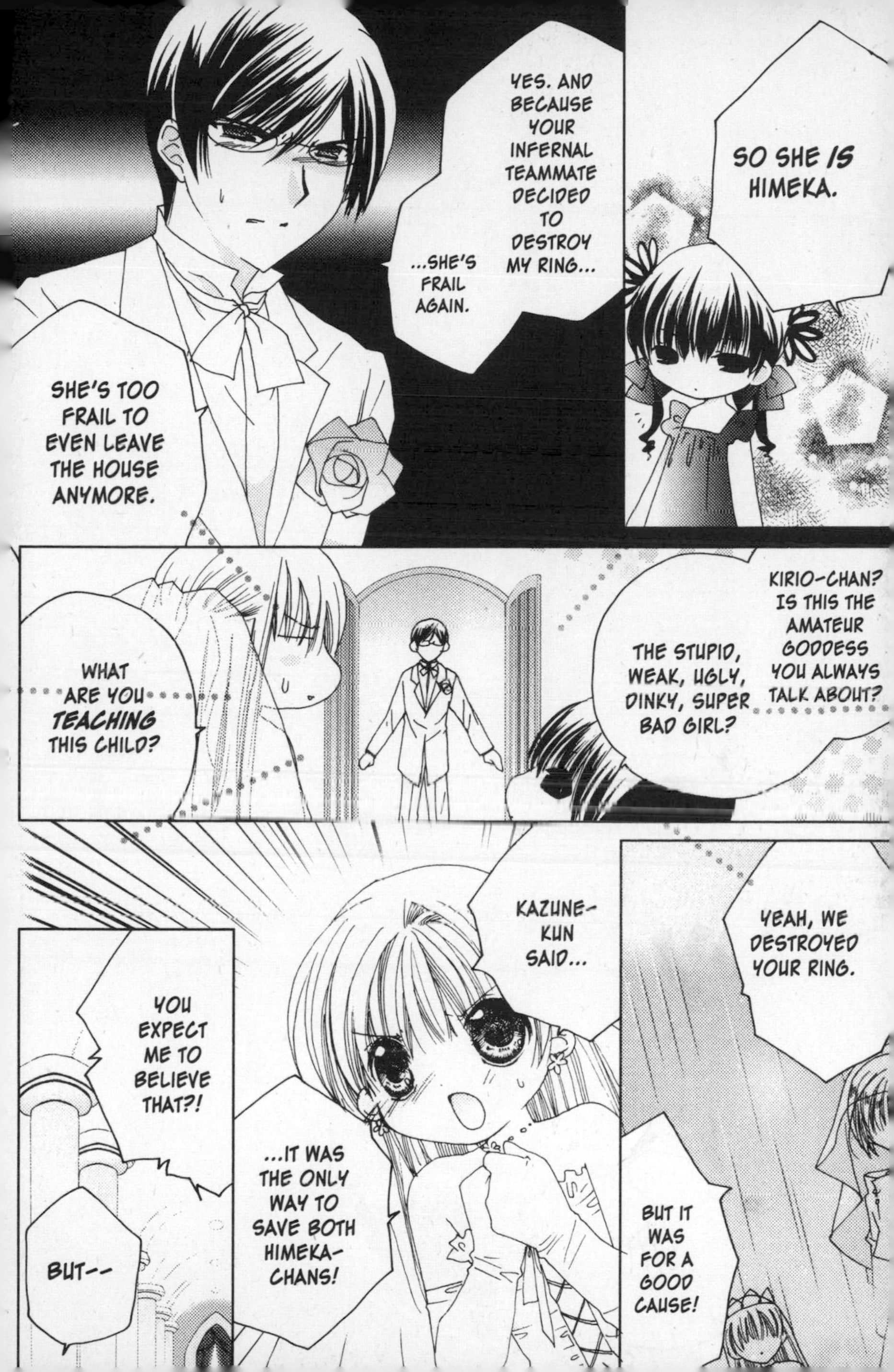
SO SHE *IS* HIMEKA.
YES. AND BECAUSE YOUR INFERNAL TEAMMATE DECIDED TO DESTROY MY RING...
...SHE'S FRAIL AGAIN.
SHE'S TOO FRAIL TO EVEN LEAVE THE HOUSE ANYMORE.
KIRIO-CHAN? IS THIS THE AMATEUR GODDESS YOU ALWAYS TALK ABOUT?
THE STUPID, WEAK, UGLY, DINKY, SUPER BAD GIRL?
WHAT ARE YOU *TEACHING* THIS CHILD?
YEAH, WE DESTROYED YOUR RING.
BUT IT WAS FOR A GOOD CAUSE!
KAZUNE-KUN SAID...
...IT WAS THE ONLY WAY TO SAVE BOTH HIMEKA-CHANS!
YOU EXPECT ME TO BELIEVE THAT?!
BUT--

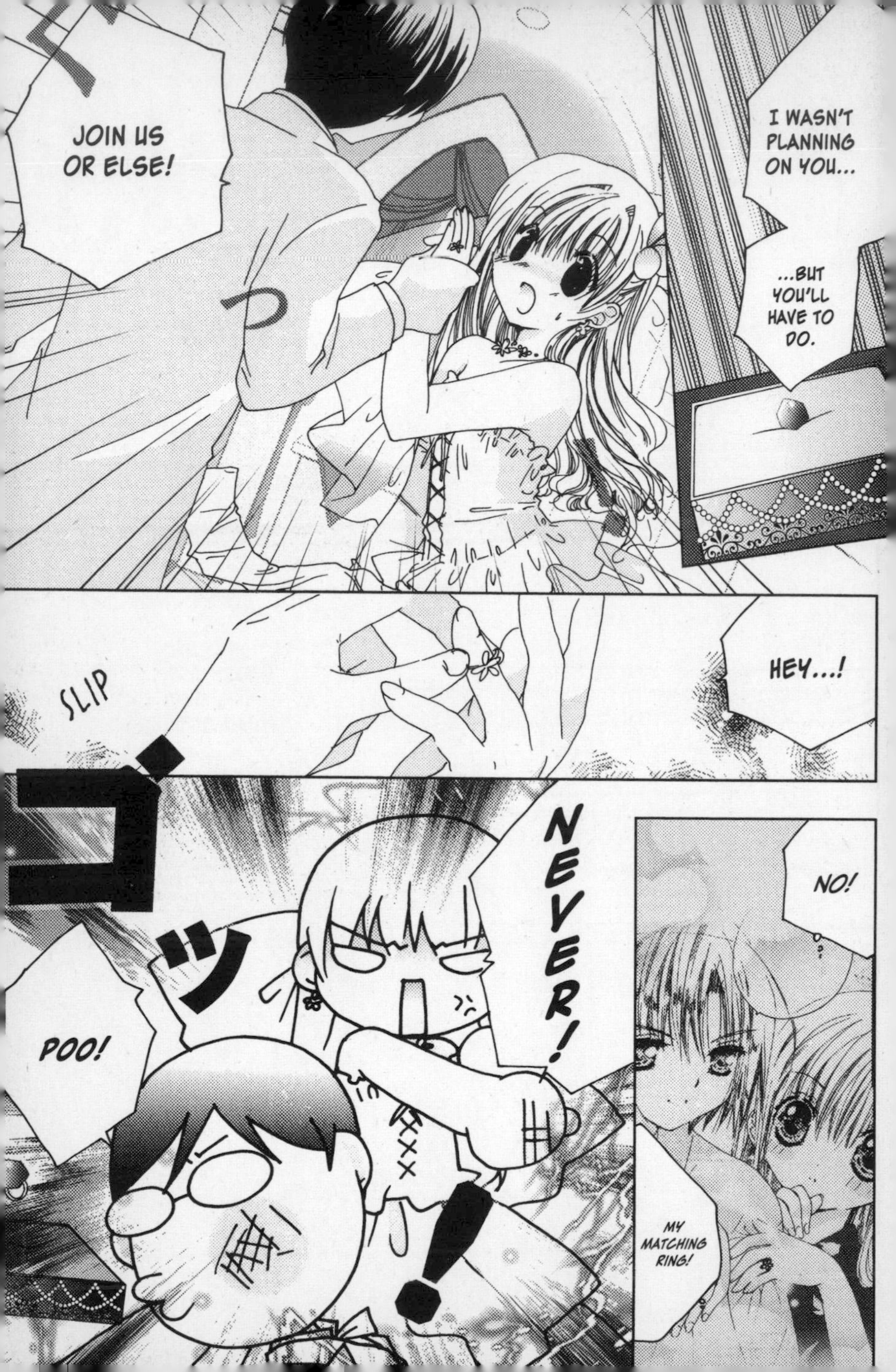

I WASN'T PLANNING ON YOU...
...BUT YOU'LL HAVE TO DO.
JOIN US OR ELSE!
HEY...!
SLIP
NO!
MY MATCHING RING!
NEVER!
ゴッ
POO!

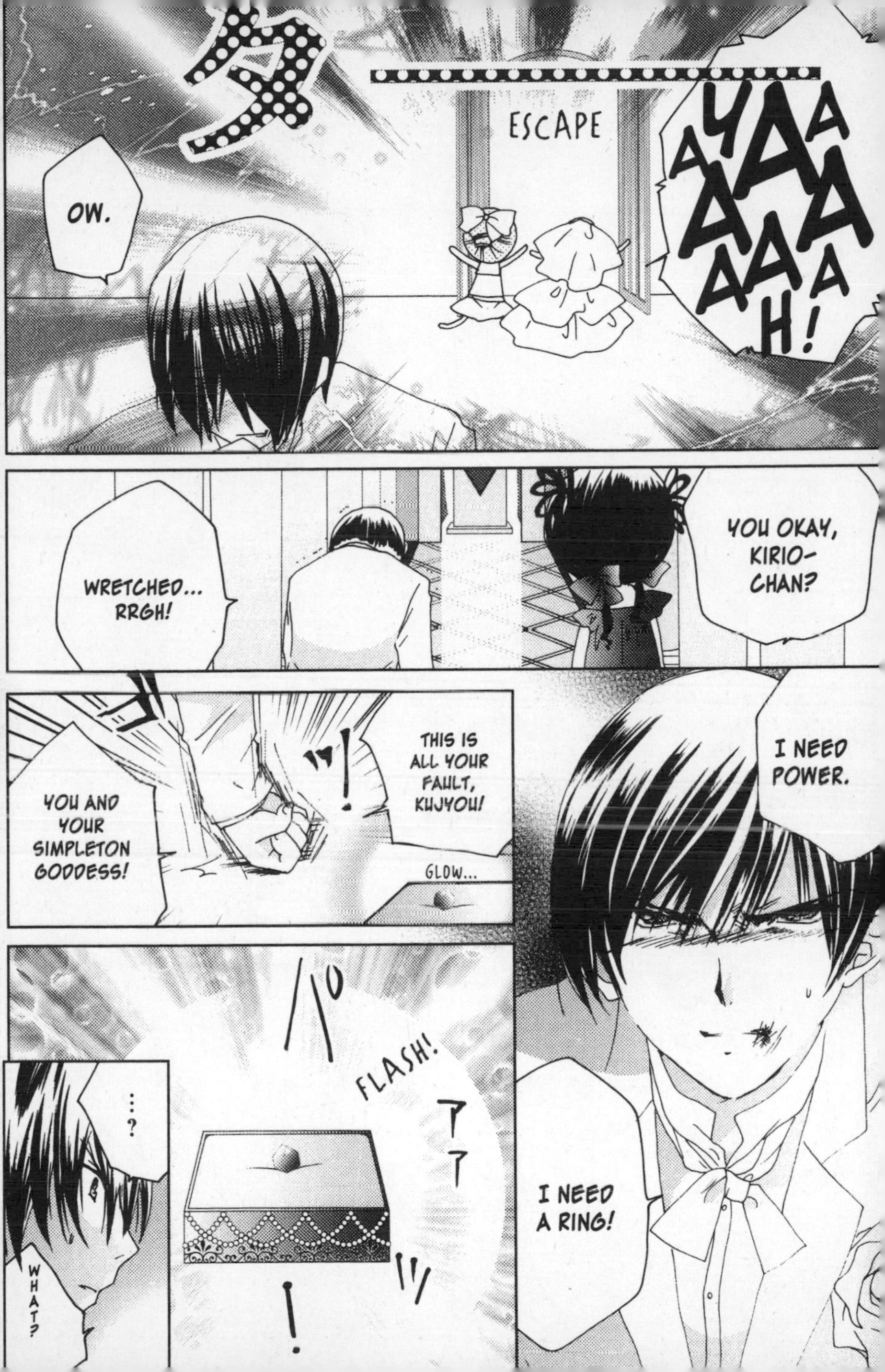
YAAAAAAAAH!
ESCAPE
OW.
YOU OKAY, KIRIO-CHAN?
WRETCHED... RRGH!
I NEED POWER.
I NEED A RING!
THIS IS ALL YOUR FAULT, KUJYOU!
YOU AND YOUR SIMPLETON GODDESS!
GLOW...
FLASH!
...?
WHAT?

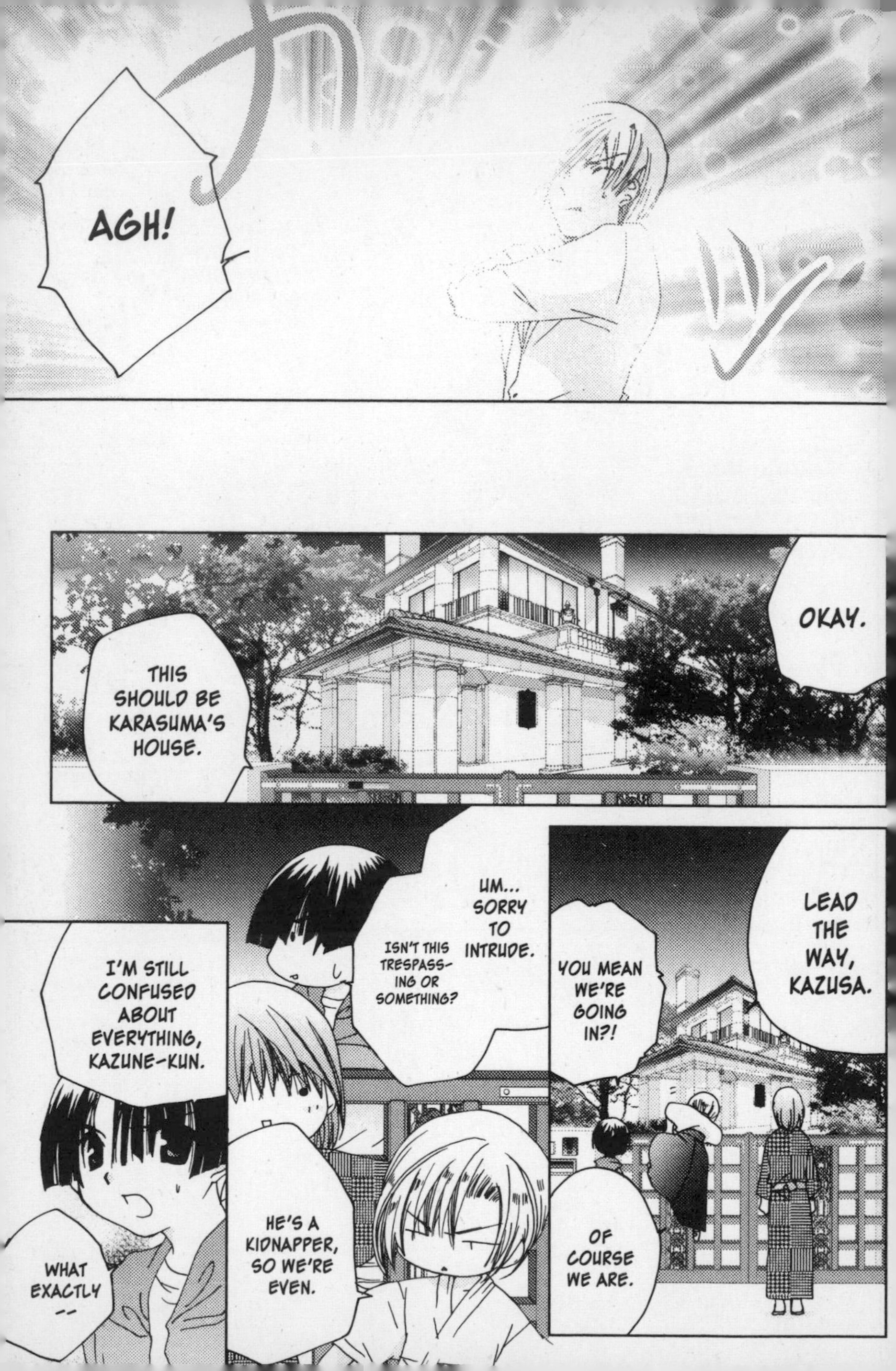
AGH!
OKAY.
THIS SHOULD BE KARASUMA'S HOUSE.
LEAD THE WAY, KAZUSA.
YOU MEAN WE'RE GOING IN?!
OF COURSE WE ARE.
UM... SORRY TO INTRUDE.
ISN'T THIS TRESPASS-ING OR SOMETHING?
I'M STILL CONFUSED ABOUT EVERYTHING, KAZUNE-KUN.
HE'S A KIDNAPPER, SO WE'RE EVEN.
WHAT EXACTLY --

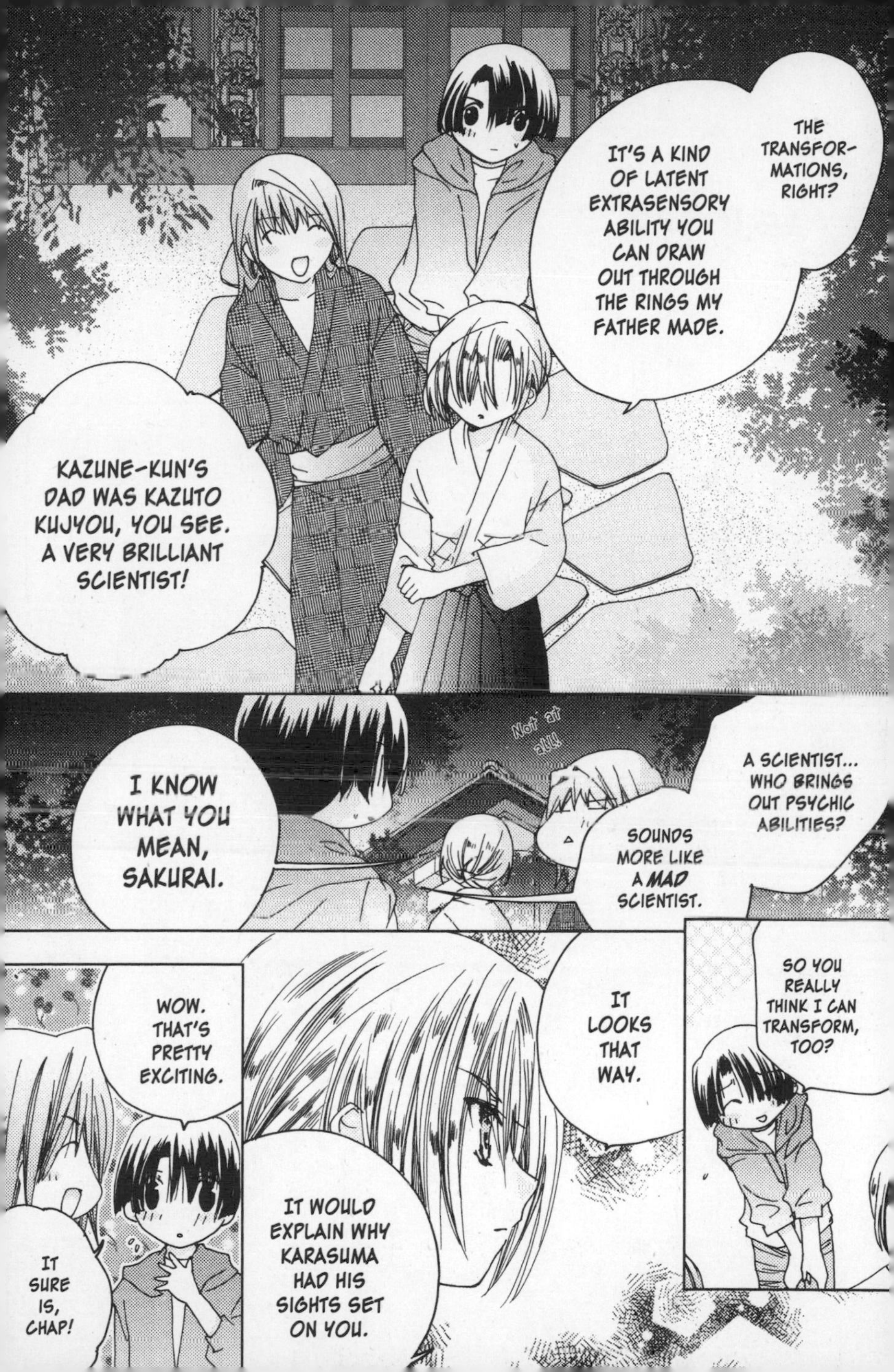
THE TRANSFORMATIONS, RIGHT?
IT'S A KIND OF LATENT EXTRASENSORY ABILITY YOU CAN DRAW OUT THROUGH THE RINGS MY FATHER MADE.
KAZUNE-KUN'S DAD WAS KAZUTO KUJYOU, YOU SEE. A VERY BRILLIANT SCIENTIST!
A SCIENTIST... WHO BRINGS OUT PSYCHIC ABILITIES?
SOUNDS MORE LIKE A MAD SCIENTIST.
Not at all!
I KNOW WHAT YOU MEAN, SAKURAI.
SO YOU REALLY THINK I CAN TRANSFORM, TOO?
IT LOOKS THAT WAY.
IT WOULD EXPLAIN WHY KARASUMA HAD HIS SIGHTS SET ON YOU.
WOW. THAT'S PRETTY EXCITING.
IT SURE IS, CHAP!

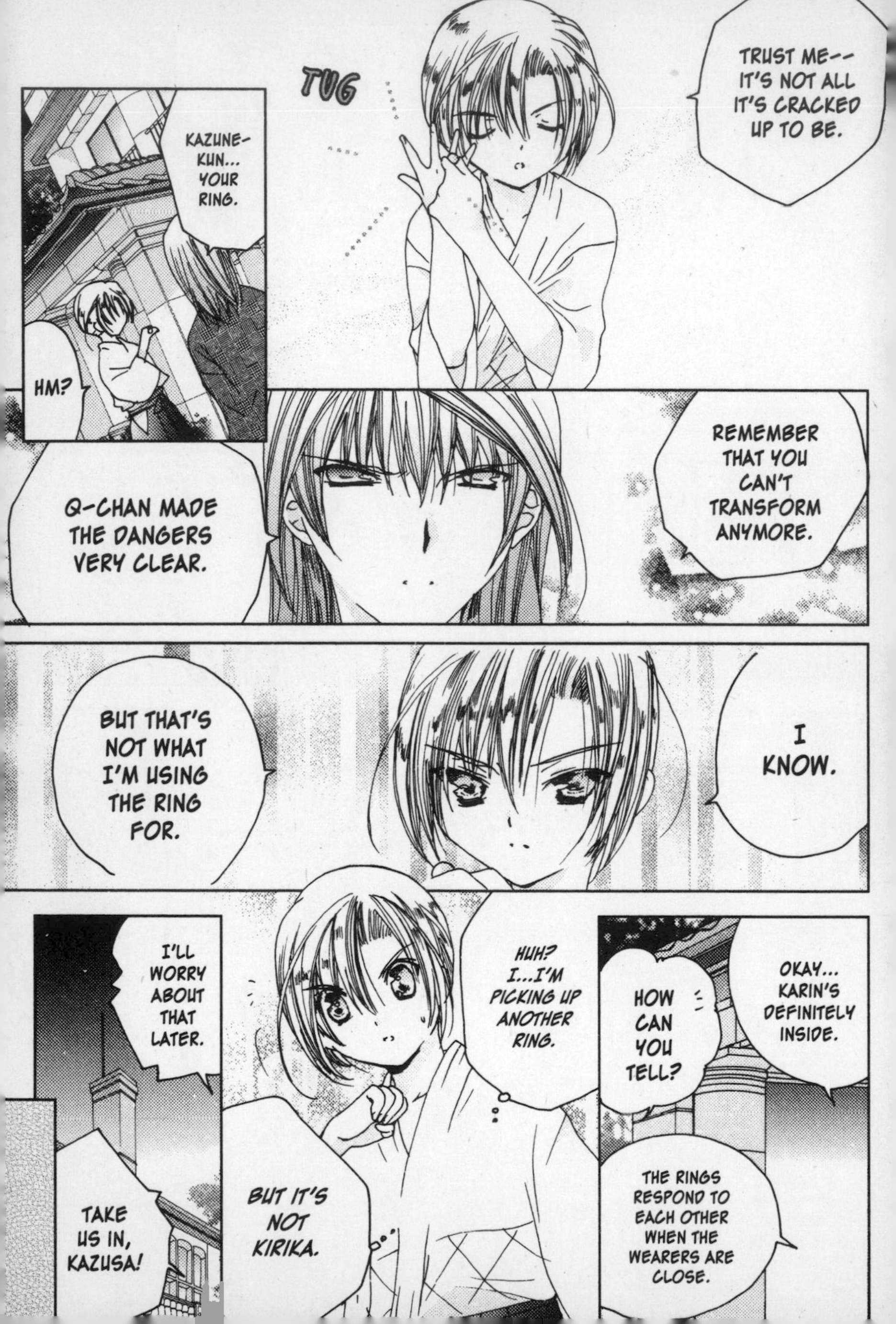
TUG
TRUST ME-- IT'S NOT ALL IT'S CRACKED UP TO BE.
KAZUNE-KUN... YOUR RING.
HM?
REMEMBER THAT YOU CAN'T TRANSFORM ANYMORE.
Q-CHAN MADE THE DANGERS VERY CLEAR.
I KNOW.
BUT THAT'S NOT WHAT I'M USING THE RING FOR.
OKAY... KARIN'S DEFINITELY INSIDE.
HOW CAN YOU TELL?
THE RINGS RESPOND TO EACH OTHER WHEN THE WEARERS ARE CLOSE.
HUH? I...I'M PICKING UP ANOTHER RING.
BUT IT'S NOT KIRIKA.
I'LL WORRY ABOUT THAT LATER.
TAKE US IN, KAZUSA!

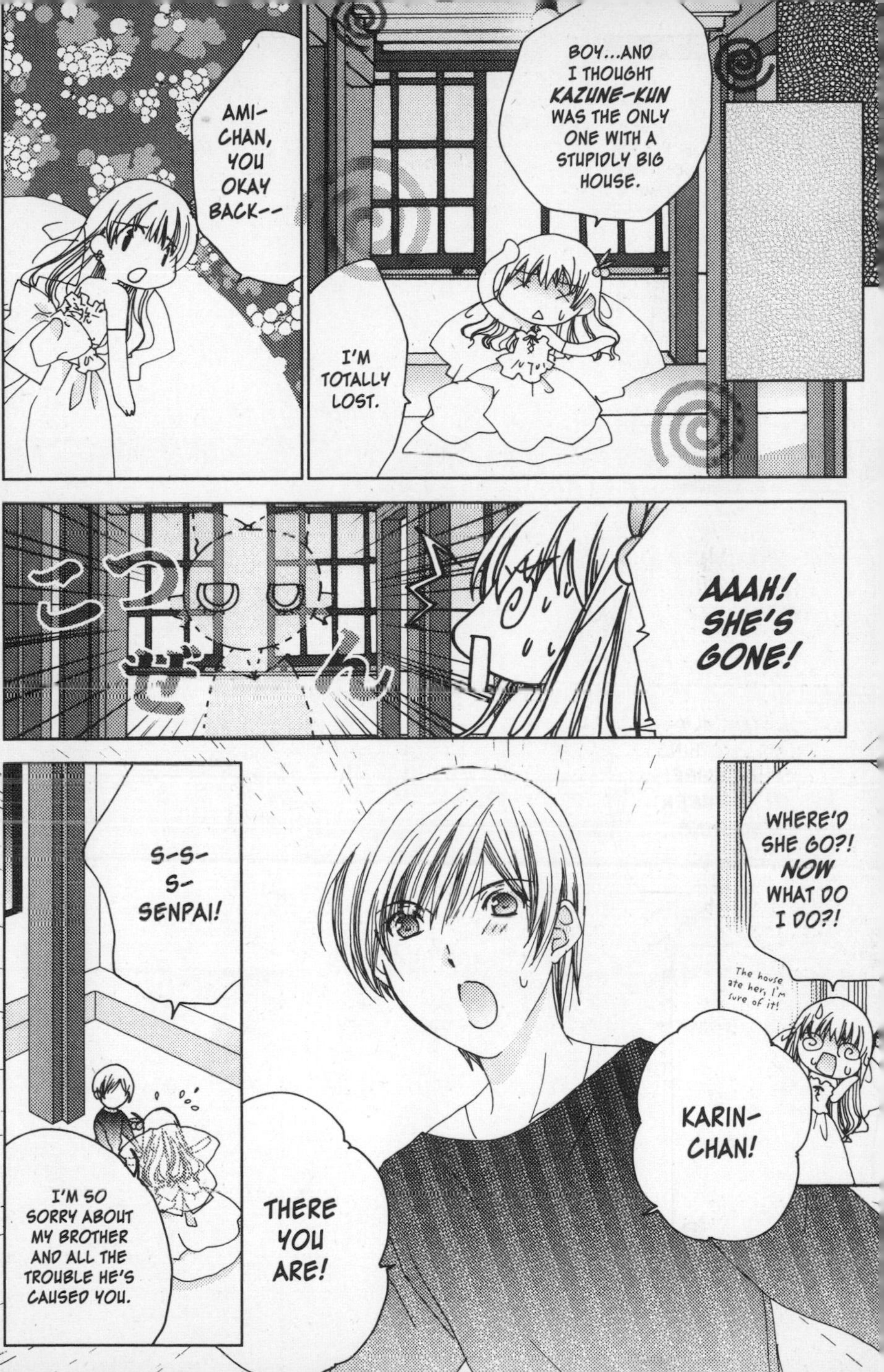
BOY...AND I THOUGHT KAZUNE-KUN WAS THE ONLY ONE WITH A STUPIDLY BIG HOUSE.
I'M TOTALLY LOST.
AMI-CHAN, YOU OKAY BACK--
AAAH! SHE'S GONE!
WHERE'D SHE GO?! NOW WHAT DO I DO?!
The house ate her, I'm sure of it!
KARIN-CHAN!
THERE YOU ARE!
S-S-S-SENPAI!
I'M SO SORRY ABOUT MY BROTHER AND ALL THE TROUBLE HE'S CAUSED YOU.

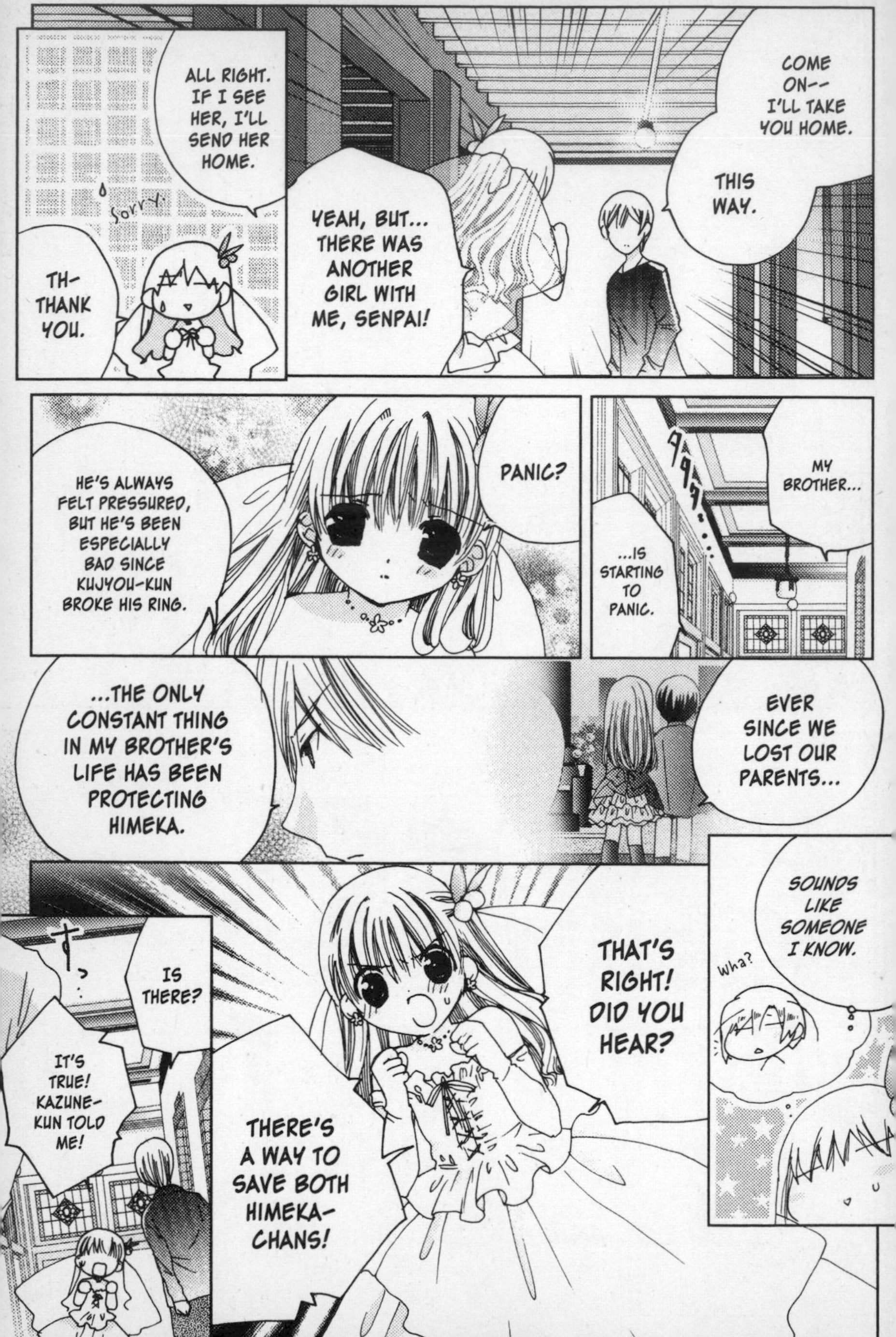
COME ON-- I'LL TAKE YOU HOME.
THIS WAY.
YEAH, BUT... THERE WAS ANOTHER GIRL WITH ME, SENPAI!
ALL RIGHT. IF I SEE HER, I'LL SEND HER HOME.
Sorry.
TH-THANK YOU.
MY BROTHER...
...IS STARTING TO PANIC.
PANIC?
HE'S ALWAYS FELT PRESSURED, BUT HE'S BEEN ESPECIALLY BAD SINCE KUJYOU-KUN BROKE HIS RING.
EVER SINCE WE LOST OUR PARENTS...
...THE ONLY CONSTANT THING IN MY BROTHER'S LIFE HAS BEEN PROTECTING HIMEKA.
SOUNDS LIKE SOMEONE I KNOW.
Wha?
THAT'S RIGHT! DID YOU HEAR?
THERE'S A WAY TO SAVE BOTH HIMEKA-CHANS!
IS THERE?
IT'S TRUE! KAZUNE-KUN TOLD ME!

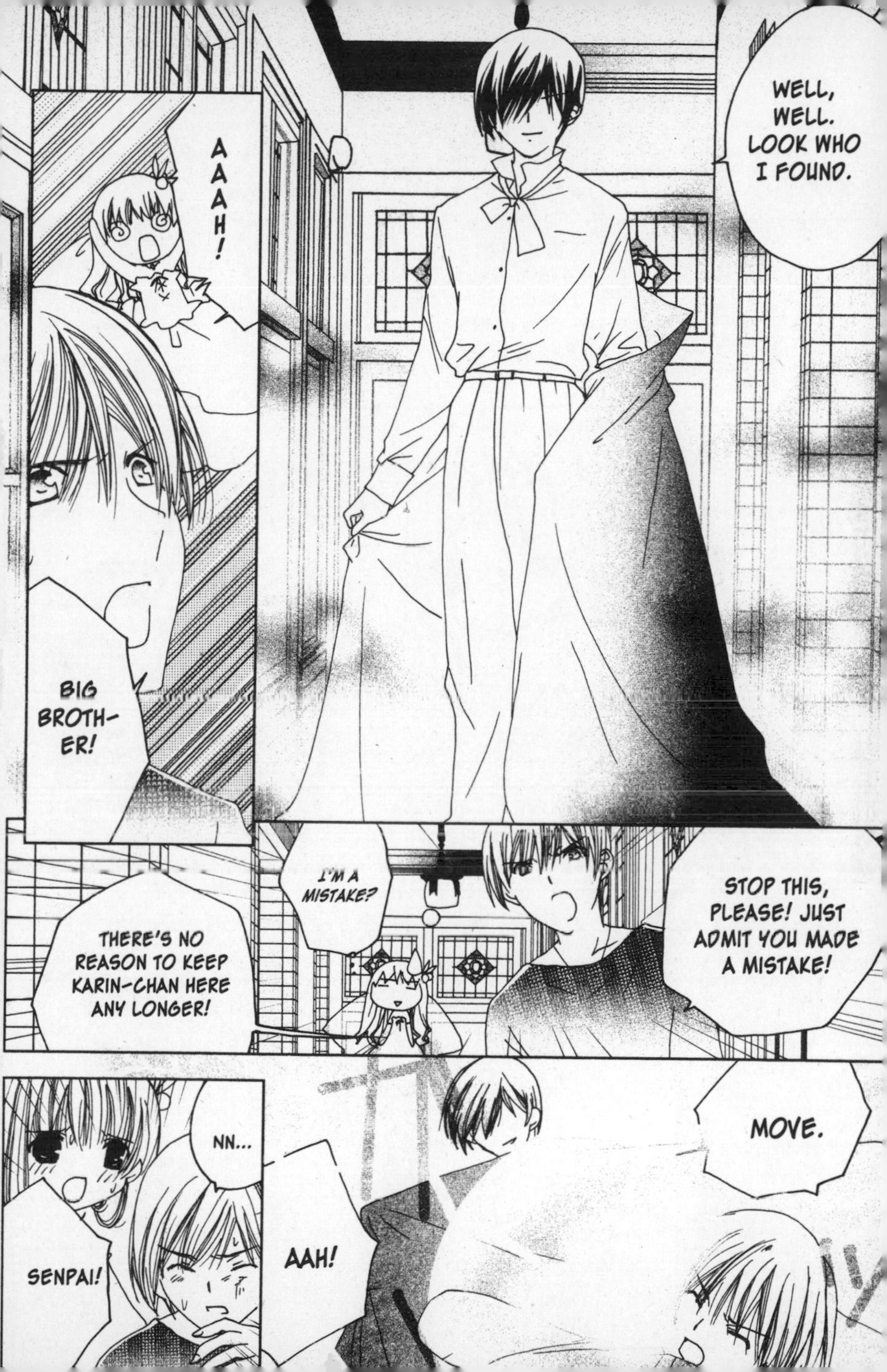
WELL, WELL. LOOK WHO I FOUND.
AAAAH!
BIG BROTHER!
STOP THIS, PLEASE! JUST ADMIT YOU MADE A MISTAKE!
I'M A MISTAKE?
THERE'S NO REASON TO KEEP KARIN-CHAN HERE ANY LONGER!
MOVE.
AAH!
NN...
SENPAI!

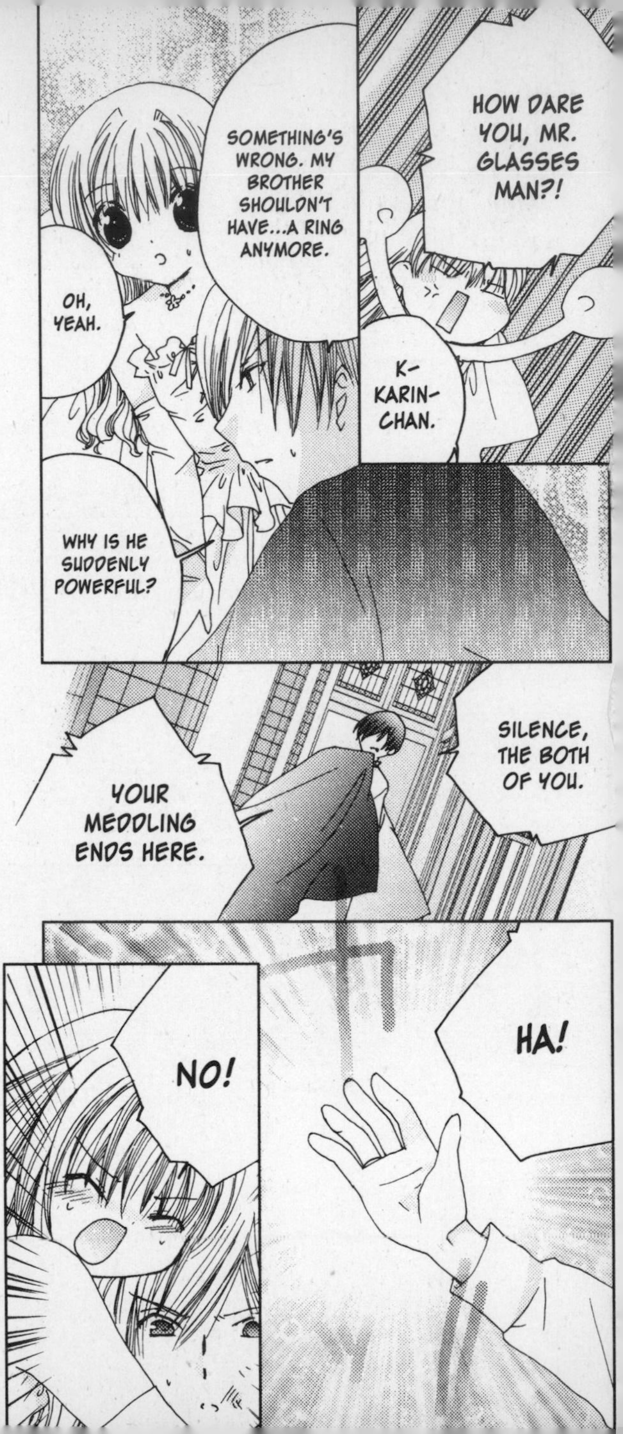
HOW DARE YOU, MR. GLASSES MAN?!
K-KARIN-CHAN.
SOMETHING'S WRONG. MY BROTHER SHOULDN'T HAVE...A RING ANYMORE.
OH, YEAH.
WHY IS HE SUDDENLY POWERFUL?
SILENCE, THE BOTH OF YOU.
YOUR MEDDLING ENDS HERE.
HA!
NO!
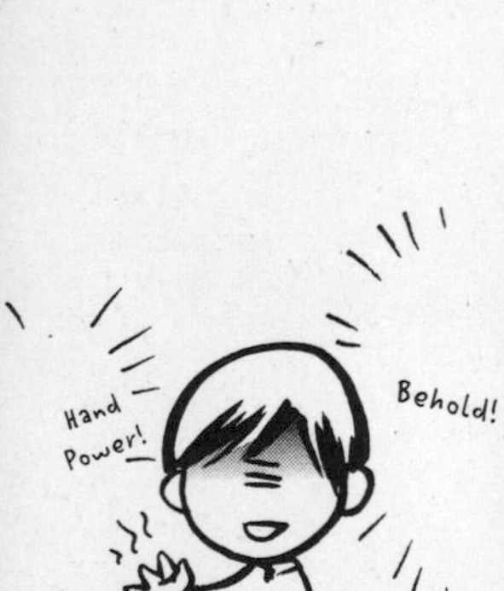
Behold!
Hand Power!

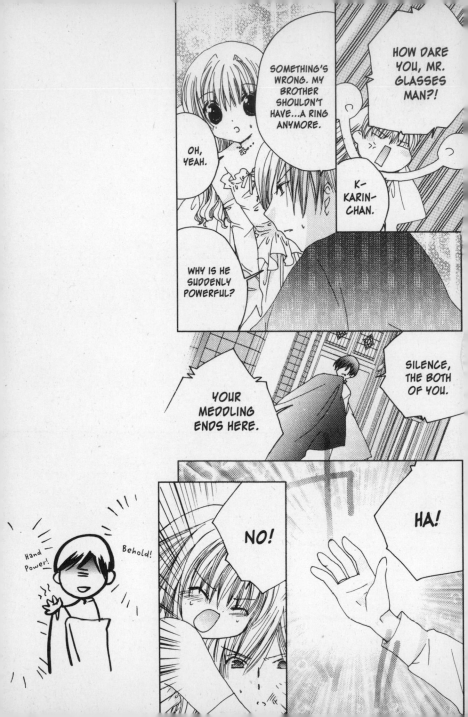

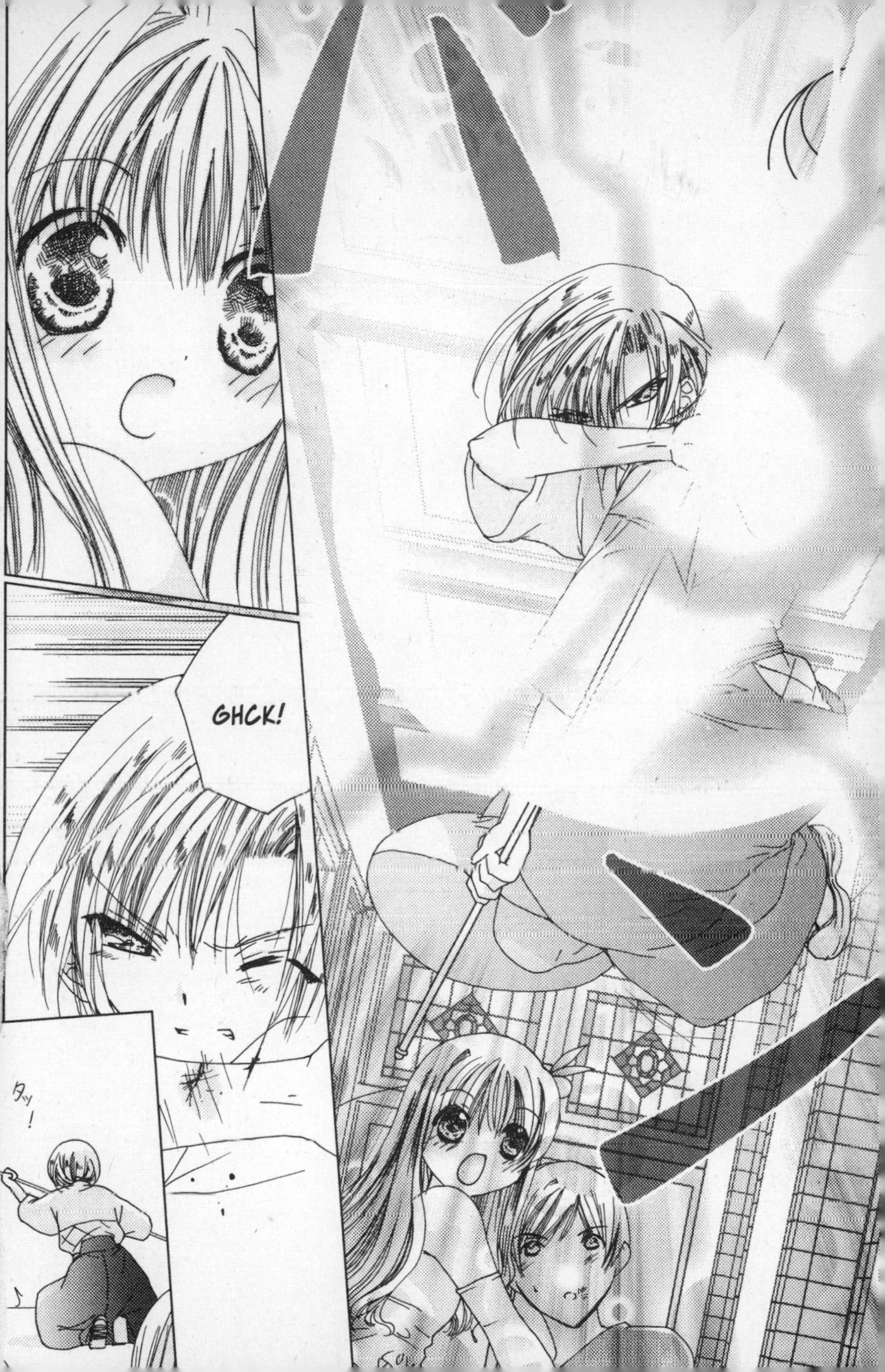
GHCK!

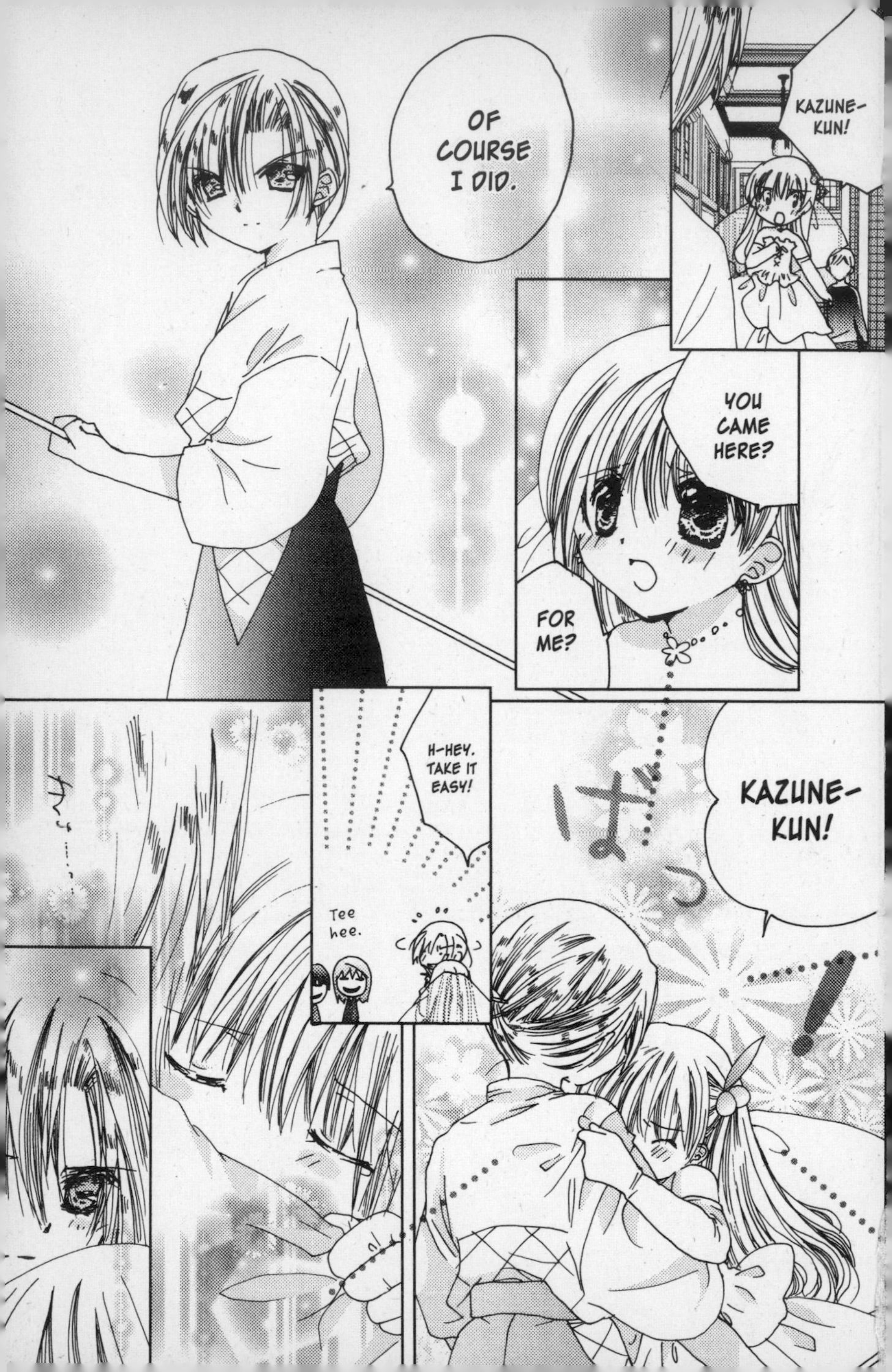
KAZUNE-KUN!
YOU CAME HERE?
FOR ME?
OF COURSE I DID.
KAZUNE-KUN!
ぱっ
H-HEY. TAKE IT EASY!
Tee hee.

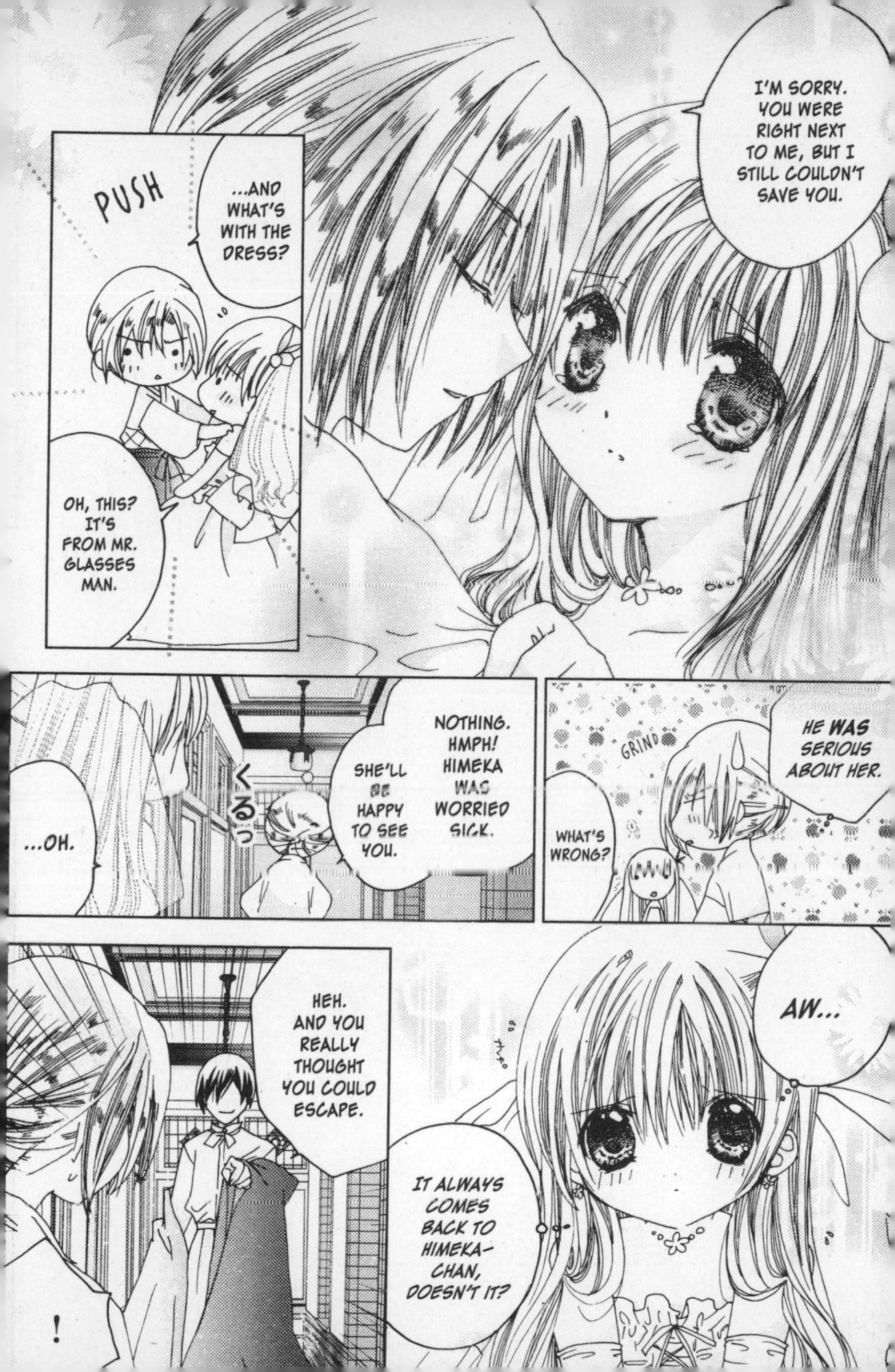
I'M SORRY. YOU WERE RIGHT NEXT TO ME, BUT I STILL COULDN'T SAVE YOU.
...AND WHAT'S WITH THE DRESS?
PUSH
OH, THIS? IT'S FROM MR. GLASSES MAN.
HE WAS SERIOUS ABOUT HER.
GRIND
WHAT'S WRONG?
NOTHING. HMPH! HIMEKA WAS WORRIED SICK.
SHE'LL BE HAPPY TO SEE YOU.
くるっ
...OH.
AW...
IT ALWAYS COMES BACK TO HIMEKA-CHAN, DOESN'T IT?
HEH. AND YOU REALLY THOUGHT YOU COULD ESCAPE.
!

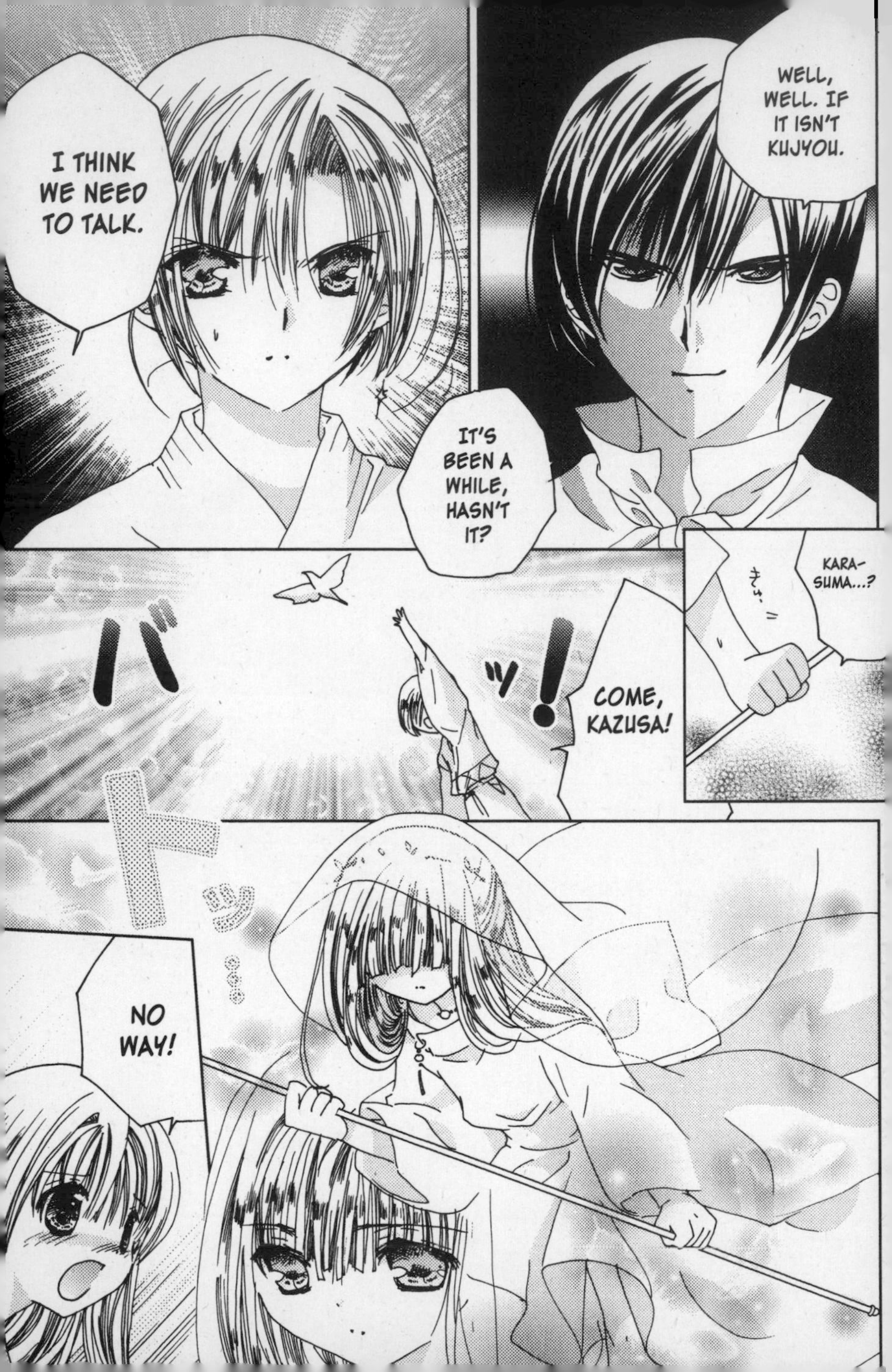
WELL, WELL. IF IT ISN'T KUJYOU.
IT'S BEEN A WHILE, HASN'T IT?
I THINK WE NEED TO TALK.
KARA-SUMA...?
COME, KAZUSA!
バッ!
NO WAY!

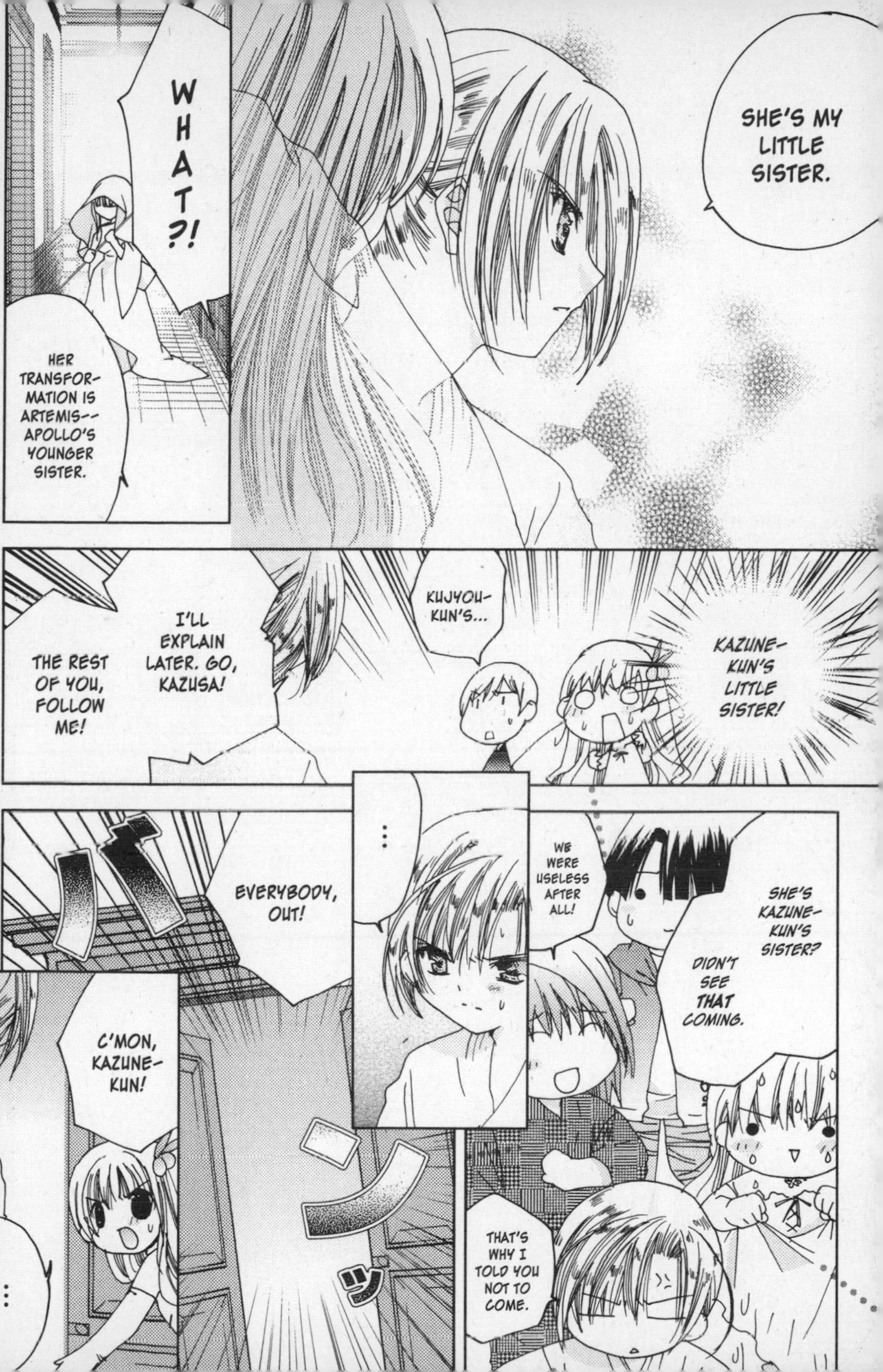
SHE'S MY LITTLE SISTER.
WHAT?!
HER TRANSFORMATION IS ARTEMIS--APOLLO'S YOUNGER SISTER.
KAZUNE-KUN'S LITTLE SISTER!
KUJYOU-KUN'S...
I'LL EXPLAIN LATER. GO, KAZUSA!
THE REST OF YOU, FOLLOW ME!
SHE'S KAZUNE-KUN'S SISTER?
WE WERE USELESS AFTER ALL!
DIDN'T SEE THAT COMING.
THAT'S WHY I TOLD YOU NOT TO COME.
...
EVERYBODY, OUT!
C'MON, KAZUNE-KUN!
...

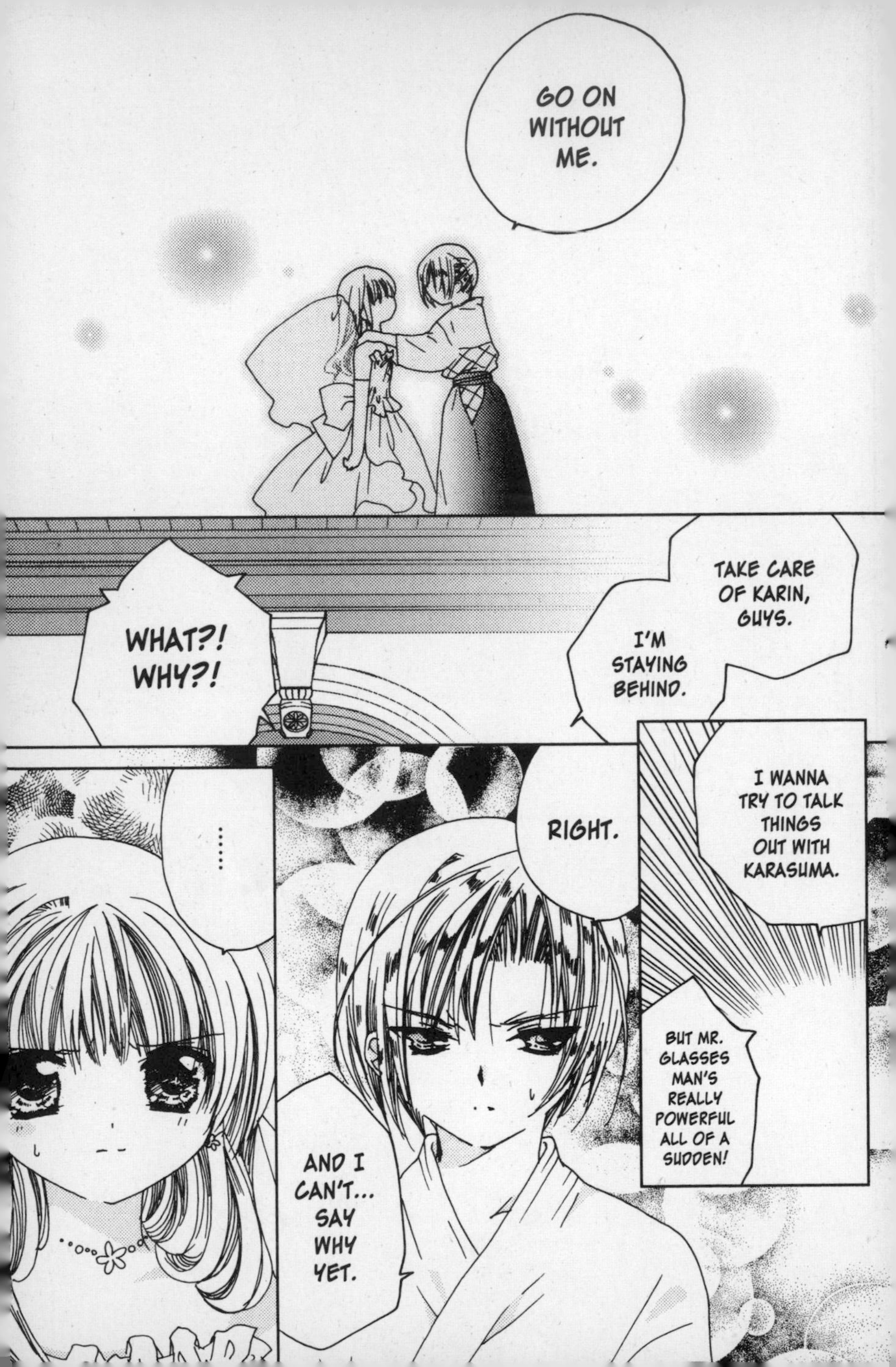
GO ON WITHOUT ME.
TAKE CARE OF KARIN, GUYS.
I'M STAYING BEHIND.
WHAT?! WHY?!
I WANNA TRY TO TALK THINGS OUT WITH KARASUMA.
BUT MR. GLASSES MAN'S REALLY POWERFUL ALL OF A SUDDEN!
RIGHT.
AND I CAN'T... SAY WHY YET.
......

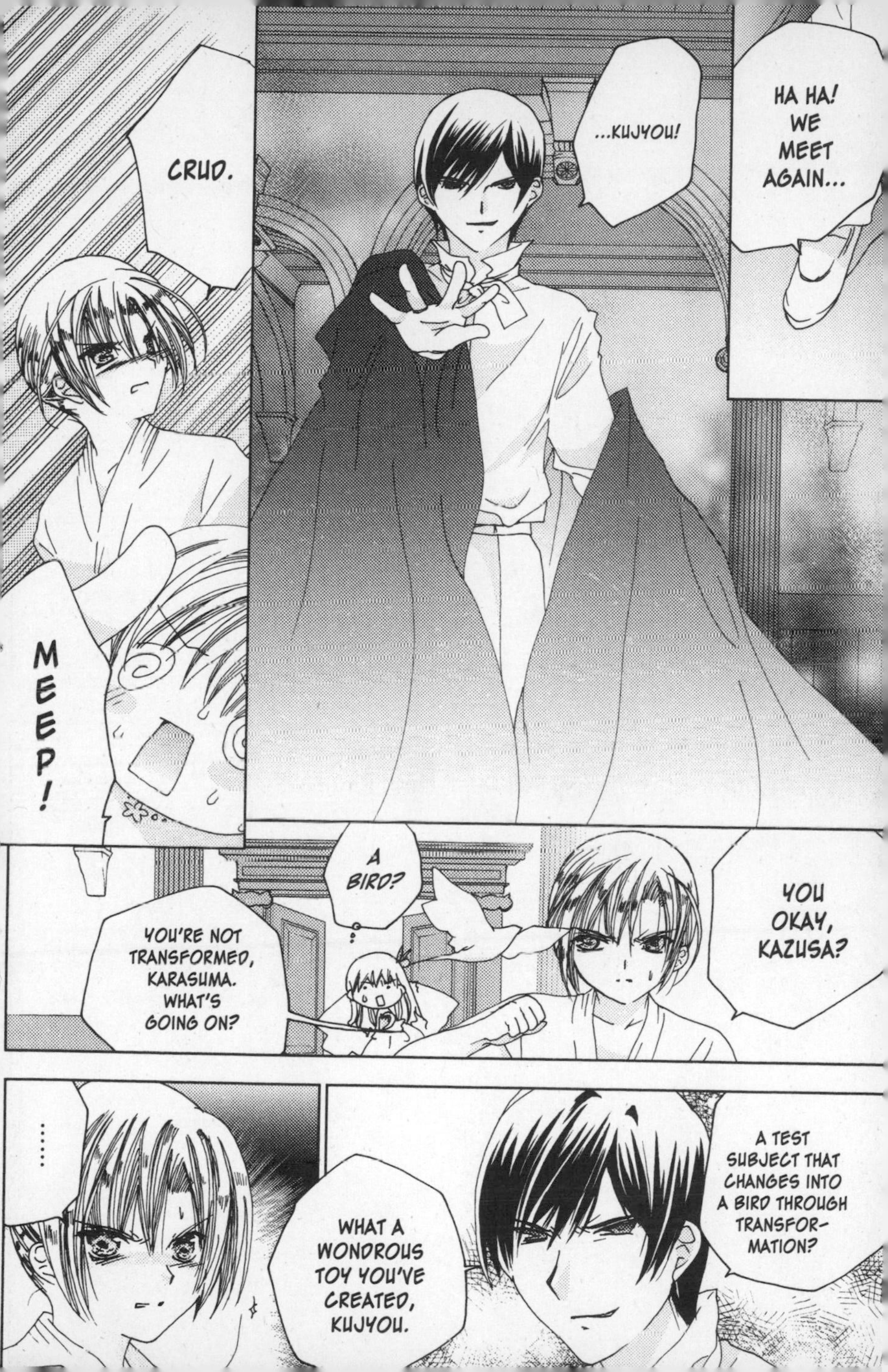
HA HA! WE MEET AGAIN...
...KUJYOU!
CRUD.
MEEP!
YOU OKAY, KAZUSA?
A BIRD?
YOU'RE NOT TRANSFORMED, KARASUMA. WHAT'S GOING ON?
A TEST SUBJECT THAT CHANGES INTO A BIRD THROUGH TRANSFOR-MATION?
WHAT A WONDROUS TOY YOU'VE CREATED, KUJYOU.
......

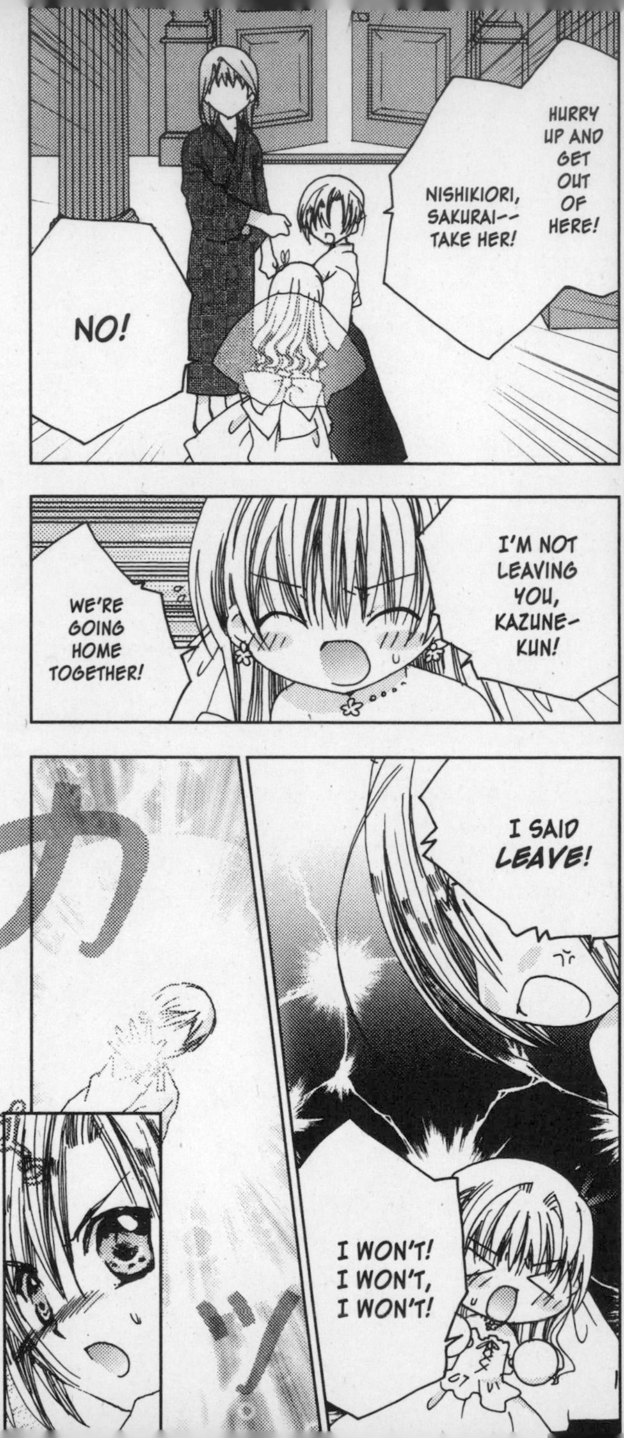
HURRY UP AND GET OUT OF HERE!
NISHIKIORI, SAKURAI-- TAKE HER!
NO!
I'M NOT LEAVING YOU, KAZUNE-KUN!
WE'RE GOING HOME TOGETHER!
I SAID *LEAVE!*
カ
I WON'T! I WON'T, I WON'T!
ッ

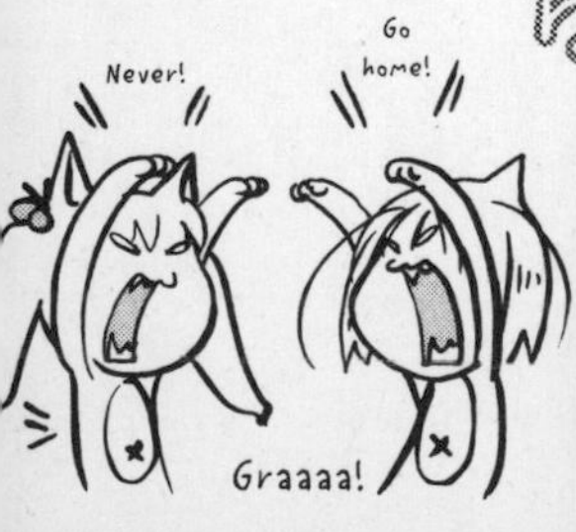
Go home!
Never!
Graaaa!

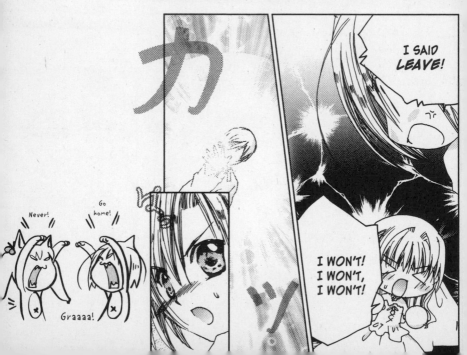

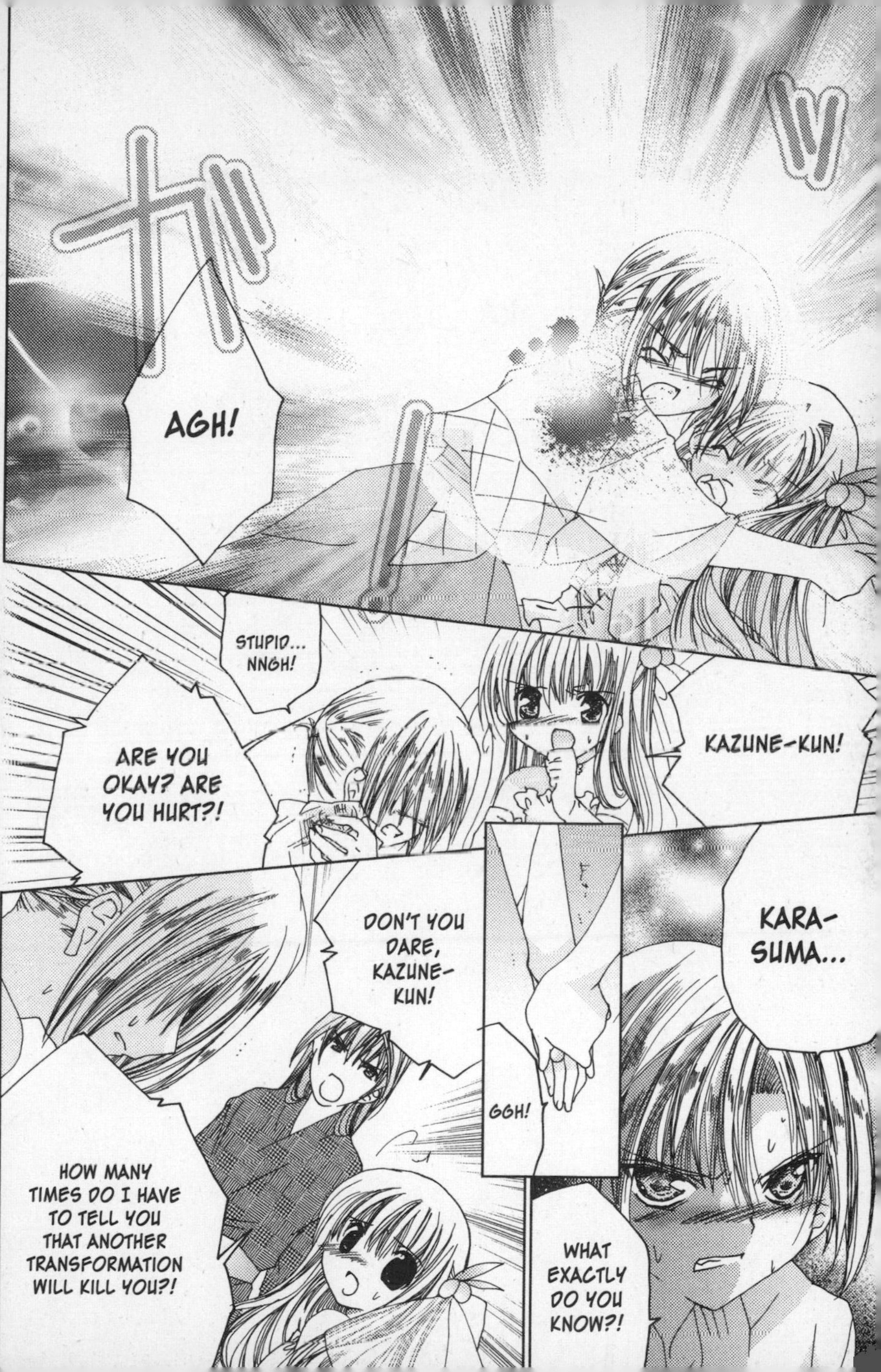
AGH!
KAZUNE-KUN!
STUPID... NNGH!
ARE YOU OKAY? ARE YOU HURT?!
KARA-SUMA...
WHAT EXACTLY DO YOU KNOW?!
GGH!
DON'T YOU DARE, KAZUNE-KUN!
HOW MANY TIMES DO I HAVE TO TELL YOU THAT ANOTHER TRANSFORMATION WILL KILL YOU?!

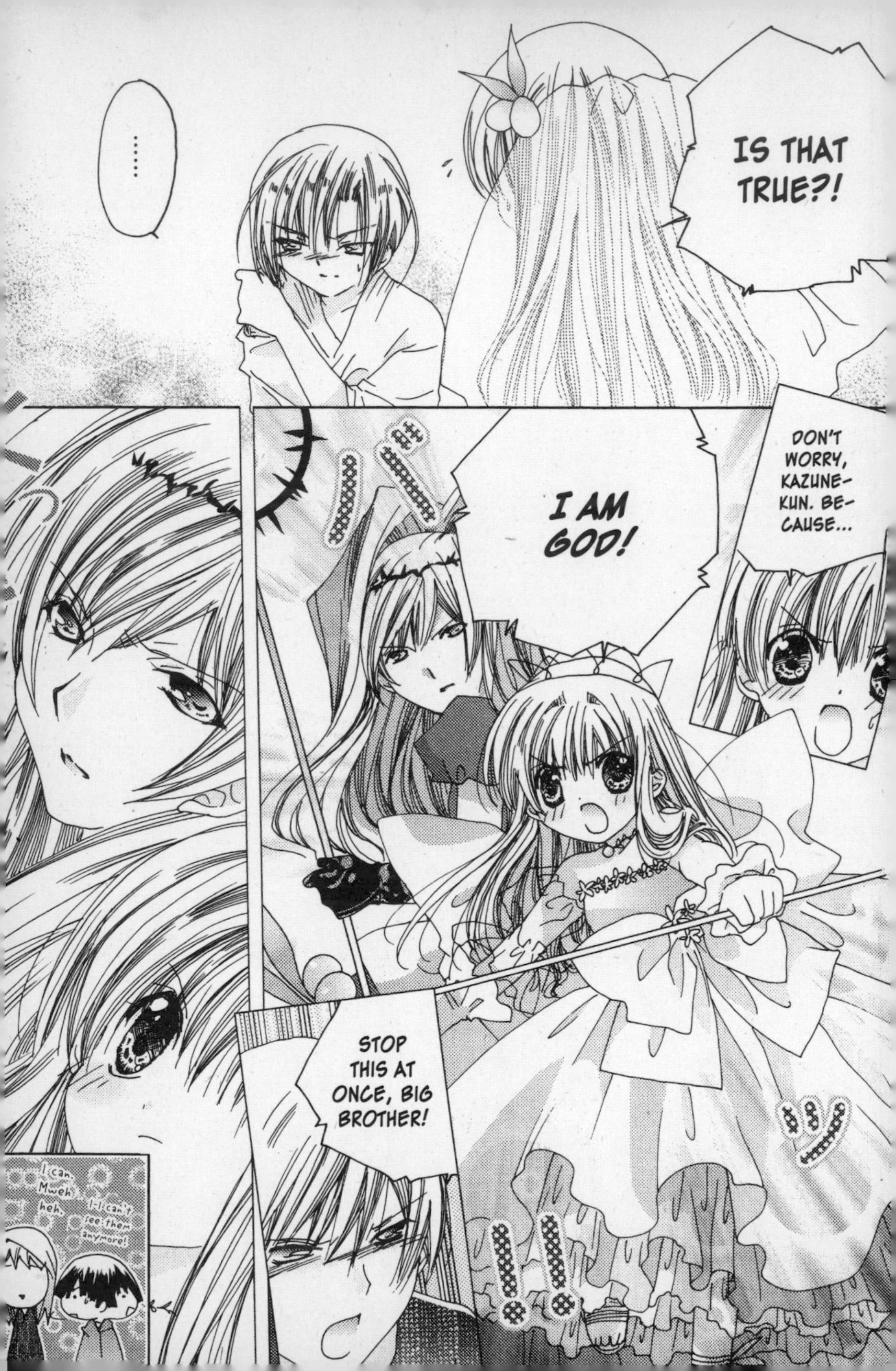
IS THAT TRUE?!
......
DON'T WORRY, KAZUNE-KUN. BE-CAUSE...
I AM GOD!
STOP THIS AT ONCE, BIG BROTHER!
I-I can't see them anymore!
I can. Mweh heh.

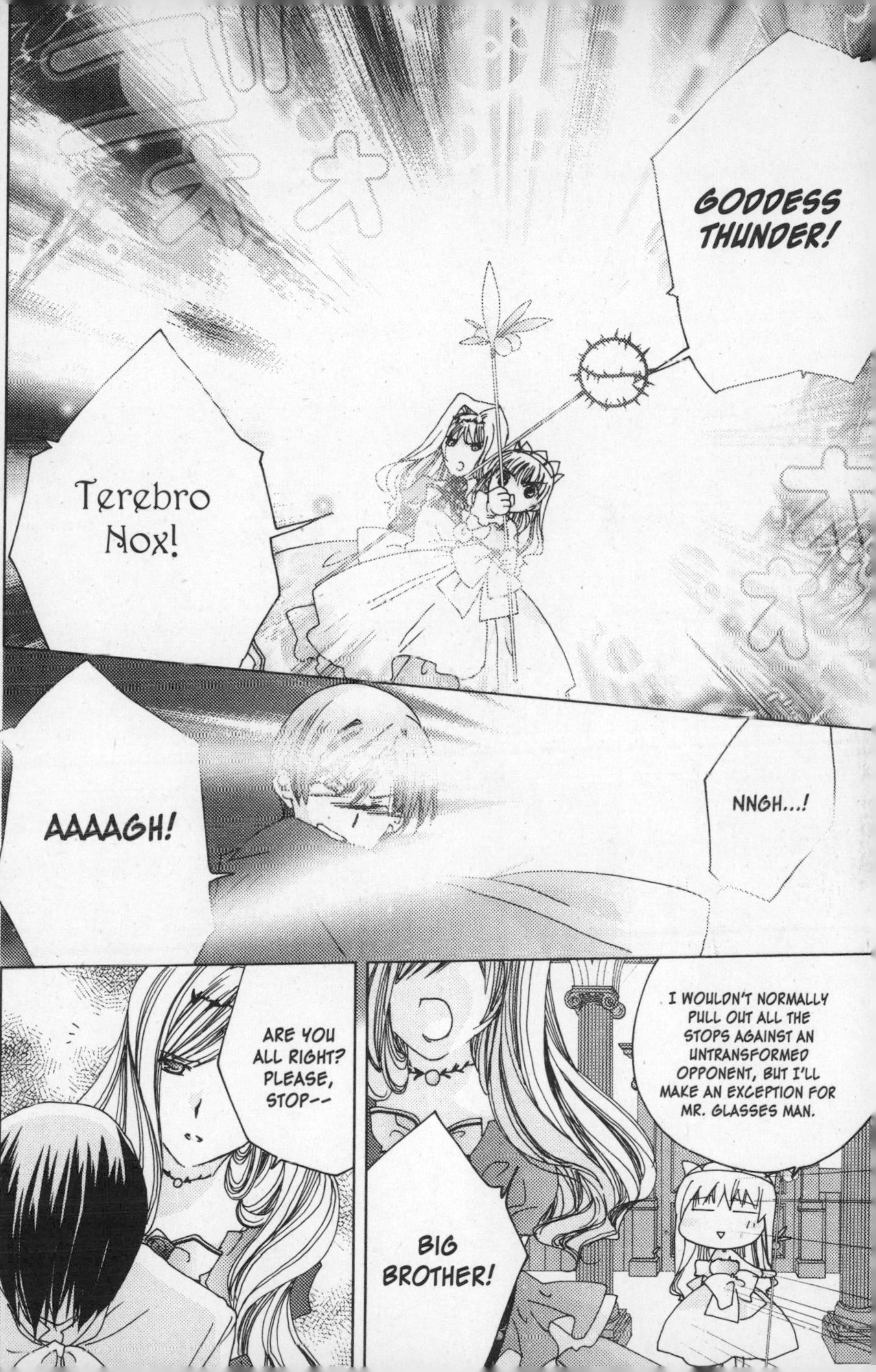
GODDESS THUNDER!
Terebro Nox!
NNGH...!
AAAAGH!
I WOULDN'T NORMALLY PULL OUT ALL THE STOPS AGAINST AN UNTRANSFORMED OPPONENT, BUT I'LL MAKE AN EXCEPTION FOR MR. GLASSES MAN.
BIG BROTHER!
ARE YOU ALL RIGHT? PLEASE, STOP--

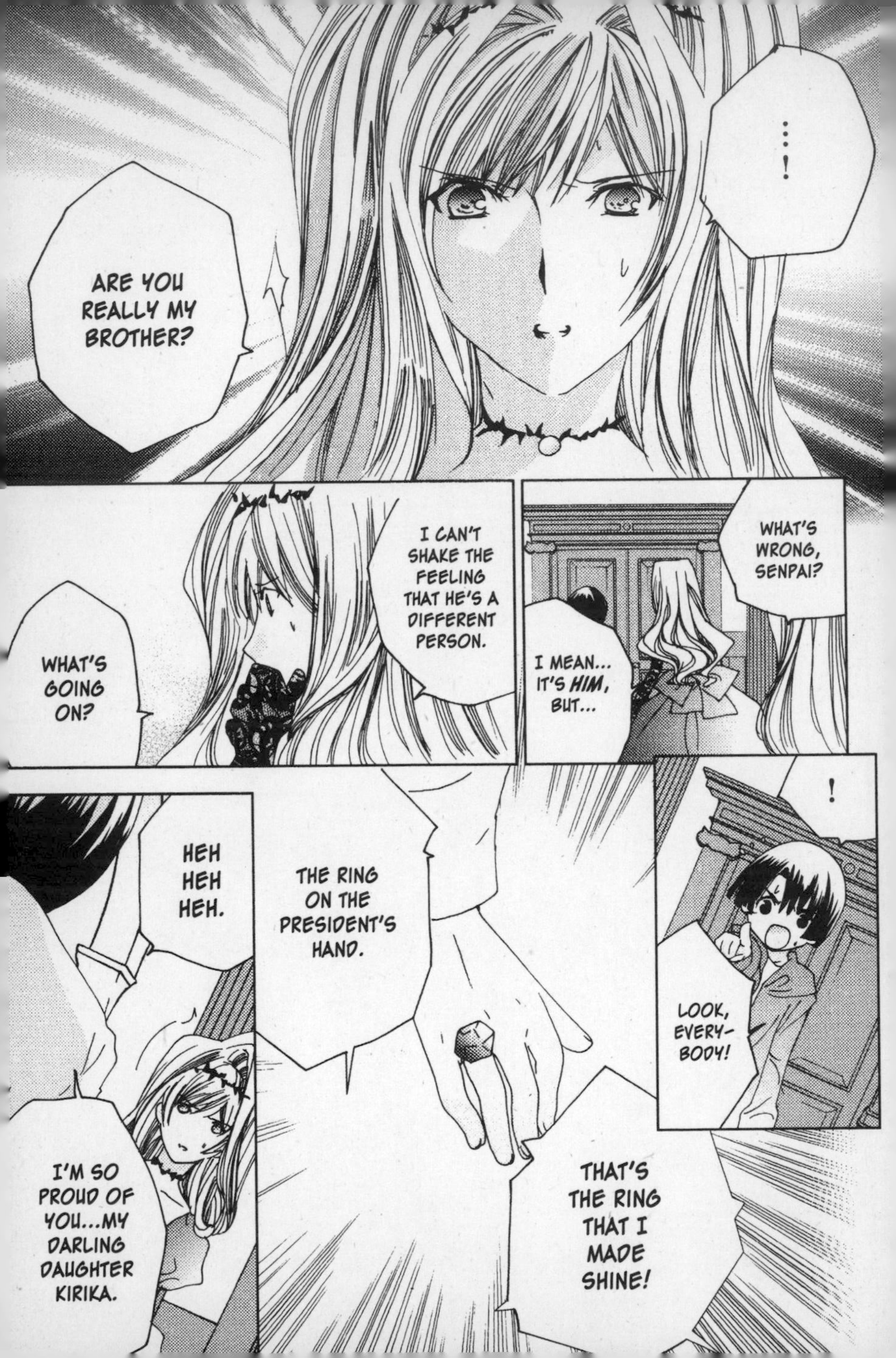
...!
ARE YOU REALLY MY BROTHER?
WHAT'S WRONG, SENPAI?
I MEAN... IT'S *HIM*, BUT...
I CAN'T SHAKE THE FEELING THAT HE'S A DIFFERENT PERSON.
WHAT'S GOING ON?
!
LOOK, EVERY-BODY!
THE RING ON THE PRESIDENT'S HAND.
THAT'S THE RING THAT I MADE SHINE!
HEH HEH HEH.
I'M SO PROUD OF YOU...MY DARLING DAUGHTER KIRIKA.

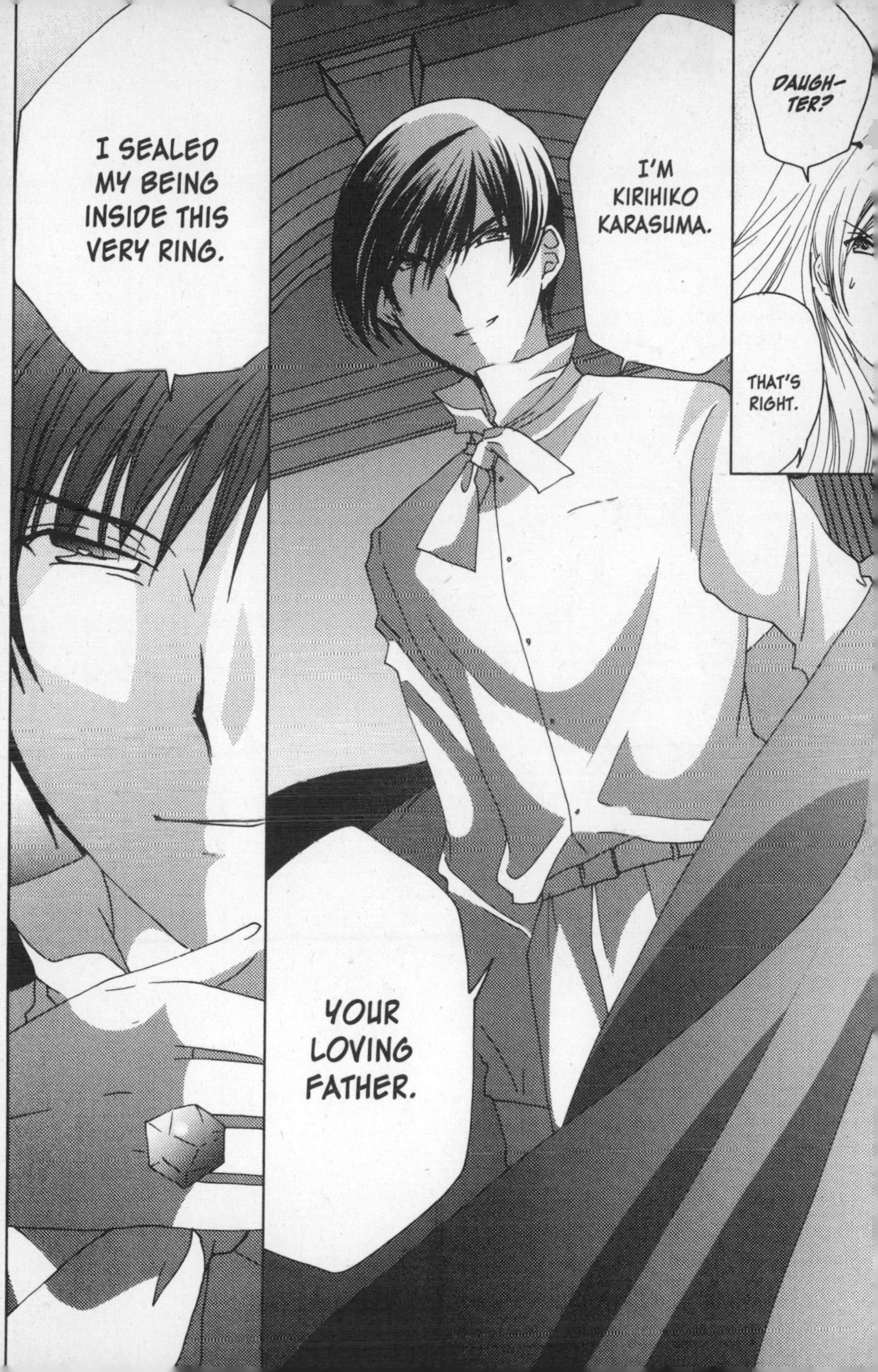
DAUGH-TER?
THAT'S RIGHT.
I'M KIRIHIKO KARASUMA.
YOUR LOVING FATHER.
I SEALED MY BEING INSIDE THIS VERY RING.

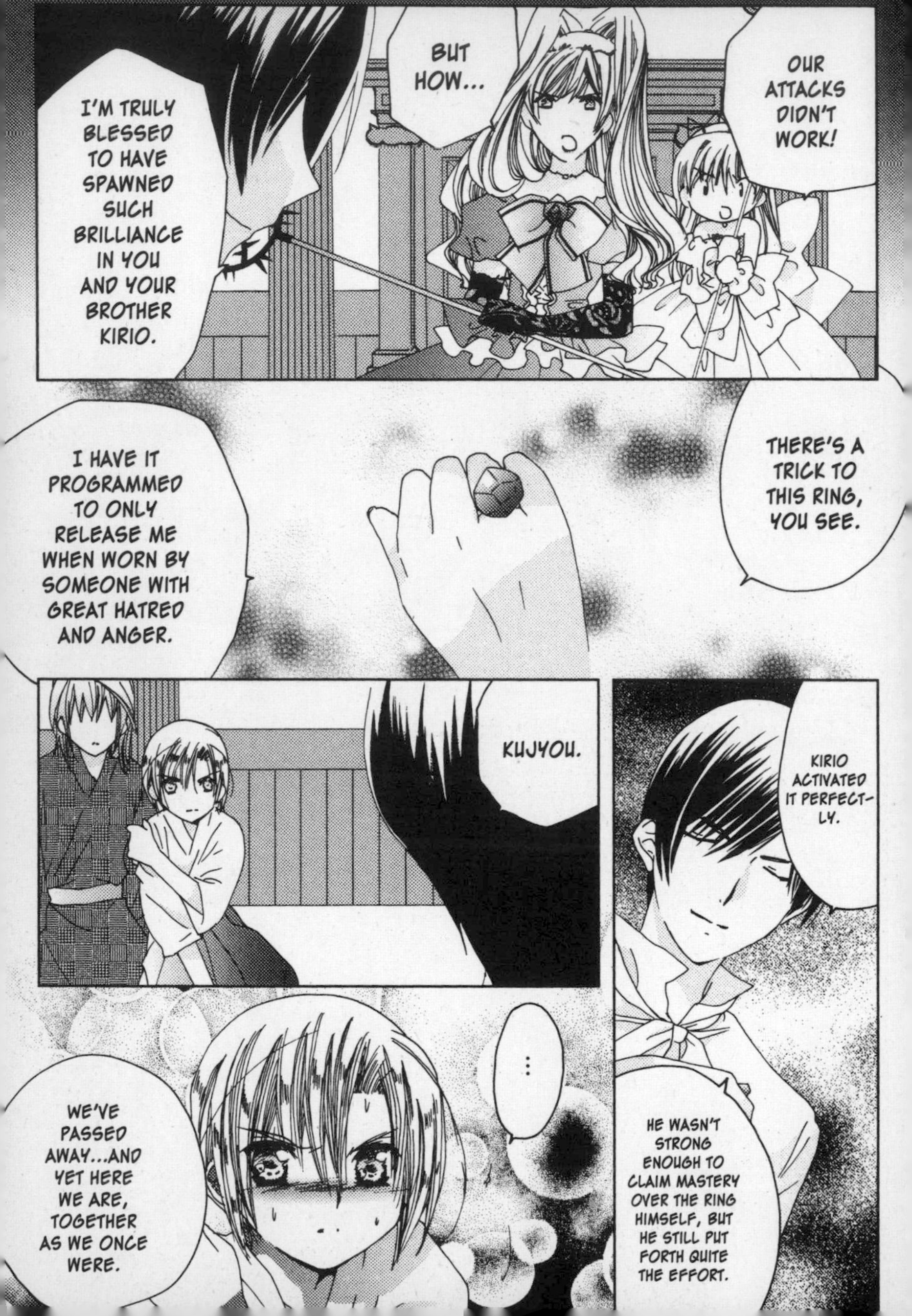
OUR ATTACKS DIDN'T WORK!
BUT HOW...
I'M TRULY BLESSED TO HAVE SPAWNED SUCH BRILLIANCE IN YOU AND YOUR BROTHER KIRIO.
THERE'S A TRICK TO THIS RING, YOU SEE.
I HAVE IT PROGRAMMED TO ONLY RELEASE ME WHEN WORN BY SOMEONE WITH GREAT HATRED AND ANGER.
KIRIO ACTIVATED IT PERFECT-LY.
HE WASN'T STRONG ENOUGH TO CLAIM MASTERY OVER THE RING HIMSELF, BUT HE STILL PUT FORTH QUITE THE EFFORT.
KUJYOU.
...
WE'VE PASSED AWAY...AND YET HERE WE ARE, TOGETHER AS WE ONCE WERE.

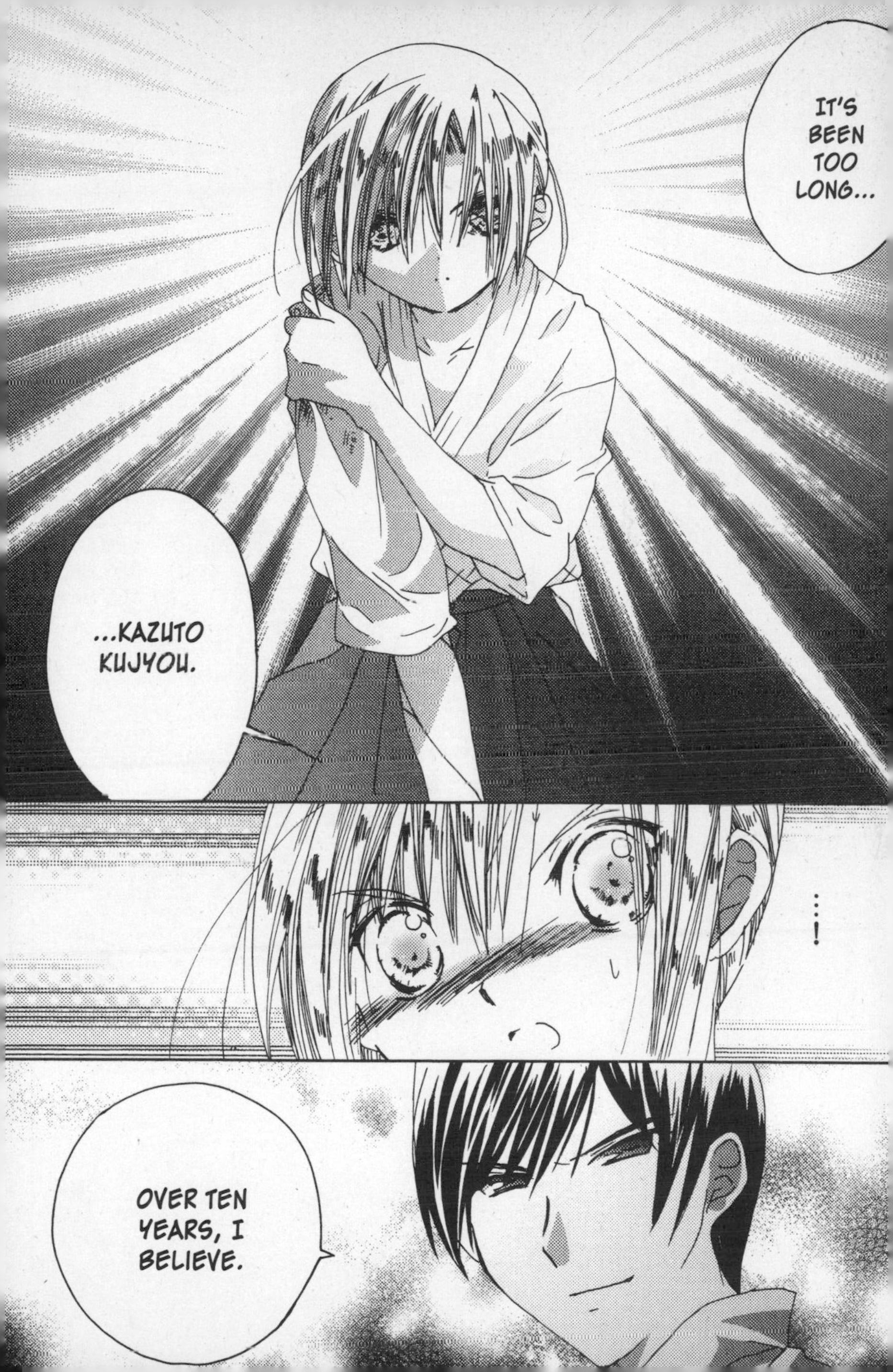
IT'S BEEN TOO LONG...
...KAZUTO KUJYOU.
...!
OVER TEN YEARS, I BELIEVE.

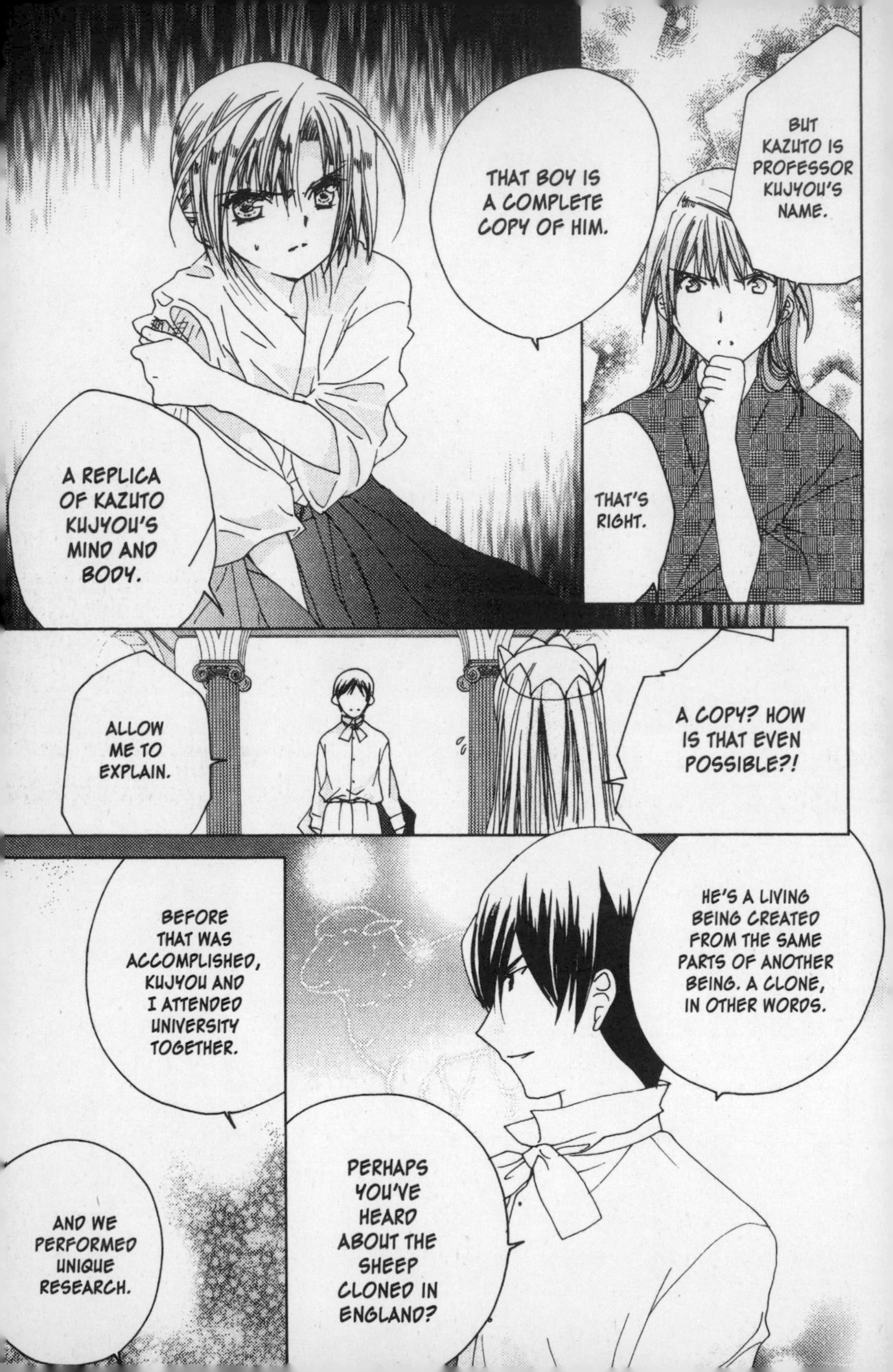
BUT KAZUTO IS PROFESSOR KUJYOU'S NAME.
THAT'S RIGHT.
THAT BOY IS A COMPLETE COPY OF HIM.
A REPLICA OF KAZUTO KUJYOU'S MIND AND BODY.
A COPY? HOW IS THAT EVEN POSSIBLE?!
ALLOW ME TO EXPLAIN.
HE'S A LIVING BEING CREATED FROM THE SAME PARTS OF ANOTHER BEING. A CLONE, IN OTHER WORDS.
PERHAPS YOU'VE HEARD ABOUT THE SHEEP CLONED IN ENGLAND?
BEFORE THAT WAS ACCOMPLISHED, KUJYOU AND I ATTENDED UNIVERSITY TOGETHER.
AND WE PERFORMED UNIQUE RESEARCH.

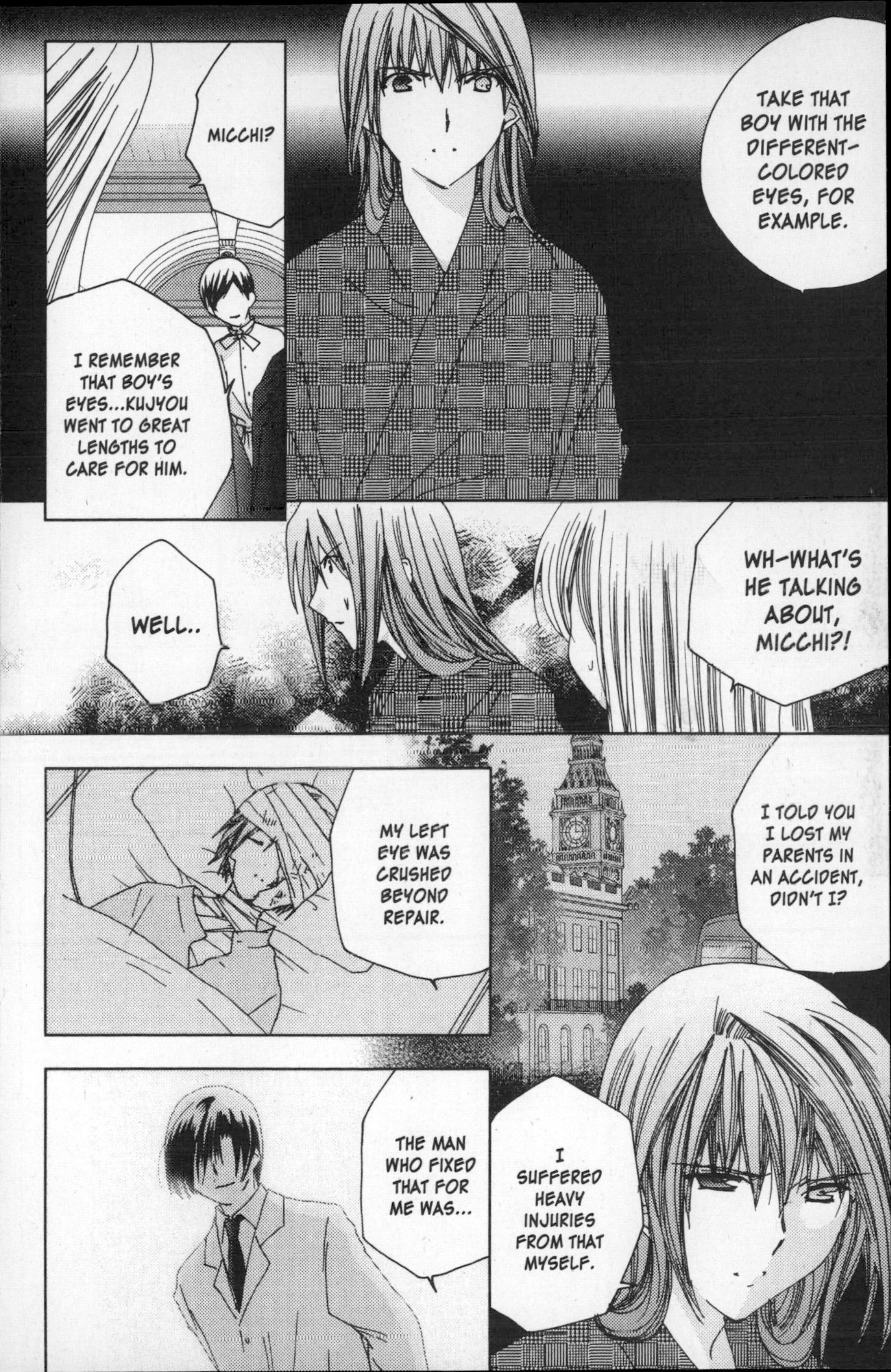
TAKE THAT BOY WITH THE DIFFERENT-COLORED EYES, FOR EXAMPLE.
MICCHI?
I REMEMBER THAT BOY'S EYES...KUJYOU WENT TO GREAT LENGTHS TO CARE FOR HIM.
WH-WHAT'S HE TALKING ABOUT, MICCHI?!
WELL..
I TOLD YOU I LOST MY PARENTS IN AN ACCIDENT, DIDN'T I?
I SUFFERED HEAVY INJURIES FROM THAT MYSELF.
MY LEFT EYE WAS CRUSHED BEYOND REPAIR.
THE MAN WHO FIXED THAT FOR ME WAS...

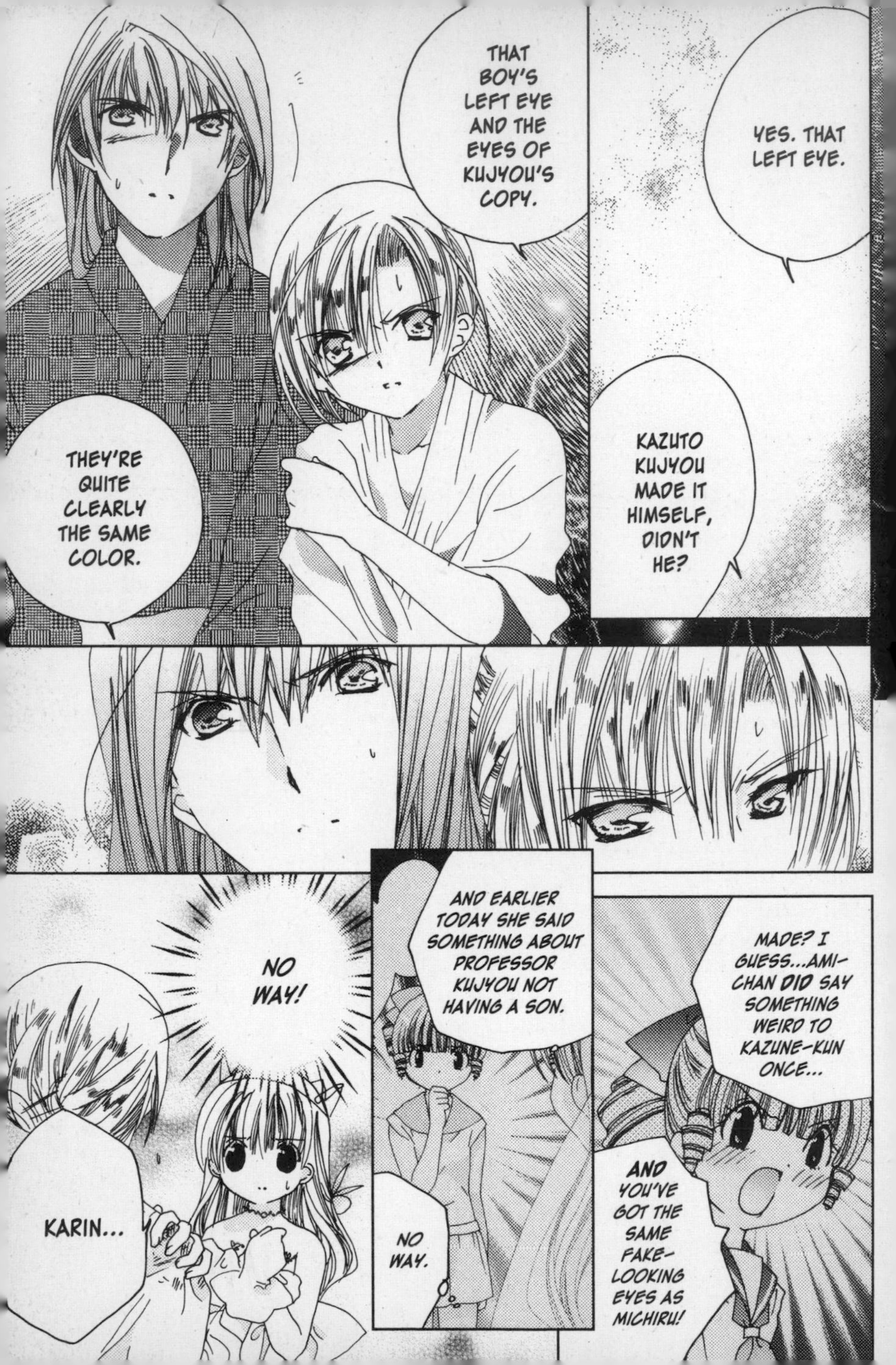
YES. THAT LEFT EYE.
KAZUTO KUJYOU MADE IT HIMSELF, DIDN'T HE?
THAT BOY'S LEFT EYE AND THE EYES OF KUJYOU'S COPY.
THEY'RE QUITE CLEARLY THE SAME COLOR.
MADE? I GUESS...AMI-CHAN DID SAY SOMETHING WEIRD TO KAZUNE-KUN ONCE...
AND YOU'VE GOT THE SAME FAKE-LOOKING EYES AS MICHIRU!
AND EARLIER TODAY SHE SAID SOMETHING ABOUT PROFESSOR KUJYOU NOT HAVING A SON.
NO WAY.
NO WAY!
KARIN...

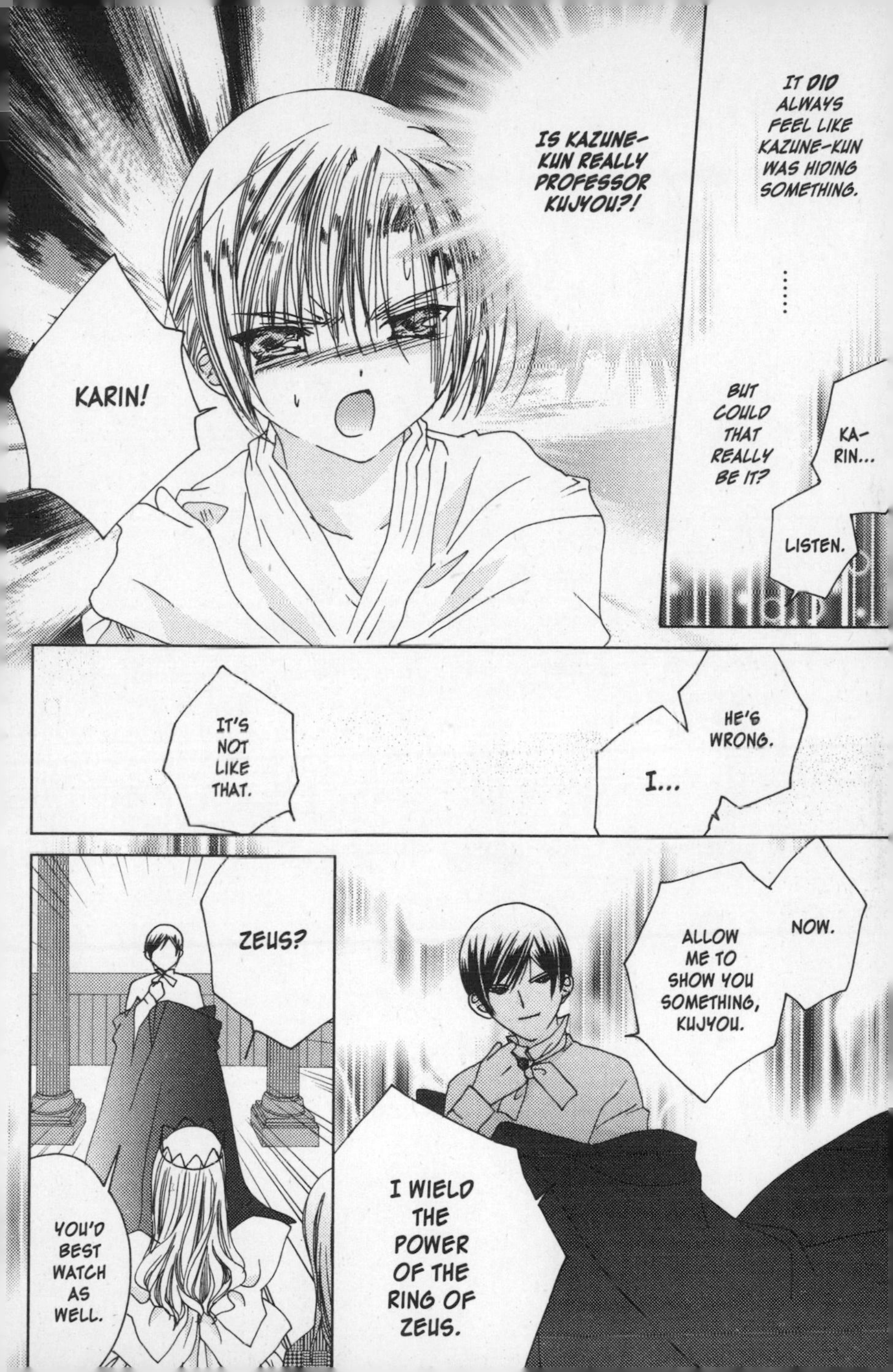
IT DID ALWAYS FEEL LIKE KAZUNE-KUN WAS HIDING SOMETHING.
……
KA-RIN...
LISTEN.
BUT COULD THAT REALLY BE IT?
IS KAZUNE-KUN REALLY PROFESSOR KUJYOU?!
KARIN!
HE'S WRONG.
I...
IT'S NOT LIKE THAT.
NOW.
ALLOW ME TO SHOW YOU SOMETHING, KUJYOU.
I WIELD THE POWER OF THE RING OF ZEUS.
ZEUS?
YOU'D BEST WATCH AS WELL.

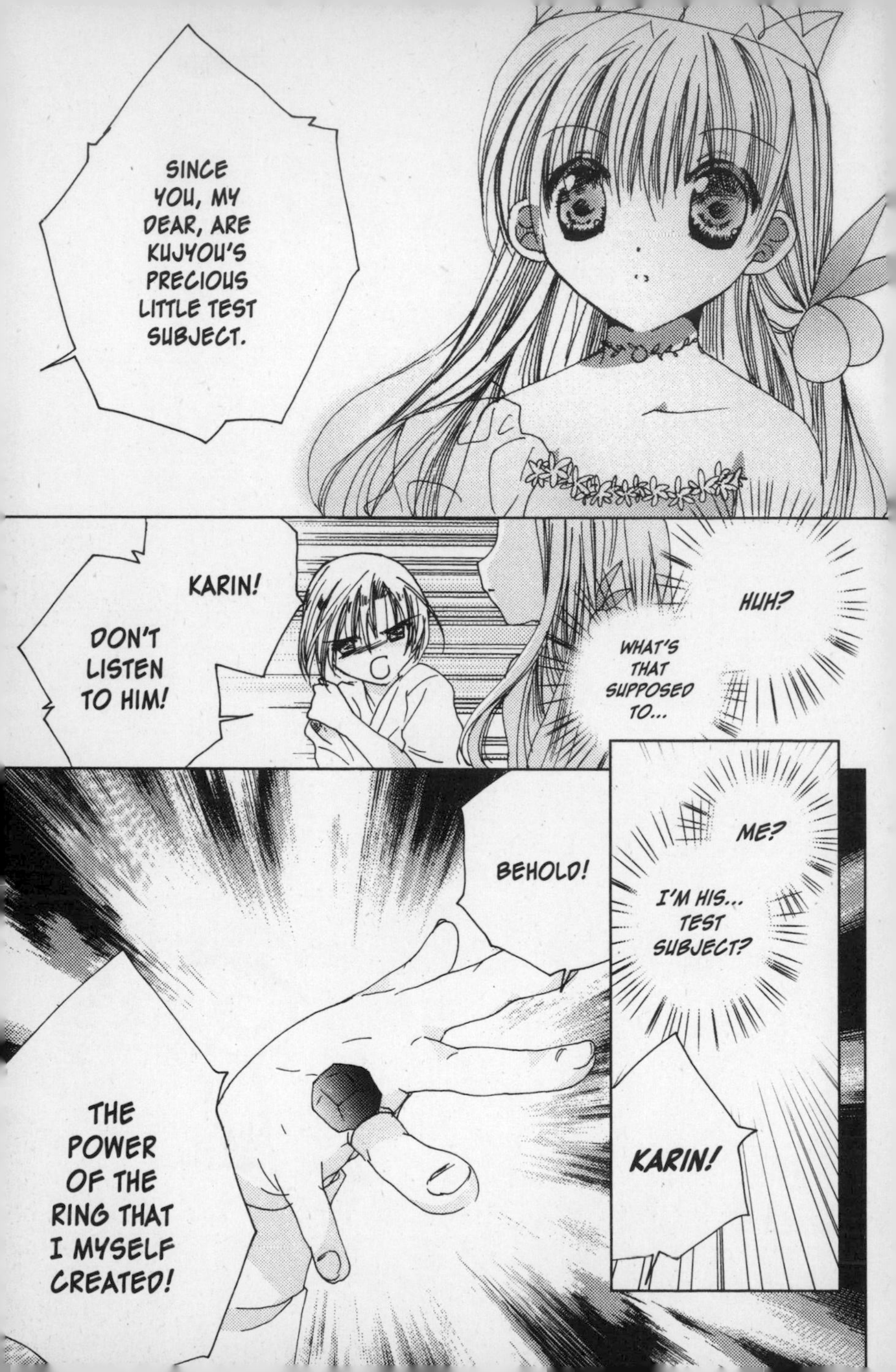
SINCE YOU, MY DEAR, ARE KUJYOU'S PRECIOUS LITTLE TEST SUBJECT.
HUH?
WHAT'S THAT SUPPOSED TO...
KARIN!
DON'T LISTEN TO HIM!
ME?
I'M HIS... TEST SUBJECT?
KARIN!
BEHOLD!
THE POWER OF THE RING THAT I MYSELF CREATED!

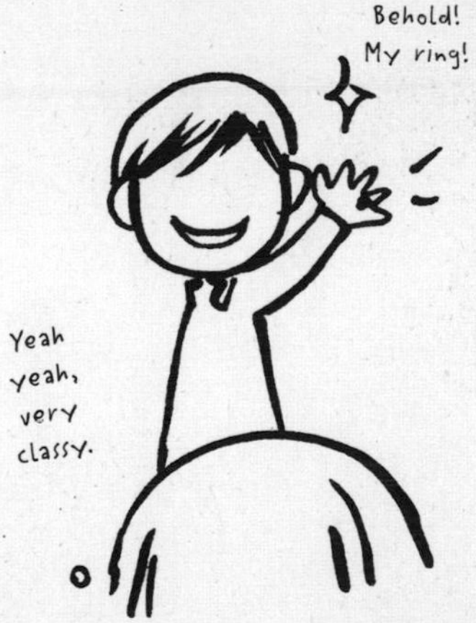
Behold! My ring!
Yeah yeah, very classy.

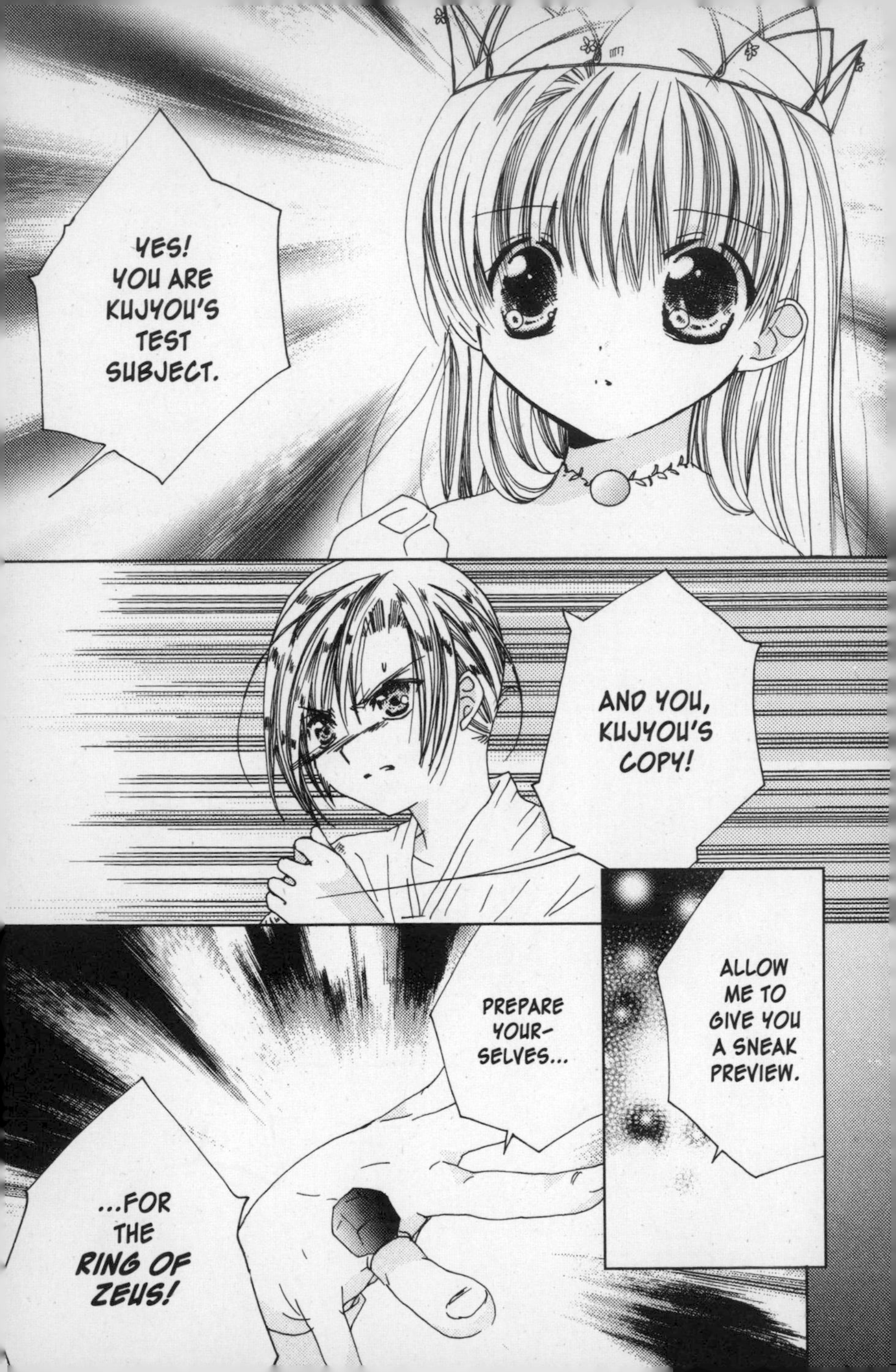
YES! YOU ARE KUJYOU'S TEST SUBJECT.
AND YOU, KUJYOU'S COPY!
ALLOW ME TO GIVE YOU A SNEAK PREVIEW.
PREPARE YOUR-SELVES...
...FOR THE *RING OF ZEUS!*

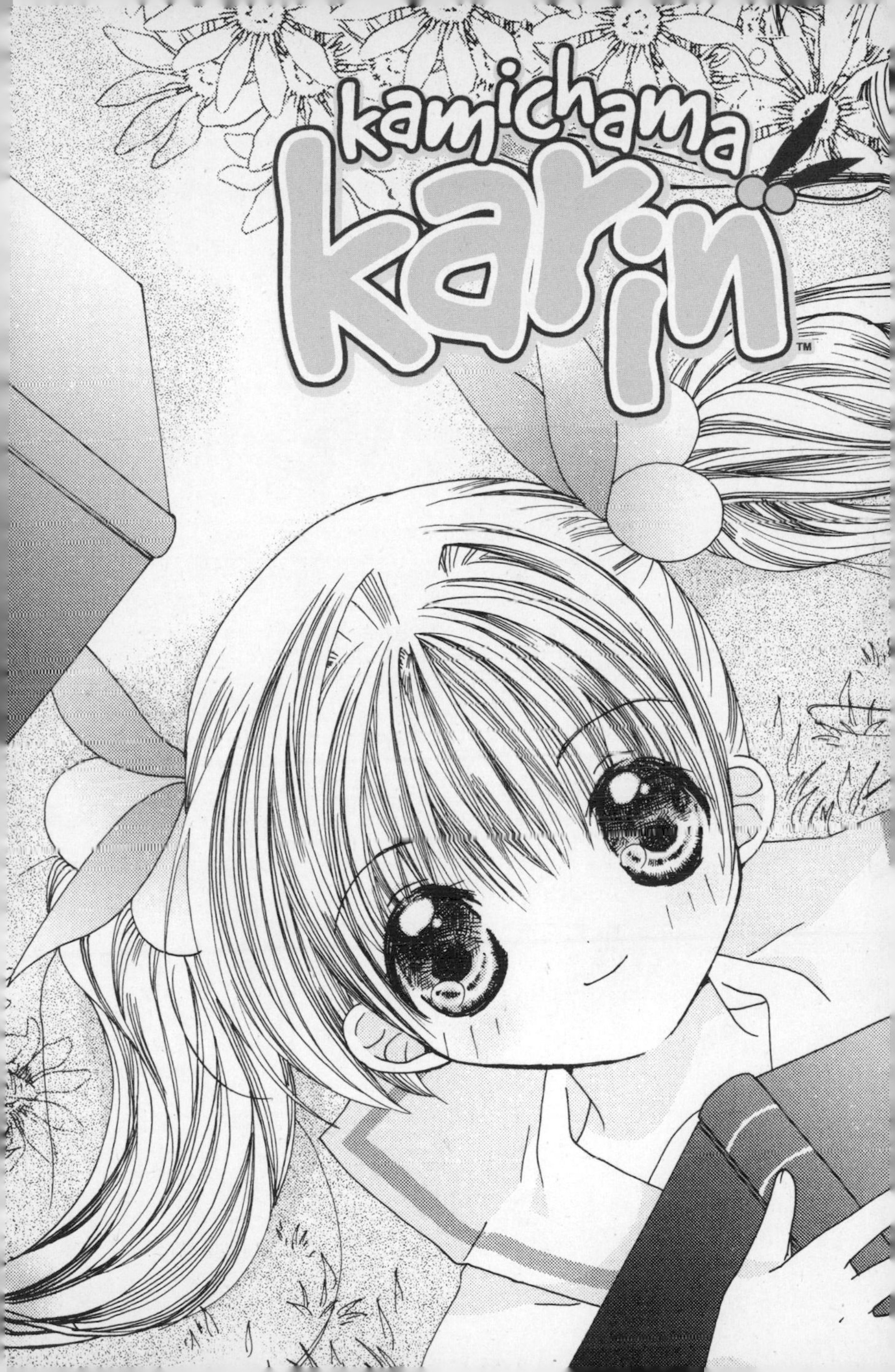
kamichama karin™

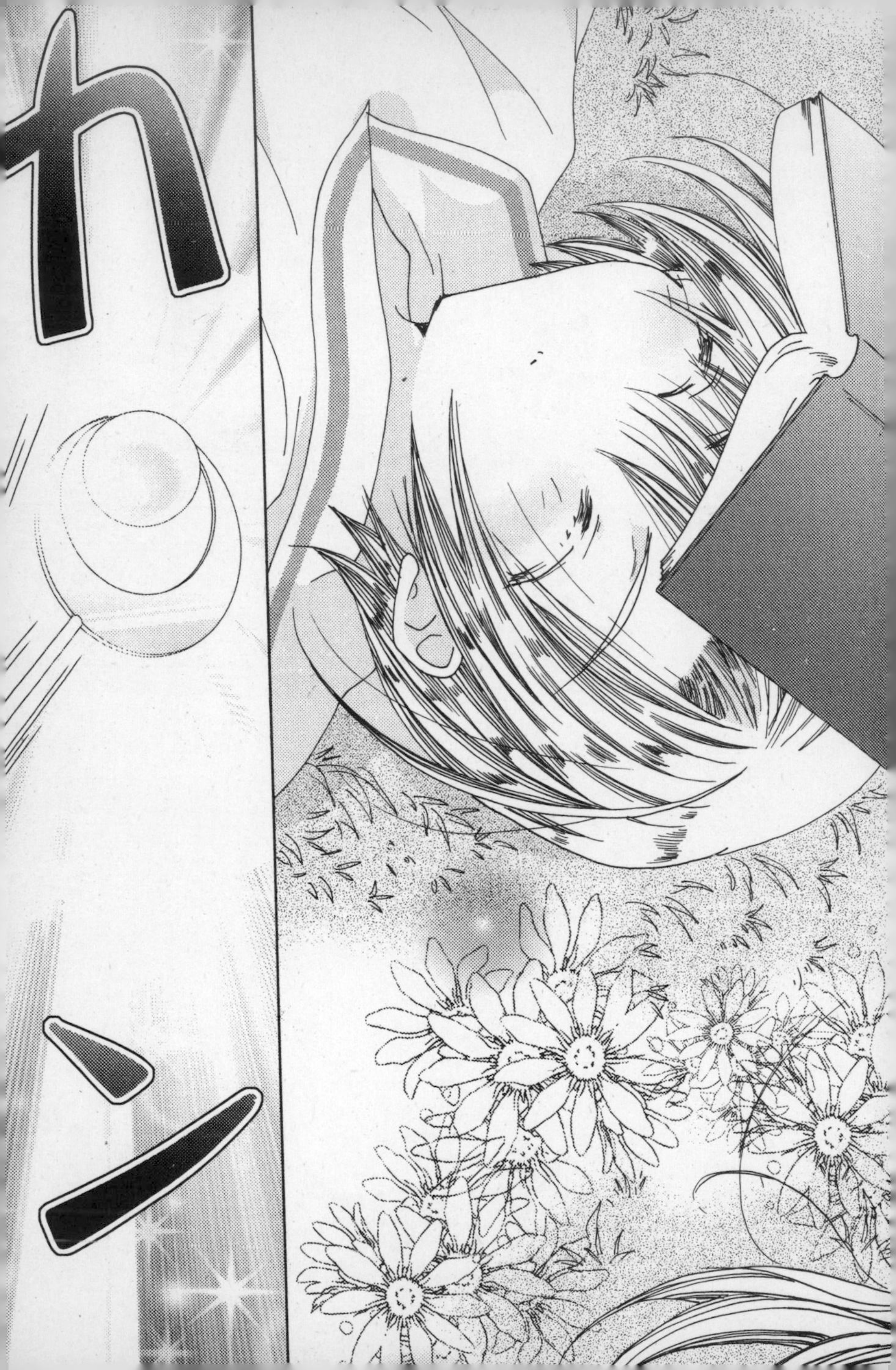
カン

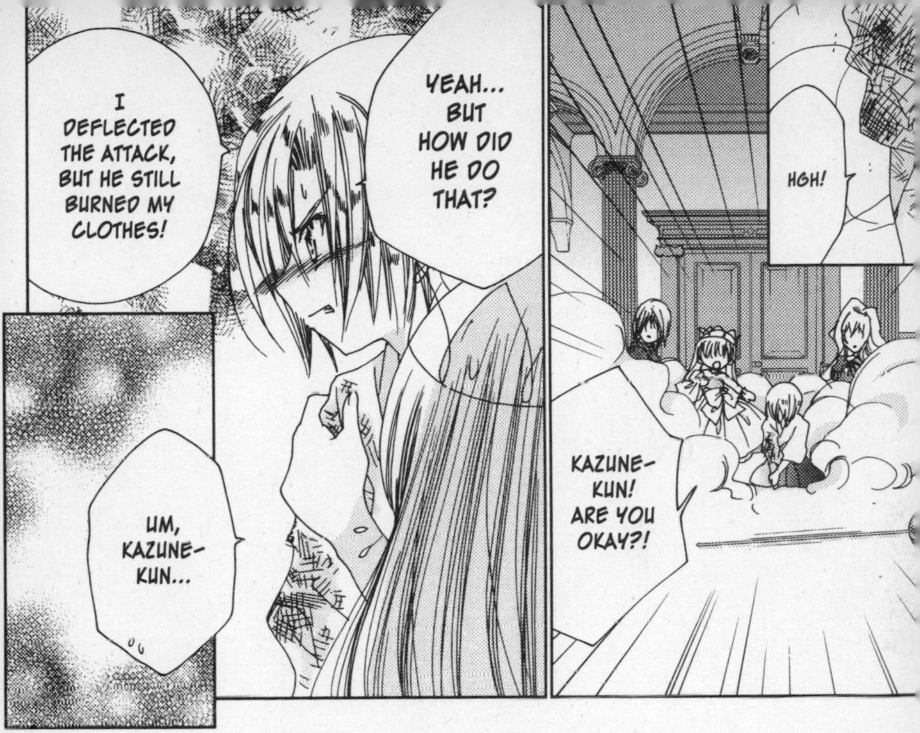
HGH!
KAZUNE-KUN! ARE YOU OKAY?!
YEAH... BUT HOW DID HE DO THAT?
I DEFLECTED THE ATTACK, BUT HE STILL BURNED MY CLOTHES!
UM, KAZUNE-KUN...

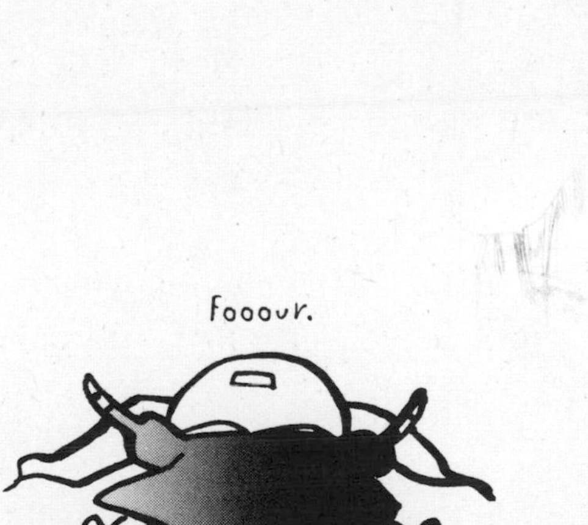
Fooour.

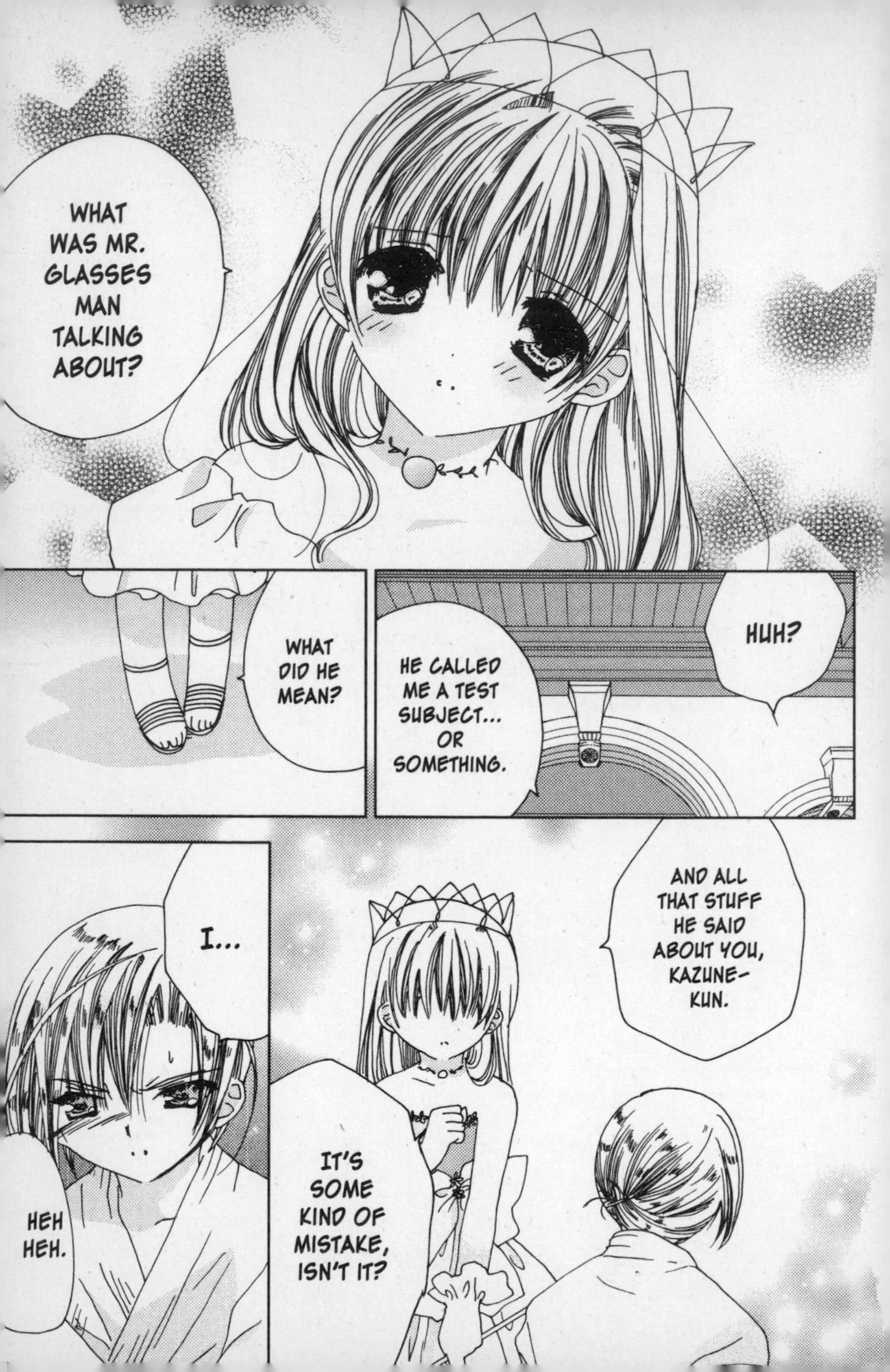
WHAT WAS MR. GLASSES MAN TALKING ABOUT?
HUH?
HE CALLED ME A TEST SUBJECT... OR SOMETHING.
WHAT DID HE MEAN?
AND ALL THAT STUFF HE SAID ABOUT YOU, KAZUNE-KUN.
IT'S SOME KIND OF MISTAKE, ISN'T IT?
I...
HEH HEH.

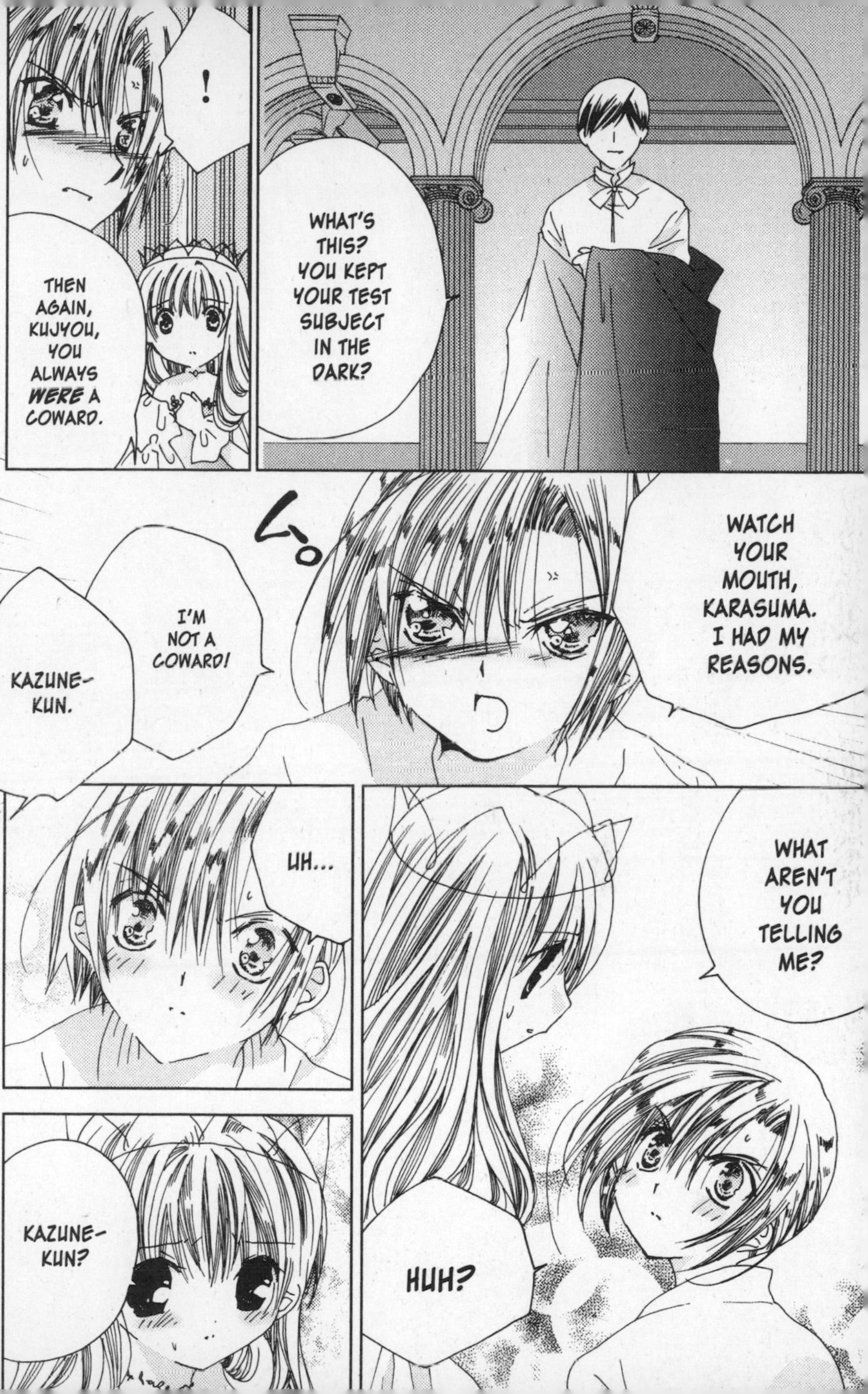
WHAT'S THIS? YOU KEPT YOUR TEST SUBJECT IN THE DARK?
!
THEN AGAIN, KUJYOU, YOU ALWAYS *WERE* A COWARD.
WATCH YOUR MOUTH, KARASUMA. I HAD MY REASONS.
むっ
I'M NOT A COWARD!
KAZUNE-KUN.
WHAT AREN'T YOU TELLING ME?
UH...
HUH?
KAZUNE-KUN?

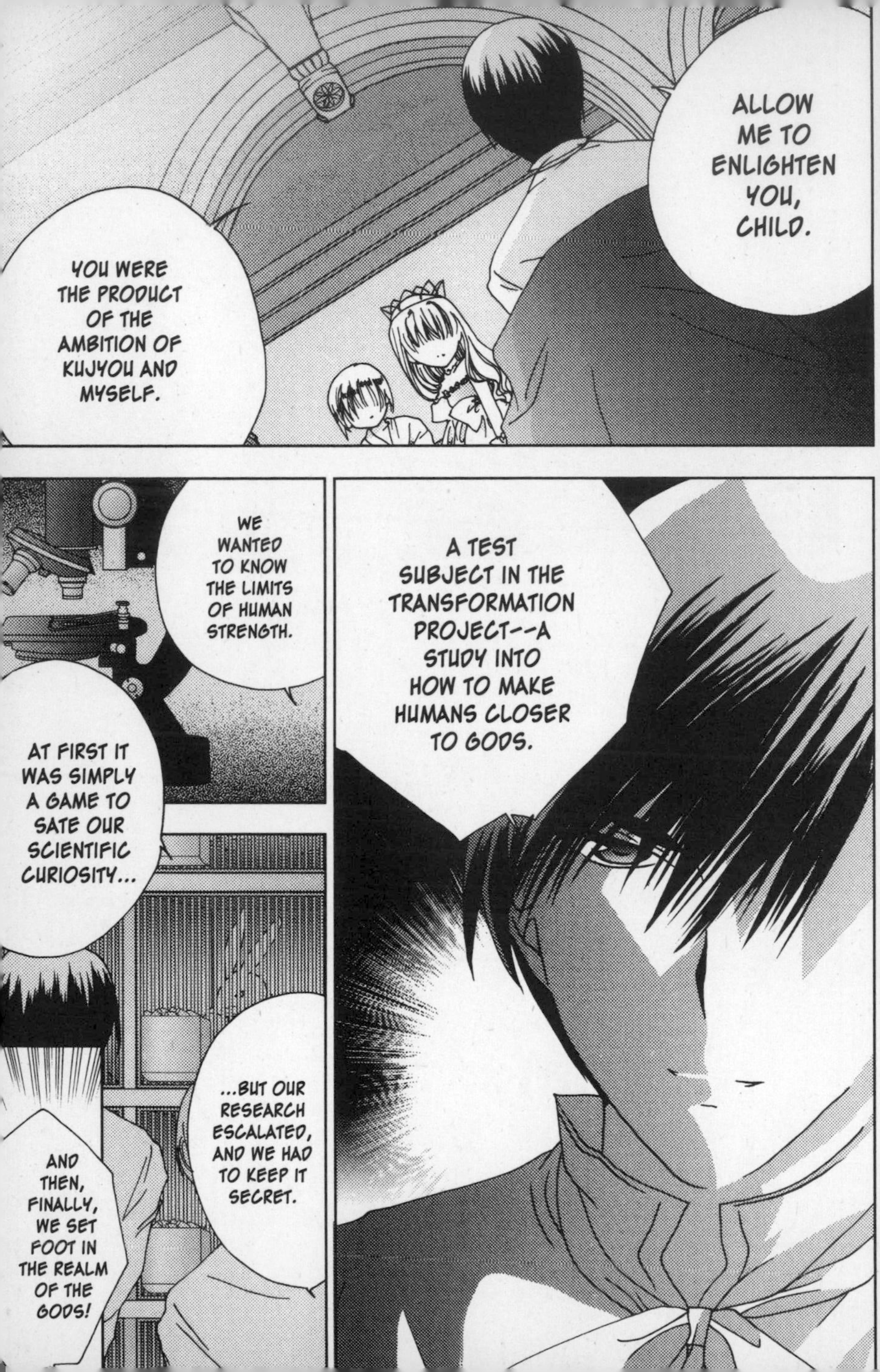
ALLOW ME TO ENLIGHTEN YOU, CHILD.
YOU WERE THE PRODUCT OF THE AMBITION OF KUJYOU AND MYSELF.
A TEST SUBJECT IN THE TRANSFORMATION PROJECT--A STUDY INTO HOW TO MAKE HUMANS CLOSER TO GODS.
WE WANTED TO KNOW THE LIMITS OF HUMAN STRENGTH.
AT FIRST IT WAS SIMPLY A GAME TO SATE OUR SCIENTIFIC CURIOSITY...
...BUT OUR RESEARCH ESCALATED, AND WE HAD TO KEEP IT SECRET.
AND THEN, FINALLY, WE SET FOOT IN THE REALM OF THE GODS!

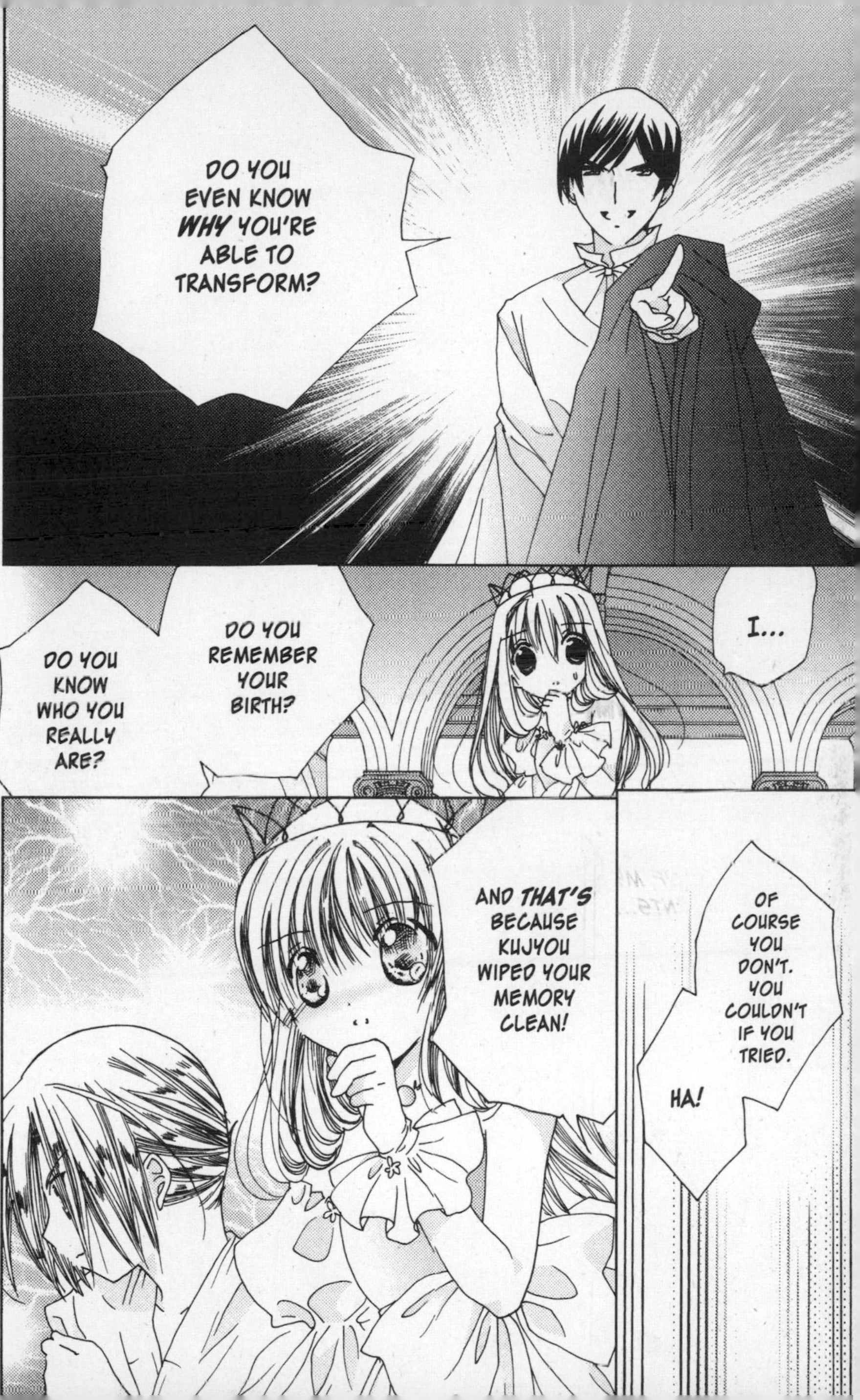
DO YOU EVEN KNOW *WHY* YOU'RE ABLE TO TRANSFORM?
I...
DO YOU REMEMBER YOUR BIRTH?
DO YOU KNOW WHO YOU REALLY ARE?
OF COURSE YOU DON'T. YOU COULDN'T IF YOU TRIED.
HA!
AND *THAT'S* BECAUSE KUJYOU WIPED YOUR MEMORY CLEAN!

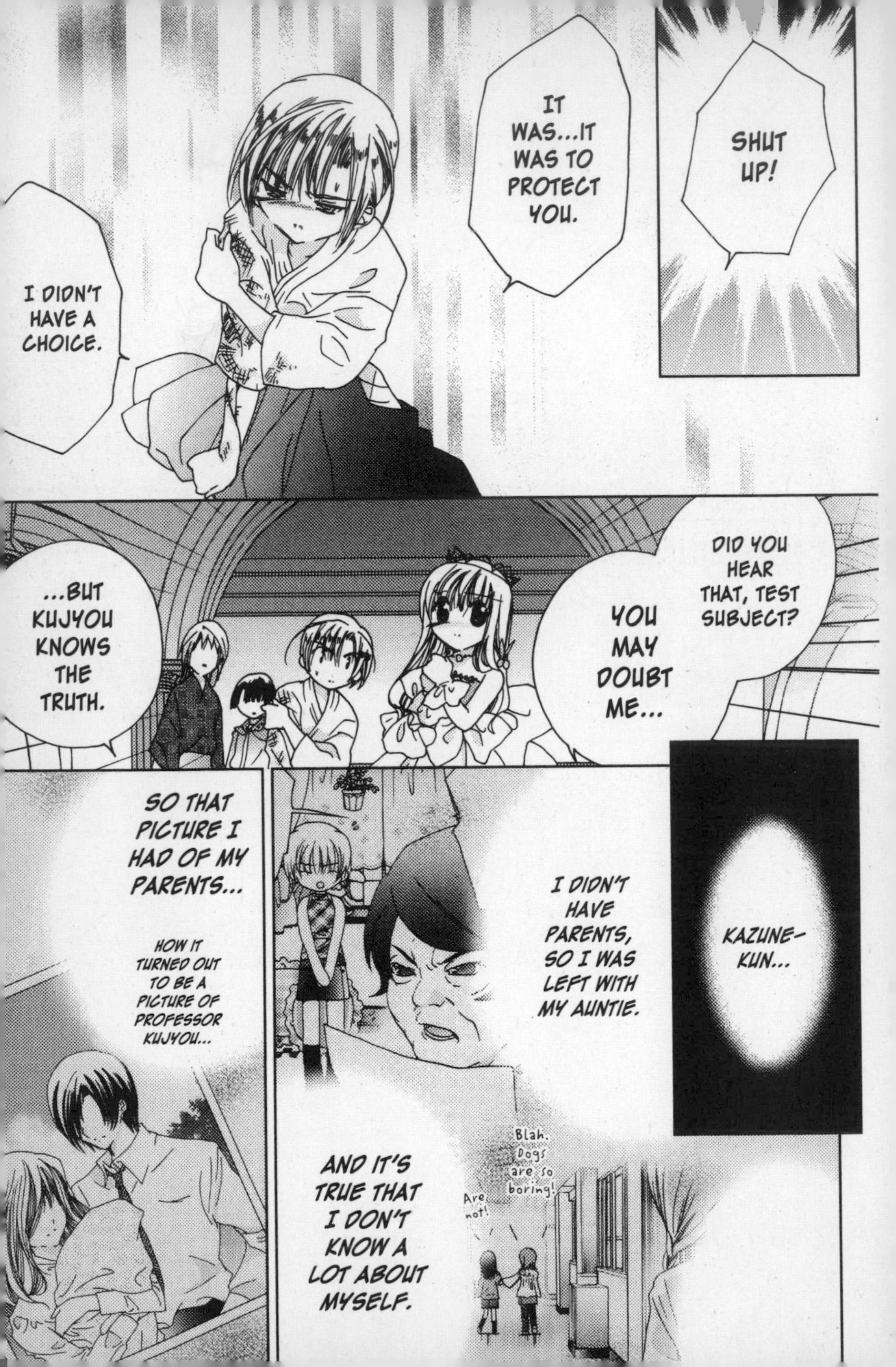
SHUT UP!
IT WAS...IT WAS TO PROTECT YOU.
I DIDN'T HAVE A CHOICE.
DID YOU HEAR THAT, TEST SUBJECT?
YOU MAY DOUBT ME...
...BUT KUJYOU KNOWS THE TRUTH.
KAZUNE-KUN...
I DIDN'T HAVE PARENTS, SO I WAS LEFT WITH MY AUNTIE.
Blah. Dogs are so boring!
Are not!
AND IT'S TRUE THAT I DON'T KNOW A LOT ABOUT MYSELF.
SO THAT PICTURE I HAD OF MY PARENTS...
HOW IT TURNED OUT TO BE A PICTURE OF PROFESSOR KUJYOU...

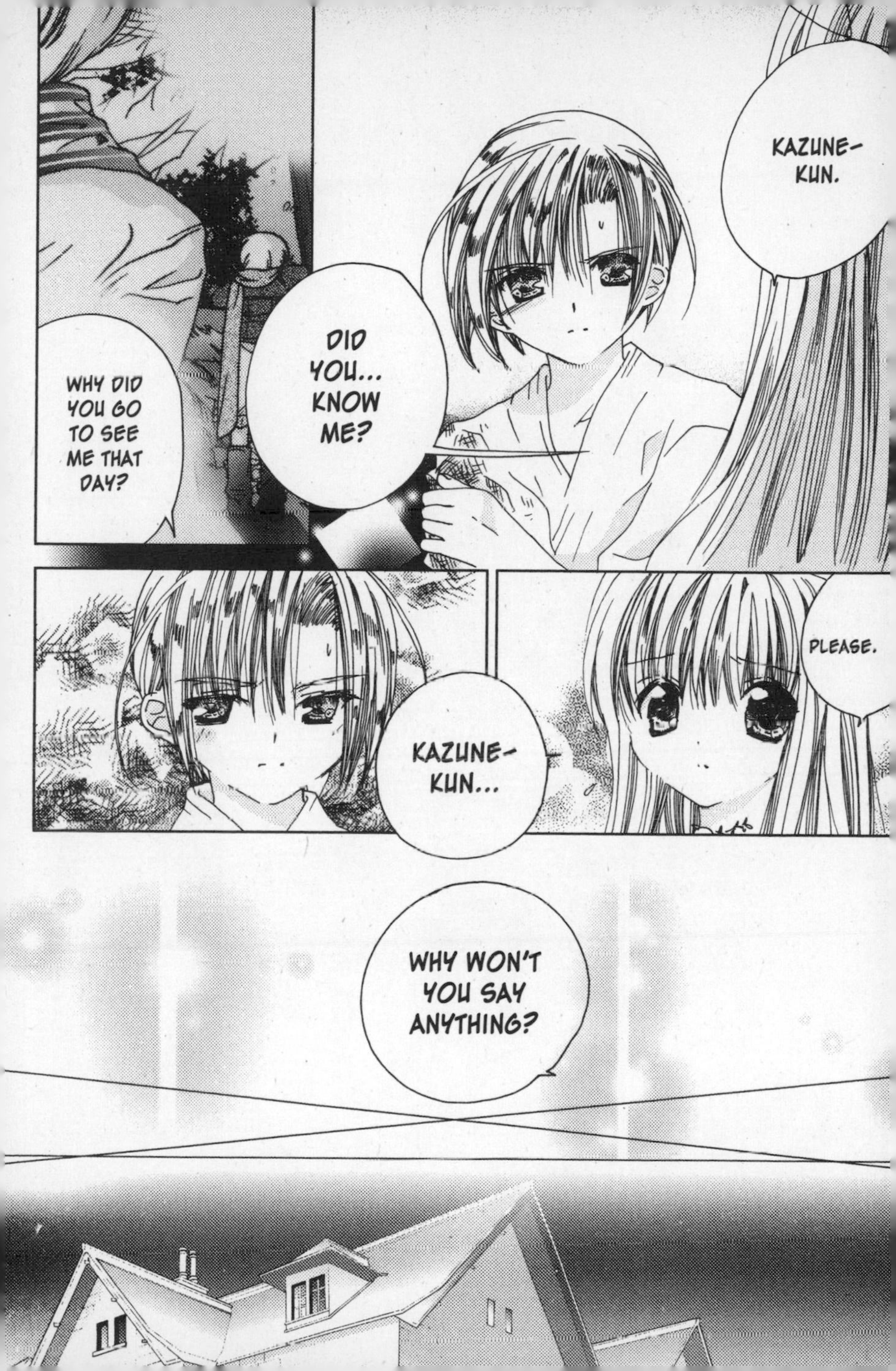
KAZUNE-KUN.
DID YOU... KNOW ME?
WHY DID YOU GO TO SEE ME THAT DAY?
PLEASE.
KAZUNE-KUN...
WHY WON'T YOU SAY ANYTHING?

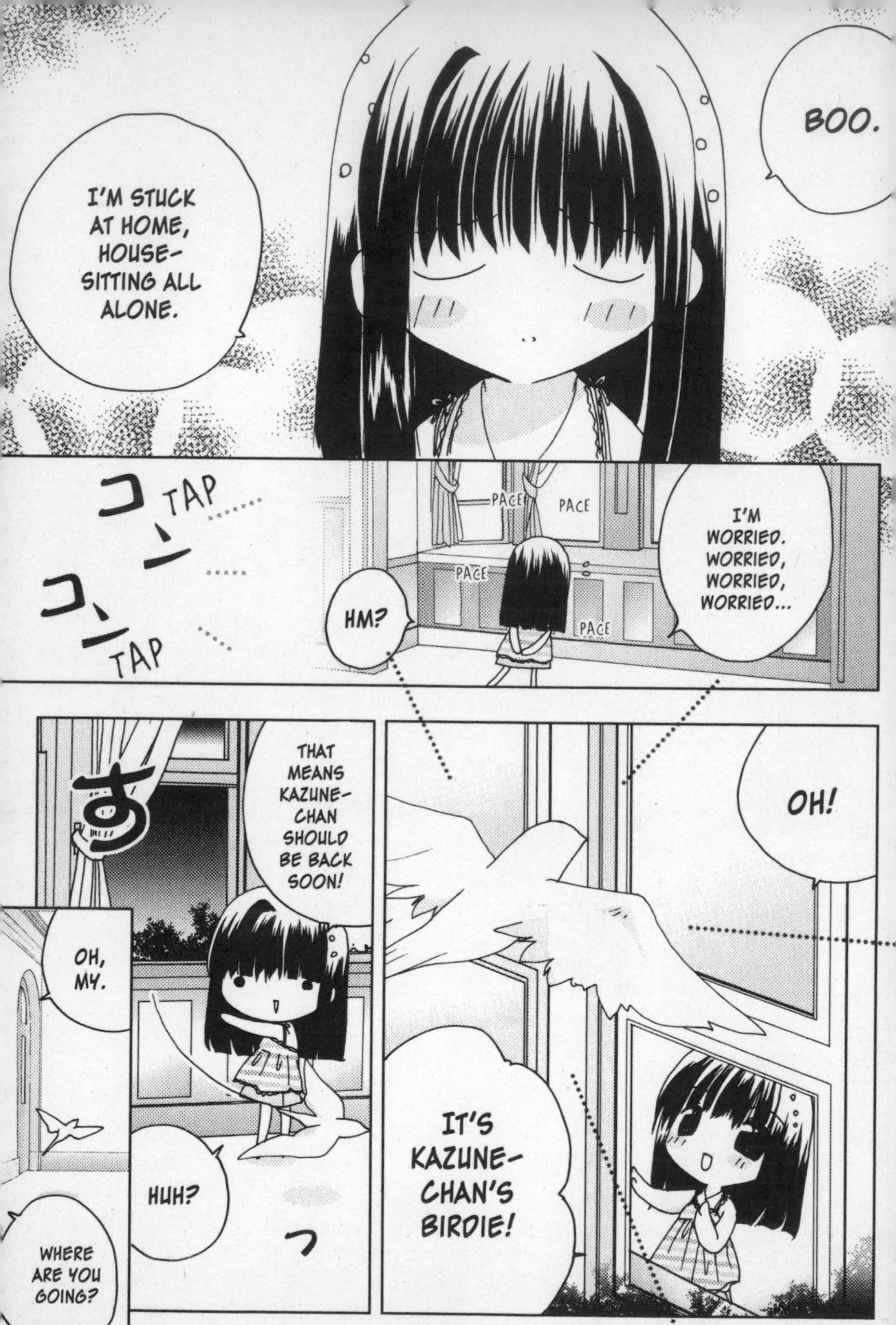
BOO.
I'M STUCK AT HOME, HOUSE-SITTING ALL ALONE.
I'M WORRIED. WORRIED, WORRIED, WORRIED...
PACE
PACE
PACE
PACE
HM?
コン TAP
コン TAP
OH!
IT'S KAZUNE-CHAN'S BIRDIE!
つ
THAT MEANS KAZUNE-CHAN SHOULD BE BACK SOON!
す
HUH?
OH, MY.
WHERE ARE YOU GOING?

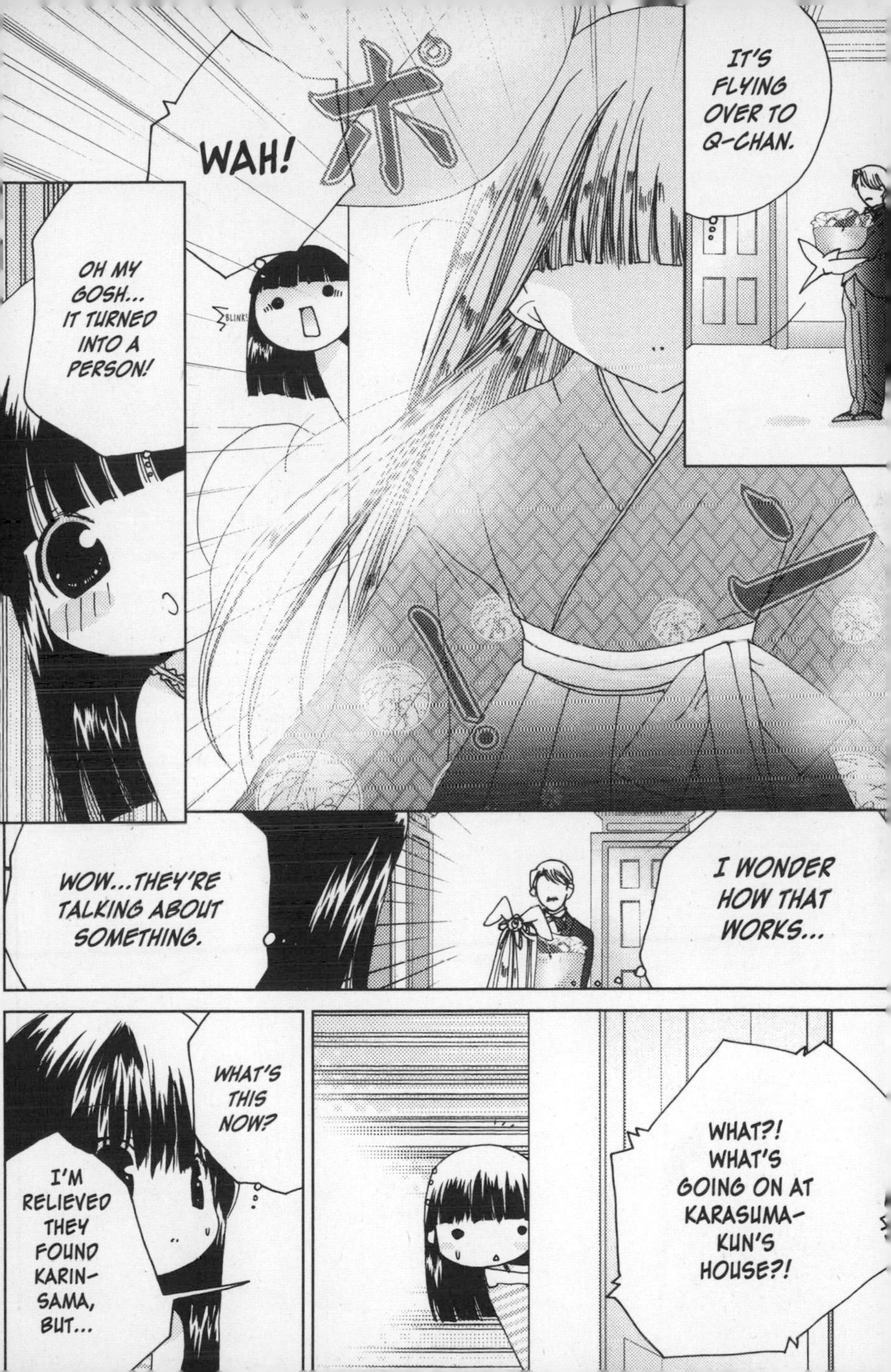
IT'S FLYING OVER TO Q-CHAN.
ポ
WAH!
BLINK!
OH MY GOSH... IT TURNED INTO A PERSON!
I WONDER HOW THAT WORKS...
WOW...THEY'RE TALKING ABOUT SOMETHING.
WHAT?! WHAT'S GOING ON AT KARASUMA-KUN'S HOUSE?!
WHAT'S THIS NOW?
I'M RELIEVED THEY FOUND KARIN-SAMA, BUT...

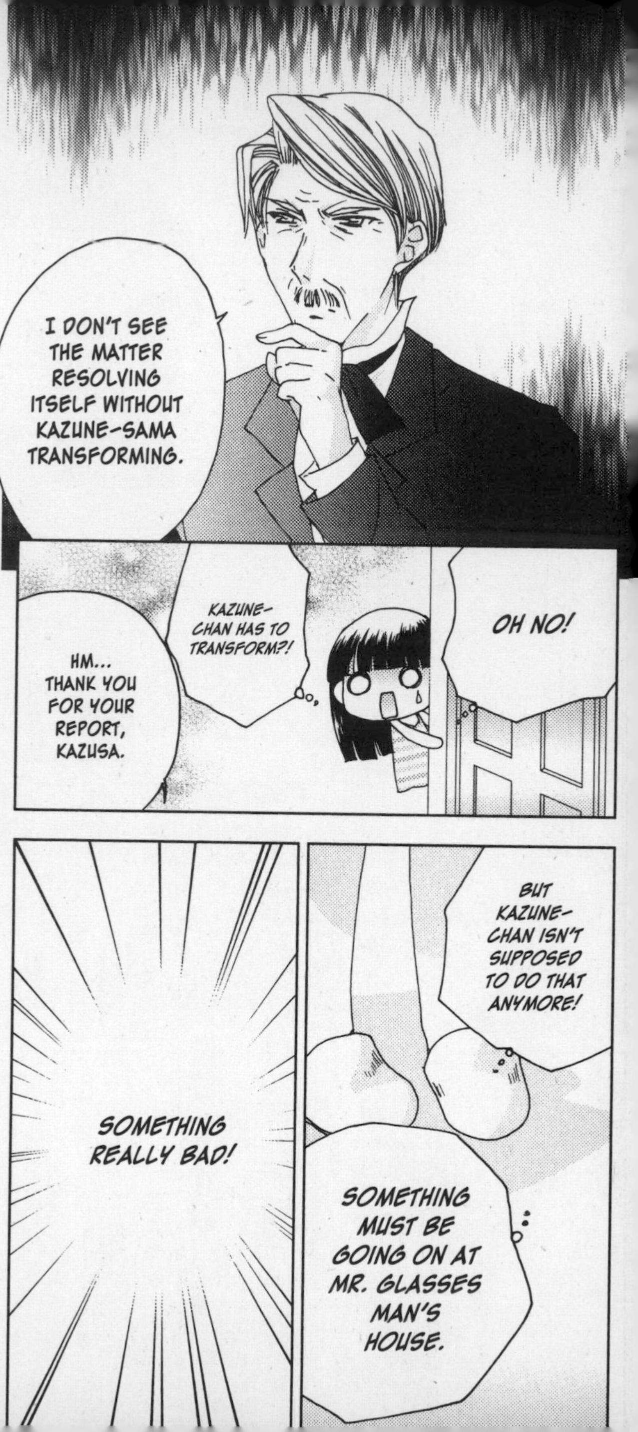
I DON'T SEE THE MATTER RESOLVING ITSELF WITHOUT KAZUNE-SAMA TRANSFORMING.
OH NO!
KAZUNE-CHAN HAS TO TRANSFORM?!
HM... THANK YOU FOR YOUR REPORT, KAZUSA.
BUT KAZUNE-CHAN ISN'T SUPPOSED TO DO THAT ANYMORE!
SOMETHING MUST BE GOING ON AT MR. GLASSES MAN'S HOUSE.
SOMETHING REALLY BAD!
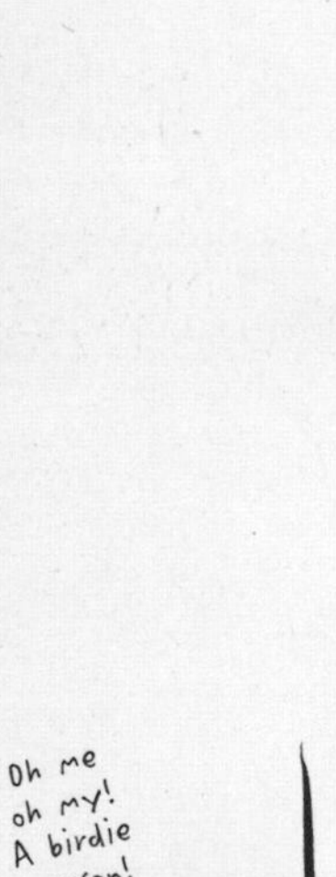
Oh me oh my! A birdie person!

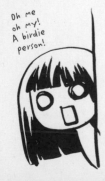

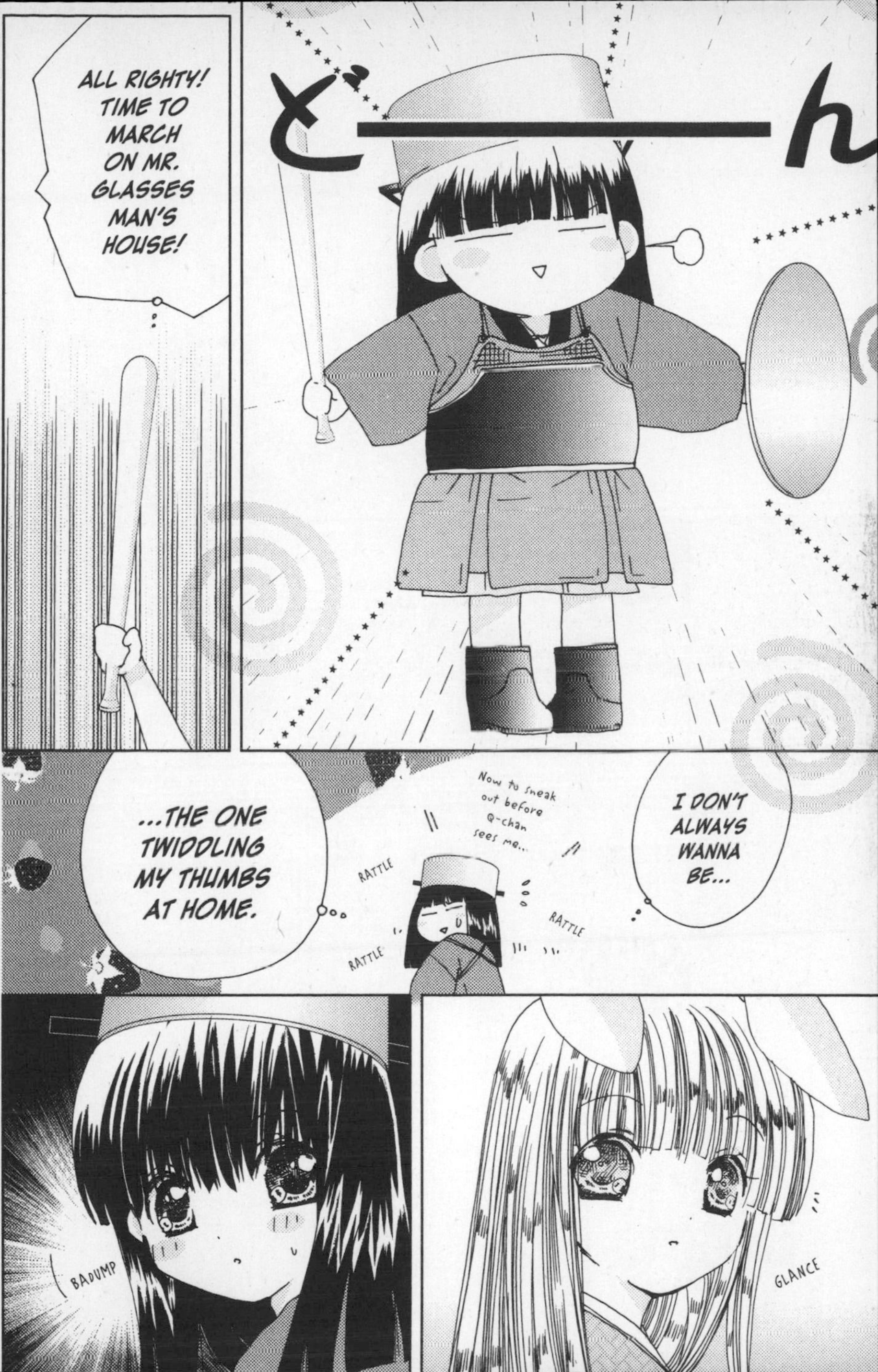

どーん
ALL RIGHTY! TIME TO MARCH ON MR. GLASSES MAN'S HOUSE!
I DON'T ALWAYS WANNA BE...
Now to sneak out before Q-chan sees me...
RATTLE
RATTLE
RATTLE
...THE ONE TWIDDLING MY THUMBS AT HOME.
GLANCE
BADUMP

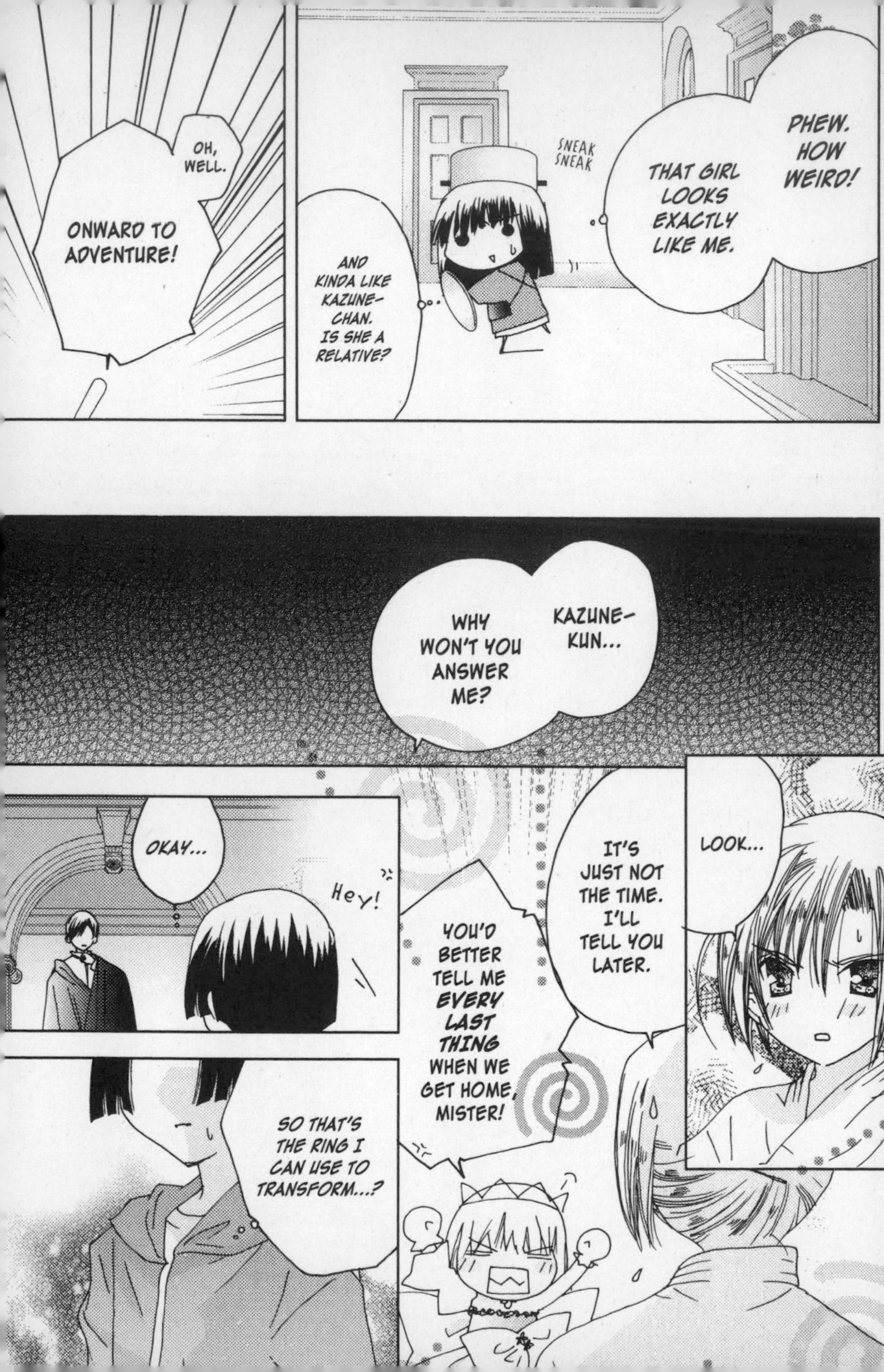
PHEW. HOW WEIRD!
THAT GIRL LOOKS EXACTLY LIKE ME.
SNEAK SNEAK
AND KINDA LIKE KAZUNE-CHAN. IS SHE A RELATIVE?
OH, WELL.
ONWARD TO ADVENTURE!
KAZUNE-KUN...
WHY WON'T YOU ANSWER ME?
LOOK...
IT'S JUST NOT THE TIME. I'LL TELL YOU LATER.
YOU'D BETTER TELL ME ***EVERY LAST THING*** WHEN WE GET HOME, MISTER!
Hey!
OKAY...
SO THAT'S THE RING I CAN USE TO TRANSFORM...?

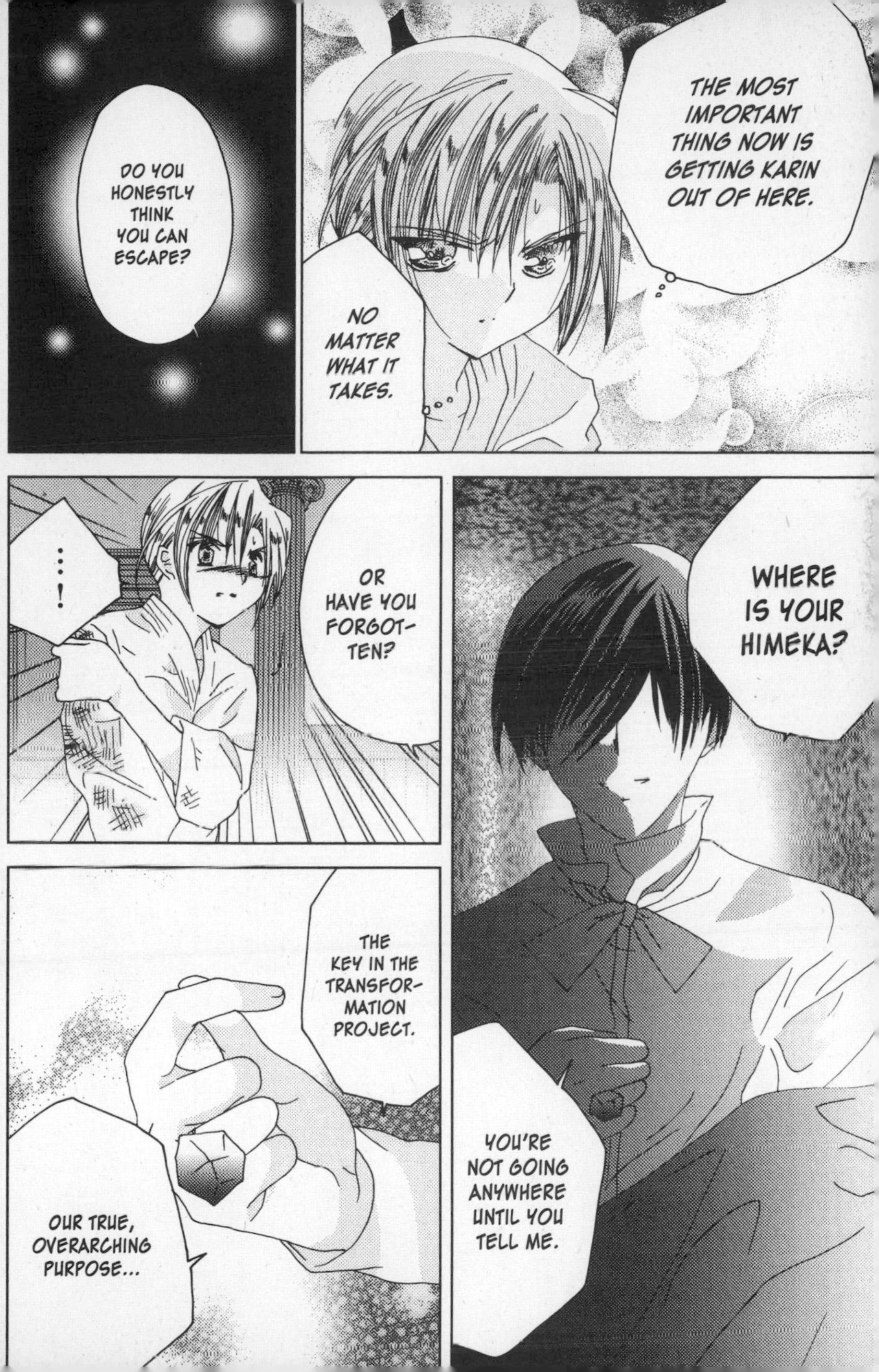
THE MOST IMPORTANT THING NOW IS GETTING KARIN OUT OF HERE.
NO MATTER WHAT IT TAKES.
DO YOU HONESTLY THINK YOU CAN ESCAPE?
WHERE IS YOUR HIMEKA?
YOU'RE NOT GOING ANYWHERE UNTIL YOU TELL ME.
OR HAVE YOU FORGOT-TEN?
...!
THE KEY IN THE TRANSFOR-MATION PROJECT.
OUR TRUE, OVERARCHING PURPOSE...

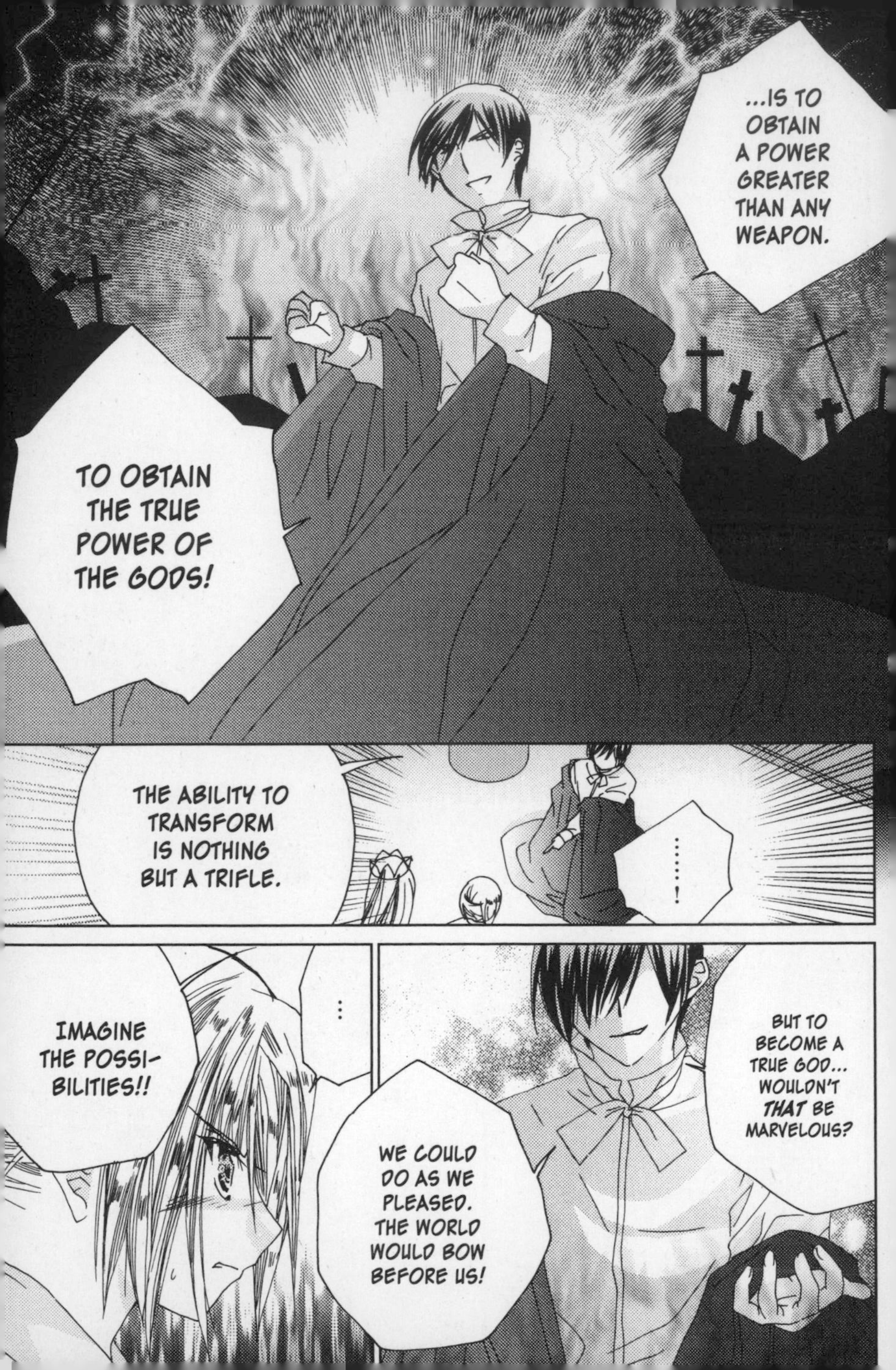
...IS TO OBTAIN A POWER GREATER THAN ANY WEAPON.
TO OBTAIN THE TRUE POWER OF THE GODS!
......!
THE ABILITY TO TRANSFORM IS NOTHING BUT A TRIFLE.
BUT TO BECOME A TRUE GOD... WOULDN'T *THAT* BE MARVELOUS?
WE COULD DO AS WE PLEASED. THE WORLD WOULD BOW BEFORE US!
...
IMAGINE THE POSSI-BILITIES!!

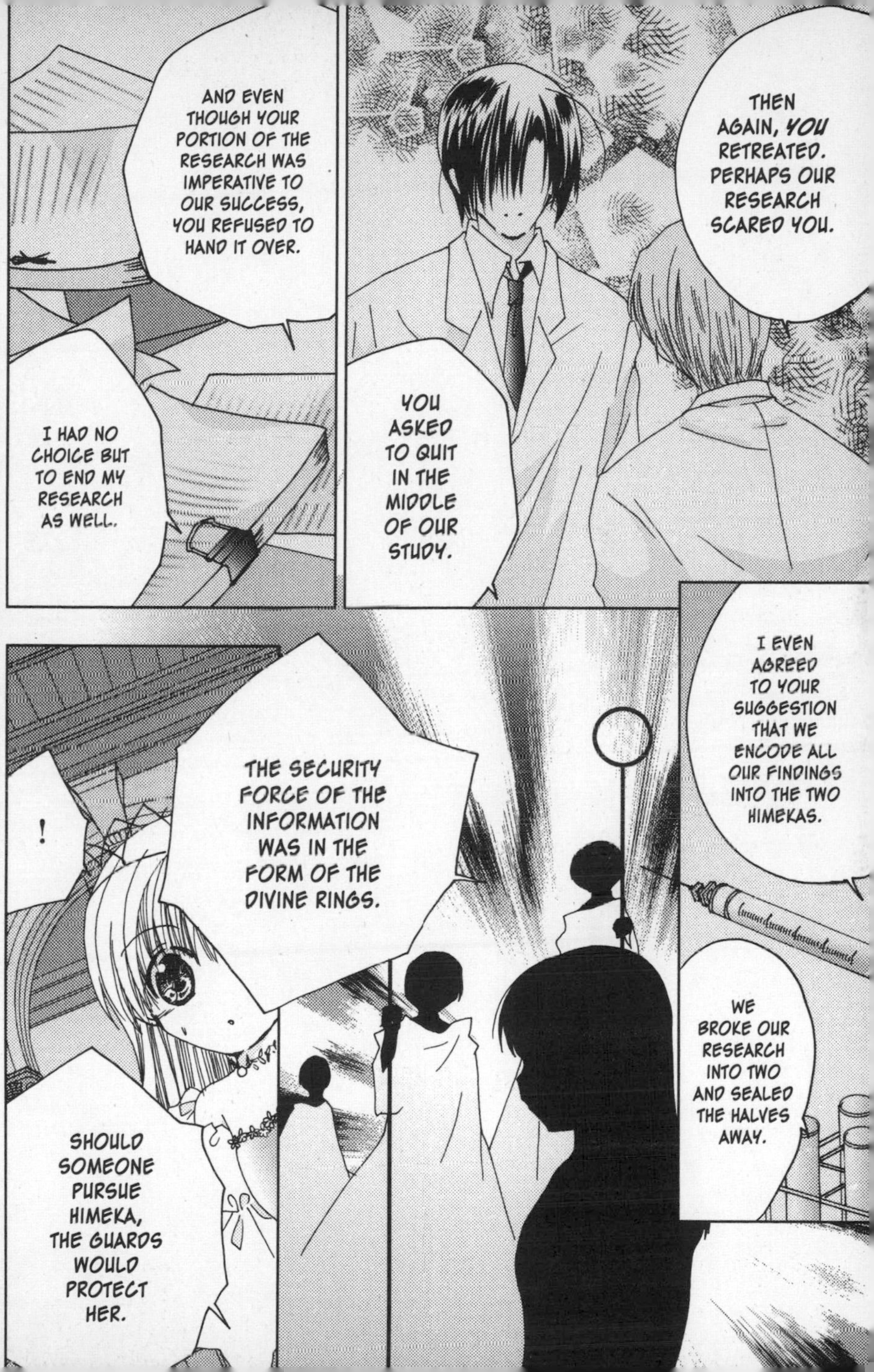
THEN AGAIN, *YOU* RETREATED. PERHAPS OUR RESEARCH SCARED YOU.
YOU ASKED TO QUIT IN THE MIDDLE OF OUR STUDY.
AND EVEN THOUGH YOUR PORTION OF THE RESEARCH WAS IMPERATIVE TO OUR SUCCESS, YOU REFUSED TO HAND IT OVER.
I HAD NO CHOICE BUT TO END MY RESEARCH AS WELL.
I EVEN AGREED TO YOUR SUGGESTION THAT WE ENCODE ALL OUR FINDINGS INTO THE TWO HIMEKAS.
WE BROKE OUR RESEARCH INTO TWO AND SEALED THE HALVES AWAY.
THE SECURITY FORCE OF THE INFORMATION WAS IN THE FORM OF THE DIVINE RINGS.
!
SHOULD SOMEONE PURSUE HIMEKA, THE GUARDS WOULD PROTECT HER.

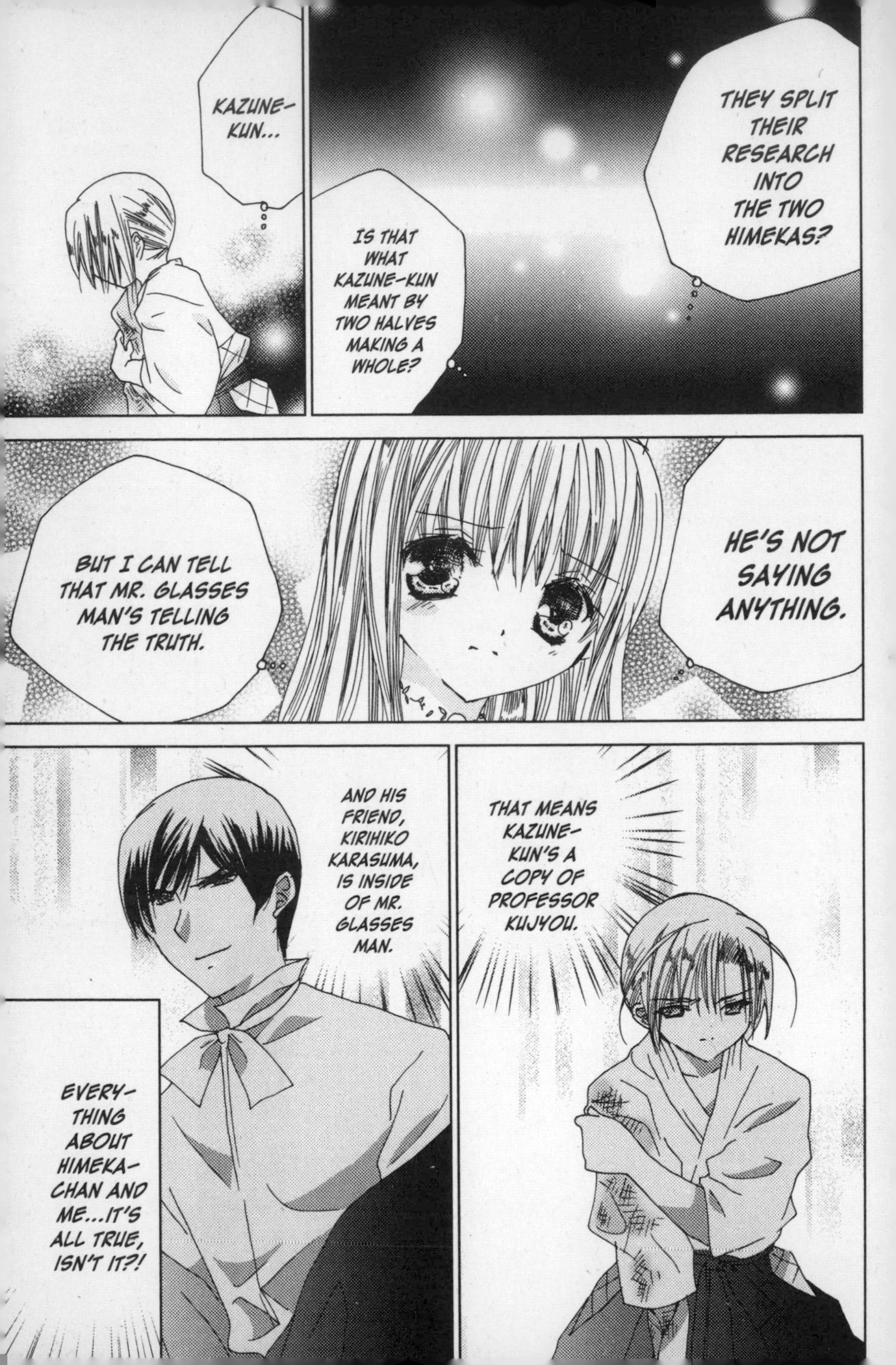
THEY SPLIT THEIR RESEARCH INTO THE TWO HIMEKAS?
IS THAT WHAT KAZUNE-KUN MEANT BY TWO HALVES MAKING A WHOLE?
KAZUNE-KUN...
HE'S NOT SAYING ANYTHING.
BUT I CAN TELL THAT MR. GLASSES MAN'S TELLING THE TRUTH.
THAT MEANS KAZUNE-KUN'S A COPY OF PROFESSOR KUJYOU.
AND HIS FRIEND, KIRIHIKO KARASUMA, IS INSIDE OF MR. GLASSES MAN.
EVERYTHING ABOUT HIMEKA-CHAN AND ME...IT'S ALL TRUE, ISN'T IT?!

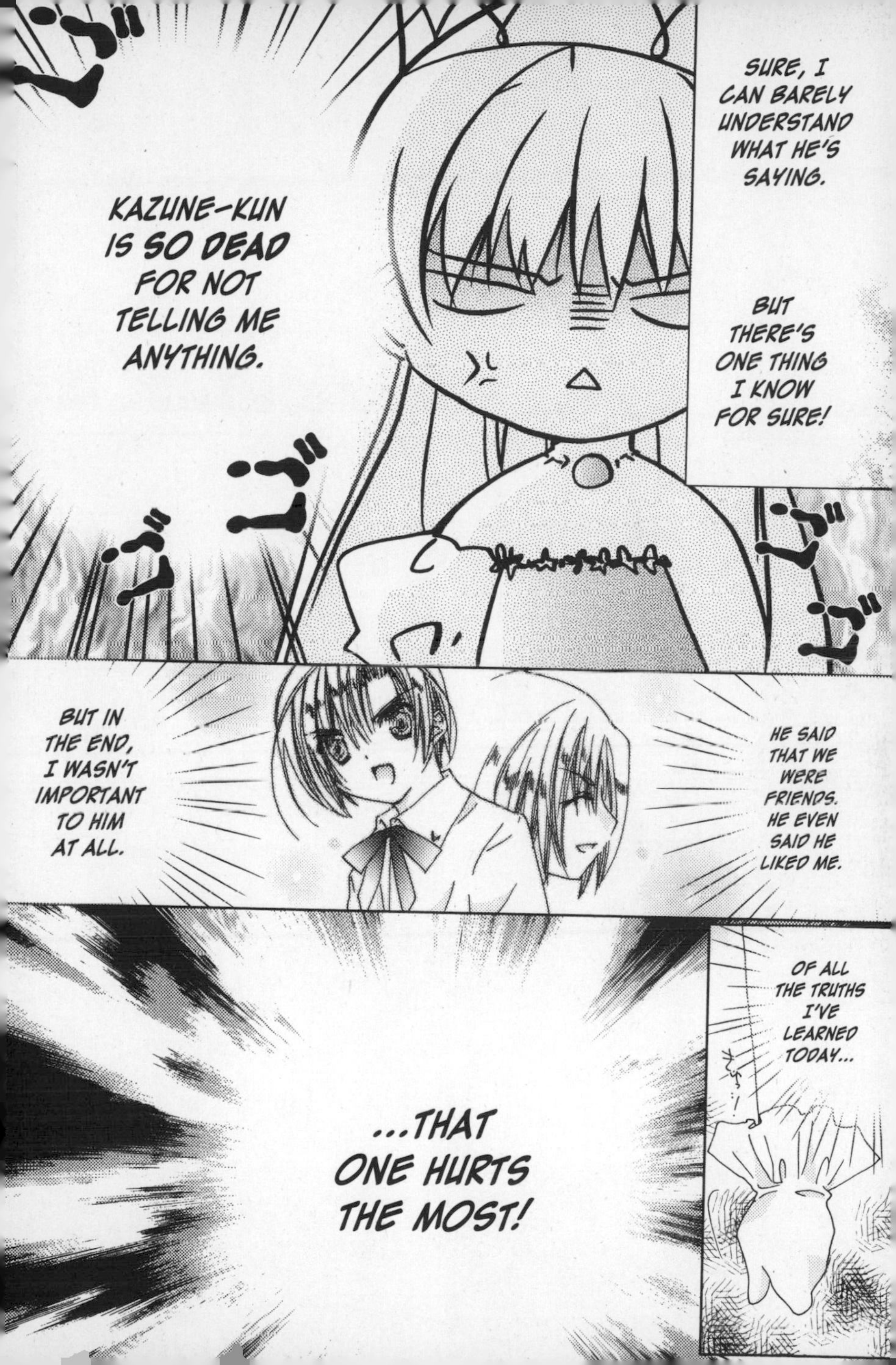
SURE, I CAN BARELY UNDERSTAND WHAT HE'S SAYING.
BUT THERE'S ONE THING I KNOW FOR SURE!
KAZUNE-KUN IS SO DEAD FOR NOT TELLING ME ANYTHING.
HE SAID THAT WE WERE FRIENDS. HE EVEN SAID HE LIKED ME.
BUT IN THE END, I WASN'T IMPORTANT TO HIM AT ALL.
OF ALL THE TRUTHS I'VE LEARNED TODAY...
...THAT ONE HURTS THE MOST!

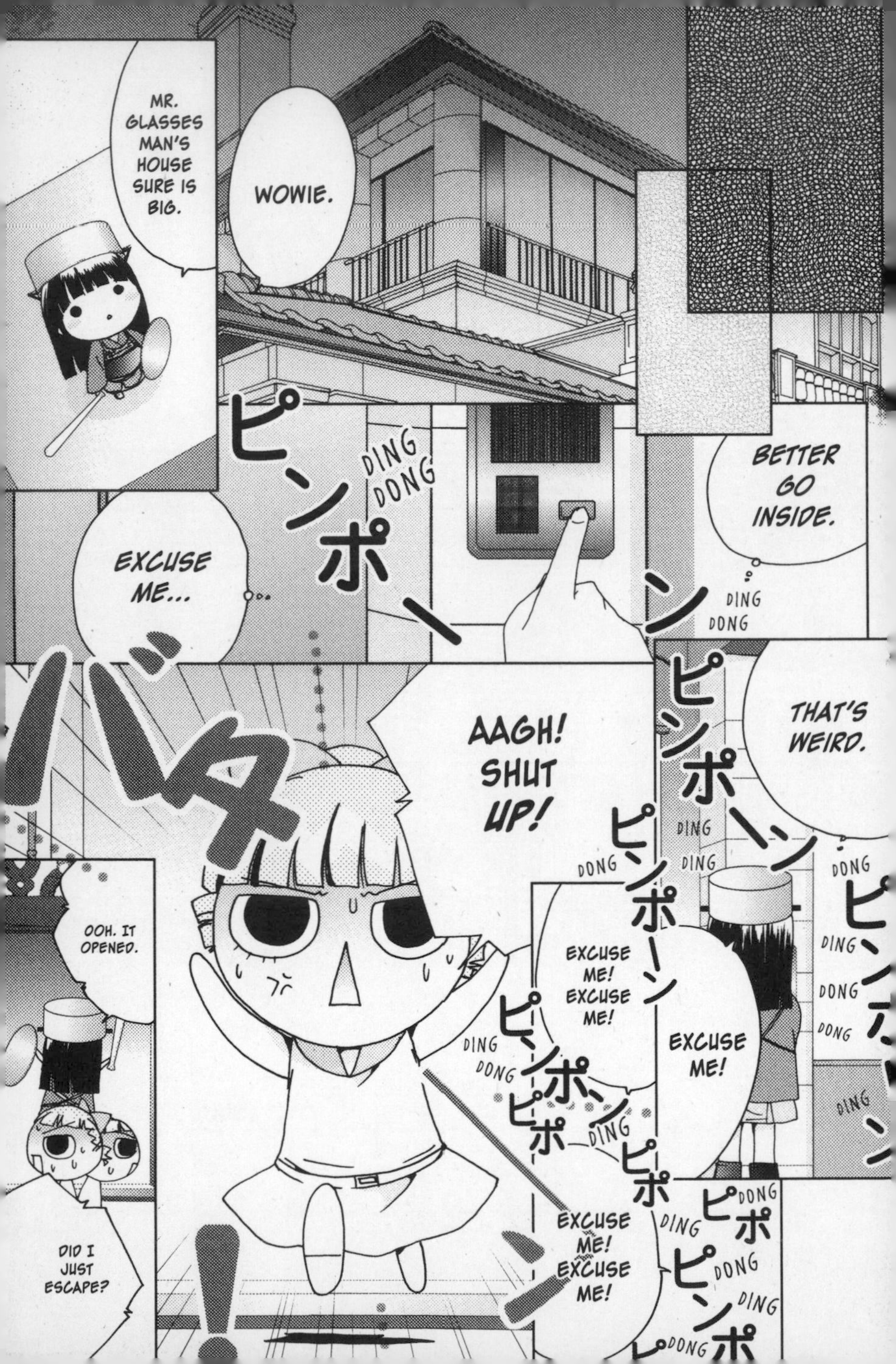
WOWIE.
MR. GLASSES MAN'S HOUSE SURE IS BIG.
BETTER GO INSIDE.
DING DONG
ピンポーン
DING DONG
EXCUSE ME...
THAT'S WEIRD.
ピンポーン
DING DING
DONG
ピンポーン
DONG
ピンポーン
DING DONG DONG
DING
EXCUSE ME!
EXCUSE ME! EXCUSE ME!
ピンポーン
DING DONG
ピポ
DING
ピポ
ピポ
DONG
DING
ピンポ
DONG DING
DONG
EXCUSE ME! EXCUSE ME!
AAGH! SHUT UP!
バタン
OOH. IT OPENED.
DID I JUST ESCAPE?

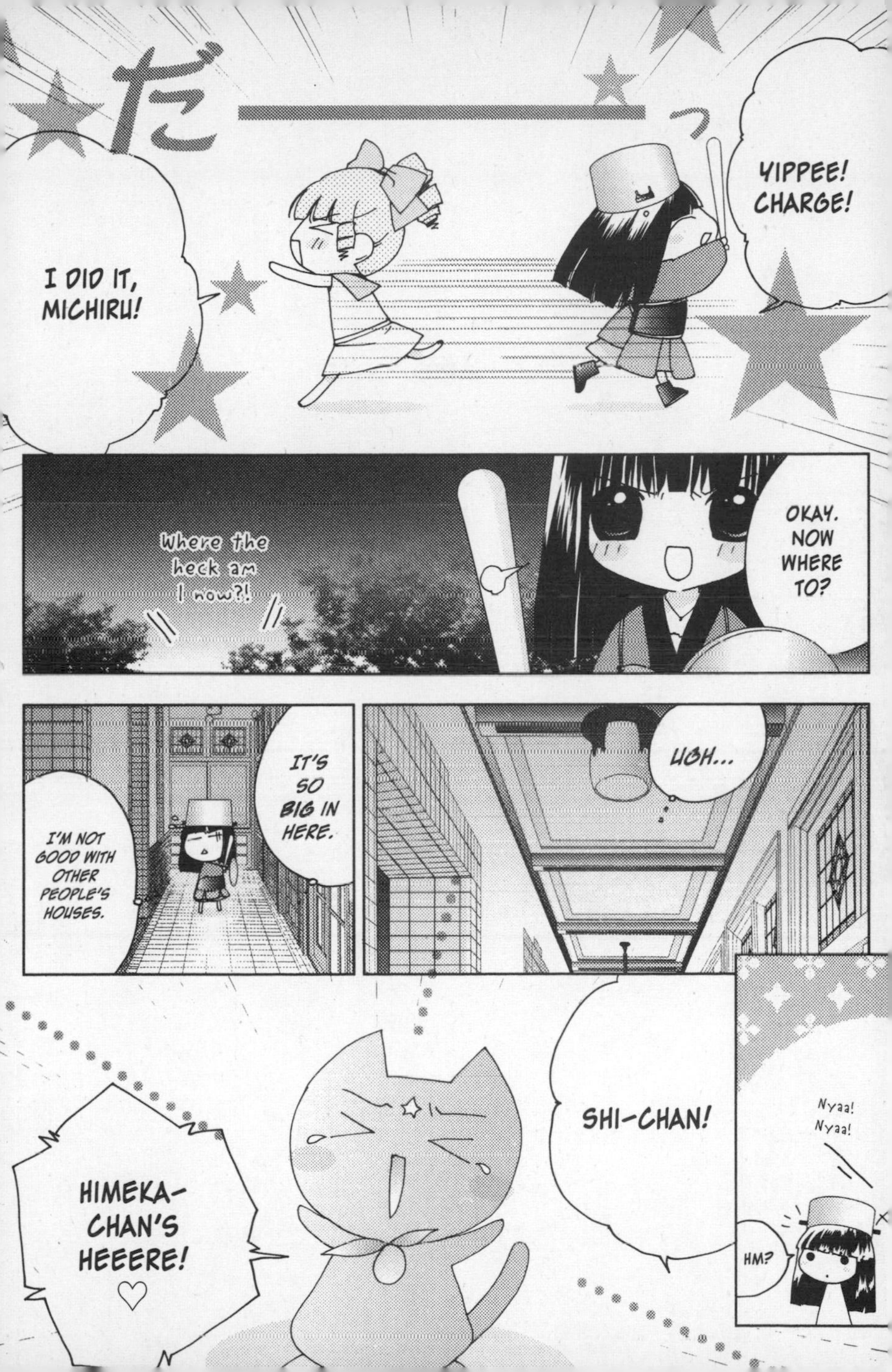
だ——っ
YIPPEE! CHARGE!
I DID IT, MICHIRU!
OKAY. NOW WHERE TO?
Where the heck am I now?!
UGH...
IT'S SO BIG IN HERE.
I'M NOT GOOD WITH OTHER PEOPLE'S HOUSES.
Nyaa! Nyaa!
HM?
SHI-CHAN!
HIMEKA-CHAN'S HEEERE! ♡

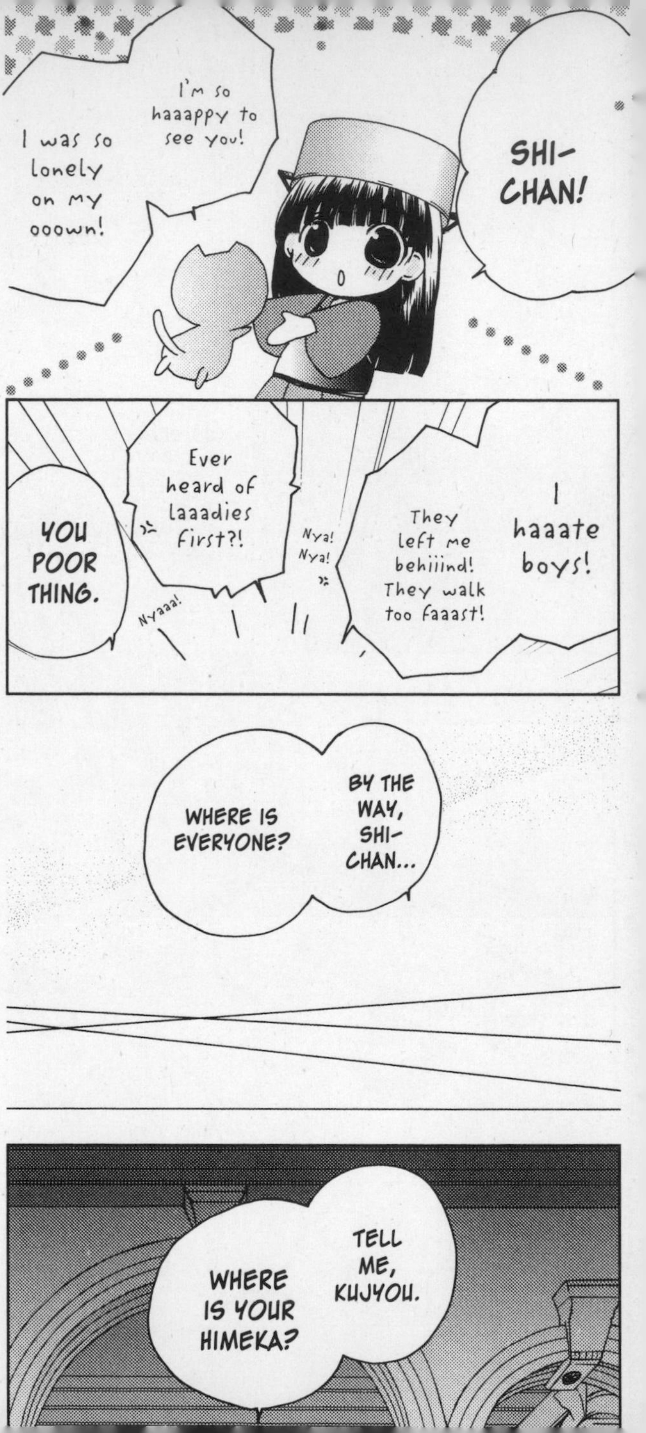
SHI-CHAN!
I'm so haaappy to see you!
I was so lonely on my ooown!
I haaate boys!
They left me behiiind! They walk too faaast!
Nya! Nya!
Ever heard of laaadies first?!
Nyaaa!
YOU POOR THING.
BY THE WAY, SHI-CHAN...
WHERE IS EVERYONE?
TELL ME, KUJYOU.
WHERE IS YOUR HIMEKA?

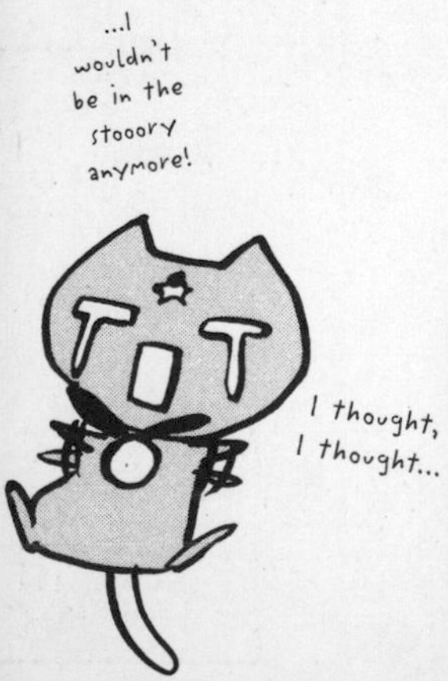
I thought, I thought...
...I wouldn't be in the stooory anymore!

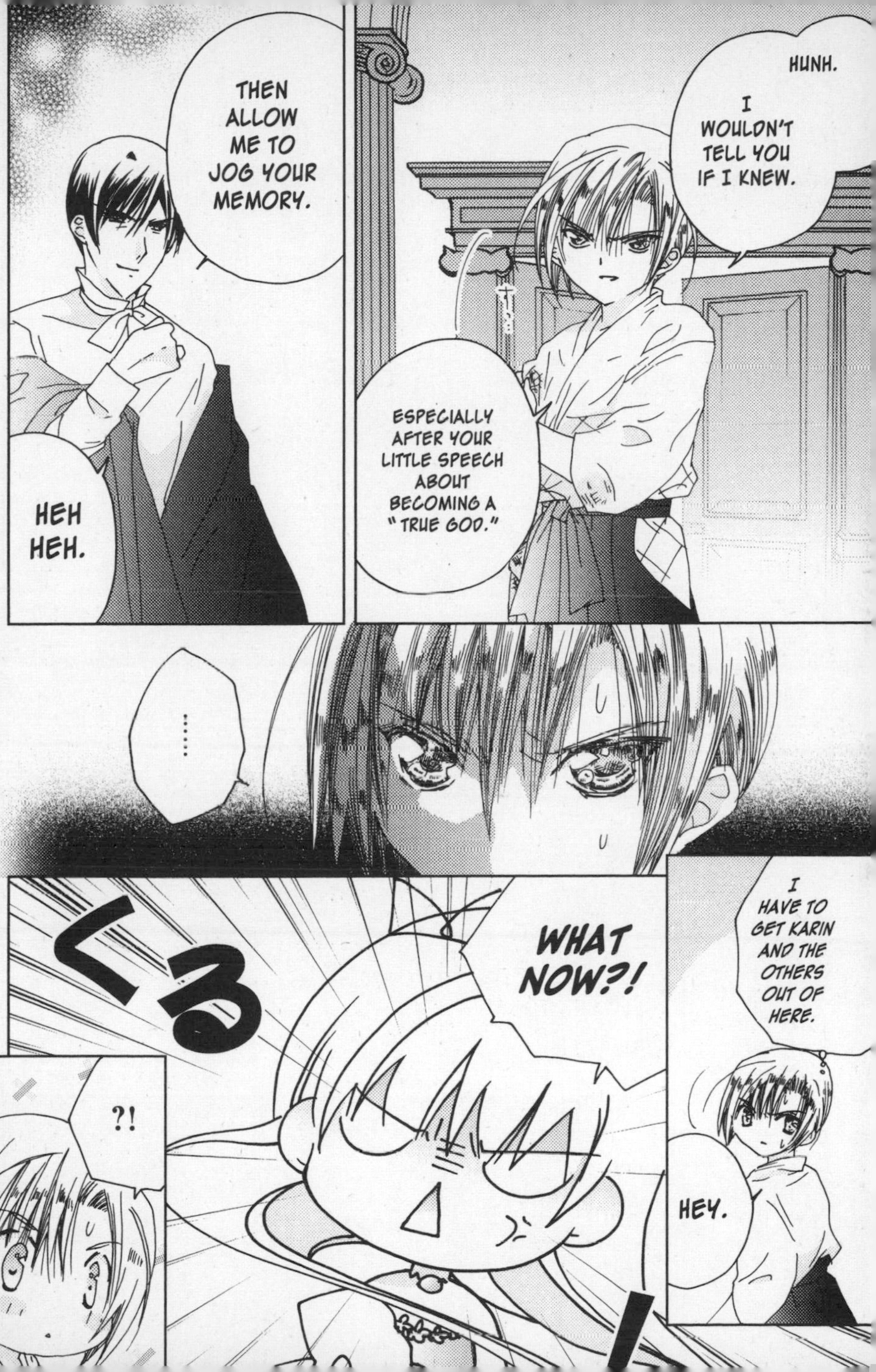
HUNH.
I WOULDN'T TELL YOU IF I KNEW.
ESPECIALLY AFTER YOUR LITTLE SPEECH ABOUT BECOMING A "TRUE GOD."
THEN ALLOW ME TO JOG YOUR MEMORY.
HEH HEH.
......
I HAVE TO GET KARIN AND THE OTHERS OUT OF HERE.
HEY.
WHAT NOW?!
くる
?!

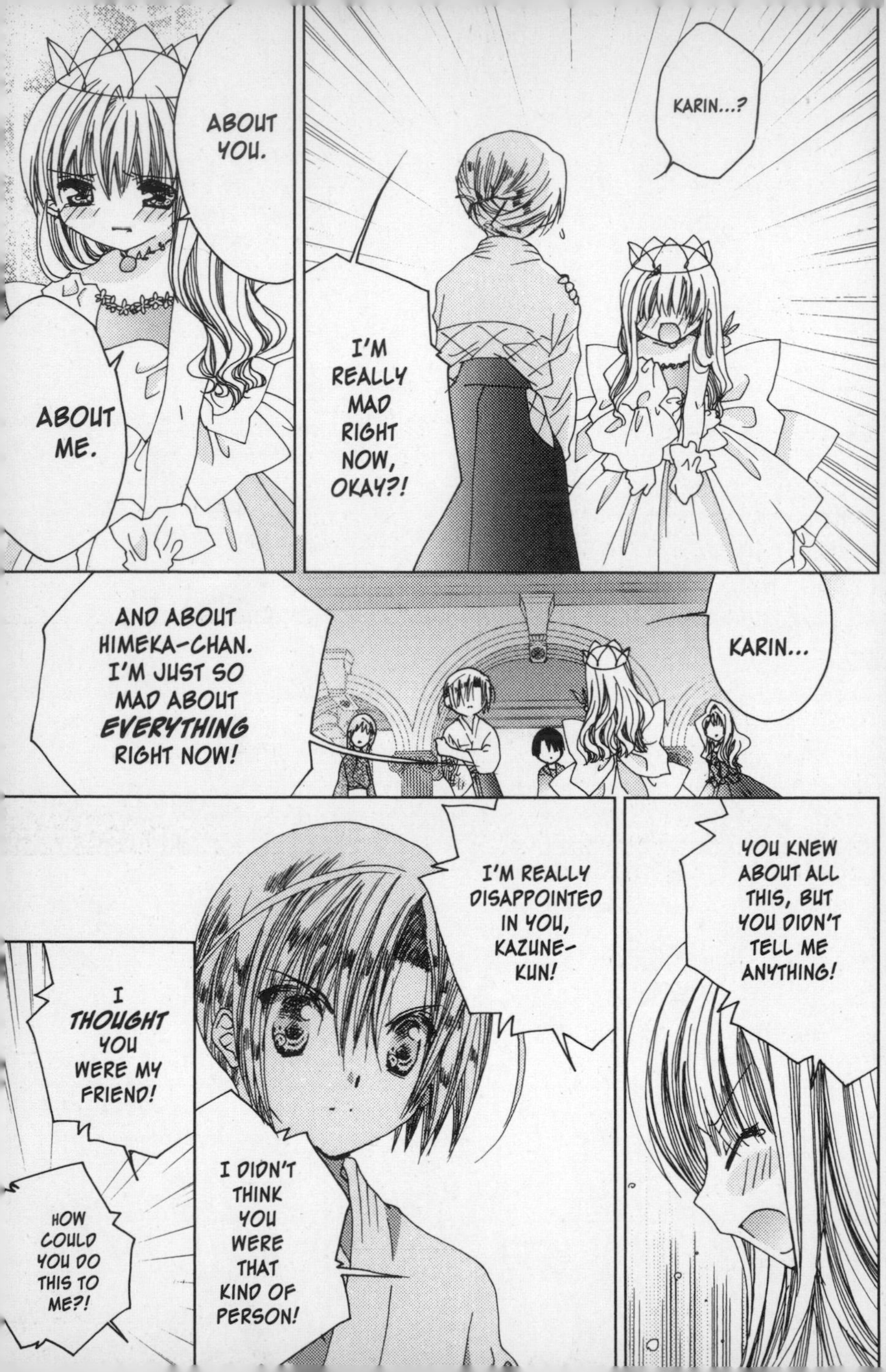

KARIN...?
I'M REALLY MAD RIGHT NOW, OKAY?!
ABOUT YOU.
ABOUT ME.
KARIN...
AND ABOUT HIMEKA-CHAN. I'M JUST SO MAD ABOUT *EVERYTHING* RIGHT NOW!
YOU KNEW ABOUT ALL THIS, BUT YOU DIDN'T TELL ME ANYTHING!
I'M REALLY DISAPPOINTED IN YOU, KAZUNE-KUN!
I *THOUGHT* YOU WERE MY FRIEND!
I DIDN'T THINK YOU WERE THAT KIND OF PERSON!
HOW COULD YOU DO THIS TO ME?!

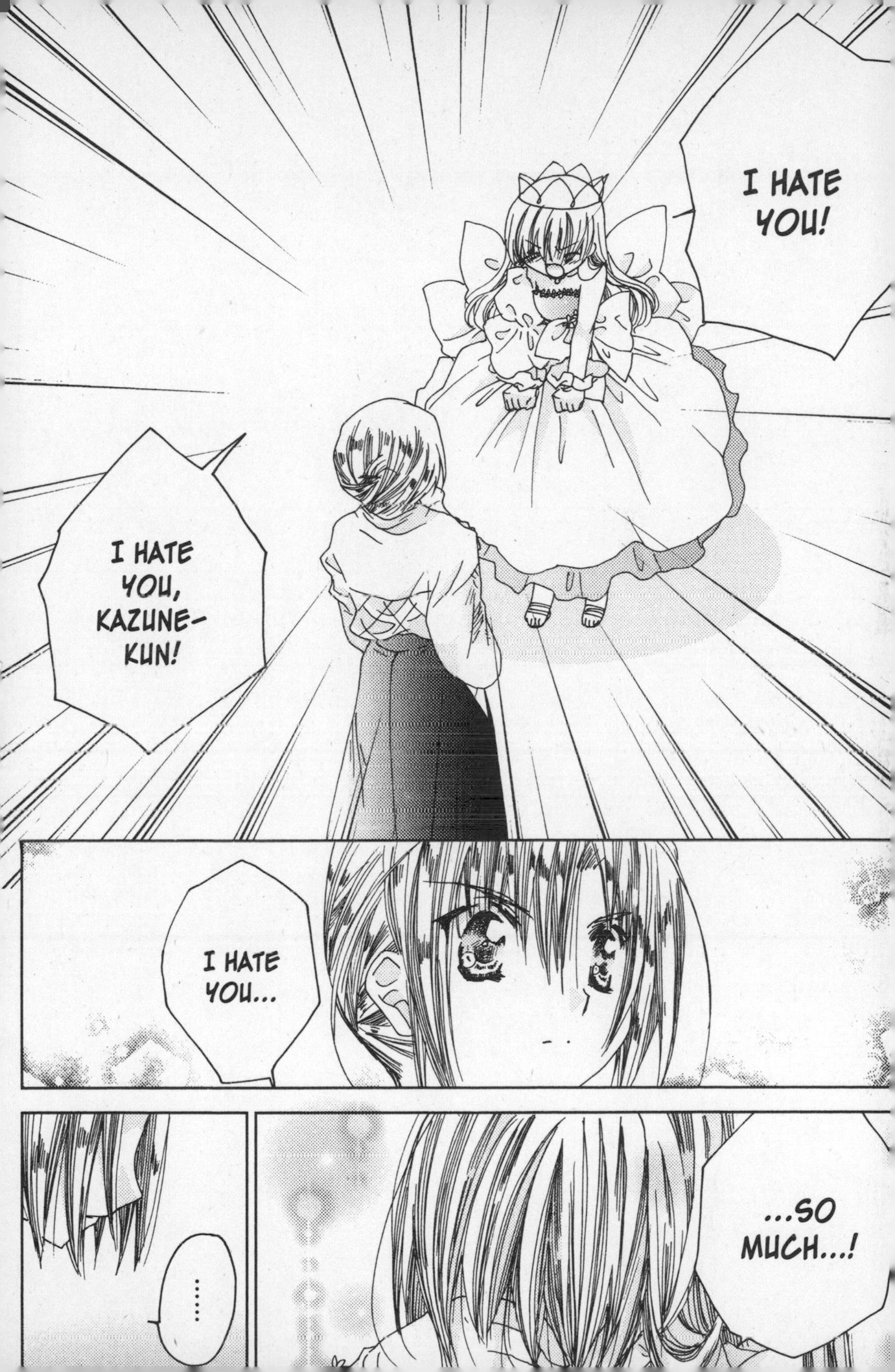
I HATE YOU!
I HATE YOU, KAZUNE-KUN!
I HATE YOU...
...SO MUCH...!
......

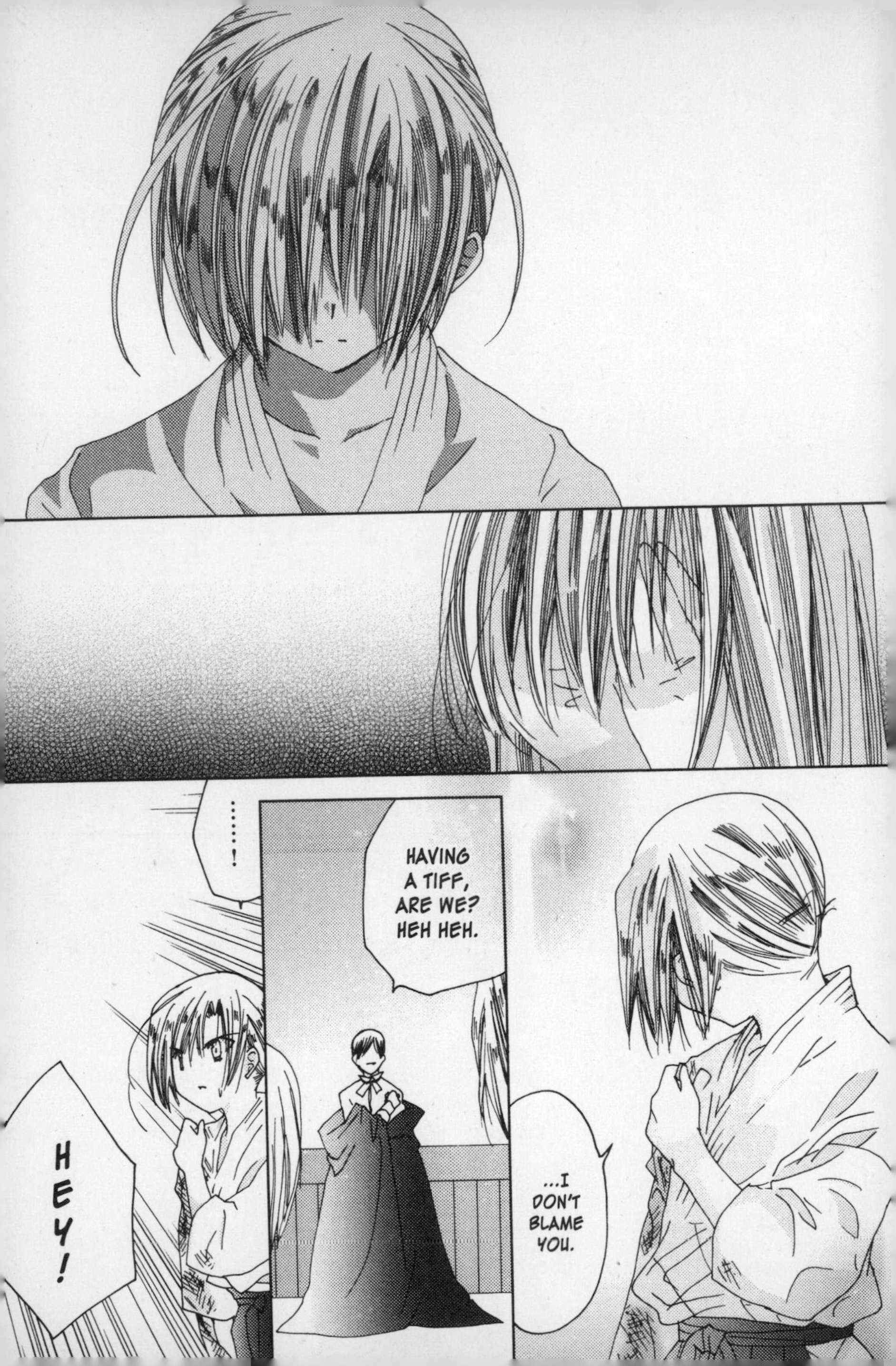
...I DON'T BLAME YOU.
HAVING A TIFF, ARE WE? HEH HEH.
......!
HEY!

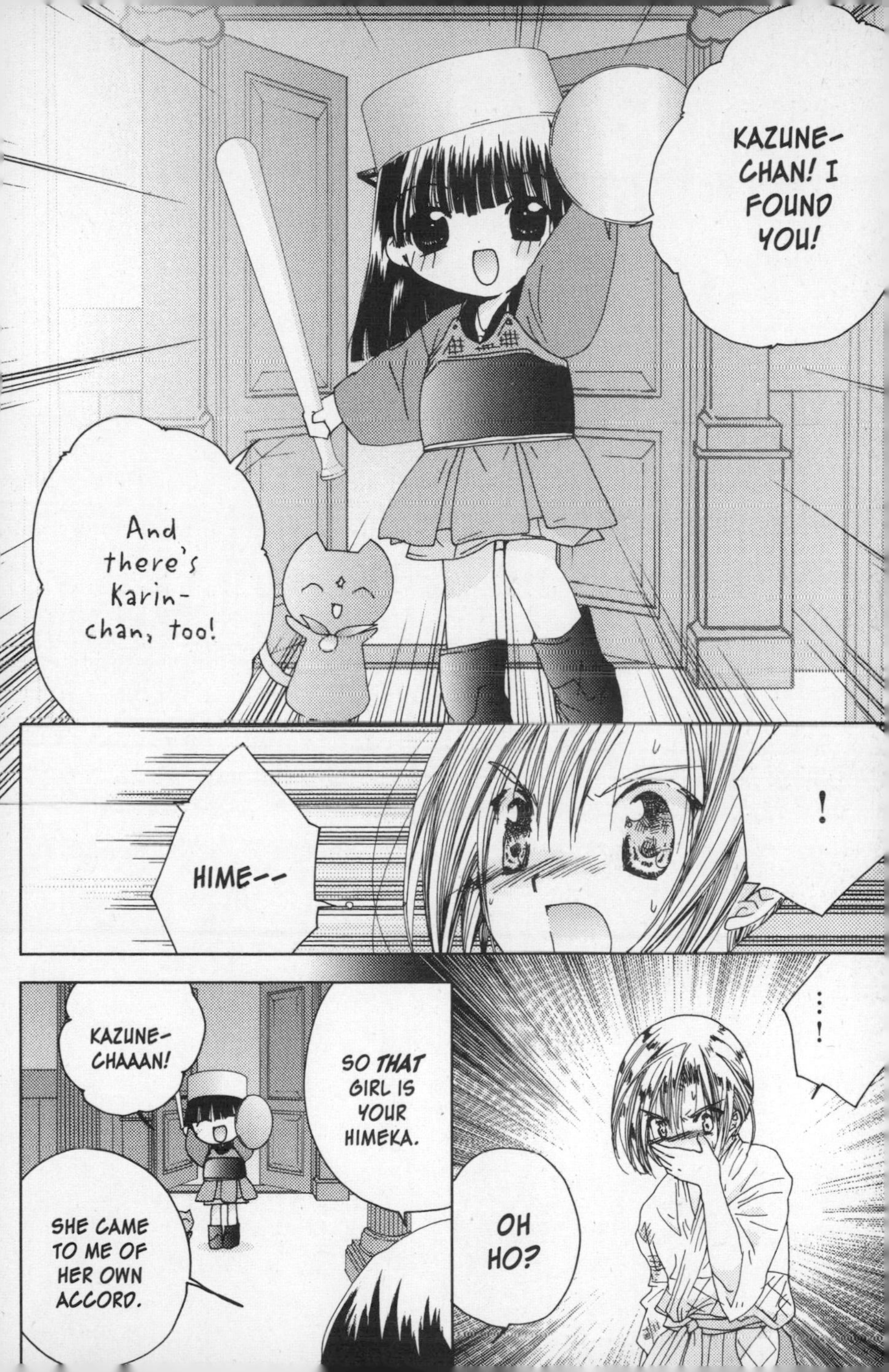
KAZUNE-CHAN! I FOUND YOU!
And there's Karin-chan, too!
!
HIME--
...!
OH HO?
SO *THAT* GIRL IS YOUR HIMEKA.
KAZUNE-CHAAAN!
SHE CAME TO ME OF HER OWN ACCORD.

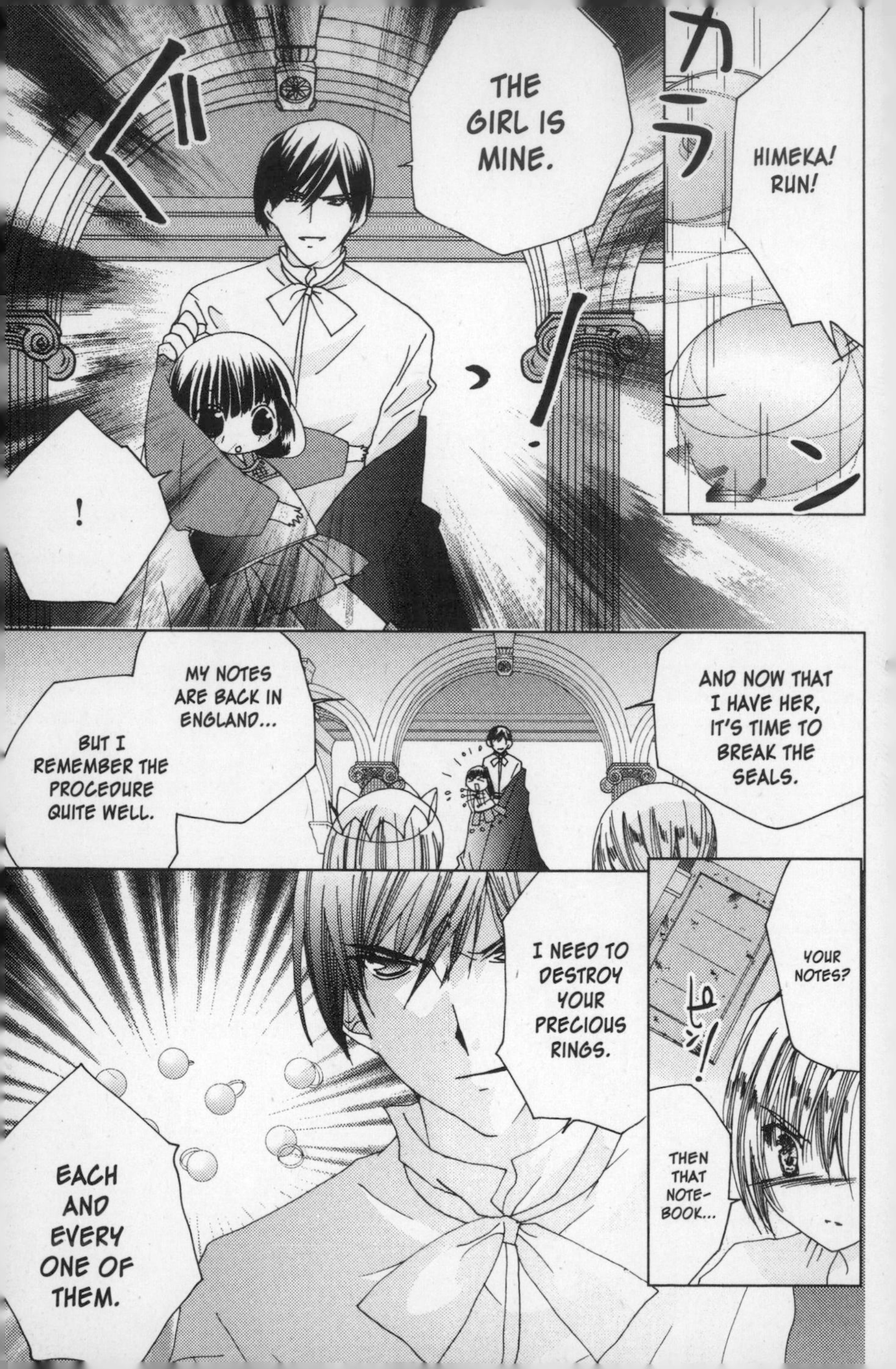
HIMEKA! RUN!
THE GIRL IS MINE.
!
AND NOW THAT I HAVE HER, IT'S TIME TO BREAK THE SEALS.
MY NOTES ARE BACK IN ENGLAND...
BUT I REMEMBER THE PROCEDURE QUITE WELL.
YOUR NOTES?
THEN THAT NOTE-BOOK...
I NEED TO DESTROY YOUR PRECIOUS RINGS.
EACH AND EVERY ONE OF THEM.

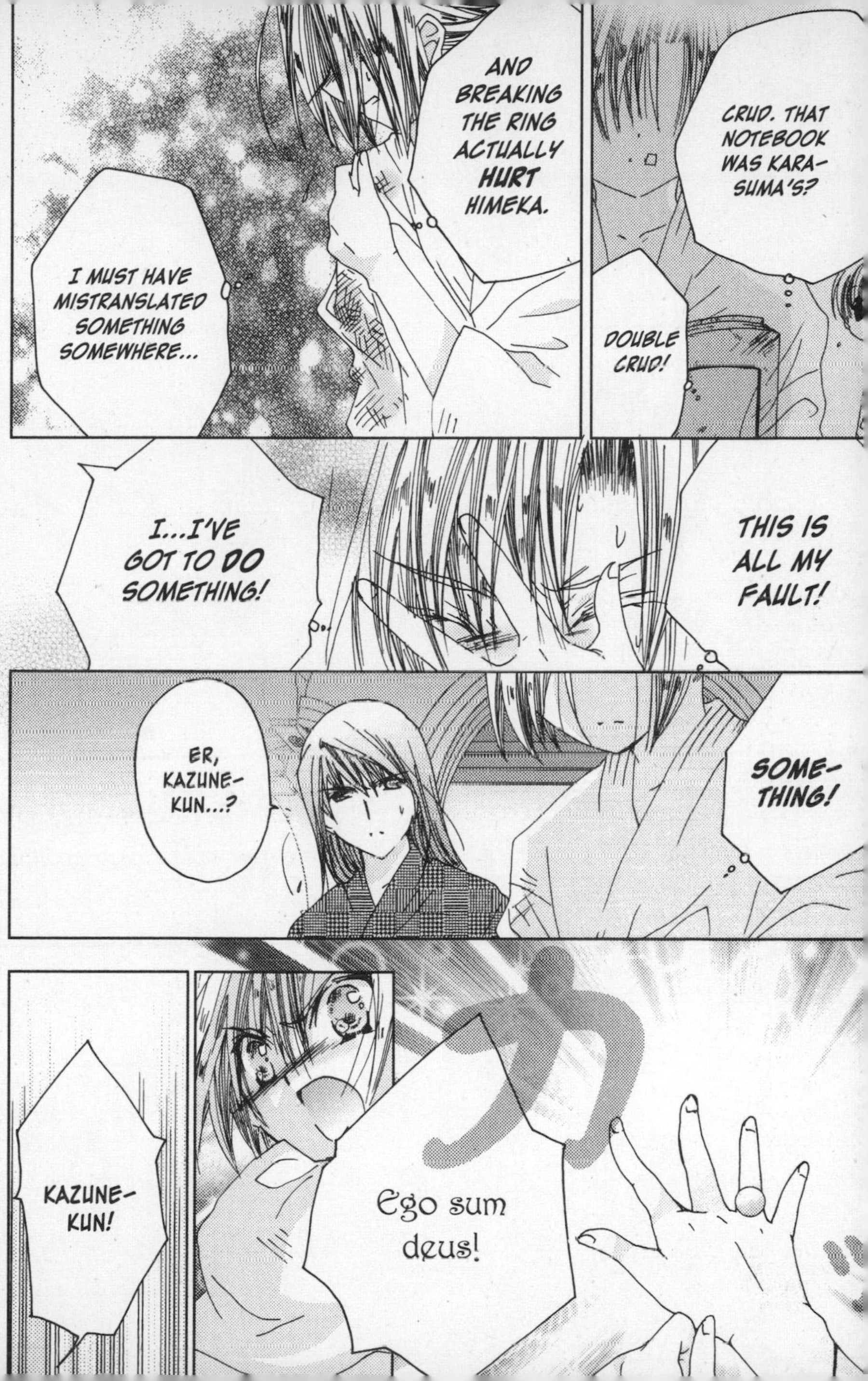

CRUD. THAT NOTEBOOK WAS KARA-SUMA'S?
DOUBLE CRUD!
AND BREAKING THE RING ACTUALLY HURT HIMEKA.
I MUST HAVE MISTRANSLATED SOMETHING SOMEWHERE...
THIS IS ALL MY FAULT!
I...I'VE GOT TO DO SOMETHING!
SOME-THING!
ER, KAZUNE-KUN...?
Ego sum deus!
KAZUNE-KUN!

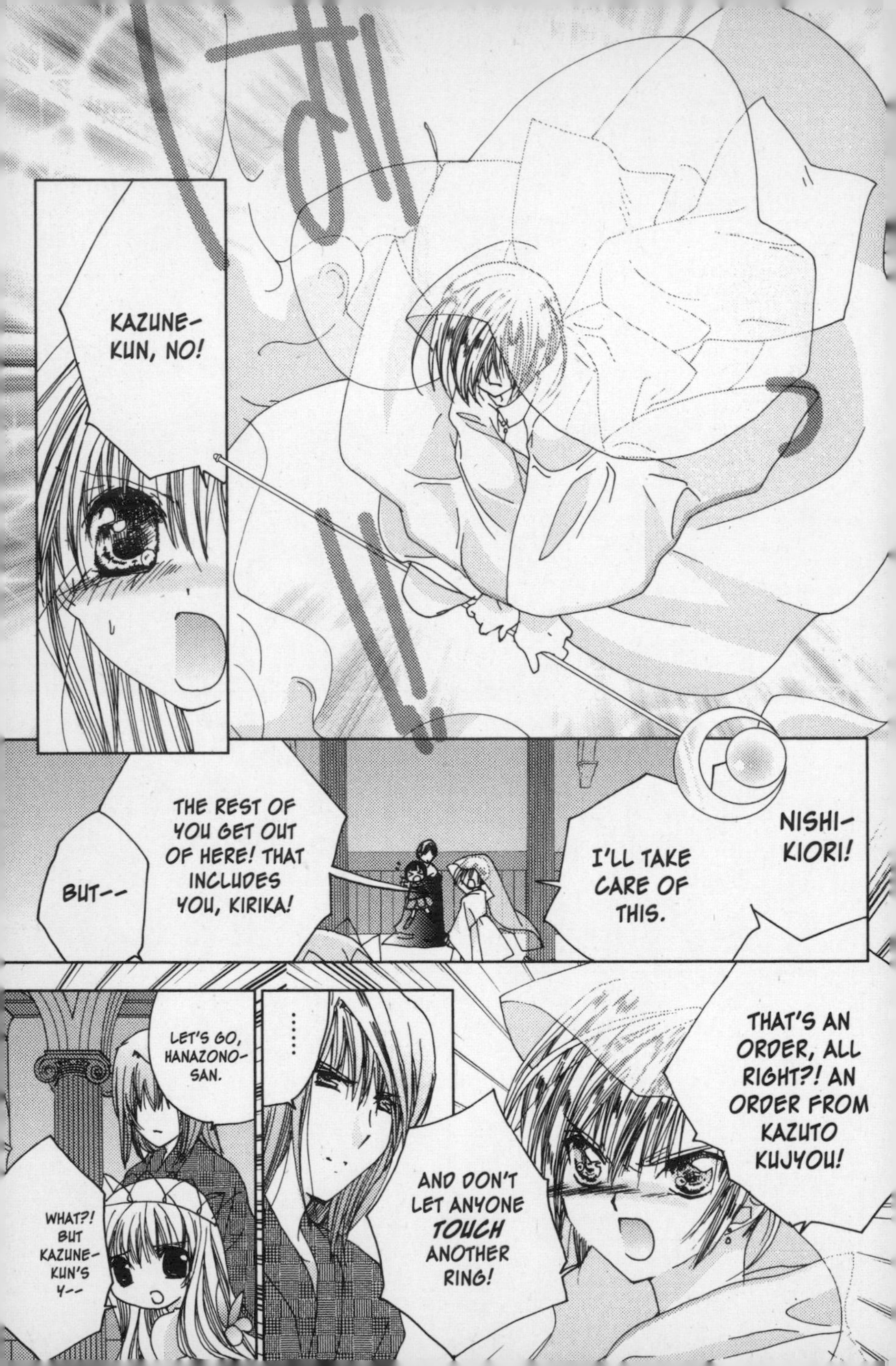
KAZUNE-KUN, NO!
NISHI-KIORI!
I'LL TAKE CARE OF THIS.
THE REST OF YOU GET OUT OF HERE! THAT INCLUDES YOU, KIRIKA!
BUT--
THAT'S AN ORDER, ALL RIGHT?! AN ORDER FROM KAZUTO KUJYOU!
AND DON'T LET ANYONE *TOUCH* ANOTHER RING!
......
LET'S GO, HANAZONO-SAN.
WHAT?! BUT KAZUNE-KUN'S Y--

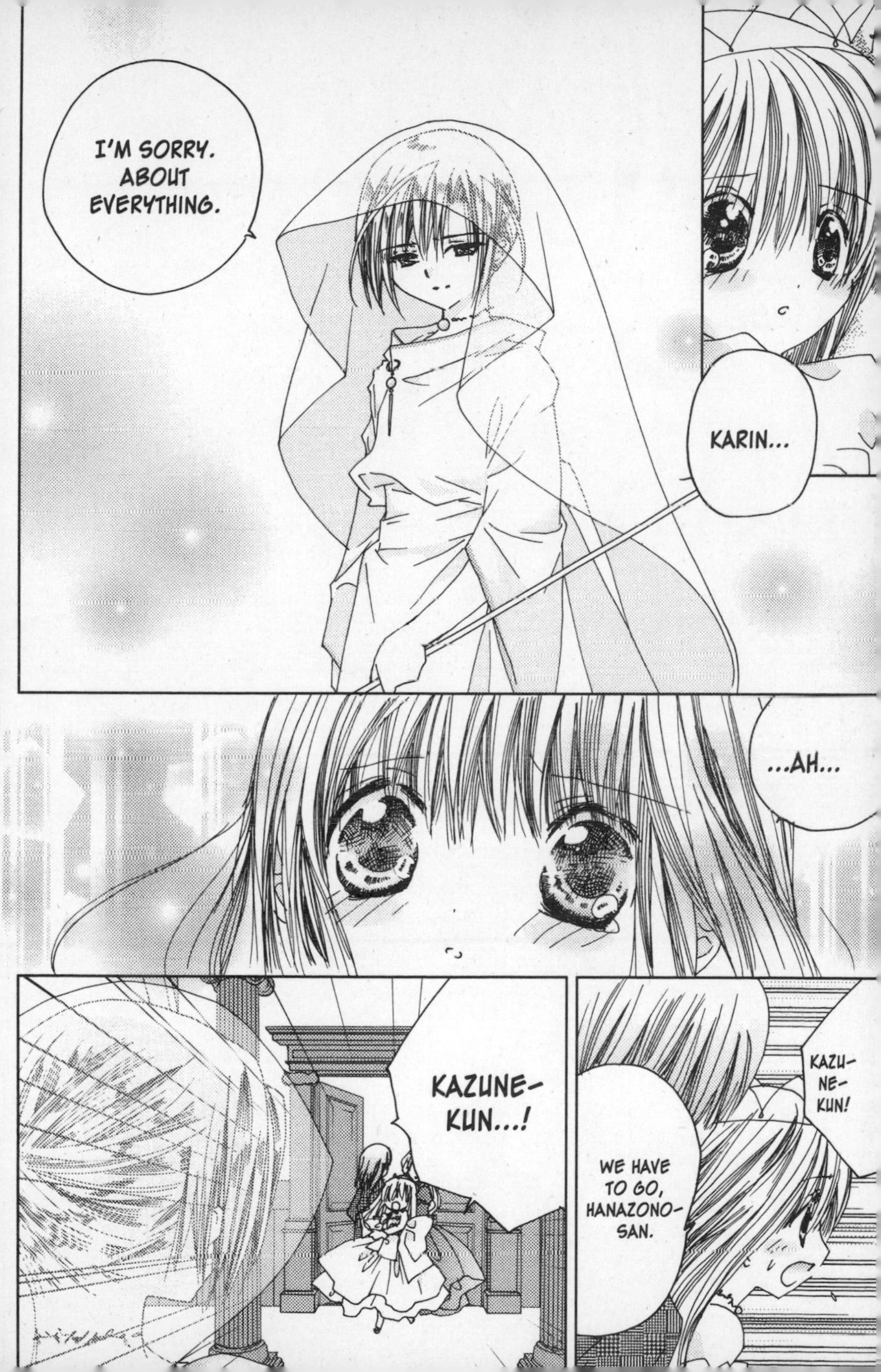
KARIN...
I'M SORRY. ABOUT EVERYTHING.
...AH...
KAZUNE-KUN!
WE HAVE TO GO, HANAZONO-SAN.
KAZUNE-KUN...!

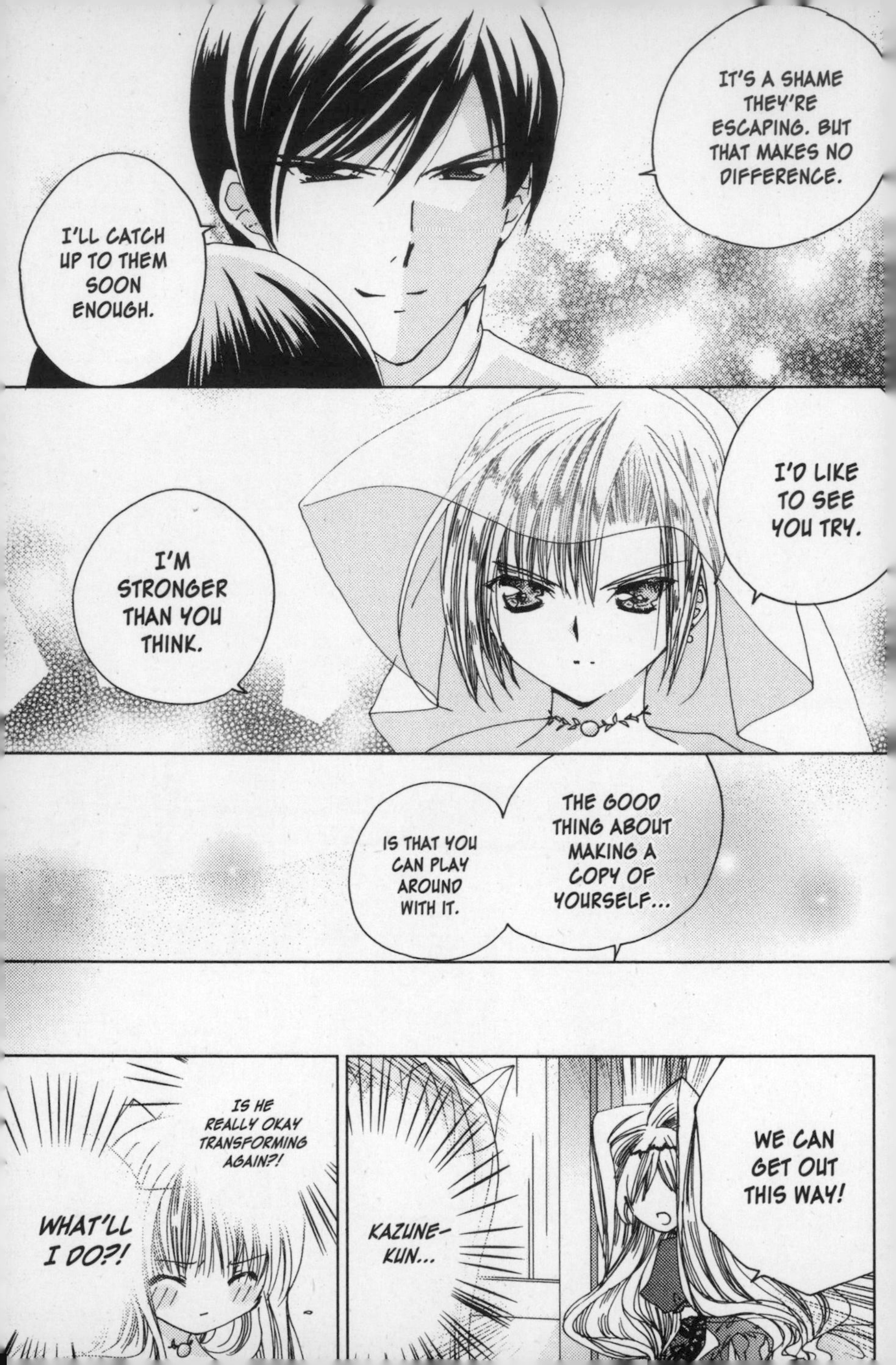
IT'S A SHAME THEY'RE ESCAPING. BUT THAT MAKES NO DIFFERENCE.
I'LL CATCH UP TO THEM SOON ENOUGH.
I'D LIKE TO SEE YOU TRY.
I'M STRONGER THAN YOU THINK.
THE GOOD THING ABOUT MAKING A COPY OF YOURSELF...
IS THAT YOU CAN PLAY AROUND WITH IT.
WE CAN GET OUT THIS WAY!
KAZUNE-KUN...
IS HE REALLY OKAY TRANSFORMING AGAIN?!
WHAT'LL I DO?!

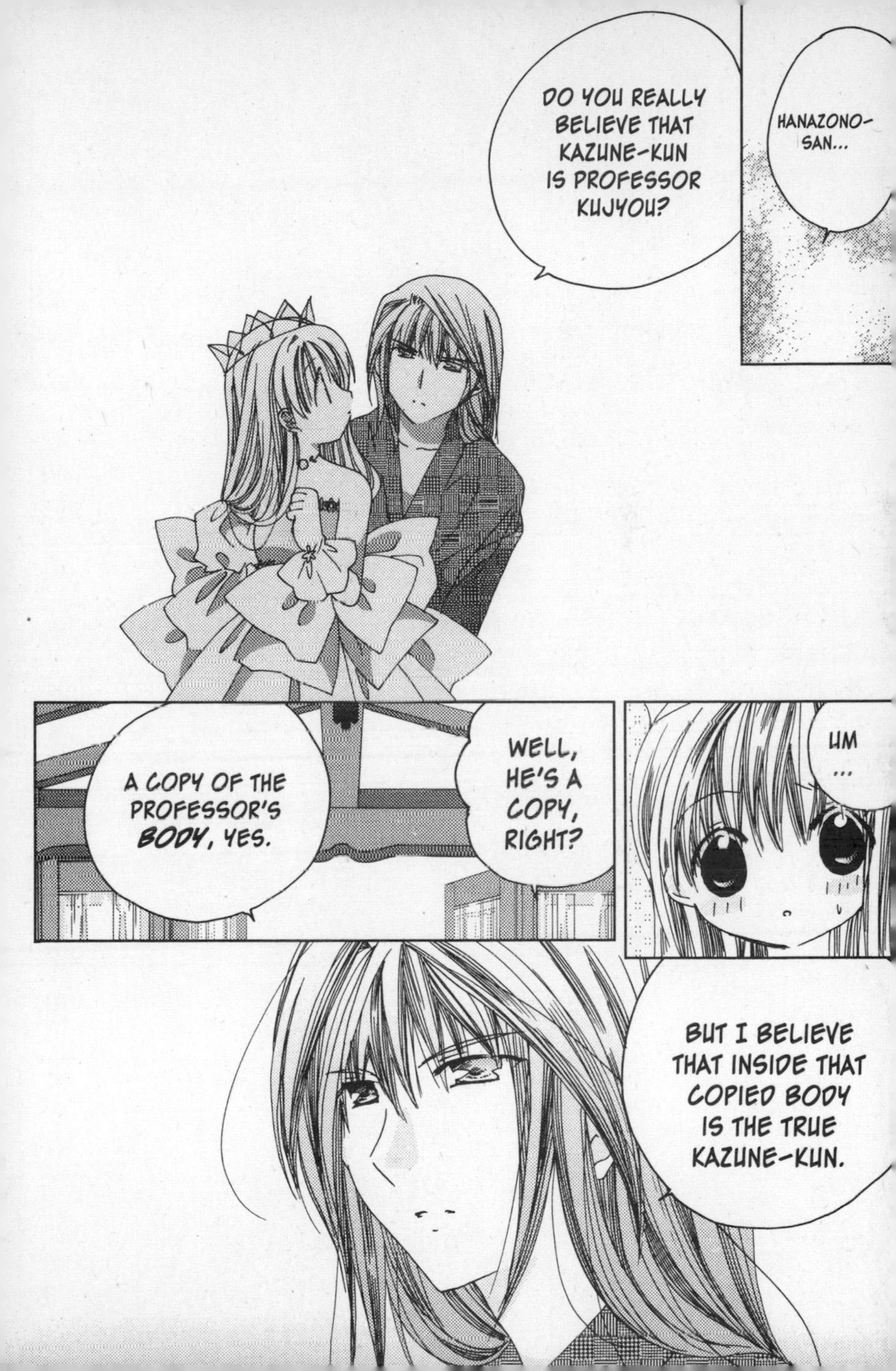
HANAZONO-SAN...
DO YOU REALLY BELIEVE THAT KAZUNE-KUN IS PROFESSOR KUJYOU?
UM ...
WELL, HE'S A COPY, RIGHT?
A COPY OF THE PROFESSOR'S *BODY*, YES.
BUT I BELIEVE THAT INSIDE THAT COPIED BODY IS THE TRUE KAZUNE-KUN.

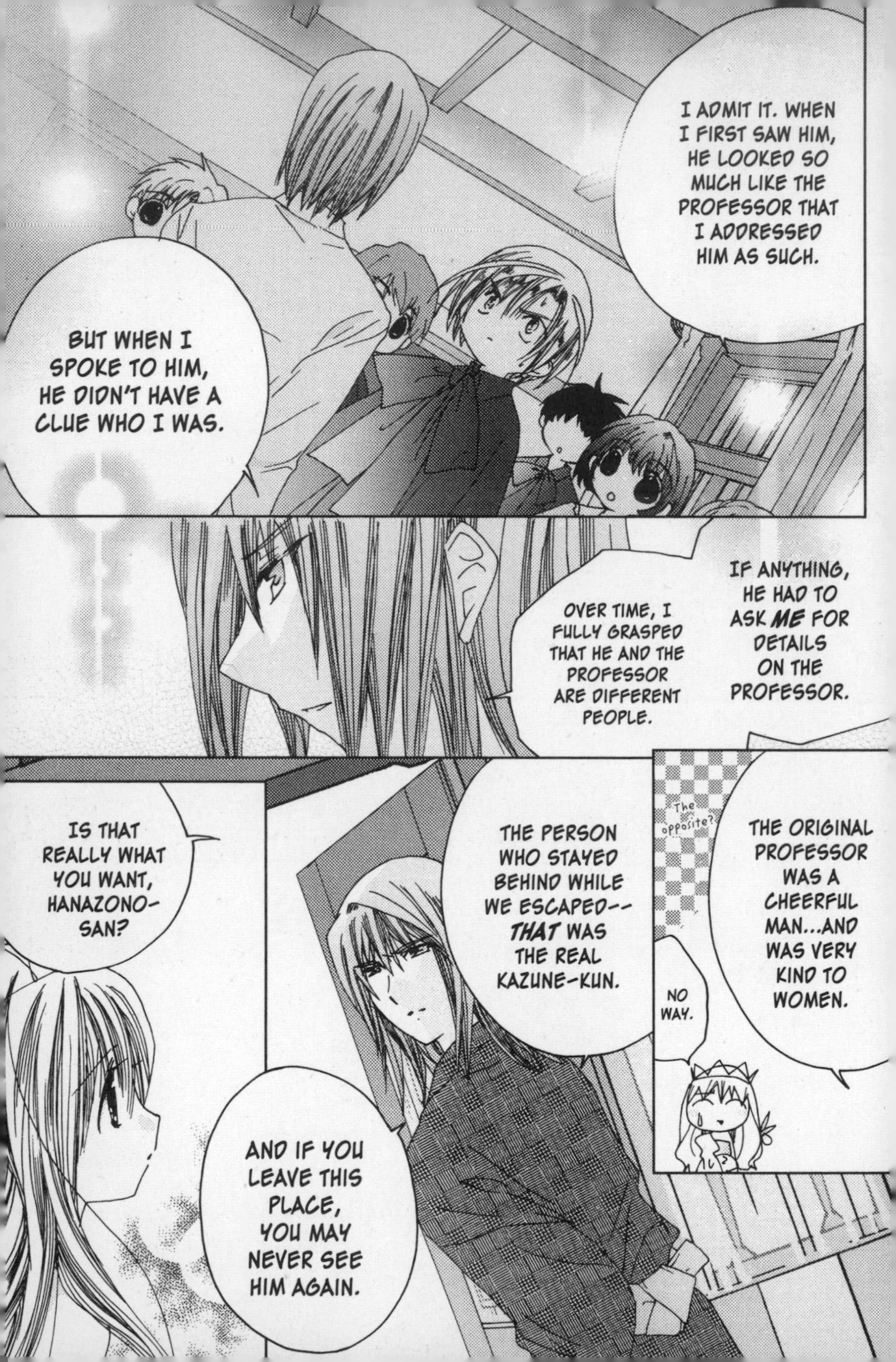
I ADMIT IT. WHEN I FIRST SAW HIM, HE LOOKED SO MUCH LIKE THE PROFESSOR THAT I ADDRESSED HIM AS SUCH.
BUT WHEN I SPOKE TO HIM, HE DIDN'T HAVE A CLUE WHO I WAS.
IF ANYTHING, HE HAD TO ASK ME FOR DETAILS ON THE PROFESSOR.
OVER TIME, I FULLY GRASPED THAT HE AND THE PROFESSOR ARE DIFFERENT PEOPLE.
THE ORIGINAL PROFESSOR WAS A CHEERFUL MAN...AND WAS VERY KIND TO WOMEN.
The opposite?
NO WAY.
THE PERSON WHO STAYED BEHIND WHILE WE ESCAPED--THAT WAS THE REAL KAZUNE-KUN.
AND IF YOU LEAVE THIS PLACE, YOU MAY NEVER SEE HIM AGAIN.
IS THAT REALLY WHAT YOU WANT, HANAZONO-SAN?

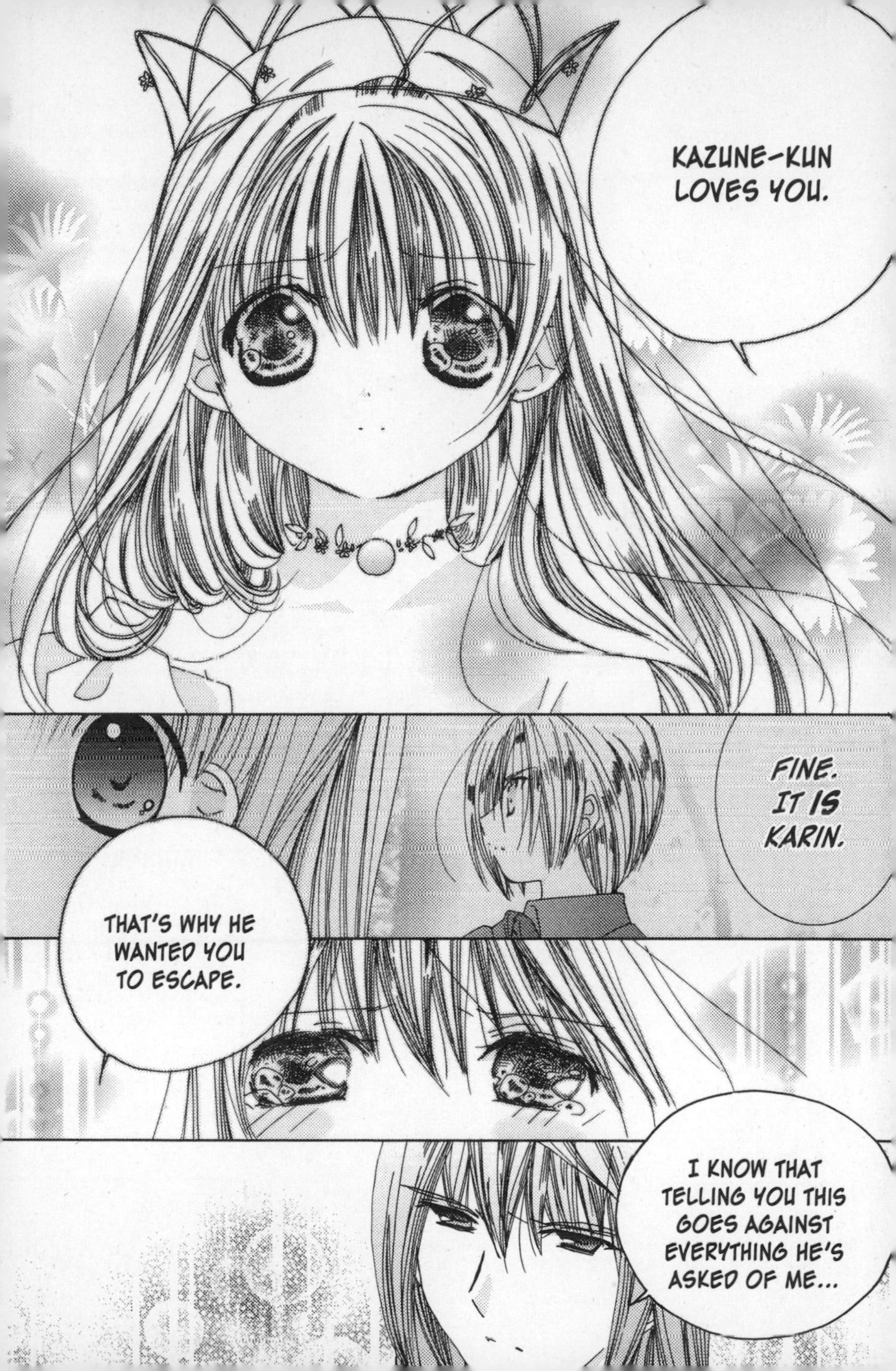
KAZUNE-KUN LOVES YOU.
FINE. IT *IS* KARIN.
THAT'S WHY HE WANTED YOU TO ESCAPE.
I KNOW THAT TELLING YOU THIS GOES AGAINST EVERYTHING HE'S ASKED OF ME...

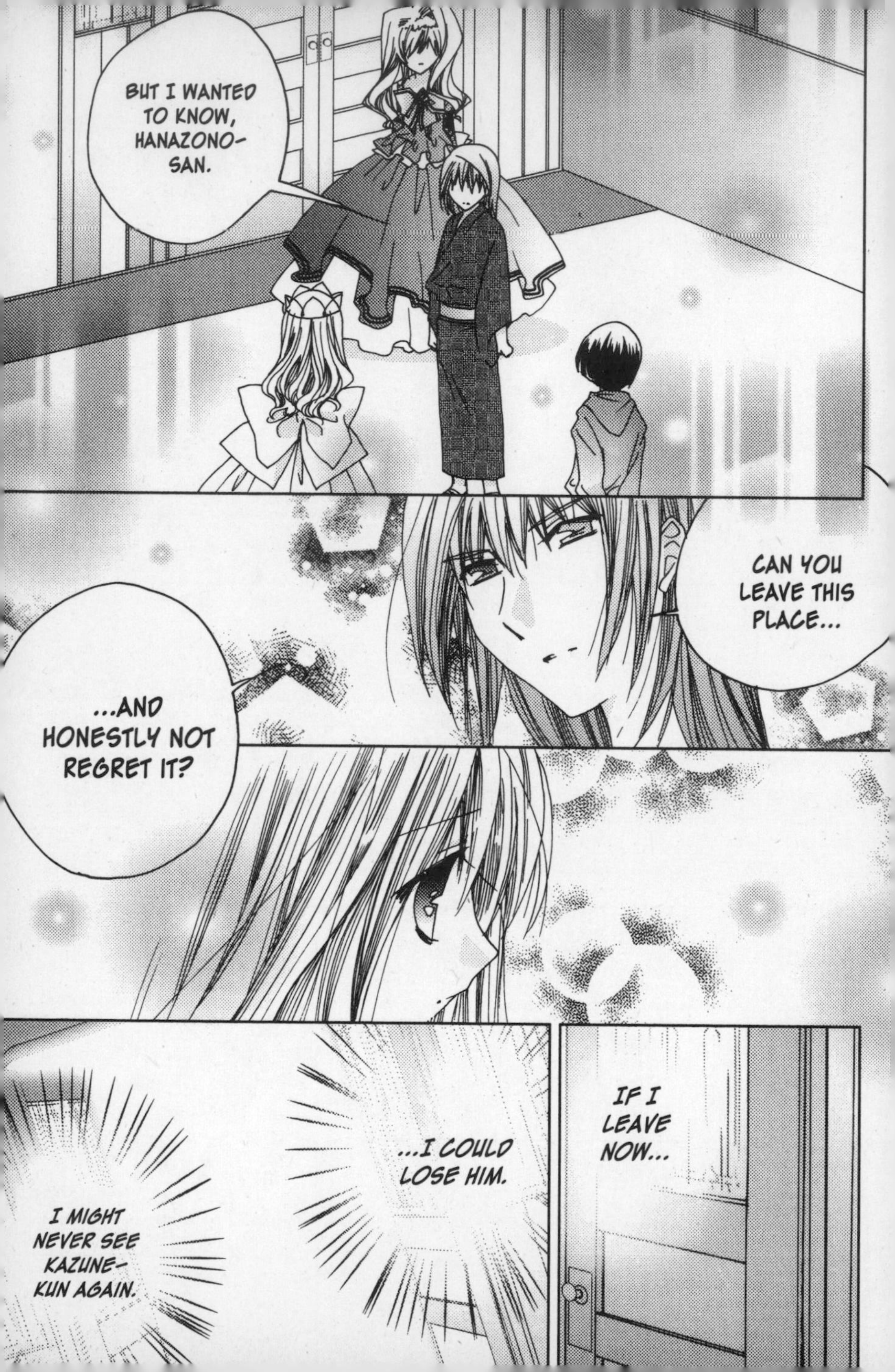
BUT I WANTED TO KNOW, HANAZONO-SAN.
CAN YOU LEAVE THIS PLACE...
...AND HONESTLY NOT REGRET IT?
IF I LEAVE NOW...
...I COULD LOSE HIM.
I MIGHT NEVER SEE KAZUNE-KUN AGAIN.

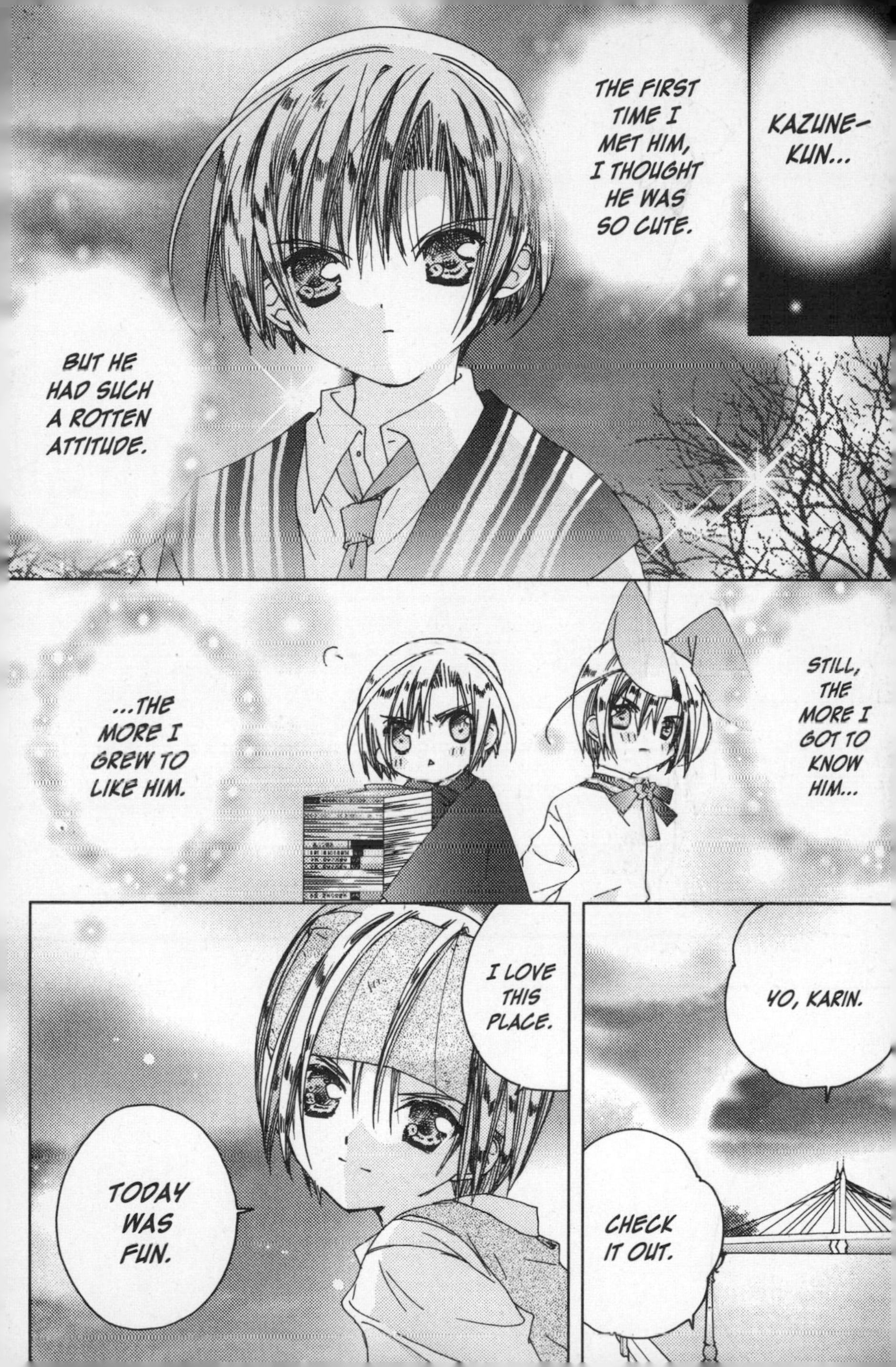
KAZUNE-KUN...
THE FIRST TIME I MET HIM, I THOUGHT HE WAS SO CUTE.
BUT HE HAD SUCH A ROTTEN ATTITUDE.
STILL, THE MORE I GOT TO KNOW HIM...
...THE MORE I GREW TO LIKE HIM.
YO, KARIN.
CHECK IT OUT.
I LOVE THIS PLACE.
TODAY WAS FUN.

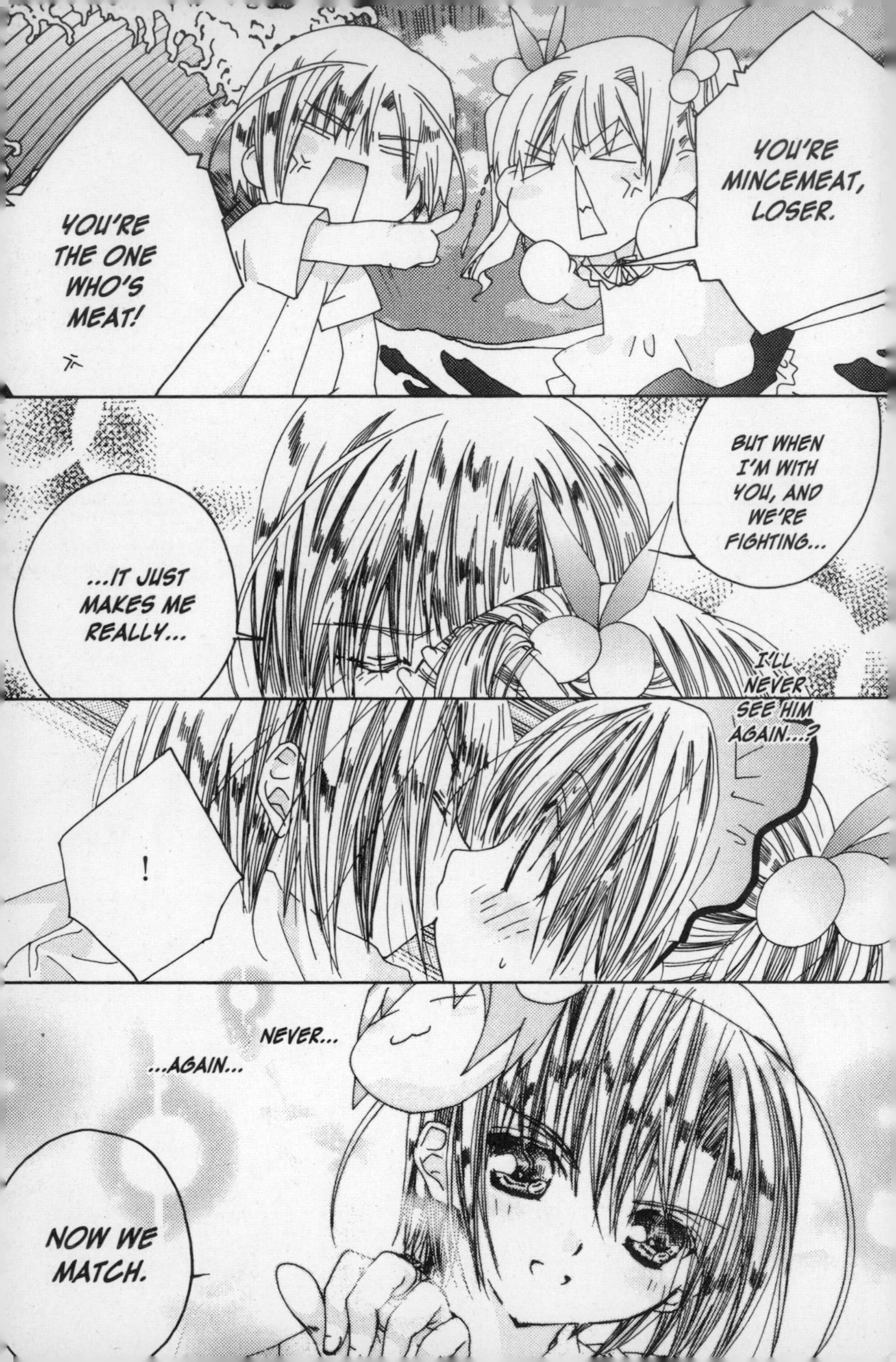
YOU'RE MINCEMEAT, LOSER.
YOU'RE THE ONE WHO'S MEAT!
BUT WHEN I'M WITH YOU, AND WE'RE FIGHTING...
...IT JUST MAKES ME REALLY...
I'LL NEVER SEE HIM AGAIN...?
!
NEVER...
...AGAIN...
NOW WE MATCH.

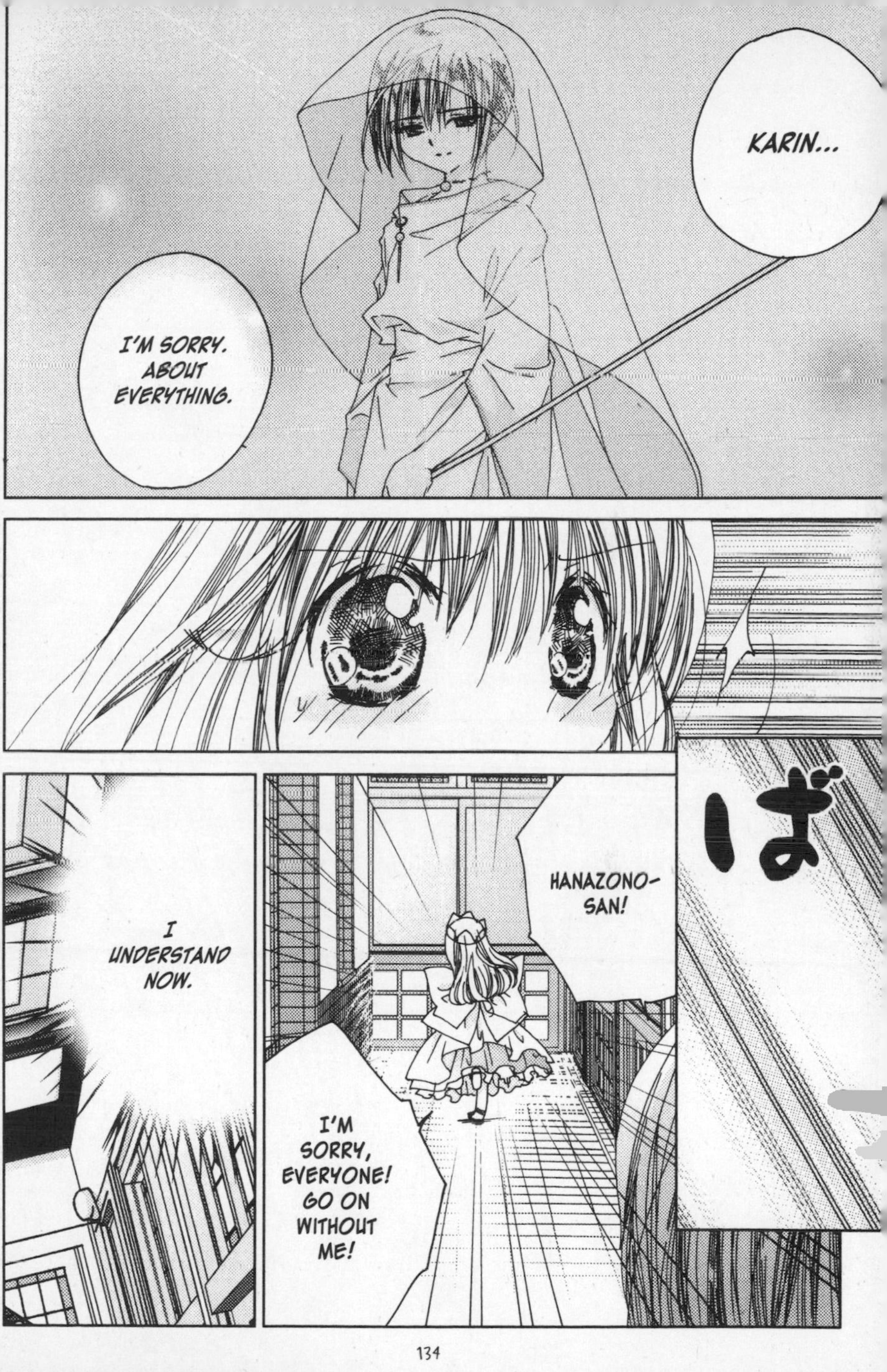
KARIN...
I'M SORRY. ABOUT EVERYTHING.
ば
HANAZONO-SAN!
I'M SORRY, EVERYONE! GO ON WITHOUT ME!
I UNDERSTAND NOW.

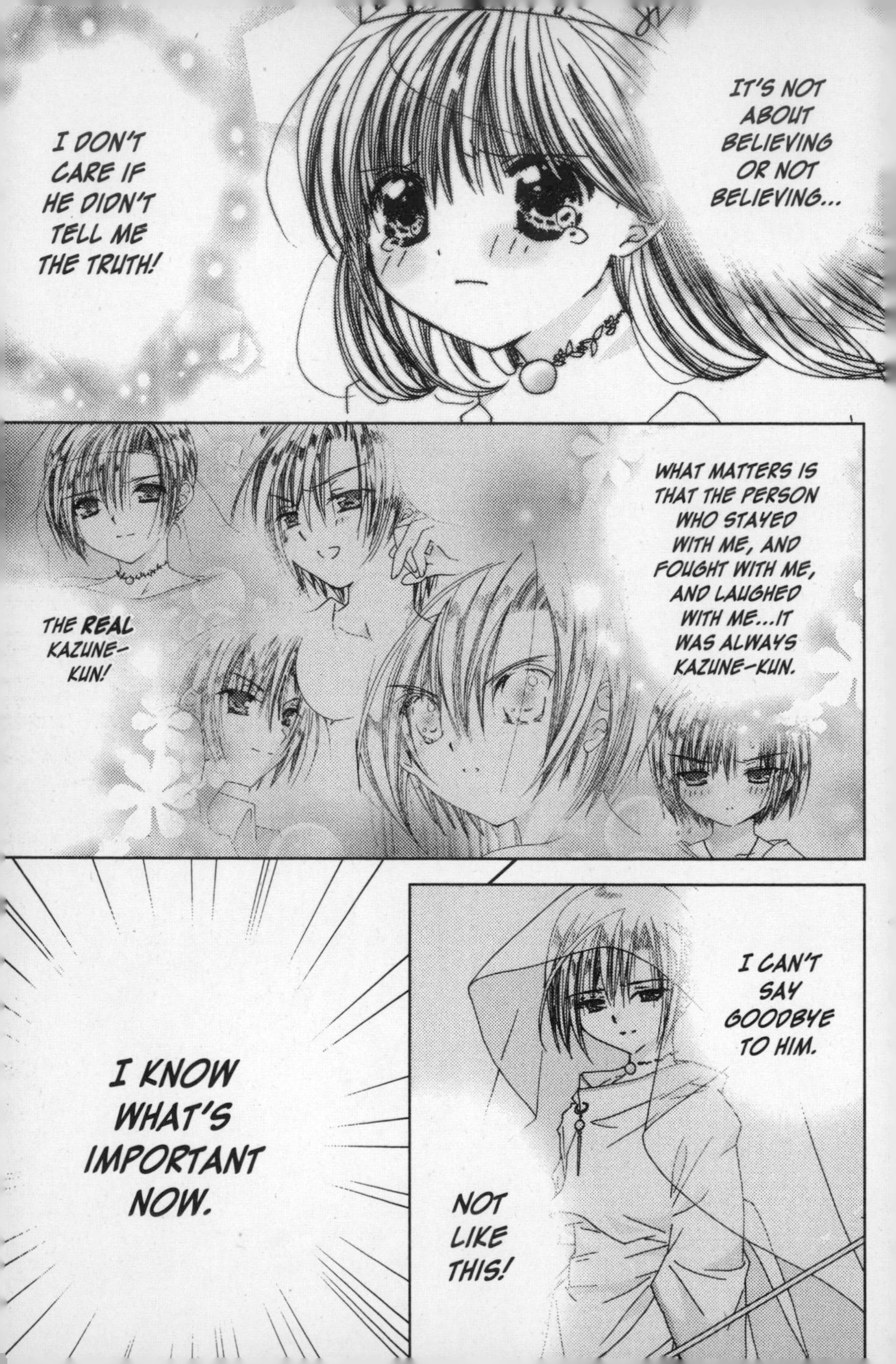
IT'S NOT ABOUT BELIEVING OR NOT BELIEVING...
I DON'T CARE IF HE DIDN'T TELL ME THE TRUTH!
WHAT MATTERS IS THAT THE PERSON WHO STAYED WITH ME, AND FOUGHT WITH ME, AND LAUGHED WITH ME...IT WAS ALWAYS KAZUNE-KUN.
THE REAL KAZUNE-KUN!
I CAN'T SAY GOODBYE TO HIM.
NOT LIKE THIS!
I KNOW WHAT'S IMPORTANT NOW.

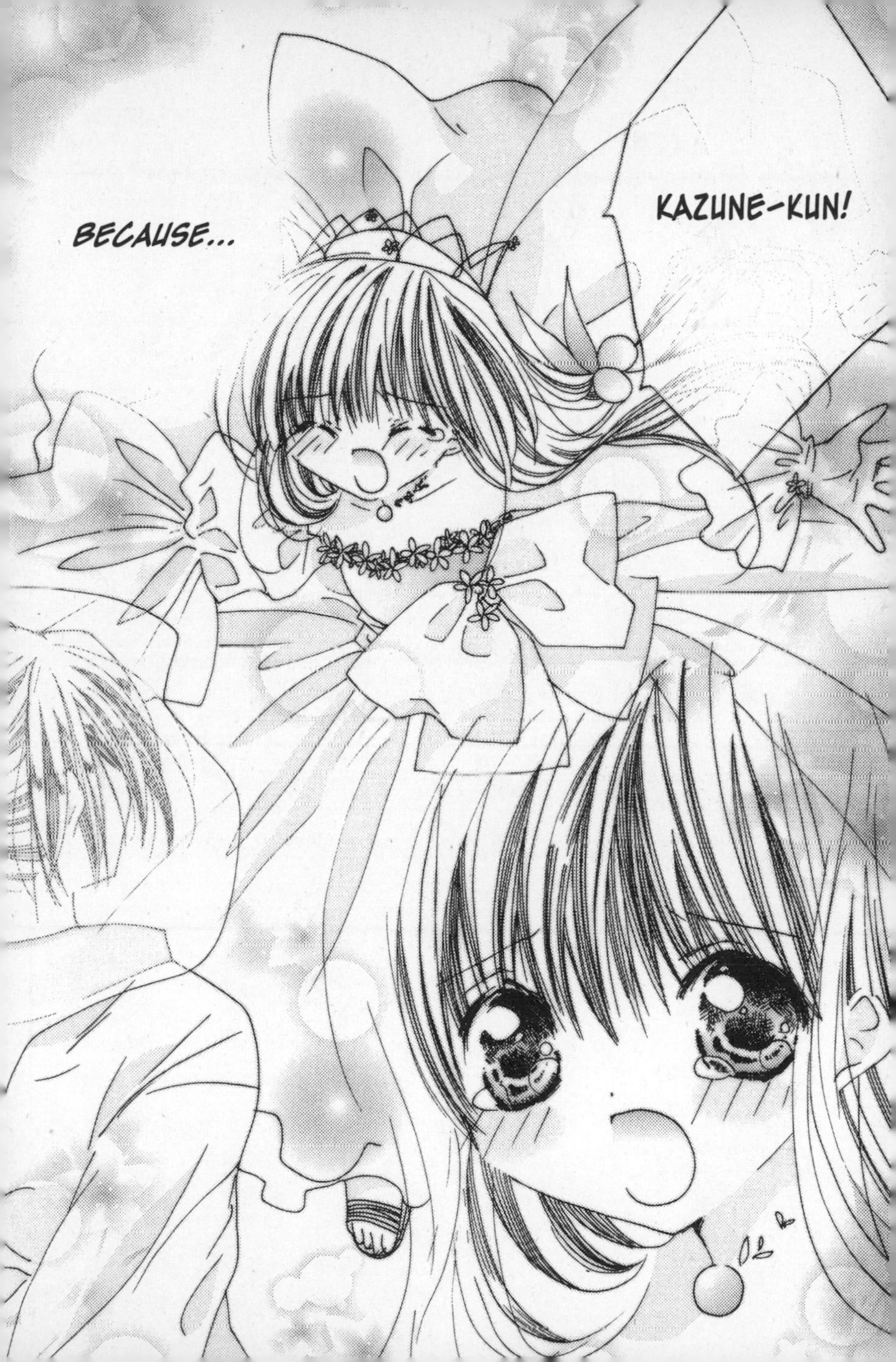
KAZUNE-KUN!
BECAUSE...

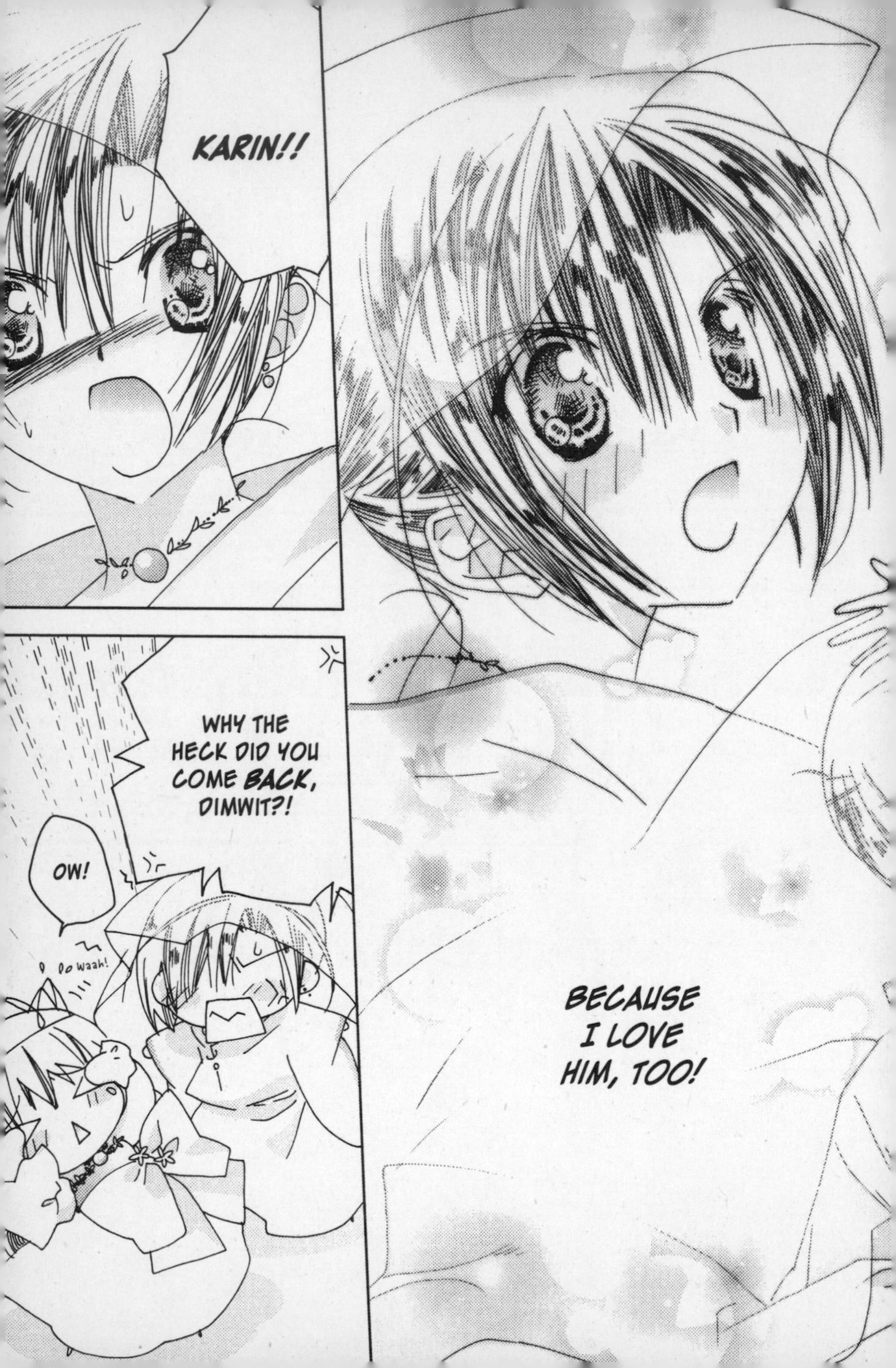
KARIN!!
WHY THE HECK DID YOU COME BACK, DIMWIT?!
OW!
Oo waah!
BECAUSE I LOVE HIM, TOO!

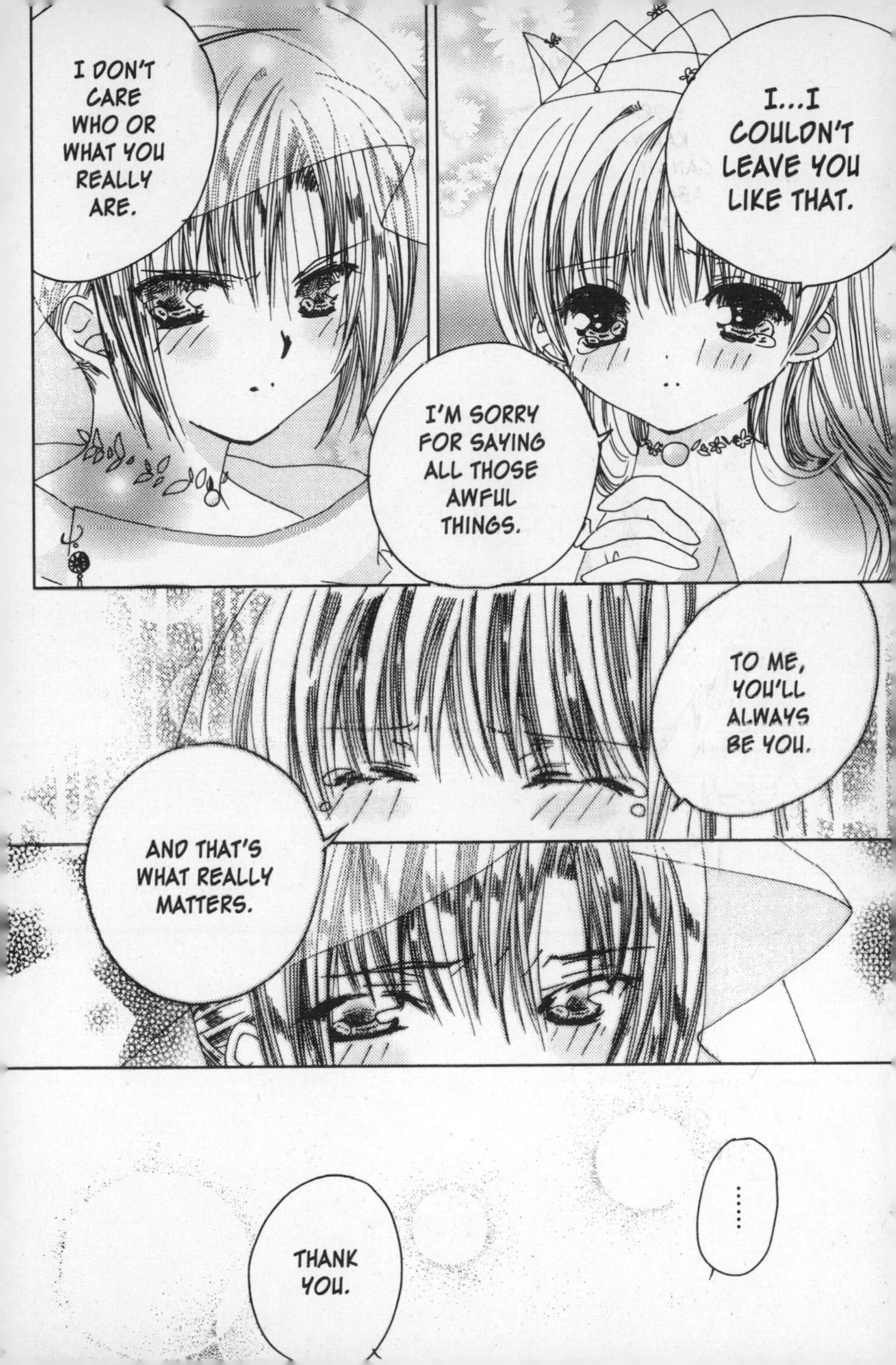
I...I COULDN'T LEAVE YOU LIKE THAT.
I'M SORRY FOR SAYING ALL THOSE AWFUL THINGS.
I DON'T CARE WHO OR WHAT YOU REALLY ARE.
TO ME, YOU'LL ALWAYS BE YOU.
AND THAT'S WHAT REALLY MATTERS.
......
THANK YOU.

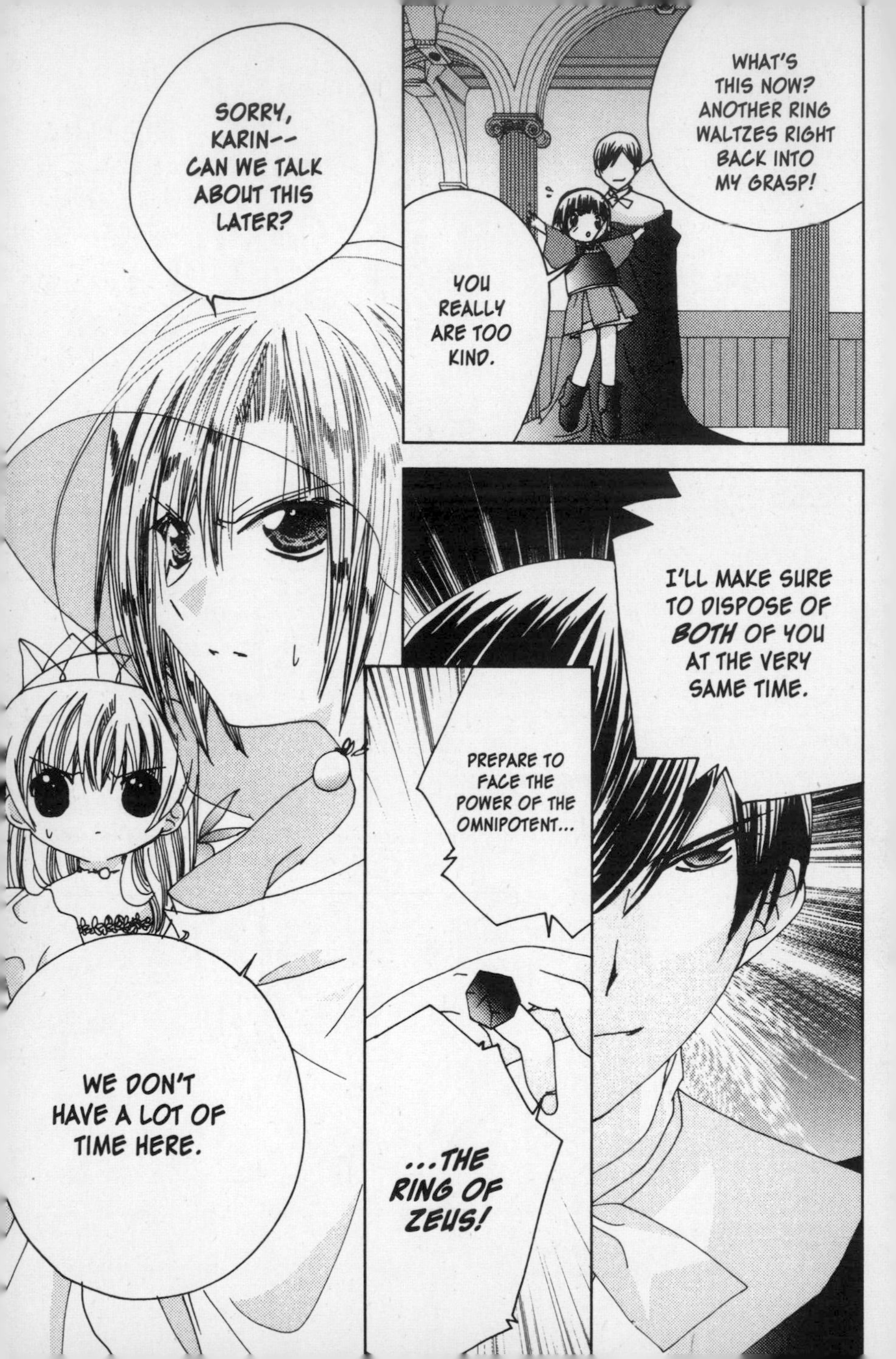
WHAT'S THIS NOW? ANOTHER RING WALTZES RIGHT BACK INTO MY GRASP!
YOU REALLY ARE TOO KIND.
I'LL MAKE SURE TO DISPOSE OF *BOTH* OF YOU AT THE VERY SAME TIME.
PREPARE TO FACE THE POWER OF THE OMNIPOTENT...
...THE RING OF ZEUS!
SORRY, KARIN-- CAN WE TALK ABOUT THIS LATER?
WE DON'T HAVE A LOT OF TIME HERE.

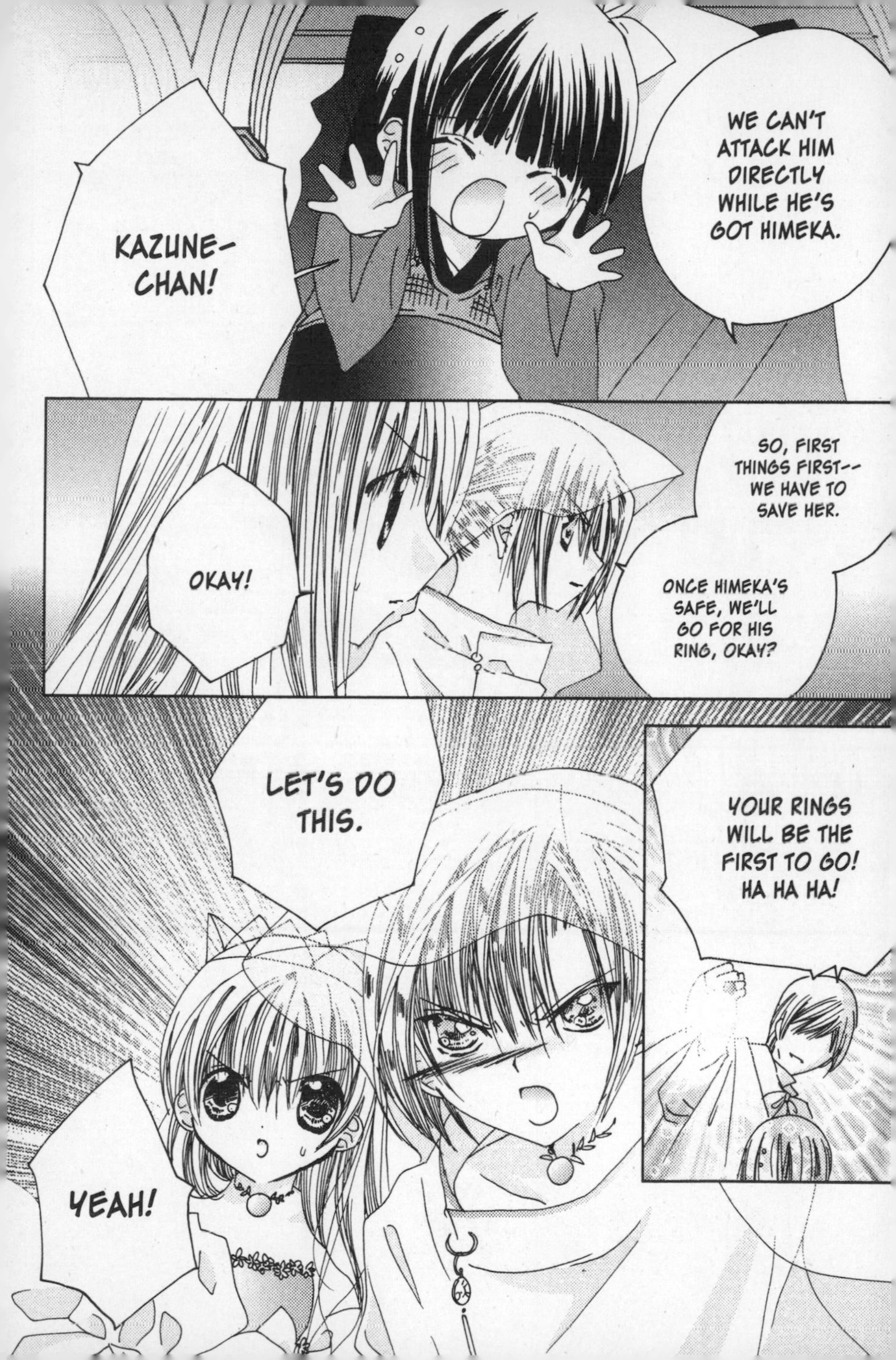
WE CAN'T ATTACK HIM DIRECTLY WHILE HE'S GOT HIMEKA.
KAZUNE-CHAN!
SO, FIRST THINGS FIRST-- WE HAVE TO SAVE HER.
ONCE HIMEKA'S SAFE, WE'LL GO FOR HIS RING, OKAY?
OKAY!
YOUR RINGS WILL BE THE FIRST TO GO! HA HA HA!
LET'S DO THIS.
YEAH!

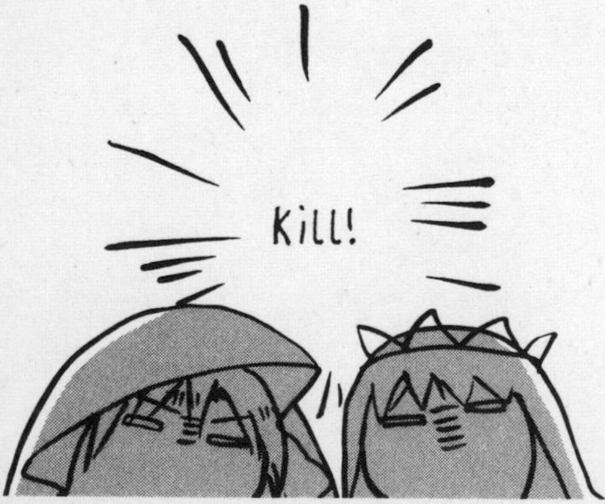
KILL!

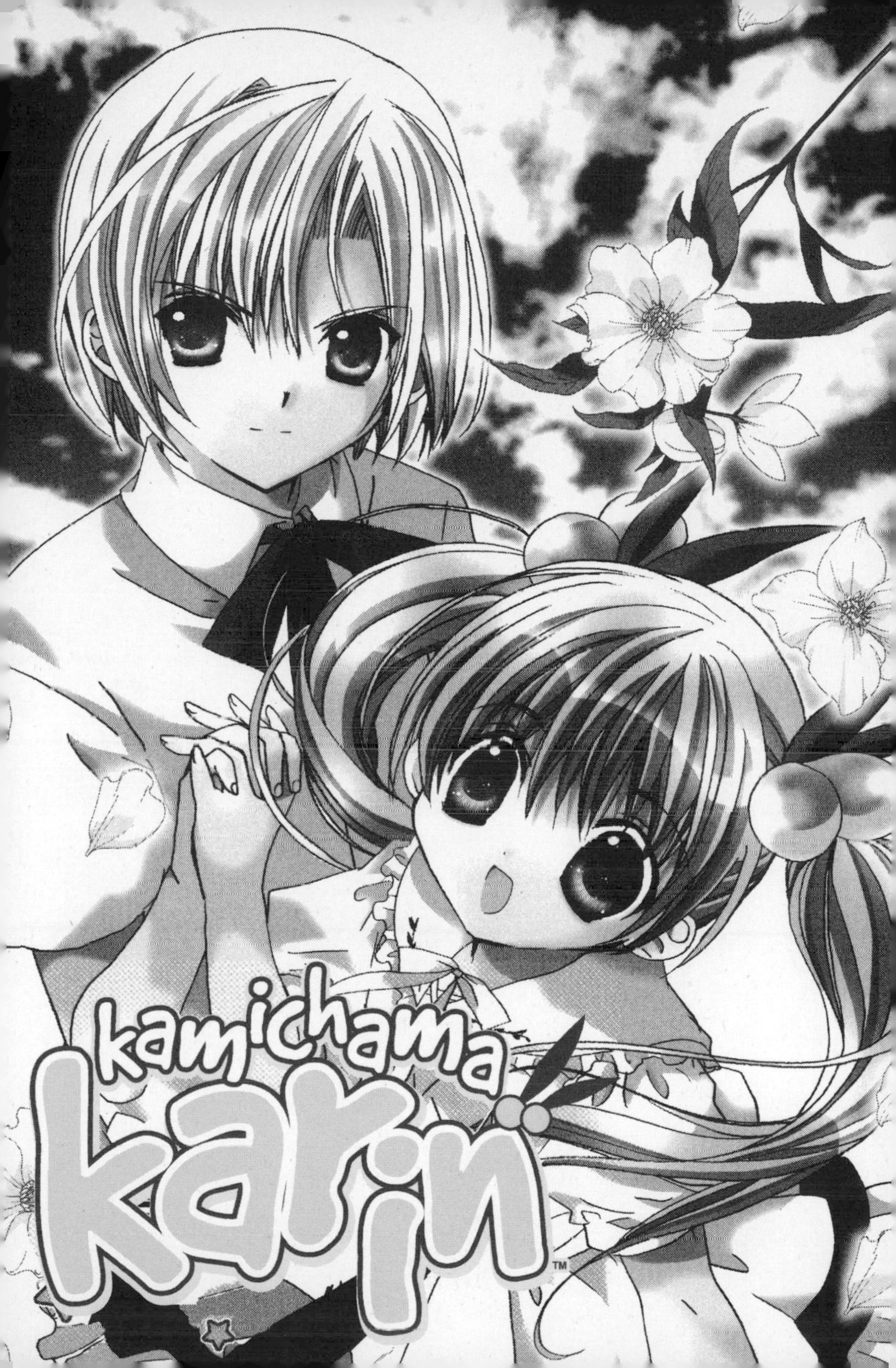
kamichama
karin™

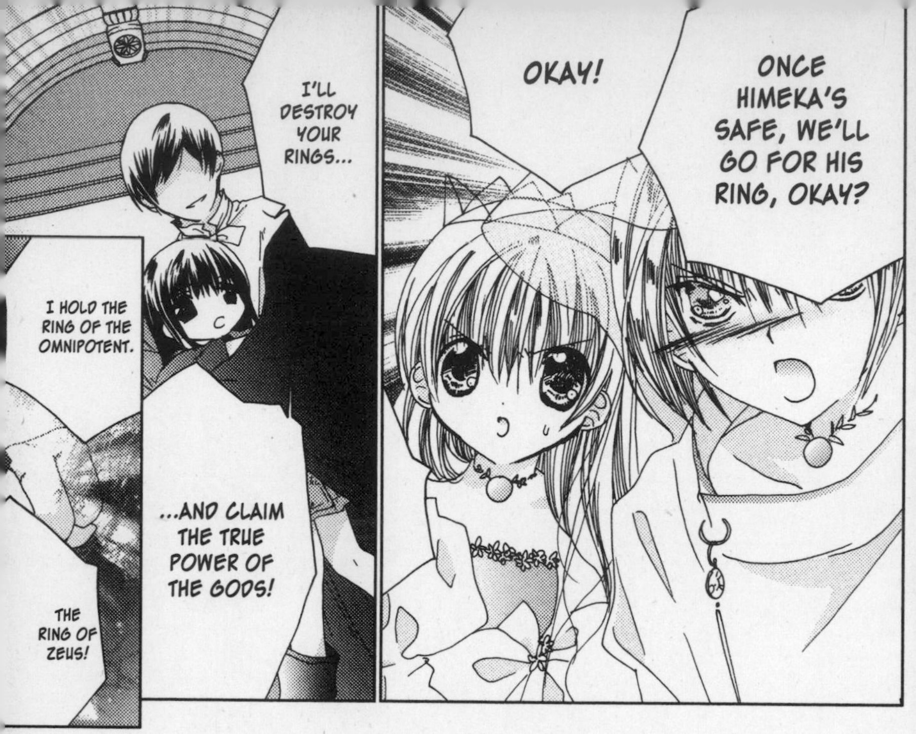
ONCE HIMEKA'S SAFE, WE'LL GO FOR HIS RING, OKAY?
OKAY!
I'LL DESTROY YOUR RINGS...
...AND CLAIM THE TRUE POWER OF THE GODS!
I HOLD THE RING OF THE OMNIPOTENT.
THE RING OF ZEUS!

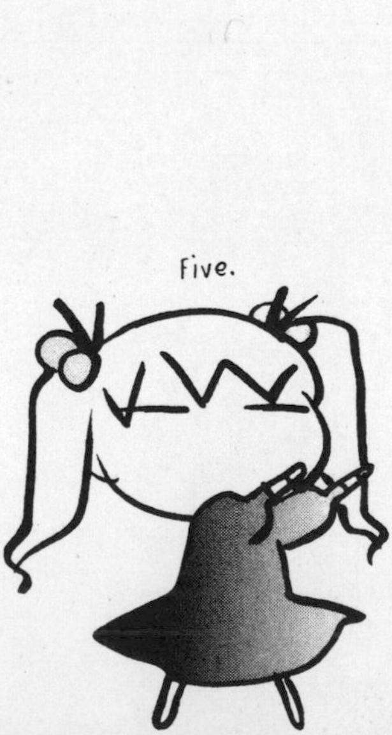
Five.

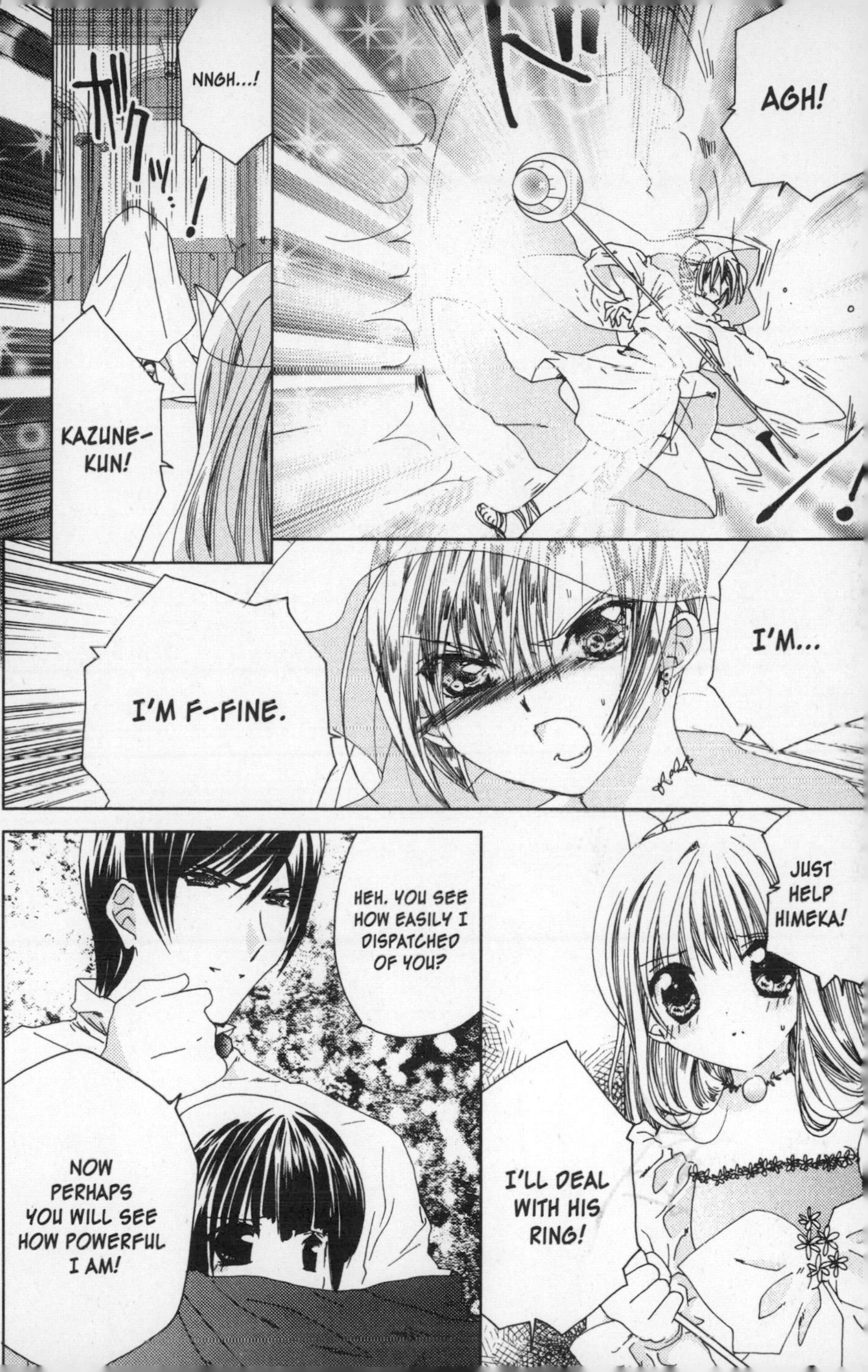
AGH!
NNGH...!
KAZUNE-KUN!
I'M...
I'M F-FINE.
JUST HELP HIMEKA!
I'LL DEAL WITH HIS RING!
HEH. YOU SEE HOW EASILY I DISPATCHED OF YOU?
NOW PERHAPS YOU WILL SEE HOW POWERFUL I AM!

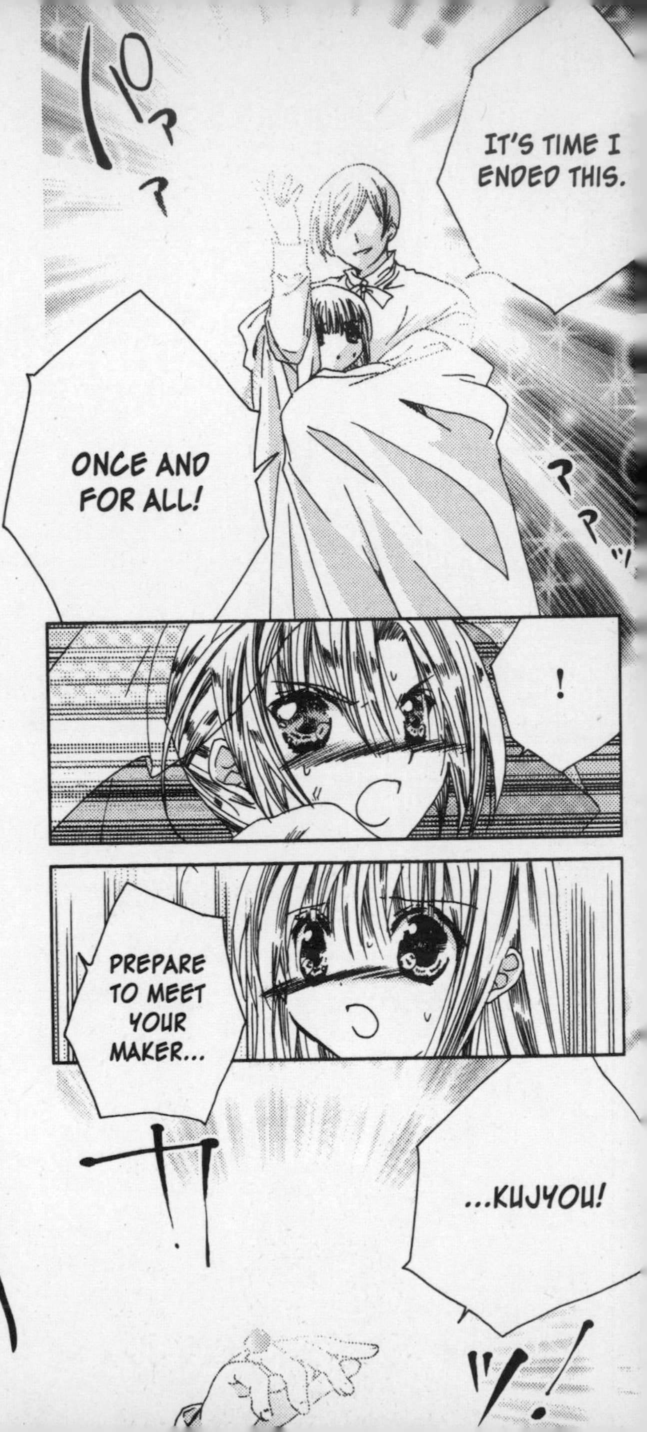
IT'S TIME I ENDED THIS.
ONCE AND FOR ALL!
!
PREPARE TO MEET YOUR MAKER...
...KUJYOU!
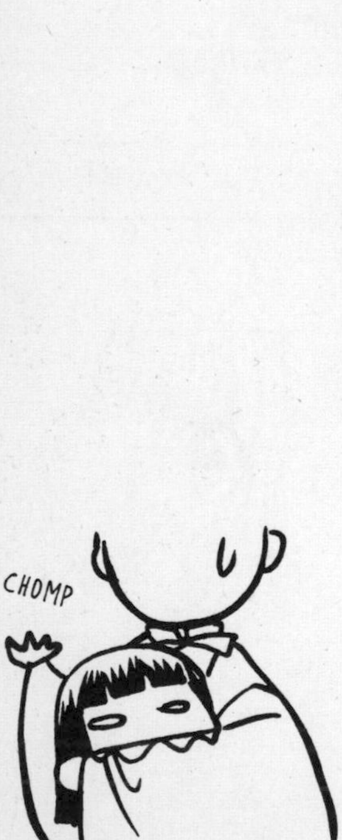
CHOMP

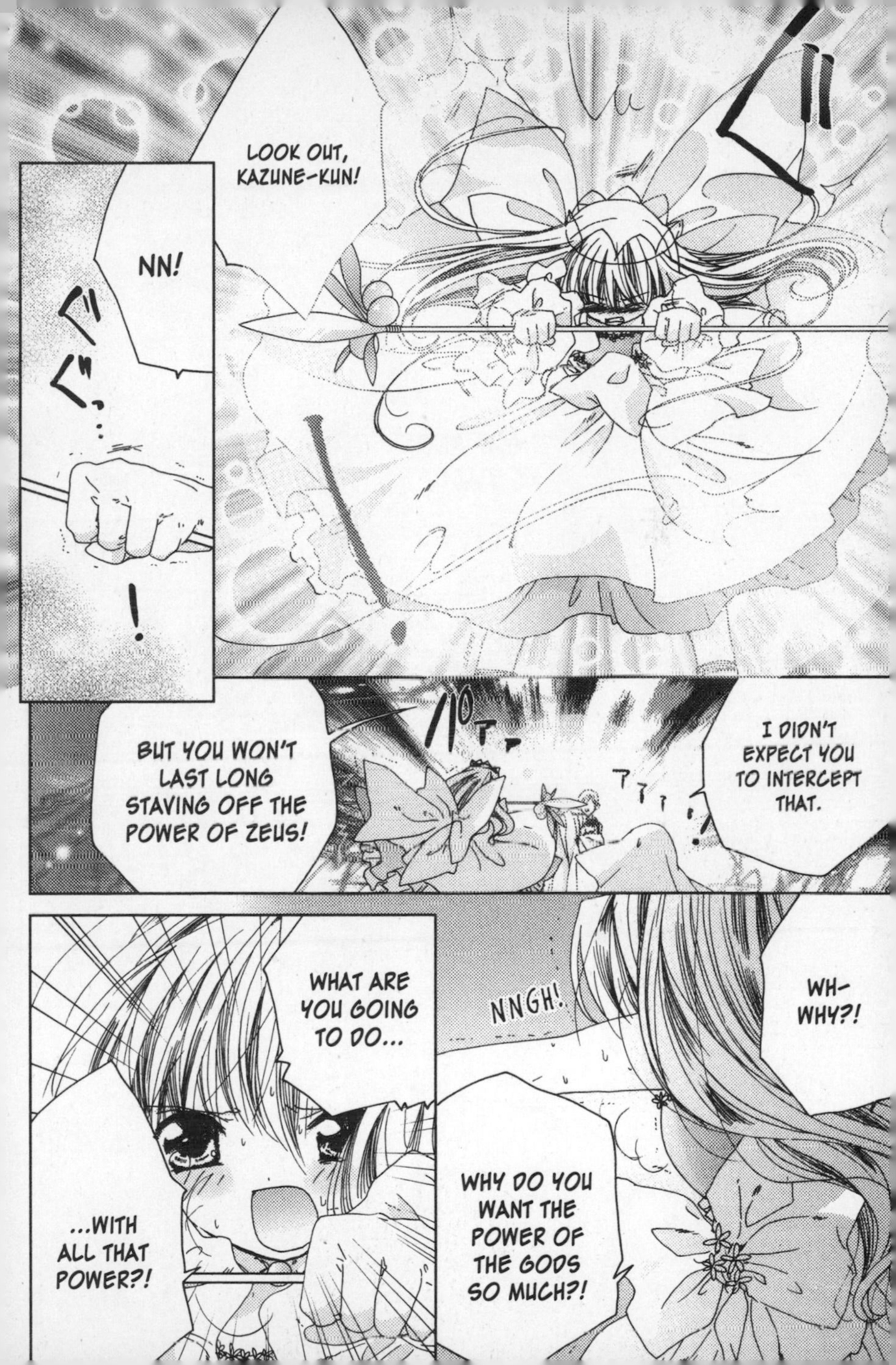
LOOK OUT, KAZUNE-KUN!
NN!
!
I DIDN'T EXPECT YOU TO INTERCEPT THAT.
BUT YOU WON'T LAST LONG STAVING OFF THE POWER OF ZEUS!
WH- WHY?!
NNGH!
WHY DO YOU WANT THE POWER OF THE GODS SO MUCH?!
WHAT ARE YOU GOING TO DO...
...WITH ALL THAT POWER?!

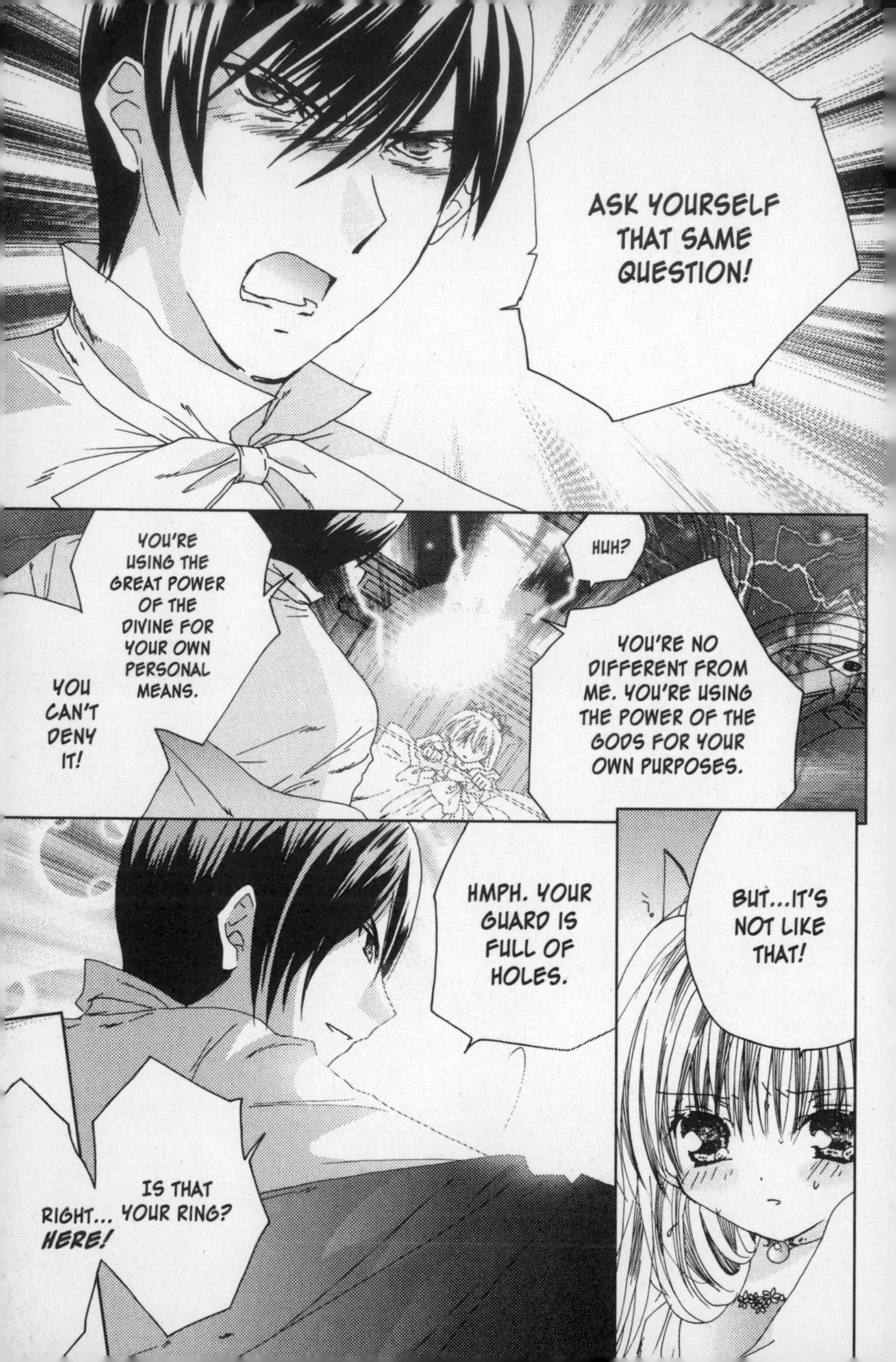
ASK YOURSELF THAT SAME QUESTION!
HUH?
YOU'RE NO DIFFERENT FROM ME. YOU'RE USING THE POWER OF THE GODS FOR YOUR OWN PURPOSES.
YOU'RE USING THE GREAT POWER OF THE DIVINE FOR YOUR OWN PERSONAL MEANS.
YOU CAN'T DENY IT!
BUT...IT'S NOT LIKE THAT!
HMPH. YOUR GUARD IS FULL OF HOLES.
IS THAT YOUR RING?
RIGHT... *HERE!*

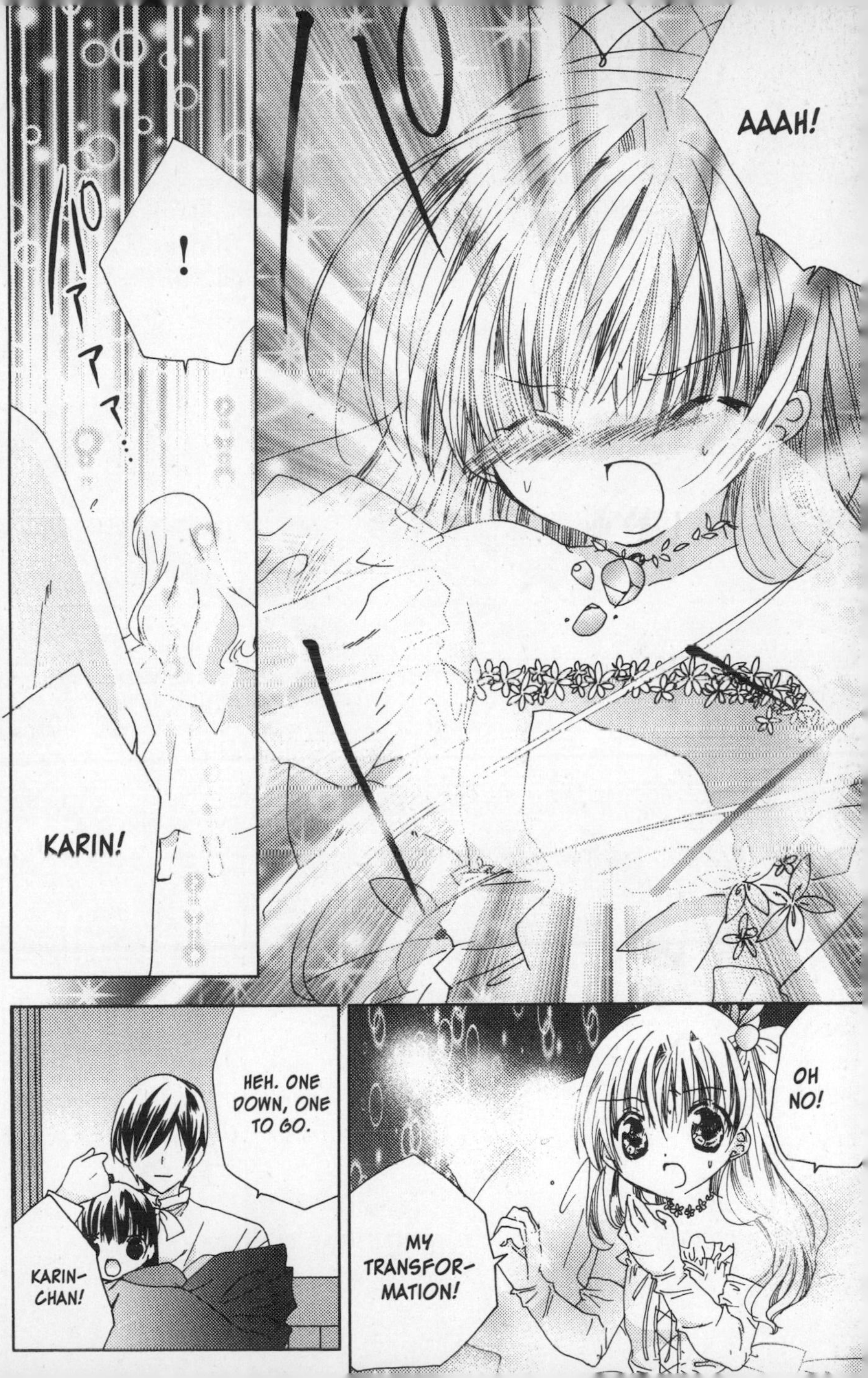
AAAH!
!
KARIN!
OH NO!
MY TRANSFORMATION!
HEH. ONE DOWN, ONE TO GO.
KARIN-CHAN!

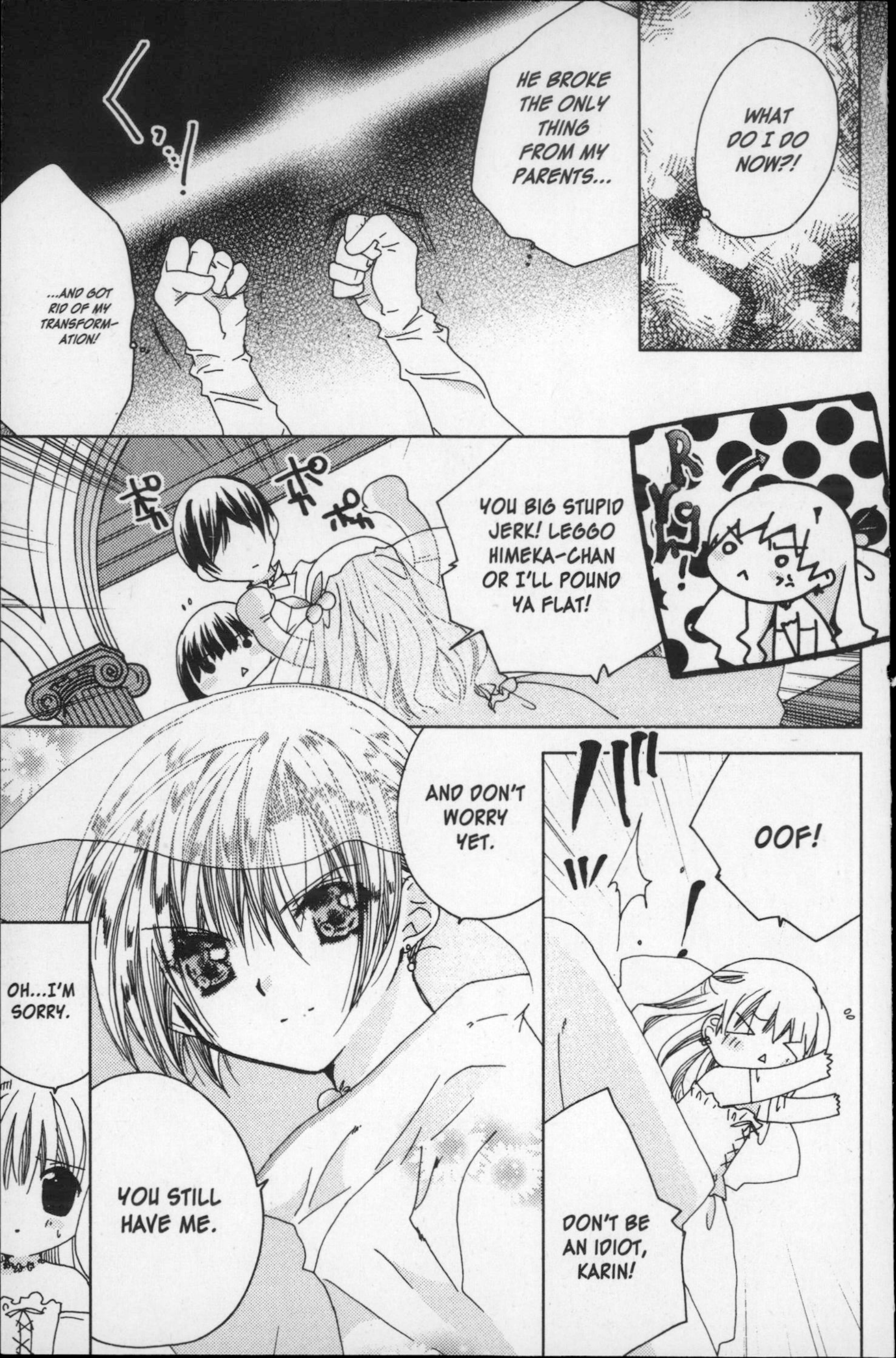
WHAT DO I DO NOW?!
HE BROKE THE ONLY THING FROM MY PARENTS...
...AND GOT RID OF MY TRANSFORMATION!
YOU BIG STUPID JERK! LEGGO HIMEKA-CHAN OR I'LL POUND YA FLAT!
OOF!
DON'T BE AN IDIOT, KARIN!
AND DON'T WORRY YET.
OH...I'M SORRY.
YOU STILL HAVE ME.

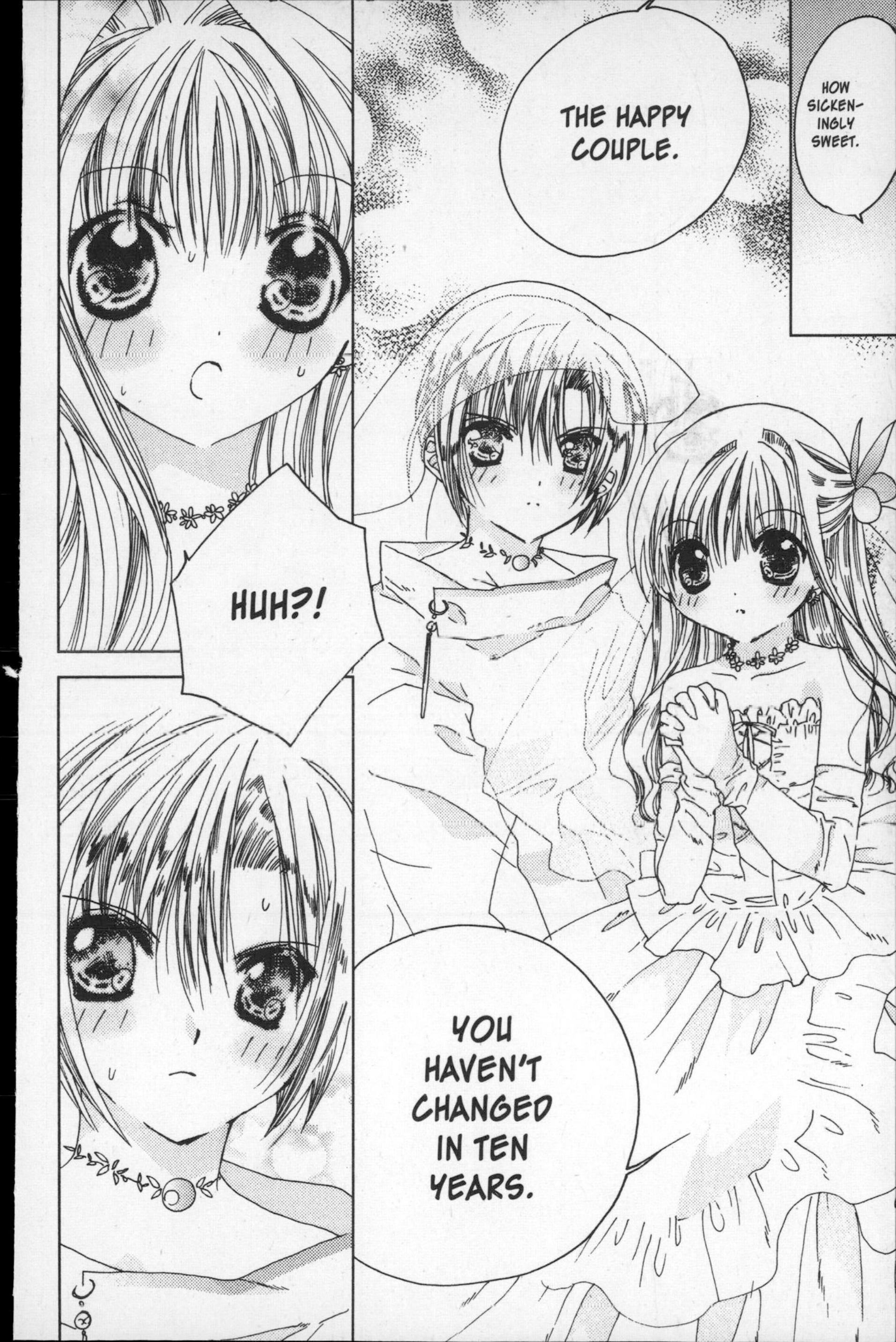
HOW SICKEN-INGLY SWEET.
THE HAPPY COUPLE.
YOU HAVEN'T CHANGED IN TEN YEARS.
HUH?!

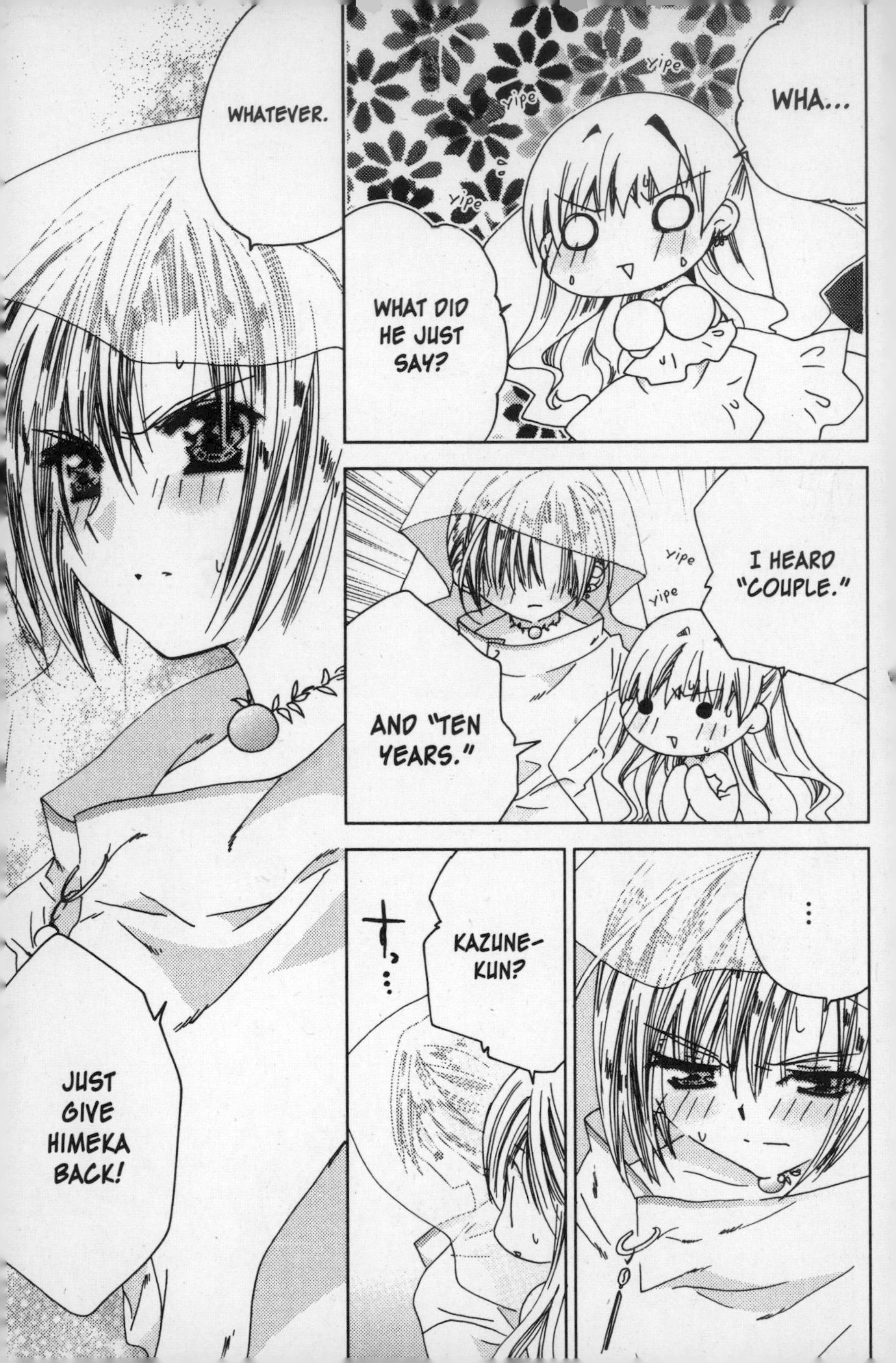
WHA...
yipe
yipe
yipe
WHAT DID HE JUST SAY?
I HEARD "COUPLE."
yipe
yipe
AND "TEN YEARS."
...
KAZUNE-KUN?
...
WHATEVER.
JUST GIVE HIMEKA BACK!

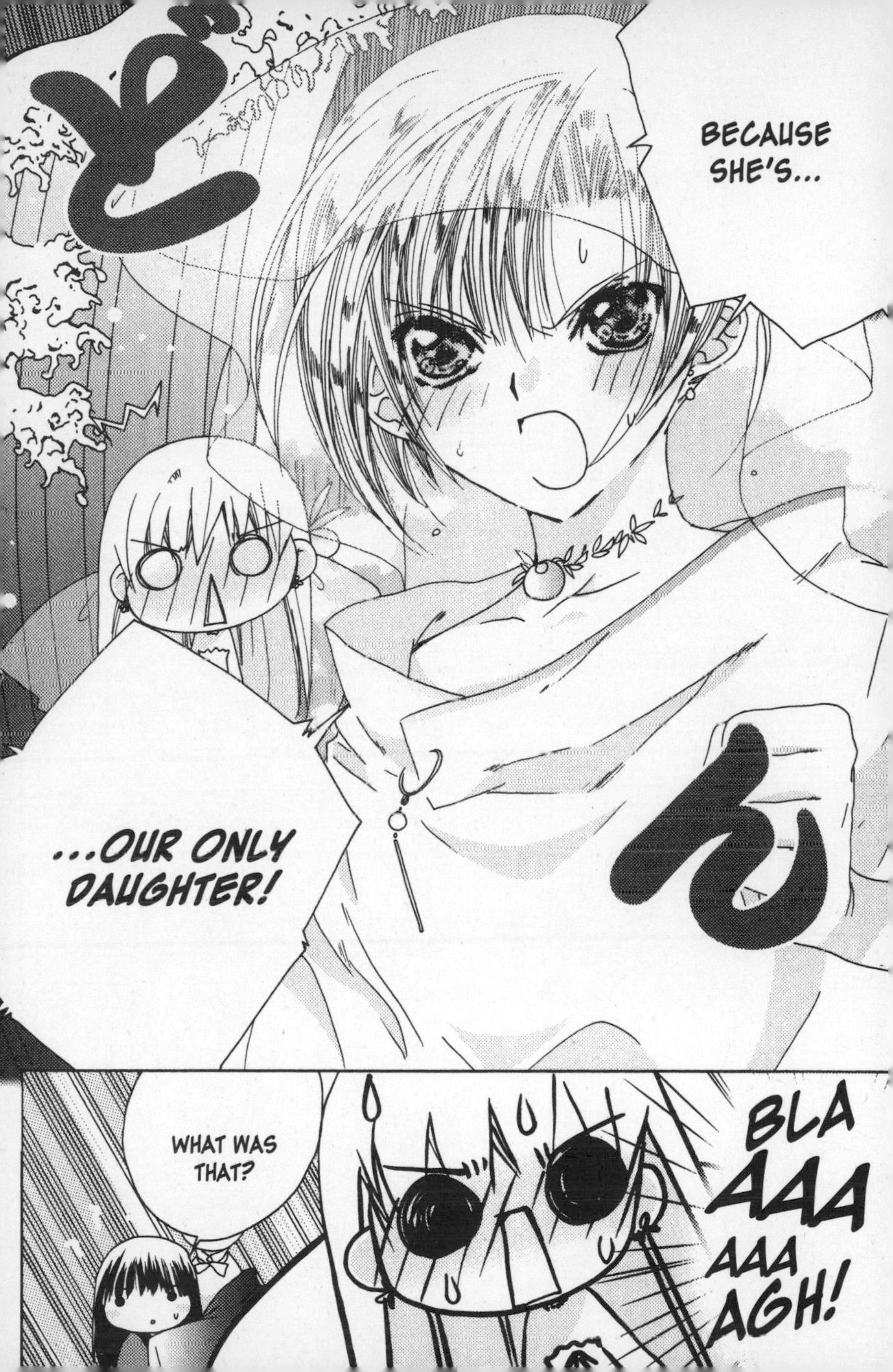
BECAUSE SHE'S...
...OUR ONLY DAUGHTER!
BLA AAA AAA AGH!
WHAT WAS THAT?

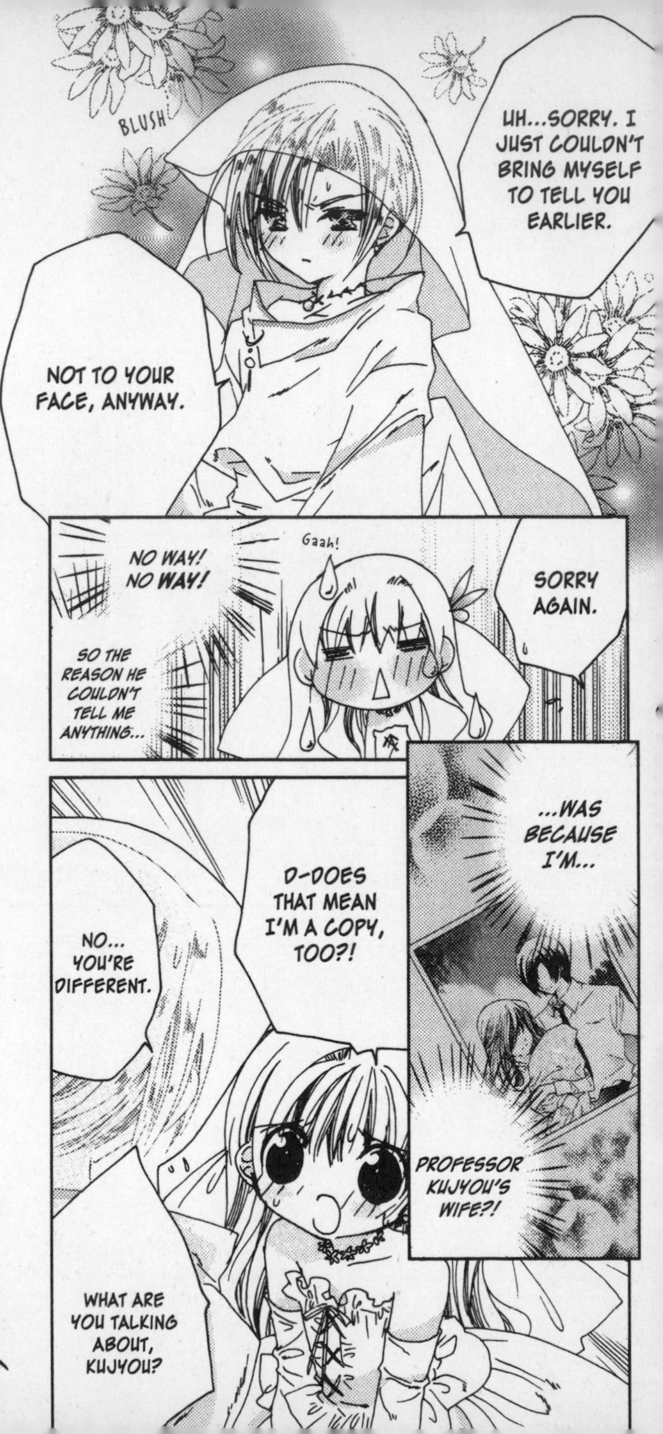
BLUSH
UH...SORRY. I JUST COULDN'T BRING MYSELF TO TELL YOU EARLIER.
NOT TO YOUR FACE, ANYWAY.
SORRY AGAIN.
Gaah!
NO WAY! NO WAY!
SO THE REASON HE COULDN'T TELL ME ANYTHING...
...WAS BECAUSE I'M...
PROFESSOR KUJYOU'S WIFE?!
D-DOES THAT MEAN I'M A COPY, TOO?!
NO... YOU'RE DIFFERENT.
WHAT ARE YOU TALKING ABOUT, KUJYOU?
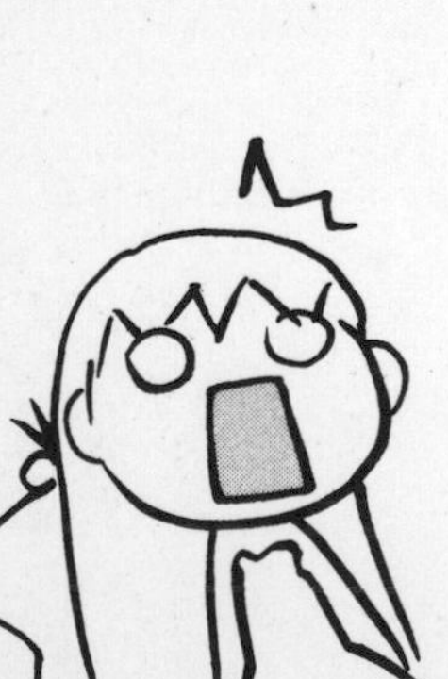

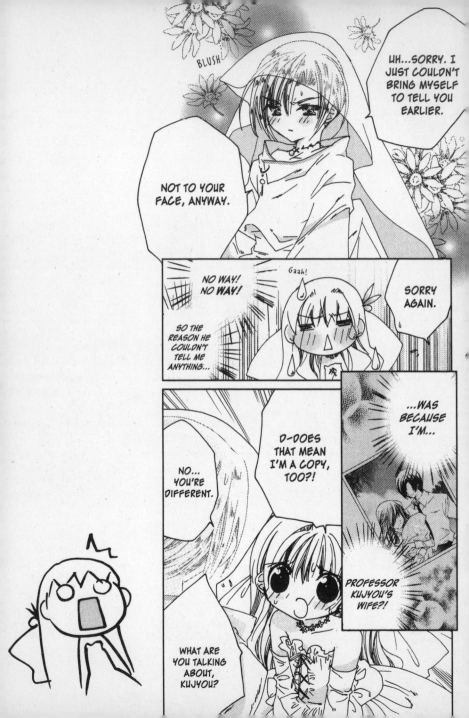

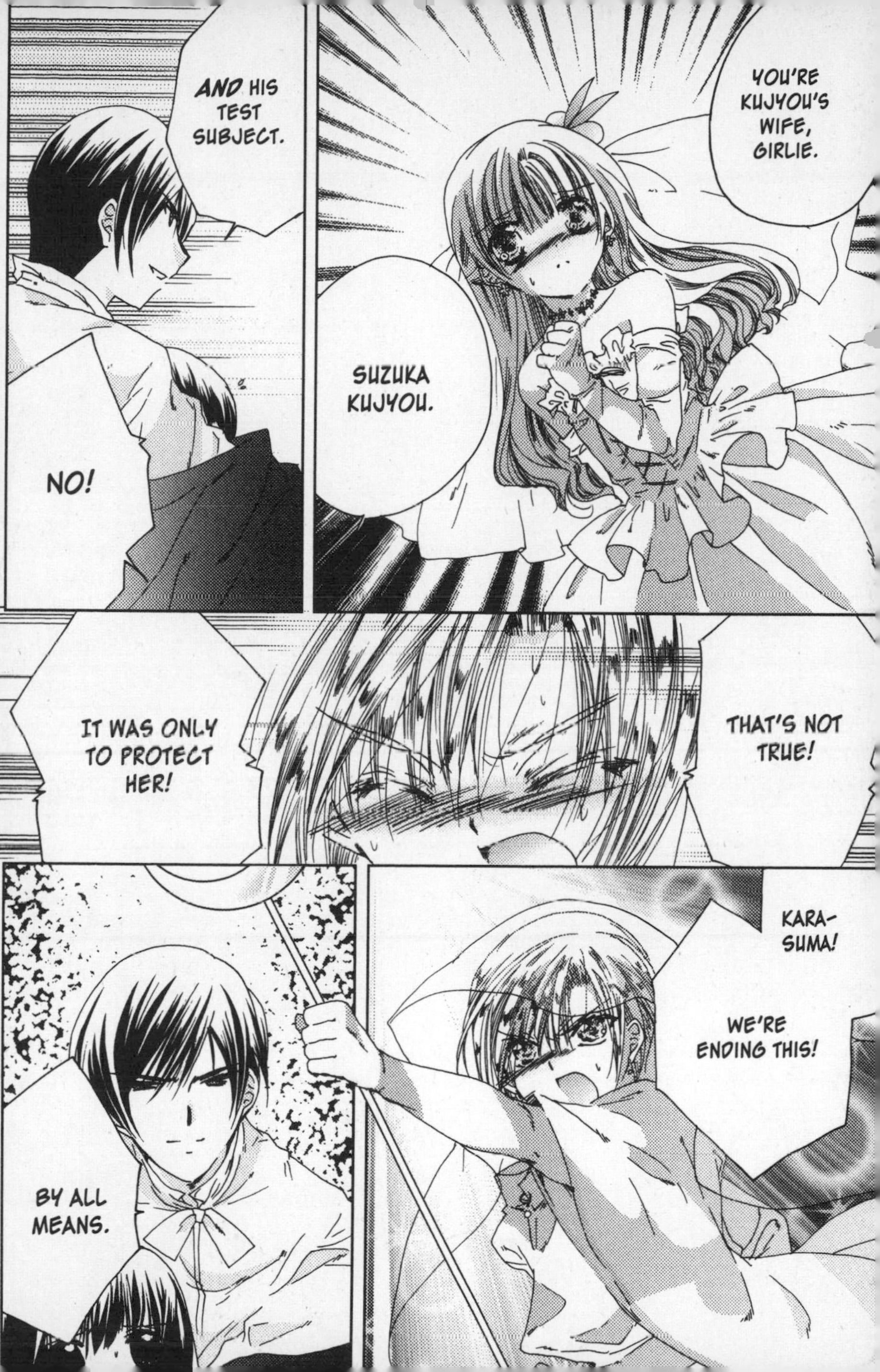
YOU'RE KUJYOU'S WIFE, GIRLIE.
SUZUKA KUJYOU.
AND HIS TEST SUBJECT.
NO!
THAT'S NOT TRUE!
IT WAS ONLY TO PROTECT HER!
KARA-SUMA!
WE'RE ENDING THIS!
BY ALL MEANS.

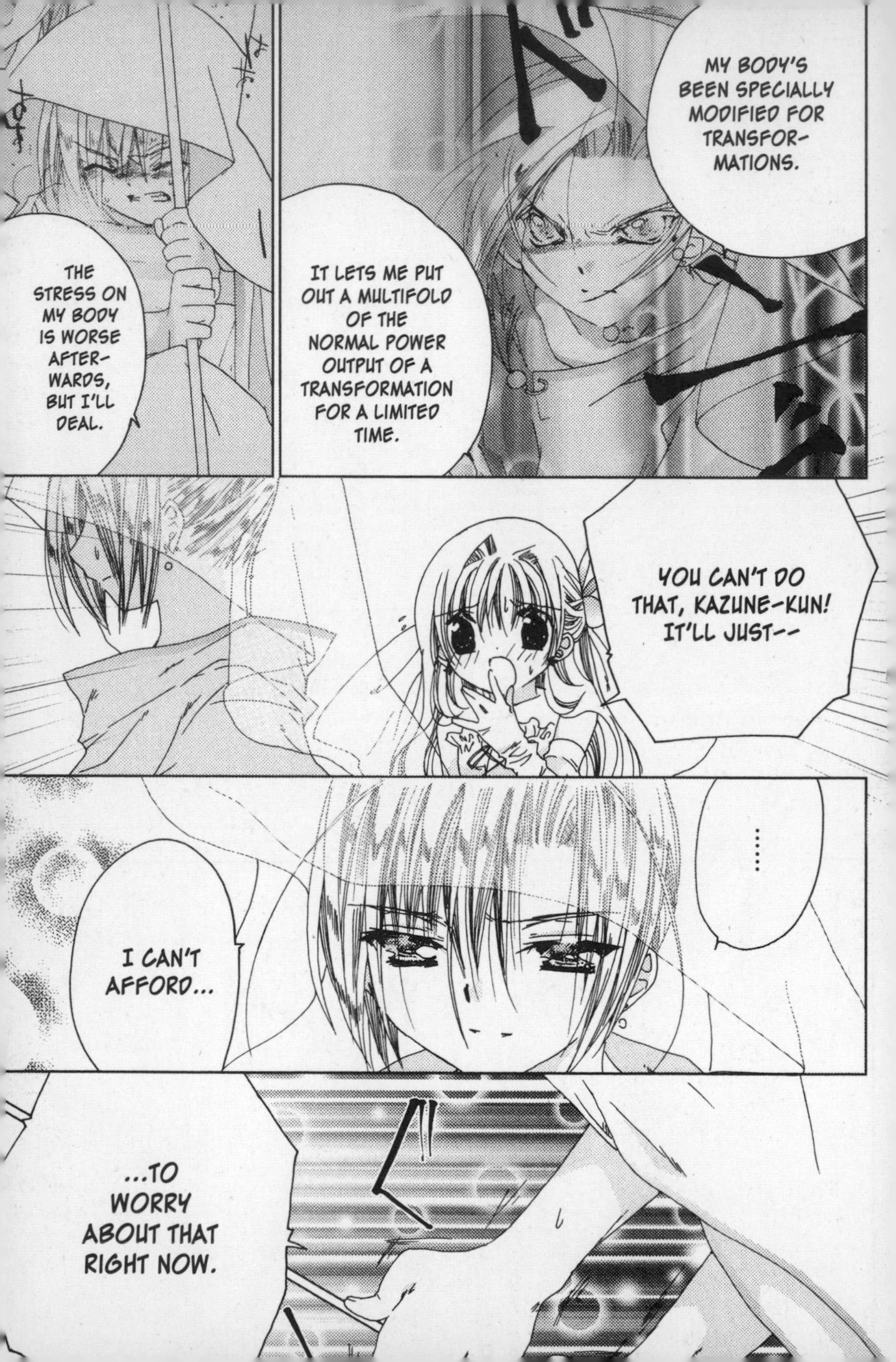
MY BODY'S BEEN SPECIALLY MODIFIED FOR TRANSFOR-MATIONS.
IT LETS ME PUT OUT A MULTIFOLD OF THE NORMAL POWER OUTPUT OF A TRANSFORMATION FOR A LIMITED TIME.
THE STRESS ON MY BODY IS WORSE AFTER-WARDS, BUT I'LL DEAL.
YOU CAN'T DO THAT, KAZUNE-KUN! IT'LL JUST--
......
I CAN'T AFFORD...
...TO WORRY ABOUT THAT RIGHT NOW.

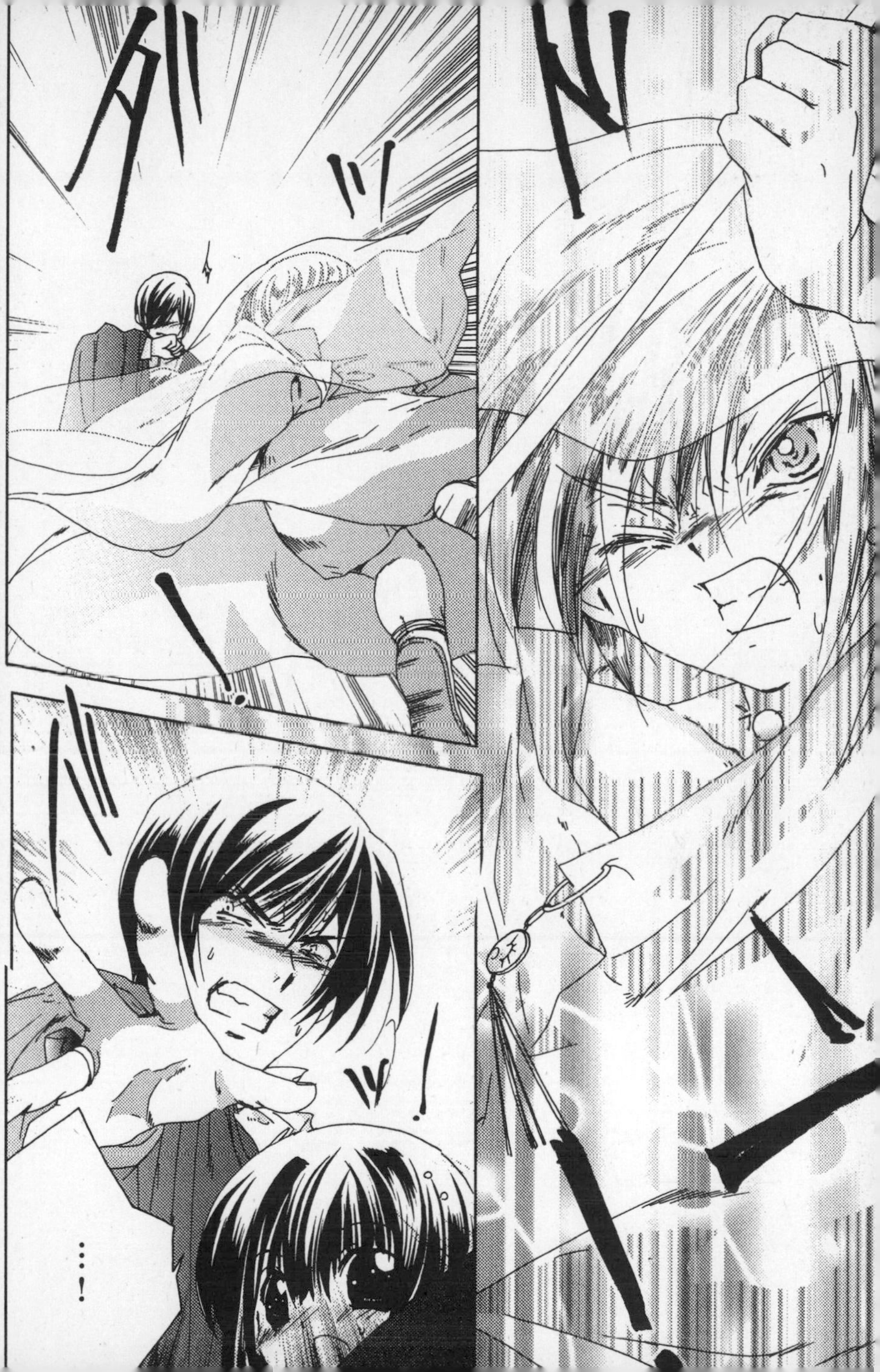
…!

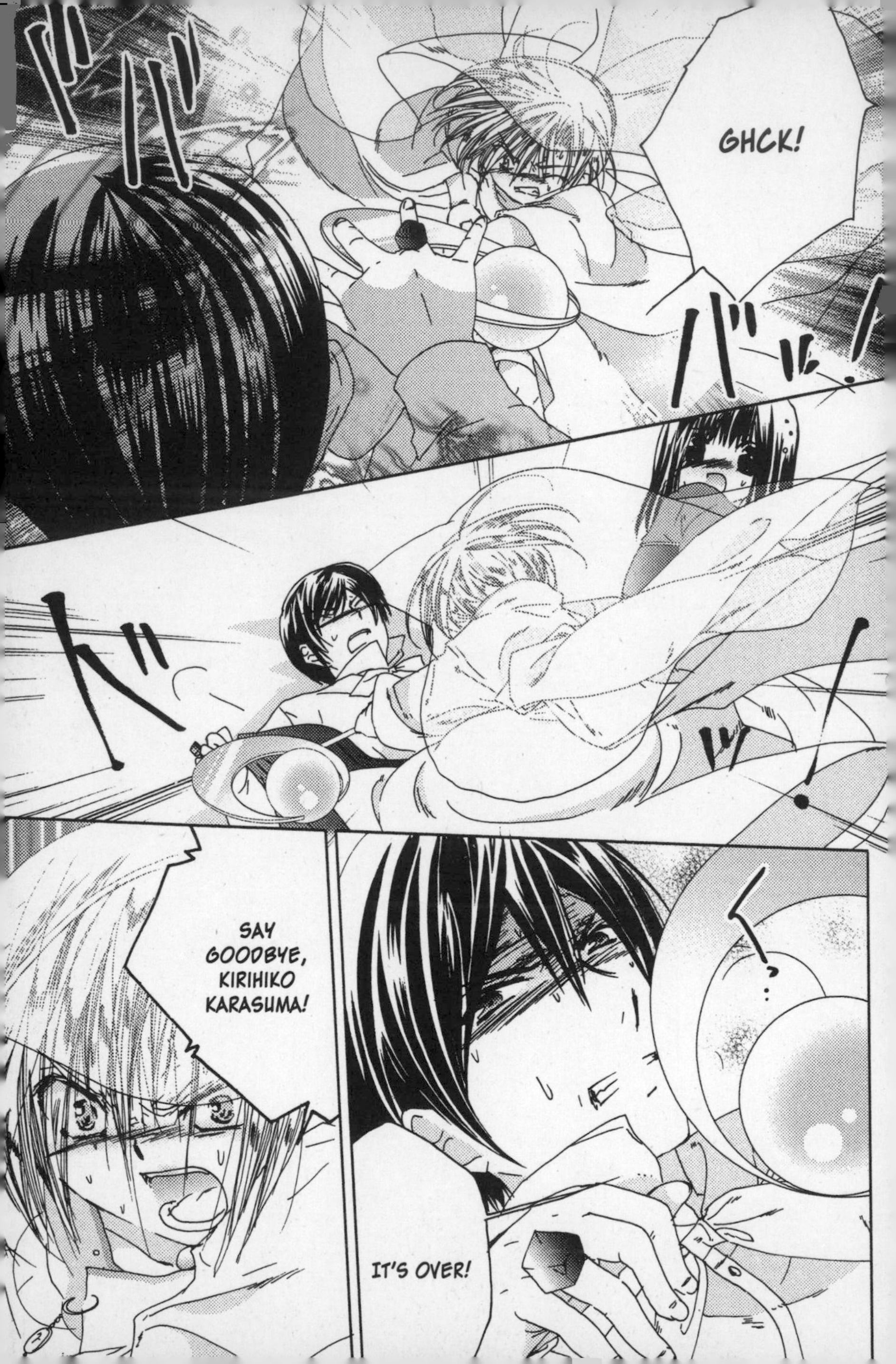
GHCK!
IT'S OVER!
SAY GOODBYE, KIRIHIKO KARASUMA!

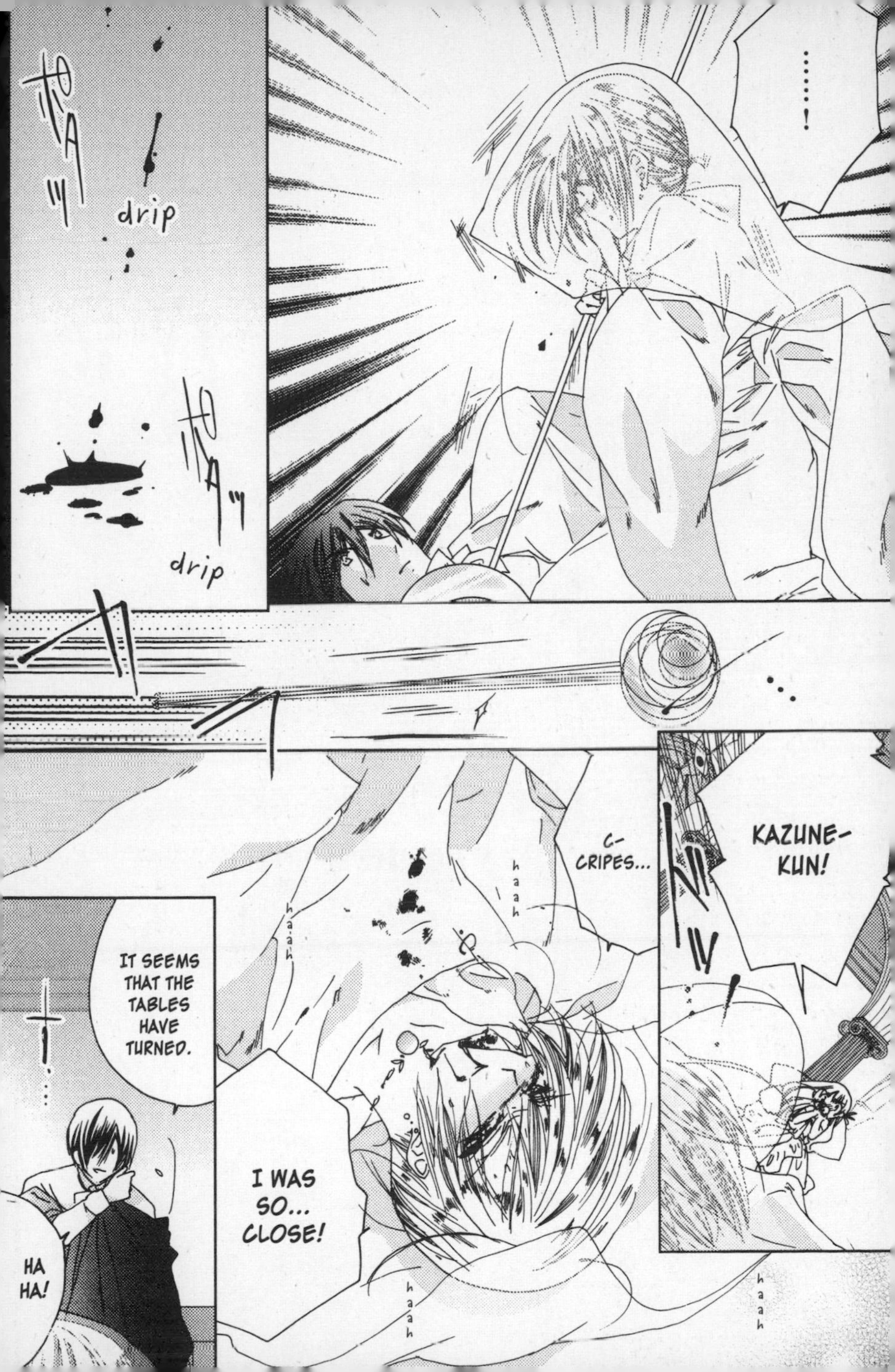
......!
drip
drip
...
KAZUNE-KUN!
C-CRIPES...
haah
haah
I WAS SO... CLOSE!
haah
haah
IT SEEMS THAT THE TABLES HAVE TURNED.
HA HA!

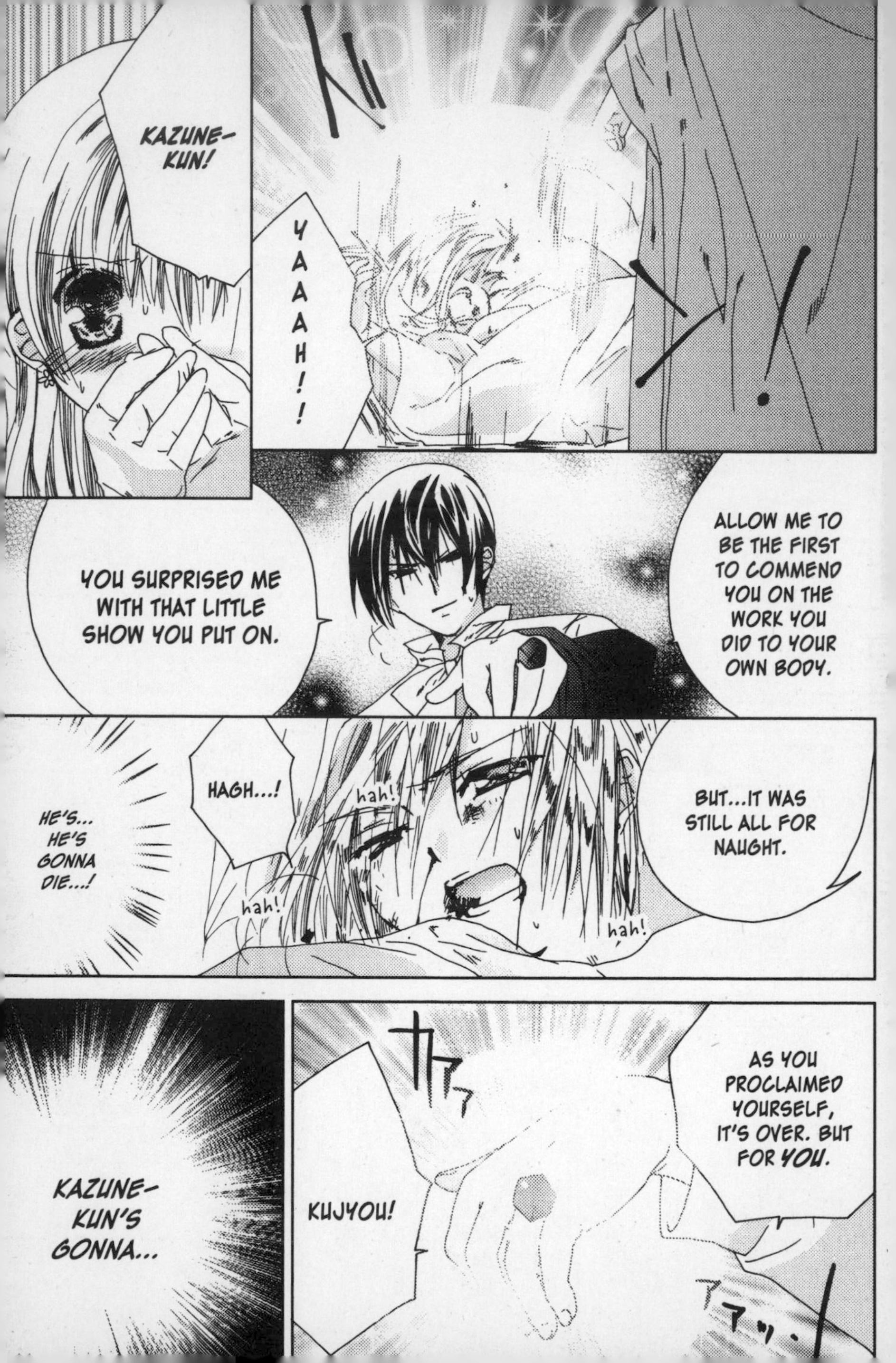
YAAAAH!!
KAZUNE-KUN!
ALLOW ME TO BE THE FIRST TO COMMEND YOU ON THE WORK YOU DID TO YOUR OWN BODY.
YOU SURPRISED ME WITH THAT LITTLE SHOW YOU PUT ON.
BUT...IT WAS STILL ALL FOR NAUGHT.
hah!
hah!
HAGH...!
hah!
HE'S... HE'S GONNA DIE...!
AS YOU PROCLAIMED YOURSELF, IT'S OVER. BUT FOR YOU.
KUJYOU!
KAZUNE-KUN'S GONNA...

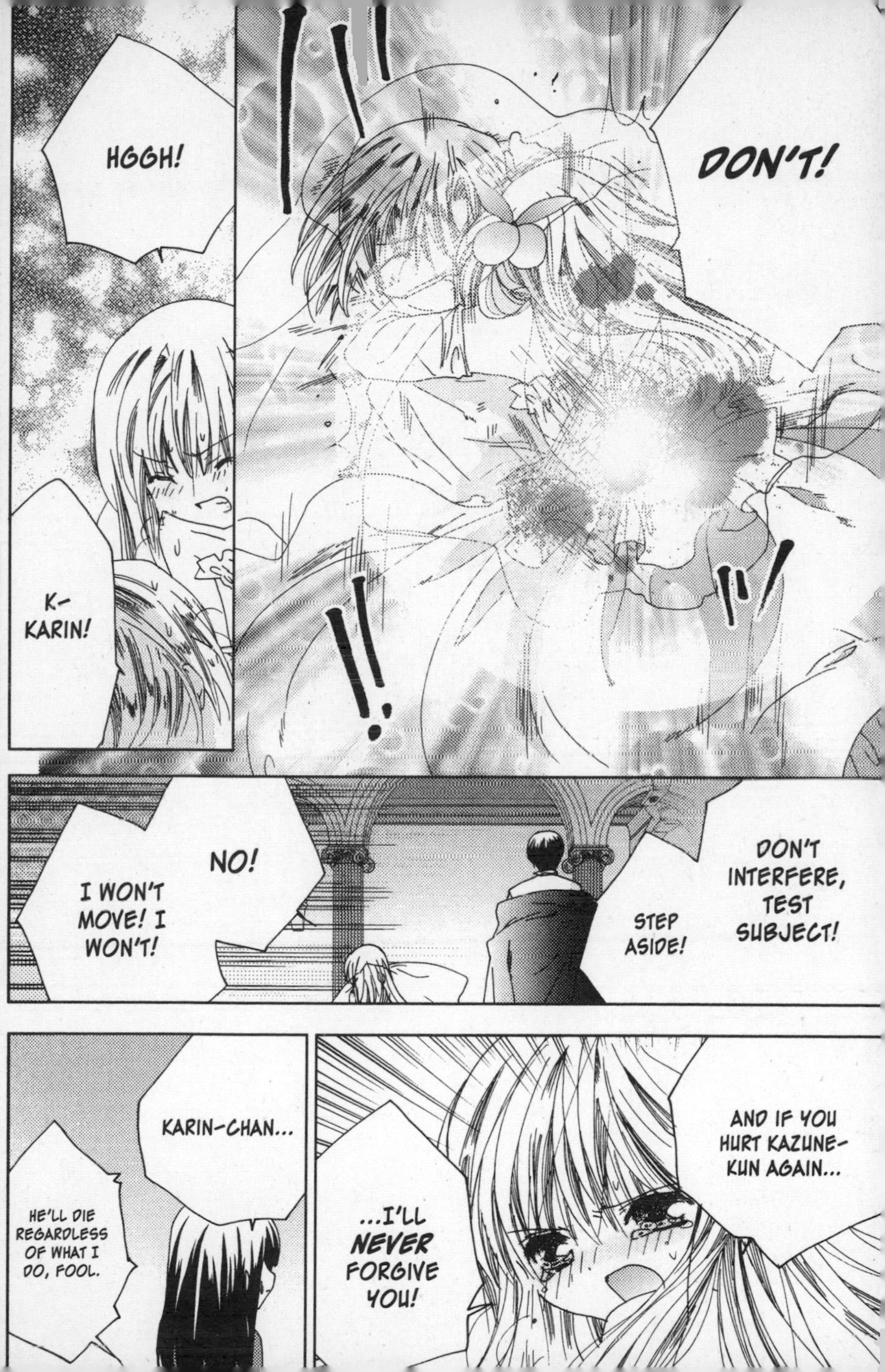
DON'T!
HGGH!
K-KARIN!
DON'T INTERFERE, TEST SUBJECT!
STEP ASIDE!
NO!
I WON'T MOVE! I WON'T!
AND IF YOU HURT KAZUNE-KUN AGAIN...
...I'LL *NEVER* FORGIVE YOU!
KARIN-CHAN...
HE'LL DIE REGARDLESS OF WHAT I DO, FOOL.

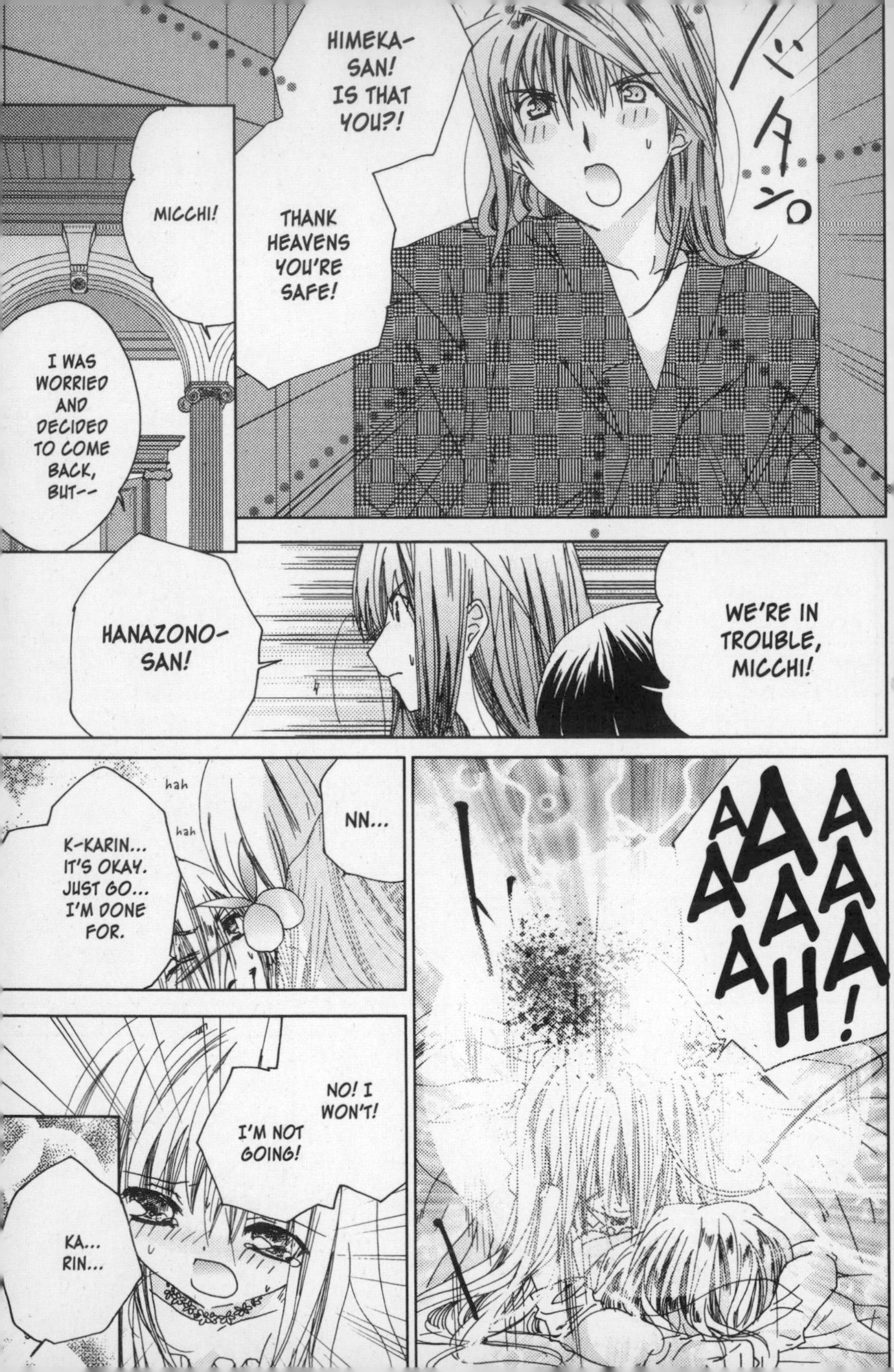
バタン
HIMEKA-SAN! IS THAT YOU?!
THANK HEAVENS YOU'RE SAFE!
MICCHI!
I WAS WORRIED AND DECIDED TO COME BACK, BUT--
WE'RE IN TROUBLE, MICCHI!
HANAZONO-SAN!
AAAAAAAH!
NN...
hah
hah
K-KARIN... IT'S OKAY. JUST GO... I'M DONE FOR.
NO! I WON'T!
I'M NOT GOING!
KA... RIN...

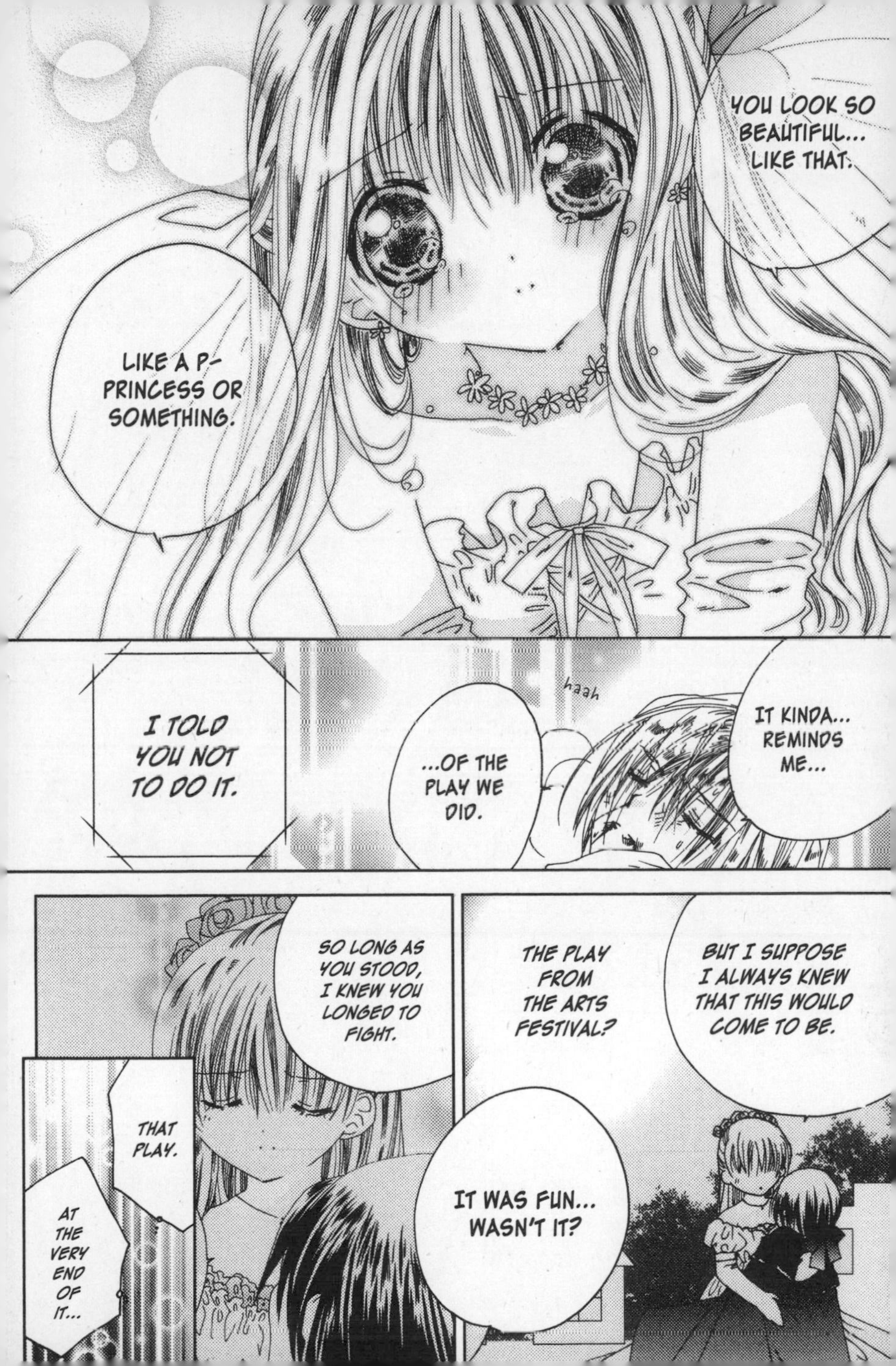
YOU LOOK SO BEAUTIFUL... LIKE THAT.
LIKE A P-PRINCESS OR SOMETHING.
IT KINDA... REMINDS ME...
haah
...OF THE PLAY WE DID.
I TOLD YOU NOT TO DO IT.
BUT I SUPPOSE I ALWAYS KNEW THAT THIS WOULD COME TO BE.
THE PLAY FROM THE ARTS FESTIVAL?
IT WAS FUN... WASN'T IT?
SO LONG AS YOU STOOD, I KNEW YOU LONGED TO FIGHT.
THAT PLAY.
AT THE VERY END OF IT...

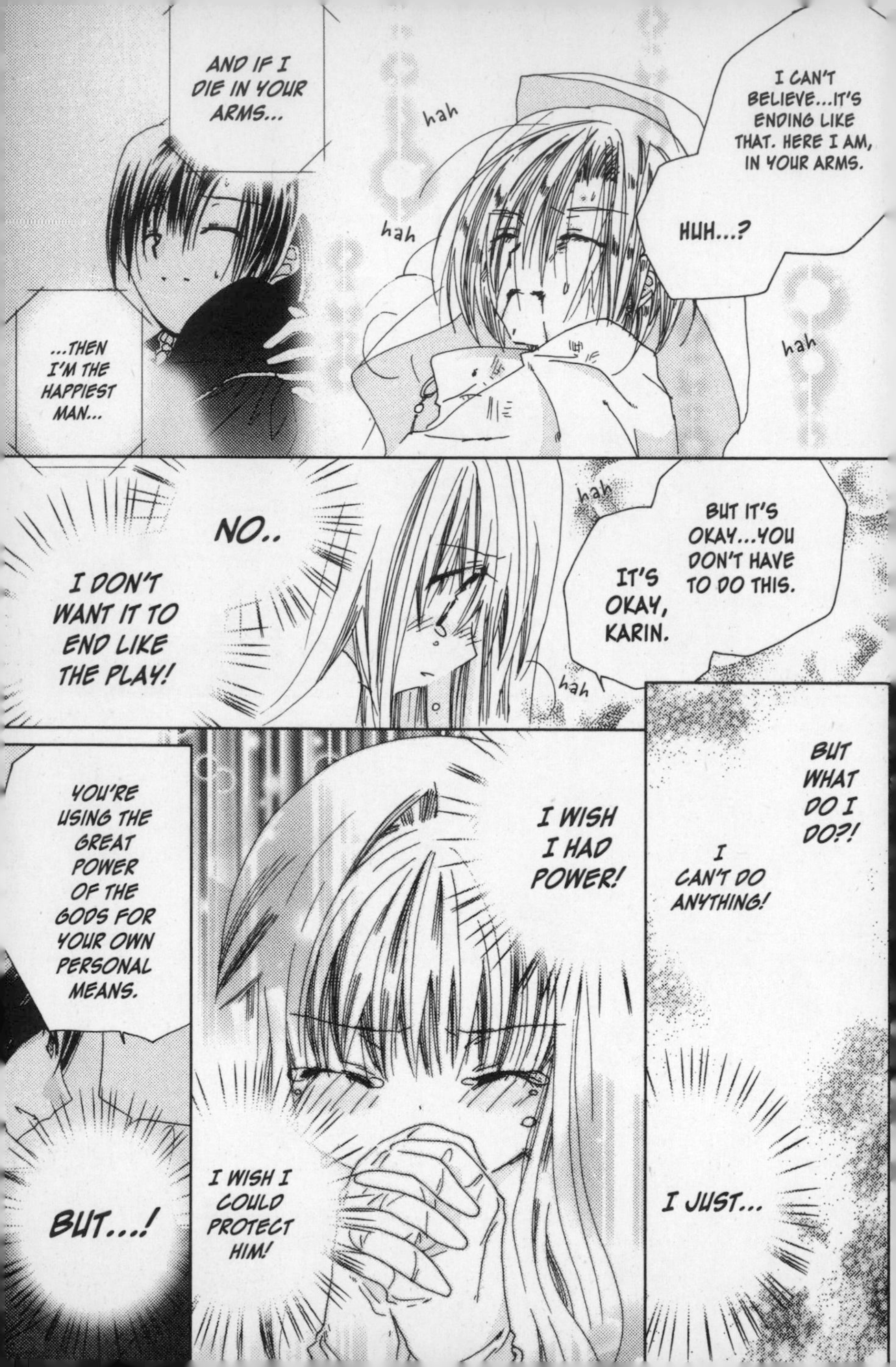
I CAN'T BELIEVE...IT'S ENDING LIKE THAT. HERE I AM, IN YOUR ARMS.
hah
HUH...?
AND IF I DIE IN YOUR ARMS...
hah
hah
...THEN I'M THE HAPPIEST MAN...
BUT IT'S OKAY...YOU DON'T HAVE TO DO THIS.
hah
IT'S OKAY, KARIN.
hah
NO..
I DON'T WANT IT TO END LIKE THE PLAY!
BUT WHAT DO I DO?!
I CAN'T DO ANYTHING!
I JUST...
I WISH I HAD POWER!
I WISH I COULD PROTECT HIM!
YOU'RE USING THE GREAT POWER OF THE GODS FOR YOUR OWN PERSONAL MEANS.
BUT...!

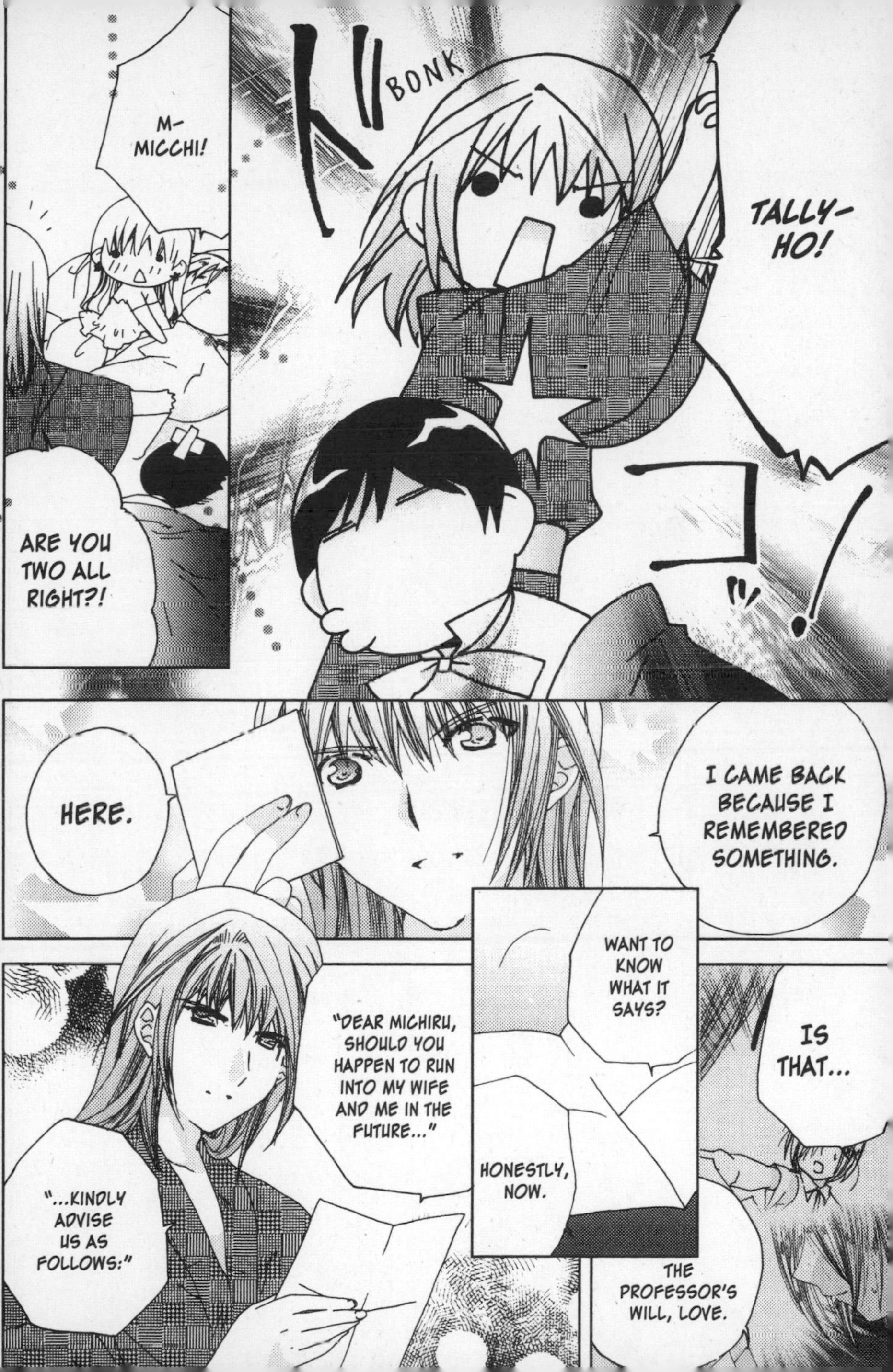
TALLY-HO!
BONK
M-MICCHI!
ARE YOU TWO ALL RIGHT?!
I CAME BACK BECAUSE I REMEMBERED SOMETHING.
HERE.
IS THAT...
THE PROFESSOR'S WILL, LOVE.
WANT TO KNOW WHAT IT SAYS?
HONESTLY, NOW.
"DEAR MICHIRU, SHOULD YOU HAPPEN TO RUN INTO MY WIFE AND ME IN THE FUTURE..."
"...KINDLY ADVISE US AS FOLLOWS:"

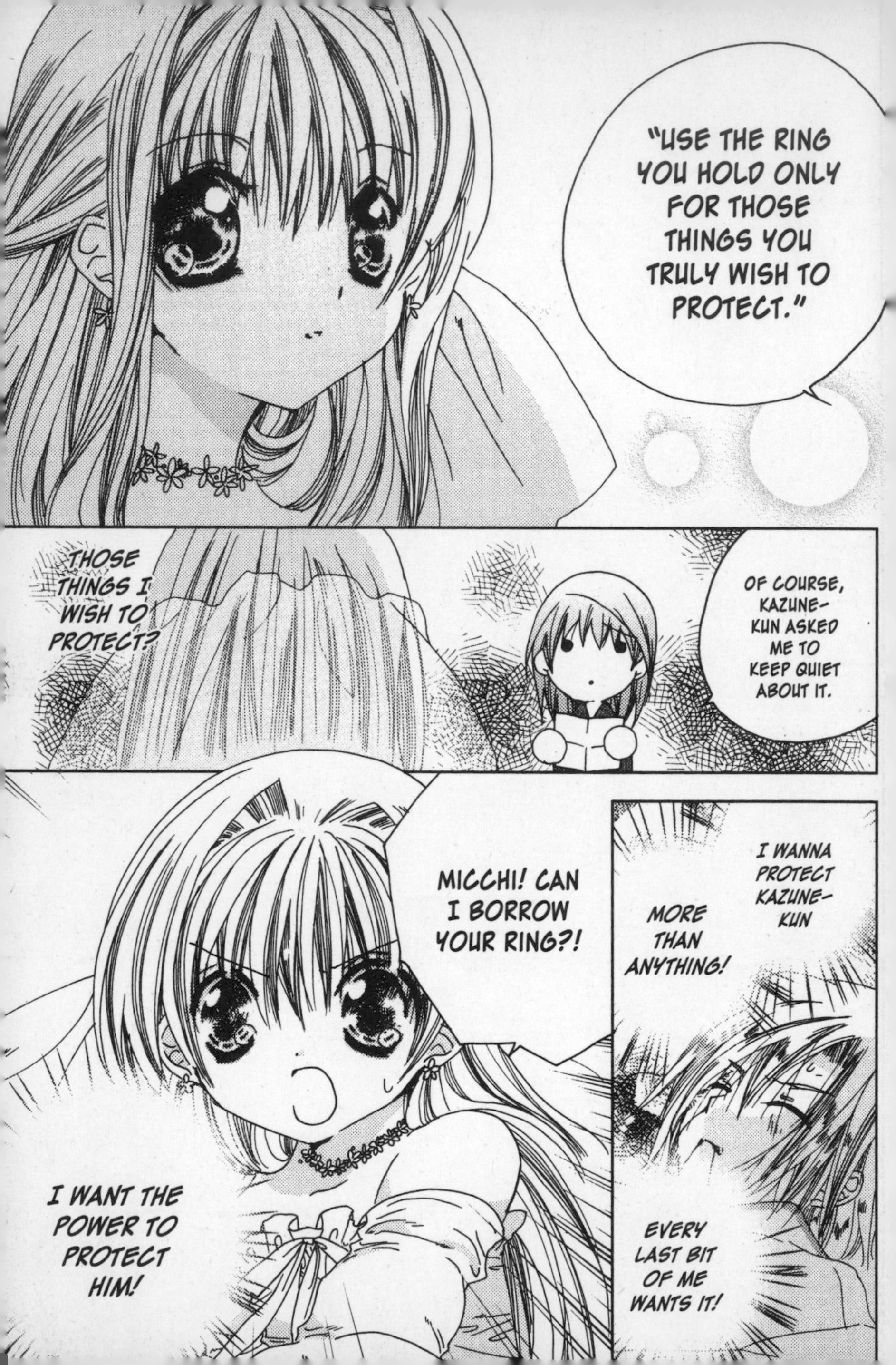
"USE THE RING YOU HOLD ONLY FOR THOSE THINGS YOU TRULY WISH TO PROTECT."
OF COURSE, KAZUNE-KUN ASKED ME TO KEEP QUIET ABOUT IT.
THOSE THINGS I WISH TO PROTECT?
I WANNA PROTECT KAZUNE-KUN
MORE THAN ANYTHING!
EVERY LAST BIT OF ME WANTS IT!
MICCHI! CAN I BORROW YOUR RING?!
I WANT THE POWER TO PROTECT HIM!

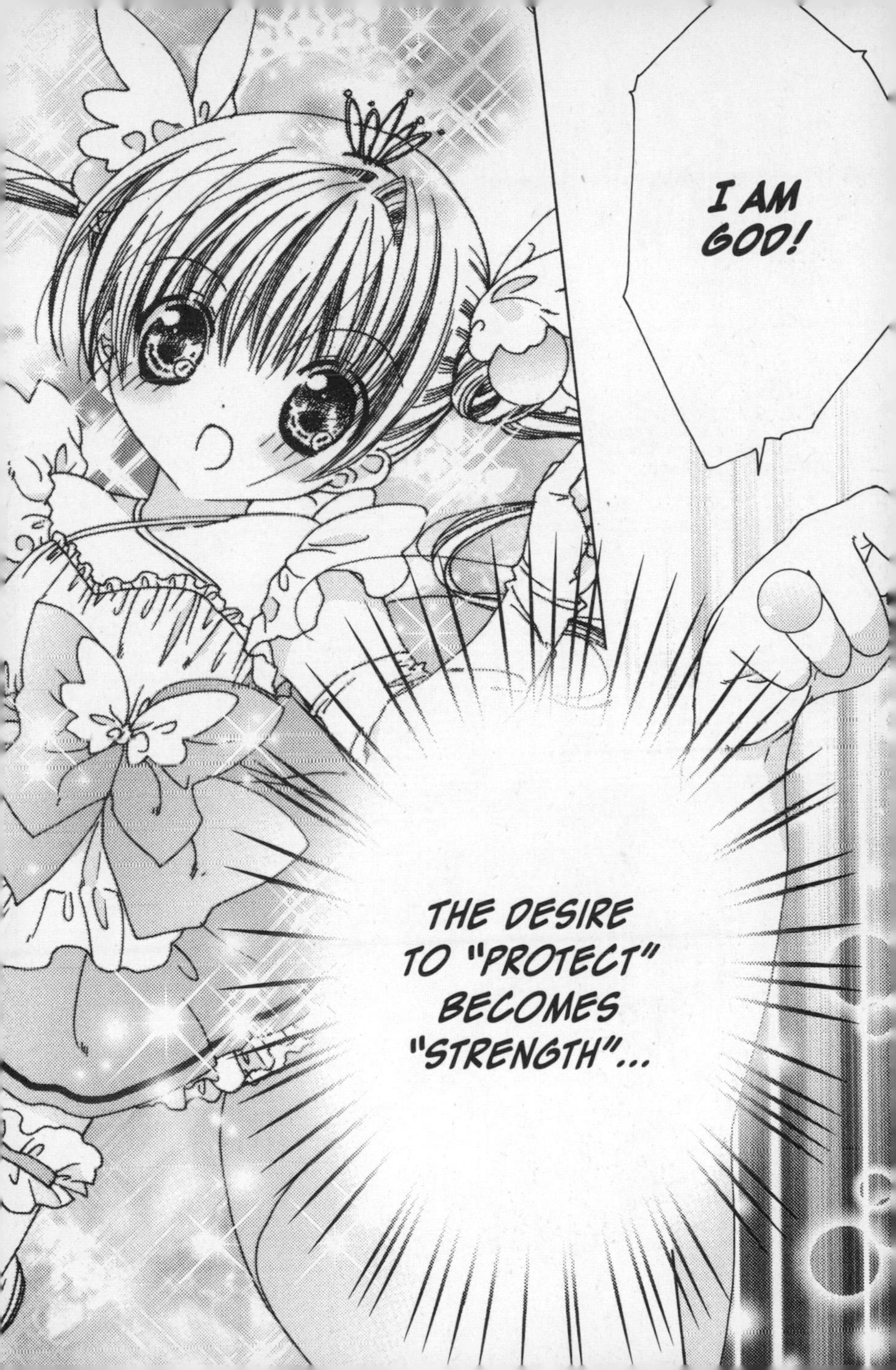
I AM GOD!
THE DESIRE TO "PROTECT" BECOMES "STRENGTH"...

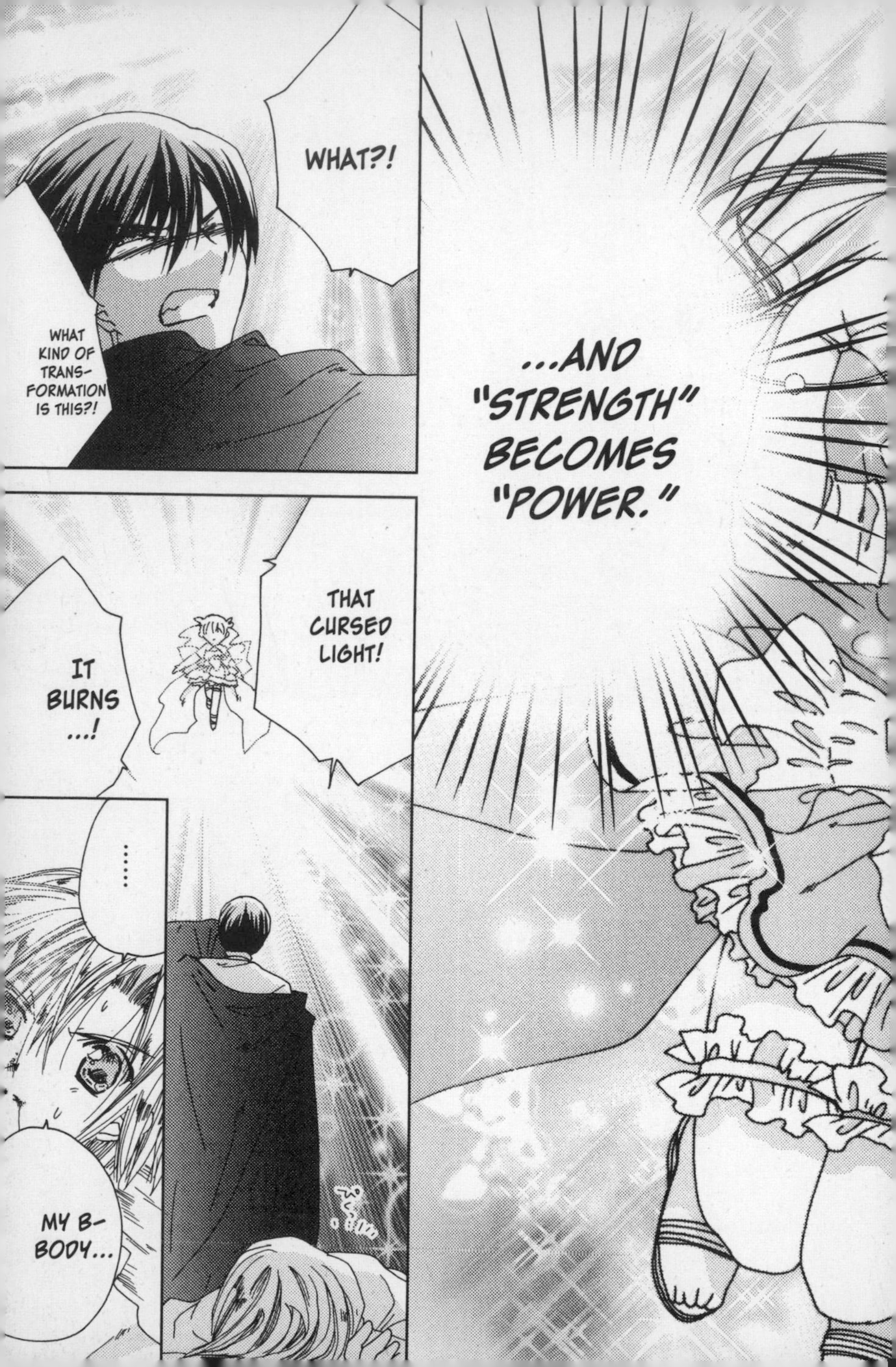
...AND "STRENGTH" BECOMES "POWER."
WHAT?!
WHAT KIND OF TRANS-FORMATION IS THIS?!
THAT CURSED LIGHT!
IT BURNS ...!
......
MY B-BODY...

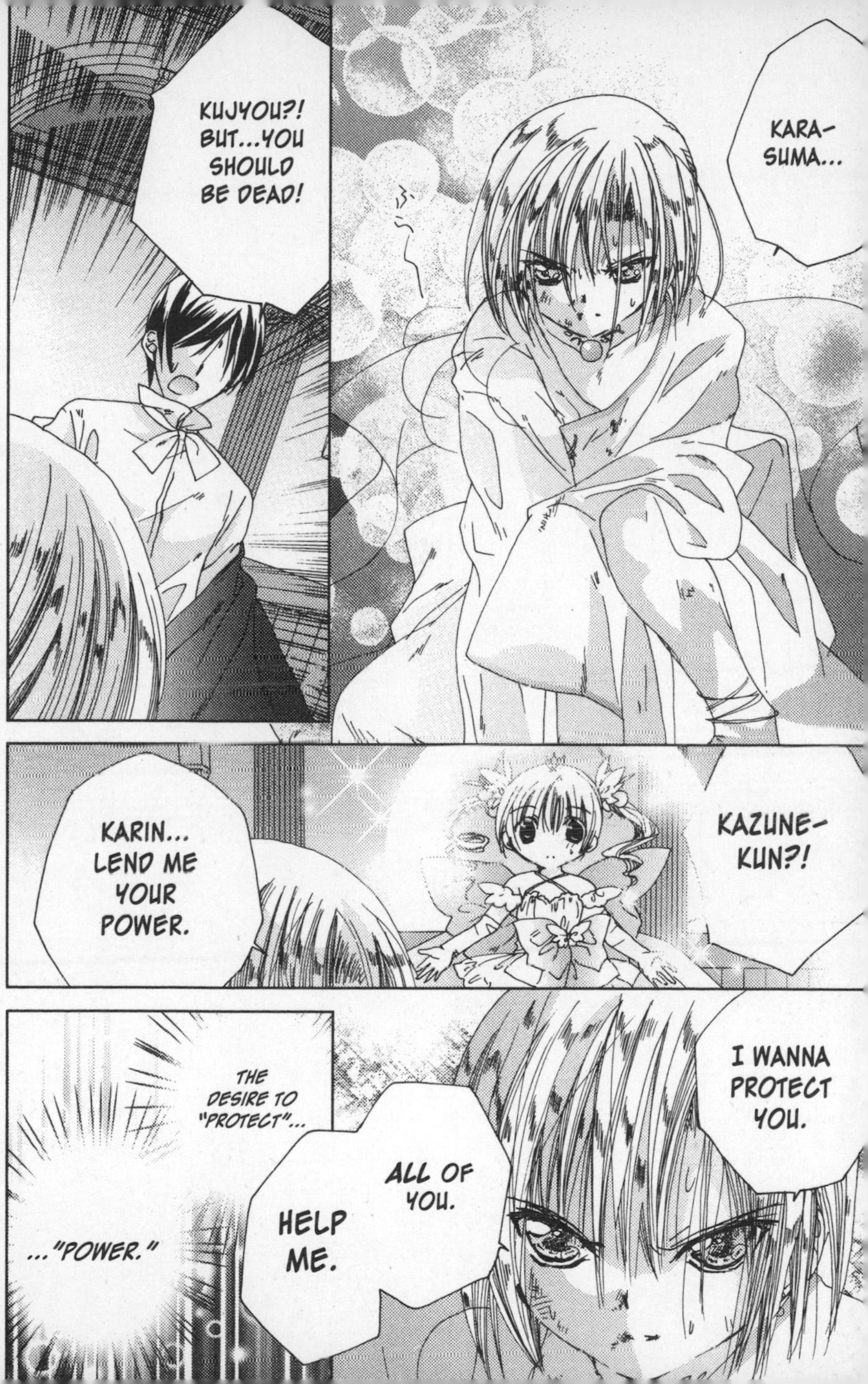
KARA-SUMA...
KUJYOU?! BUT...YOU SHOULD BE DEAD!
KAZUNE-KUN?!
KARIN... LEND ME YOUR POWER.
I WANNA PROTECT YOU.
ALL OF YOU.
HELP ME.
THE DESIRE TO "PROTECT"...
..."POWER."

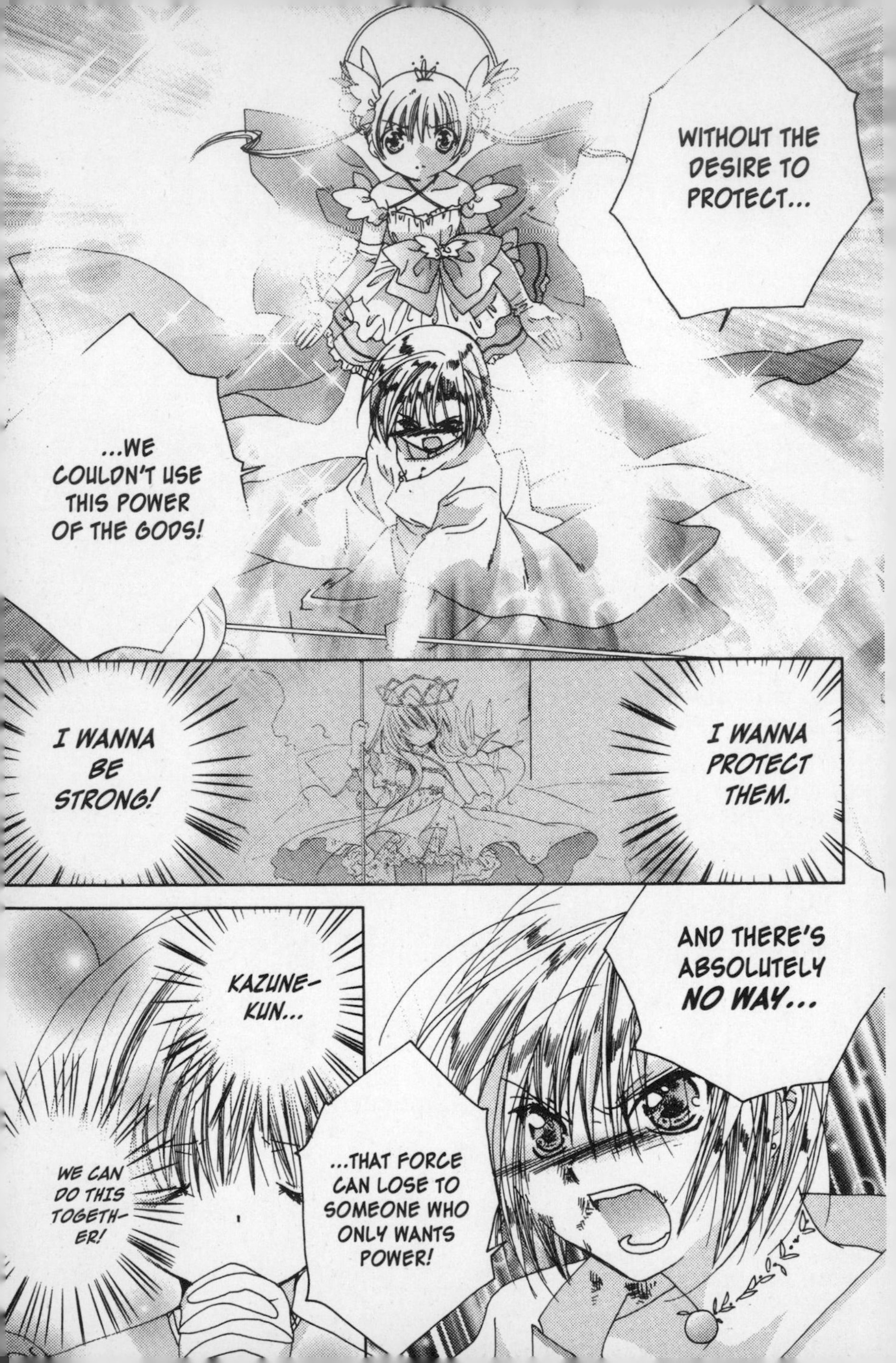
WITHOUT THE DESIRE TO PROTECT...
...WE COULDN'T USE THIS POWER OF THE GODS!
I WANNA PROTECT THEM.
I WANNA BE STRONG!
AND THERE'S ABSOLUTELY NO WAY...
...THAT FORCE CAN LOSE TO SOMEONE WHO ONLY WANTS POWER!
KAZUNE-KUN...
WE CAN DO THIS TOGETH-ER!

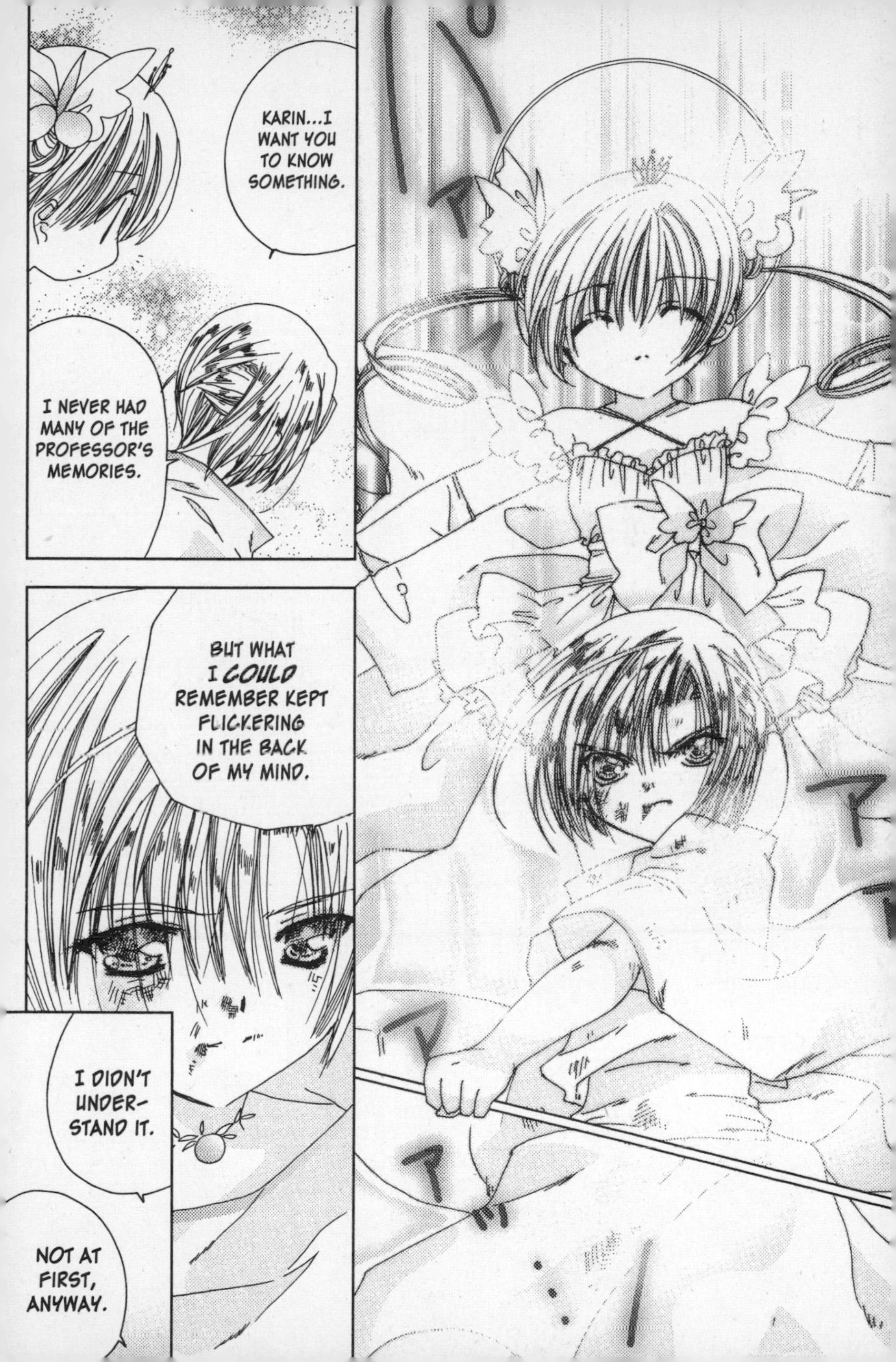
KARIN...I WANT YOU TO KNOW SOMETHING.
I NEVER HAD MANY OF THE PROFESSOR'S MEMORIES.
BUT WHAT I COULD REMEMBER KEPT FLICKERING IN THE BACK OF MY MIND.
I DIDN'T UNDER-STAND IT.
NOT AT FIRST, ANYWAY.

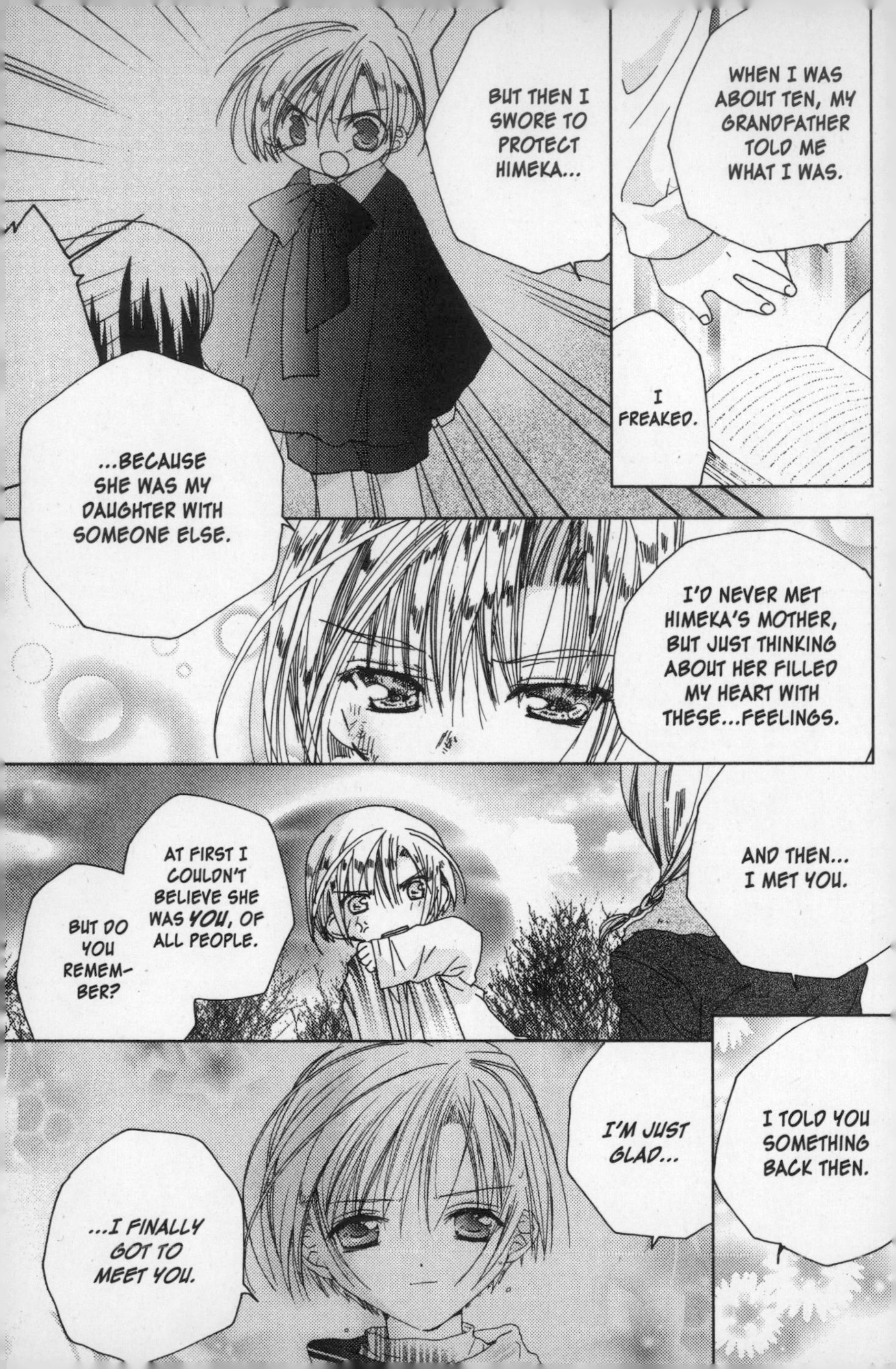
WHEN I WAS ABOUT TEN, MY GRANDFATHER TOLD ME WHAT I WAS.
I FREAKED.
BUT THEN I SWORE TO PROTECT HIMEKA...
...BECAUSE SHE WAS MY DAUGHTER WITH SOMEONE ELSE.
I'D NEVER MET HIMEKA'S MOTHER, BUT JUST THINKING ABOUT HER FILLED MY HEART WITH THESE...FEELINGS.
AND THEN... I MET YOU.
AT FIRST I COULDN'T BELIEVE SHE WAS *YOU*, OF ALL PEOPLE.
BUT DO YOU REMEM-BER?
I TOLD YOU SOMETHING BACK THEN.
I'M JUST GLAD...
...I FINALLY GOT TO MEET YOU.

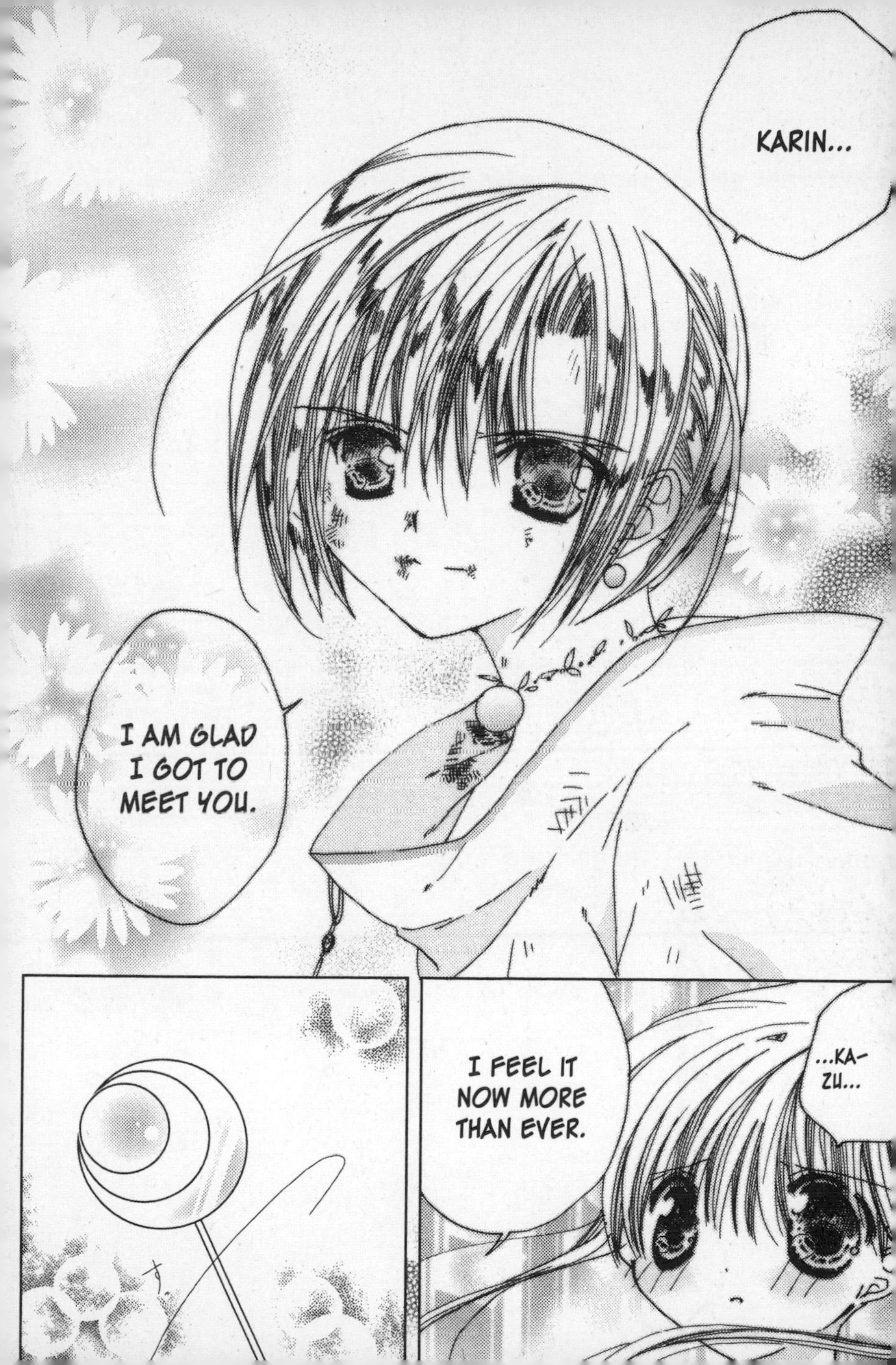
KARIN...
I AM GLAD I GOT TO MEET YOU.
...KA-ZU...
I FEEL IT NOW MORE THAN EVER.

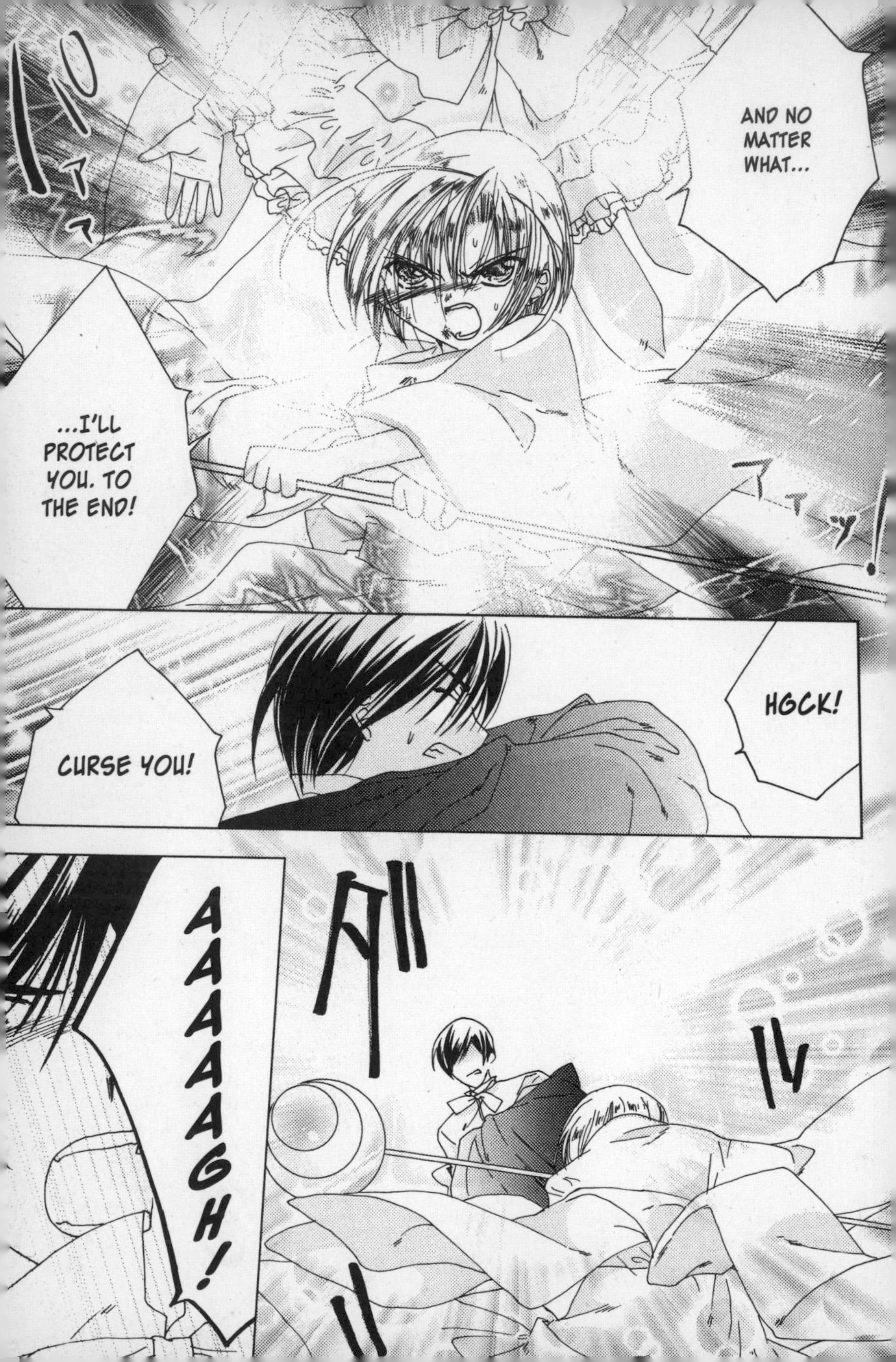
AND NO MATTER WHAT...
...I'LL PROTECT YOU. TO THE END!
HGCK!
CURSE YOU!
AAAAAAGH!

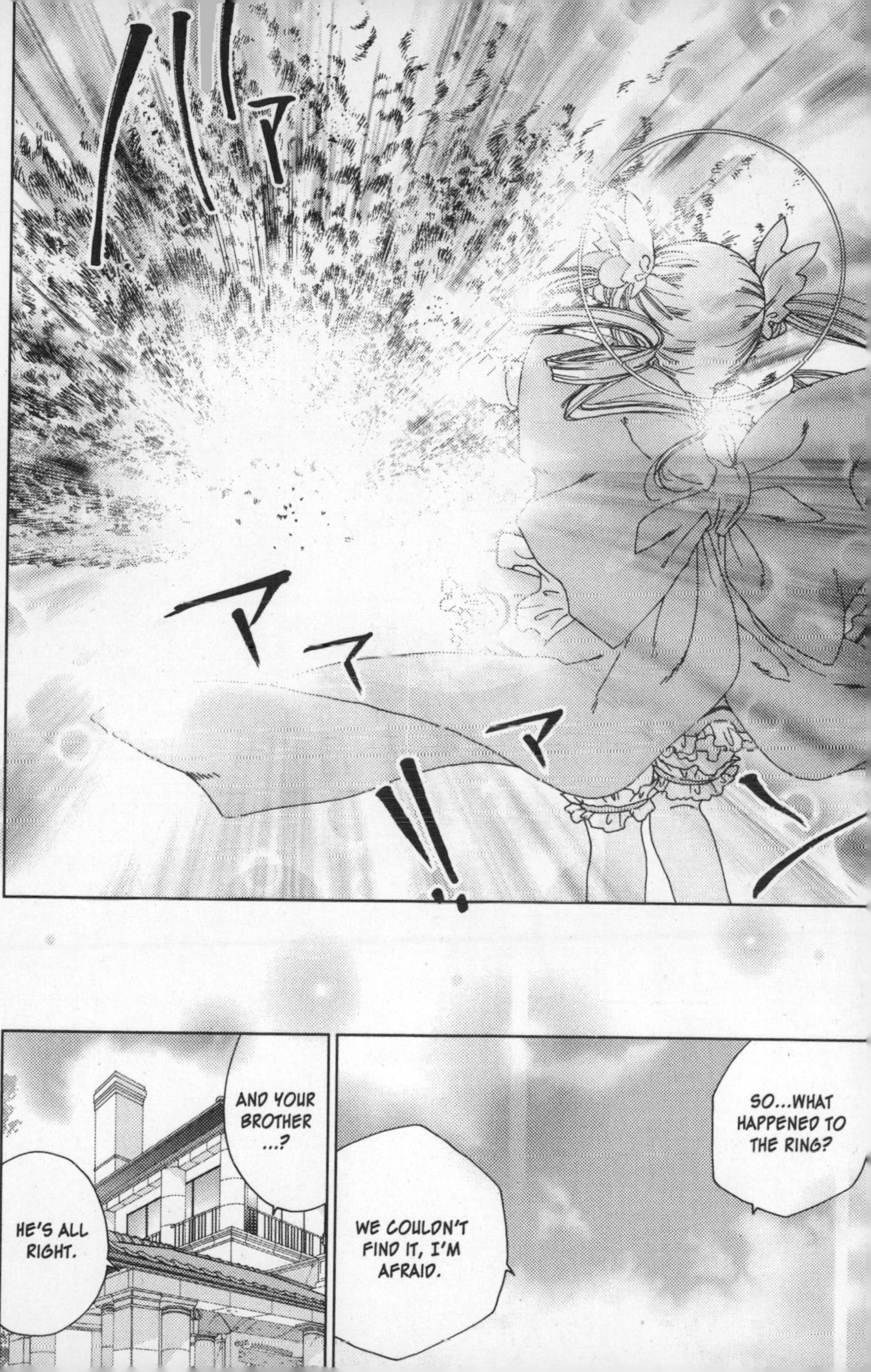
SO...WHAT HAPPENED TO THE RING?
WE COULDN'T FIND IT, I'M AFRAID.
AND YOUR BROTHER ...?
HE'S ALL RIGHT.

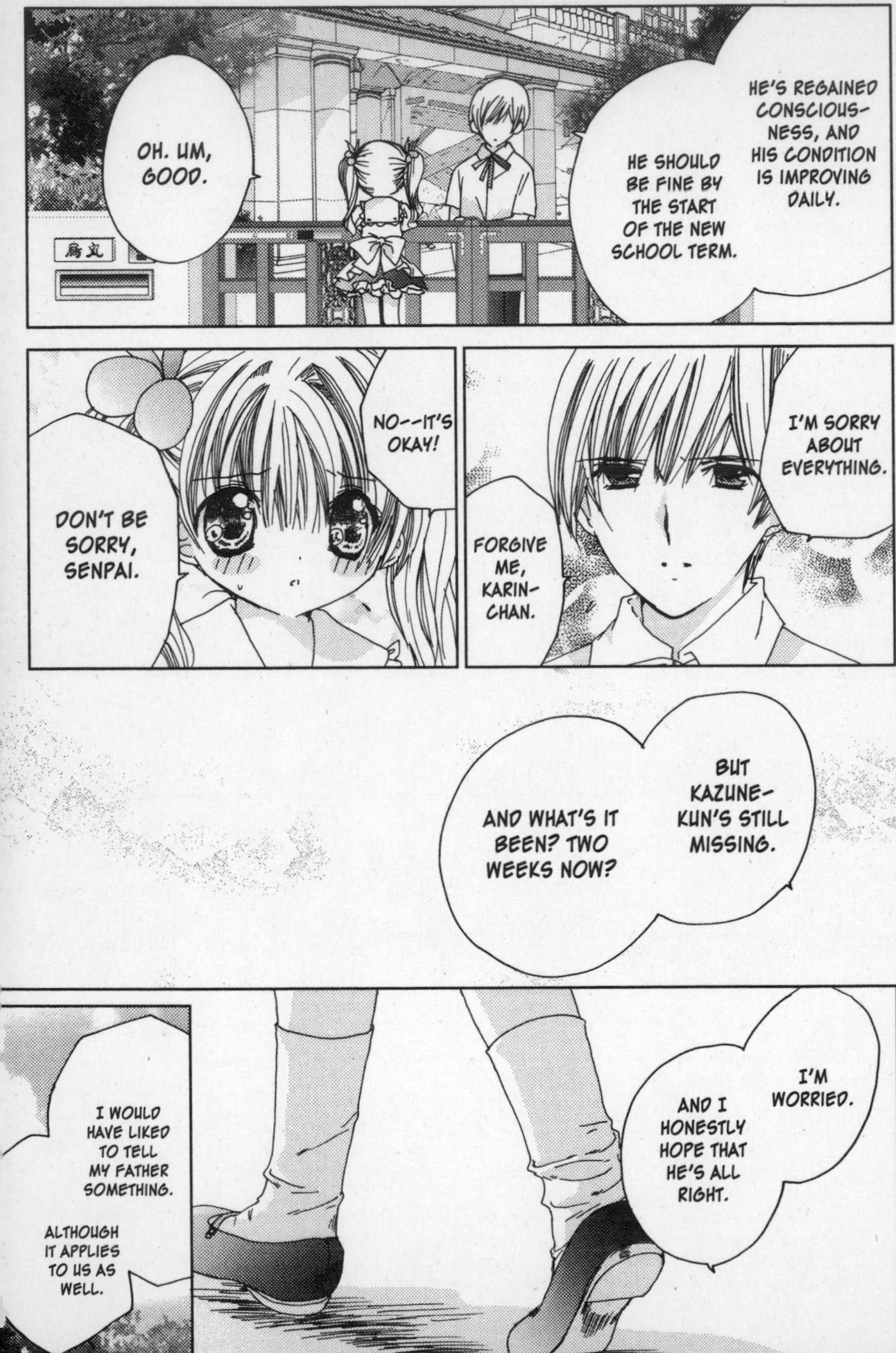
HE'S REGAINED CONSCIOUS-NESS, AND HIS CONDITION IS IMPROVING DAILY.
HE SHOULD BE FINE BY THE START OF THE NEW SCHOOL TERM.
OH. UM, GOOD.
I'M SORRY ABOUT EVERYTHING.
FORGIVE ME, KARIN-CHAN.
NO--IT'S OKAY!
DON'T BE SORRY, SENPAI.
BUT KAZUNE-KUN'S STILL MISSING.
AND WHAT'S IT BEEN? TWO WEEKS NOW?
I'M WORRIED.
AND I HONESTLY HOPE THAT HE'S ALL RIGHT.
I WOULD HAVE LIKED TO TELL MY FATHER SOMETHING.
ALTHOUGH IT APPLIES TO US AS WELL.

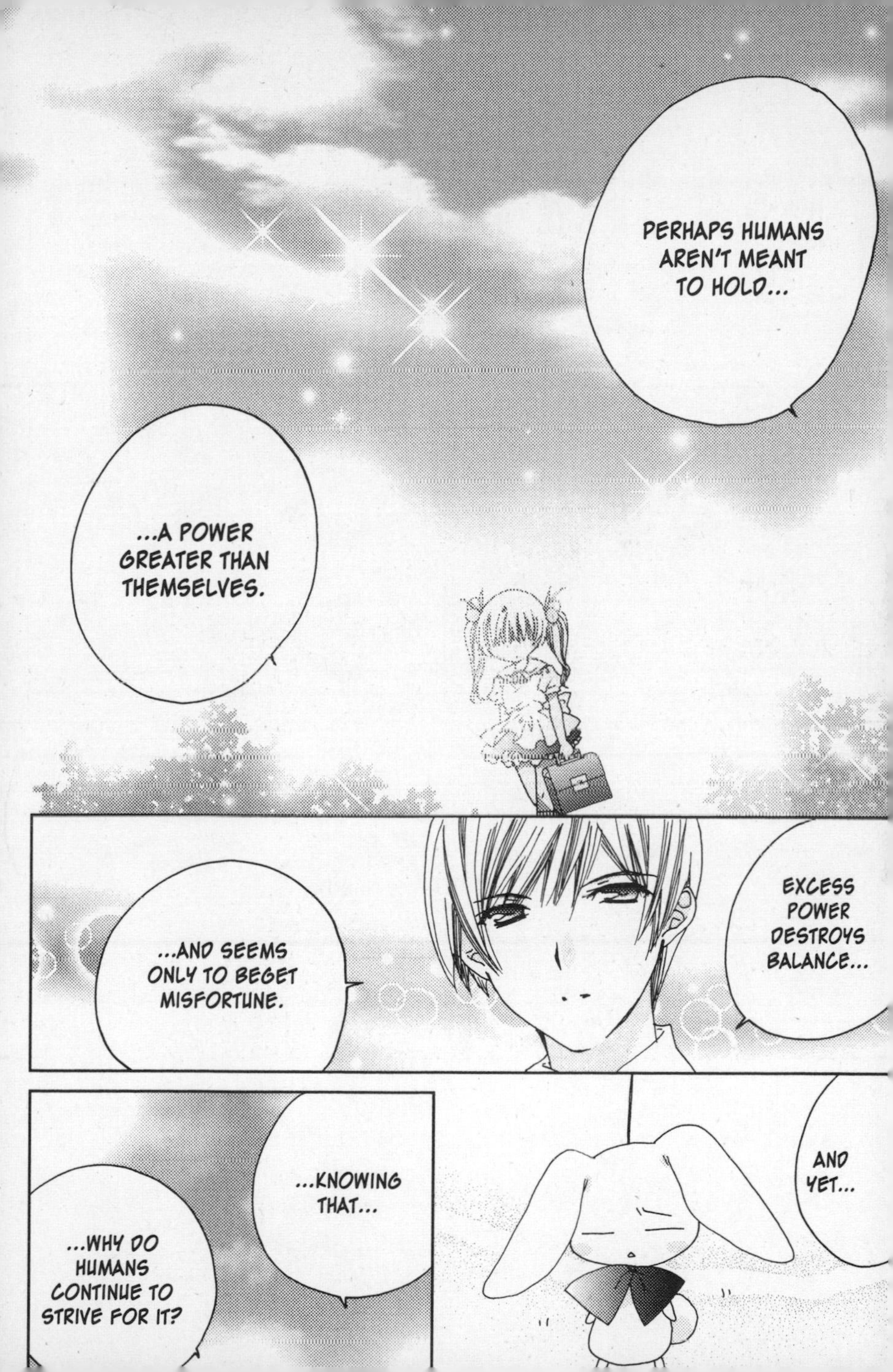
PERHAPS HUMANS AREN'T MEANT TO HOLD...
...A POWER GREATER THAN THEMSELVES.
EXCESS POWER DESTROYS BALANCE...
...AND SEEMS ONLY TO BEGET MISFORTUNE.
AND YET...
...KNOWING THAT...
...WHY DO HUMANS CONTINUE TO STRIVE FOR IT?

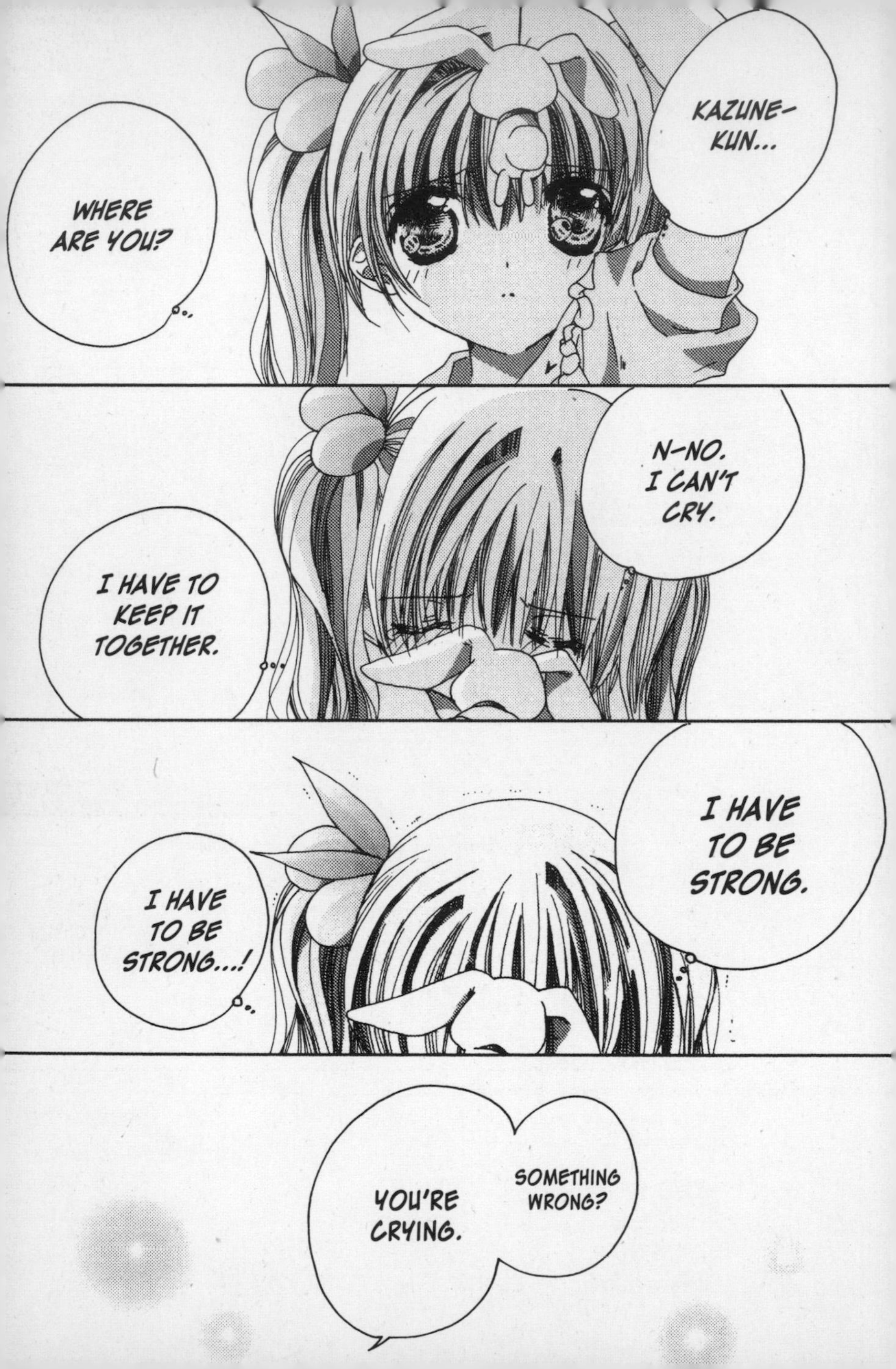
KAZUNE-KUN...
WHERE ARE YOU?
N-NO. I CAN'T CRY.
I HAVE TO KEEP IT TOGETHER.
I HAVE TO BE STRONG.
I HAVE TO BE STRONG...!
SOMETHING WRONG?
YOU'RE CRYING.

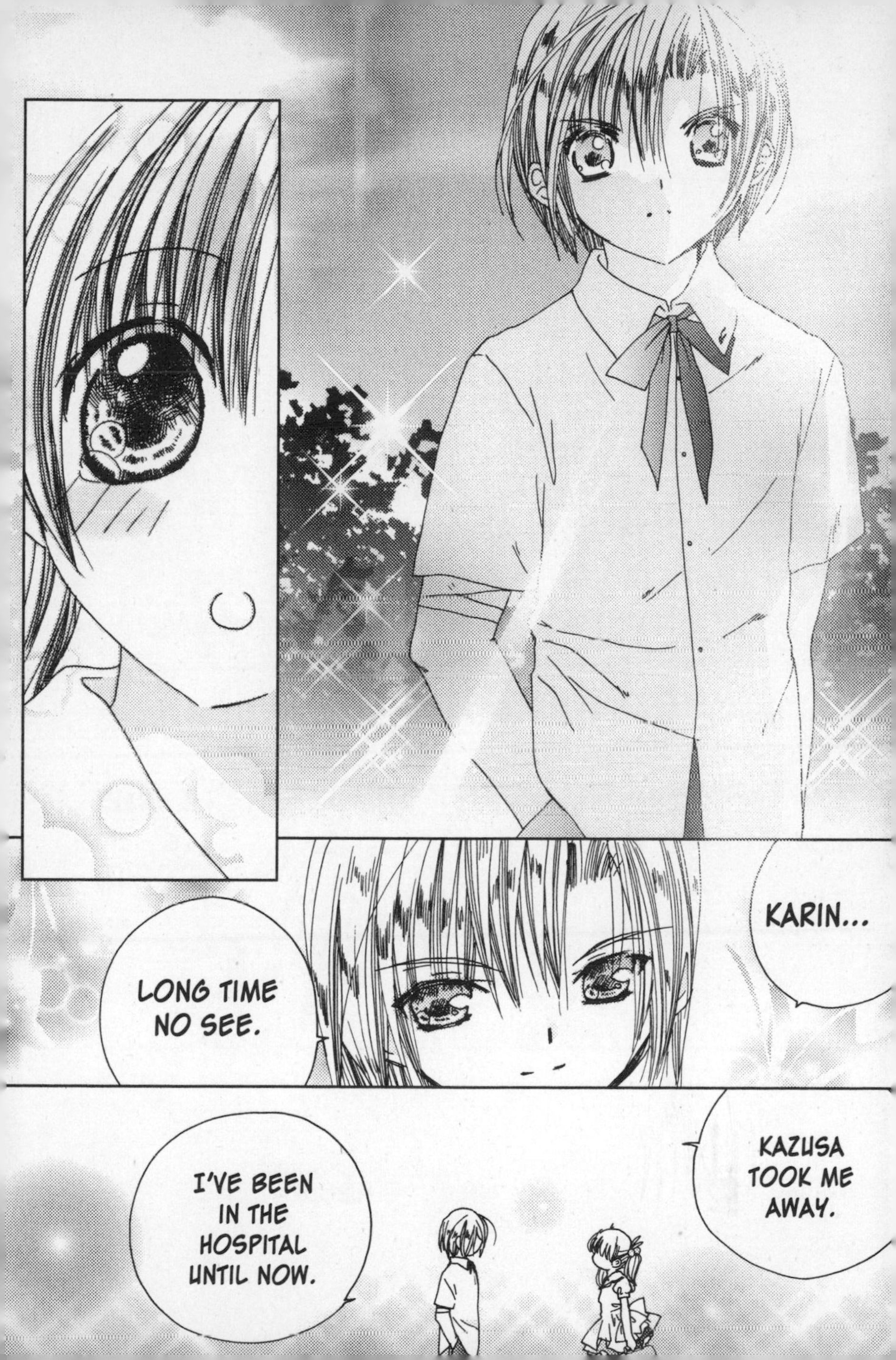
KARIN...
LONG TIME NO SEE.
KAZUSA TOOK ME AWAY.
I'VE BEEN IN THE HOSPITAL UNTIL NOW.

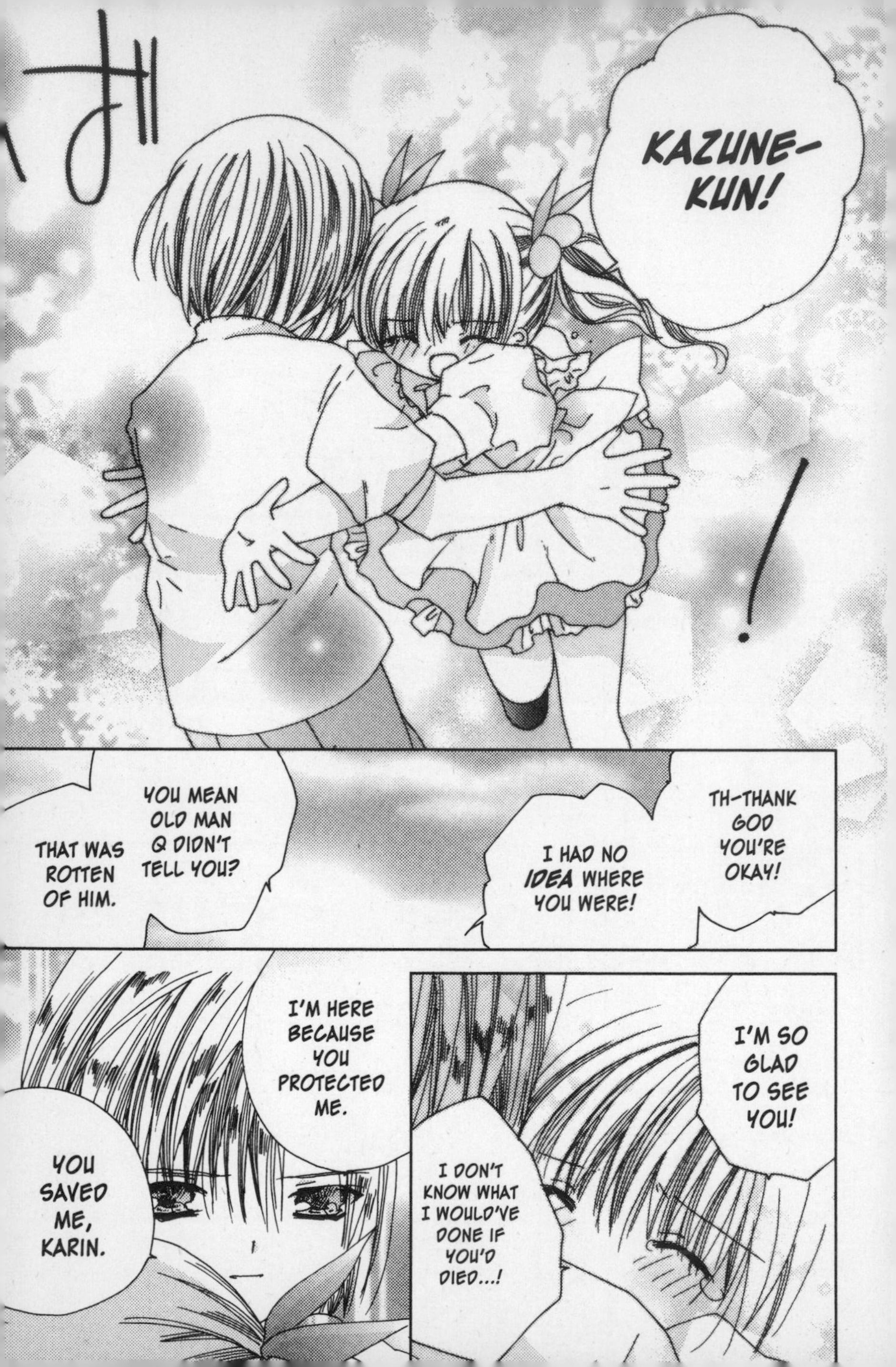
KAZUNE-KUN!
!
TH-THANK GOD YOU'RE OKAY!
I HAD NO *IDEA* WHERE YOU WERE!
YOU MEAN OLD MAN Q DIDN'T TELL YOU?
THAT WAS ROTTEN OF HIM.
I'M SO GLAD TO SEE YOU!
I DON'T KNOW WHAT I WOULD'VE DONE IF YOU'D DIED...!
I'M HERE BECAUSE YOU PROTECTED ME.
YOU SAVED ME, KARIN.

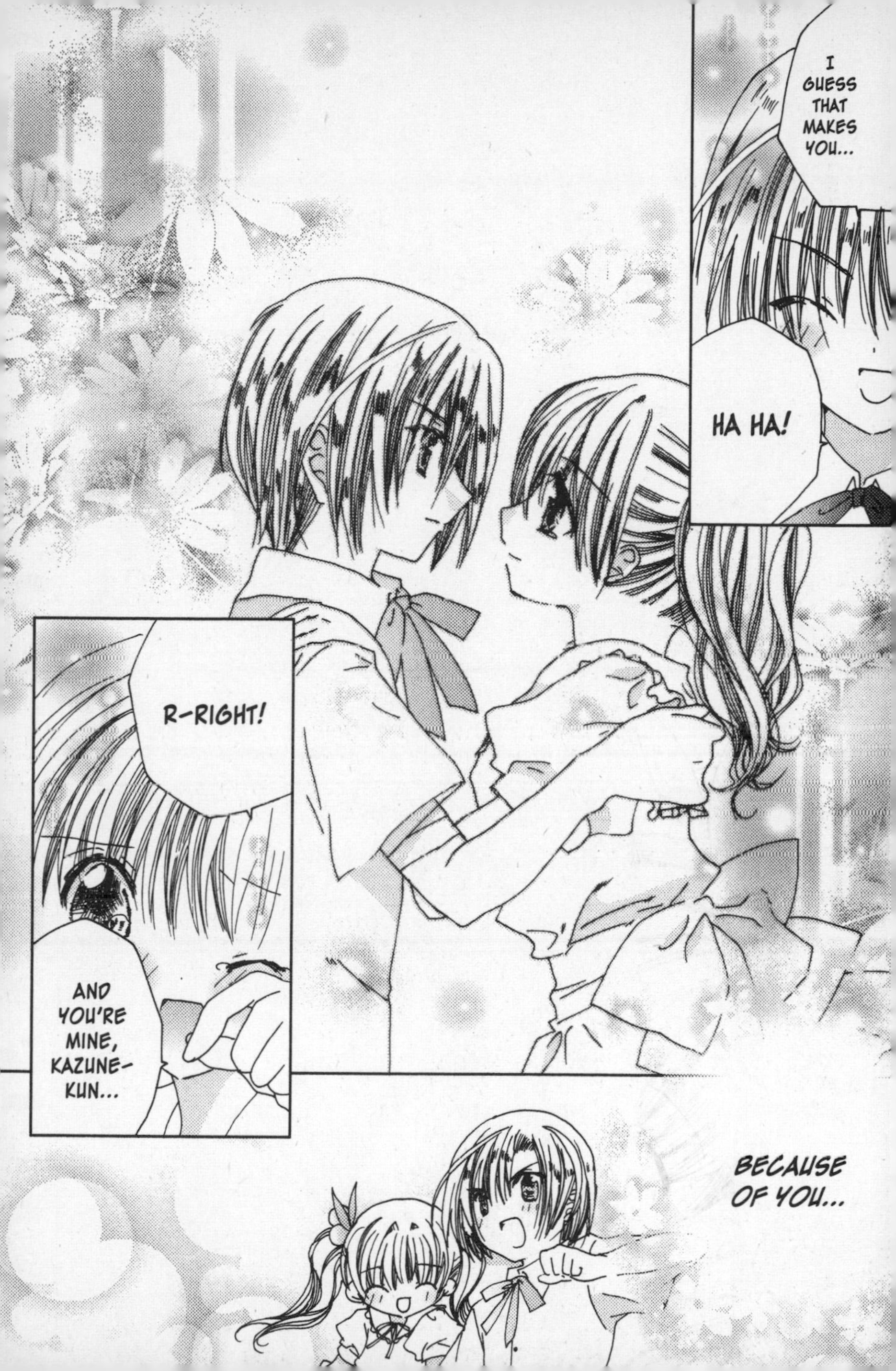
I GUESS THAT MAKES YOU...
HA HA!
R-RIGHT!
AND YOU'RE MINE, KAZUNE-KUN...
BECAUSE OF YOU...

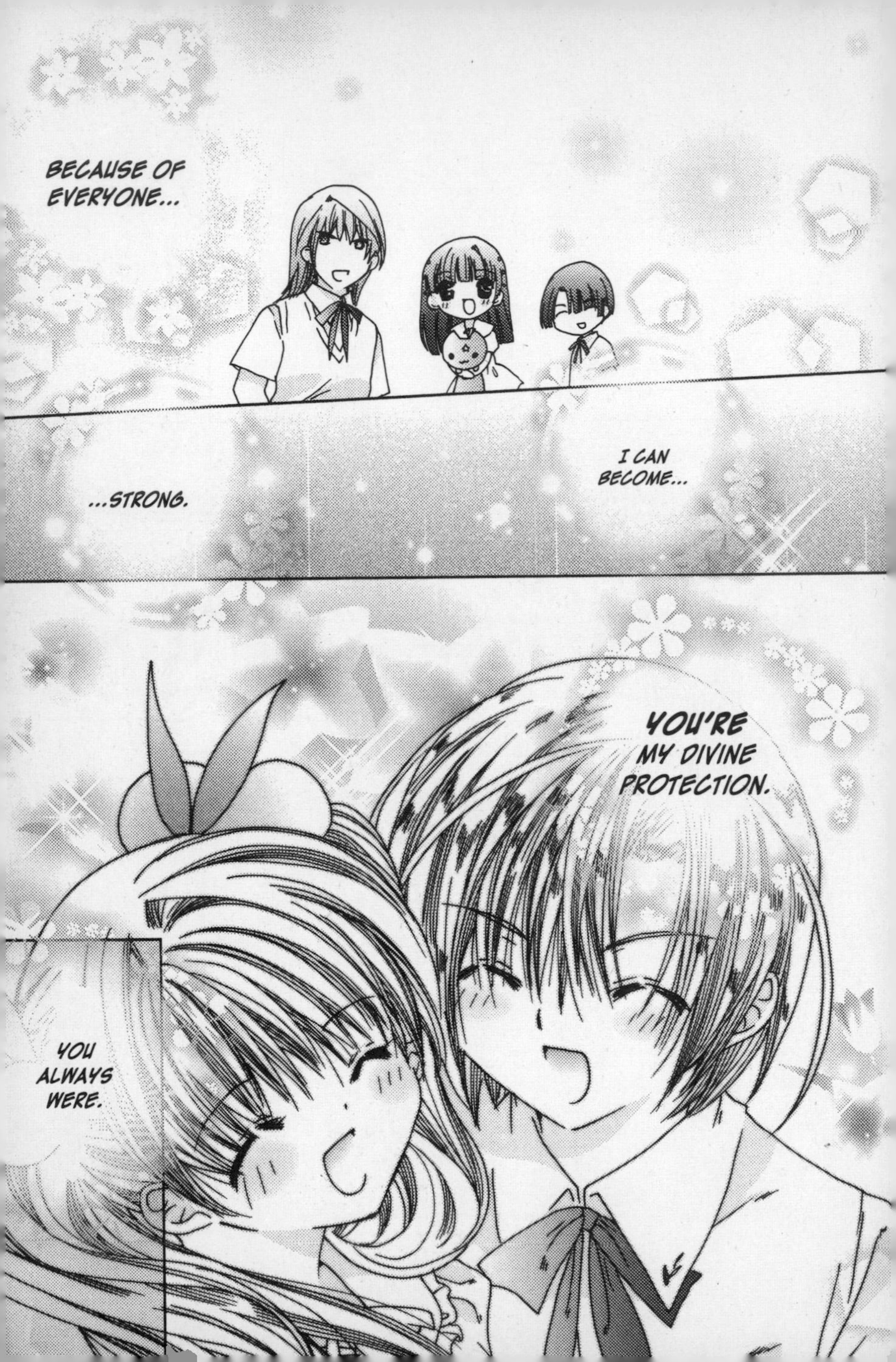
BECAUSE OF EVERYONE...
I CAN BECOME...
...STRONG.
YOU'RE MY DIVINE PROTECTION.
YOU ALWAYS WERE.

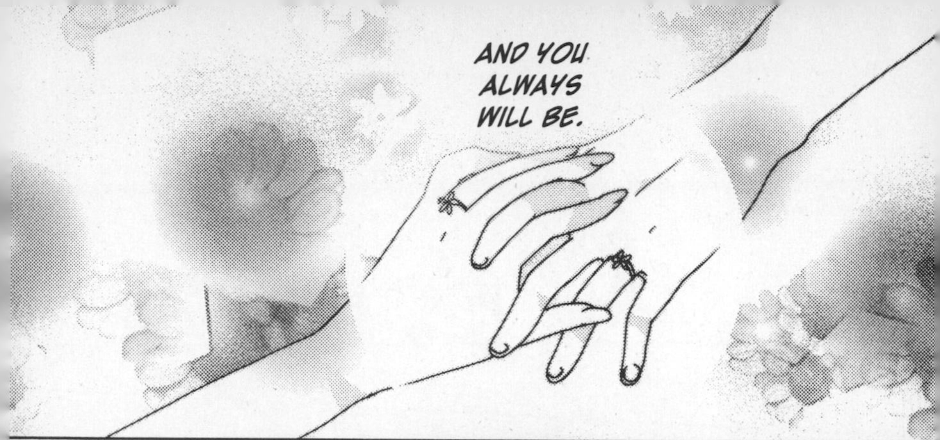
AND YOU ALWAYS WILL BE.

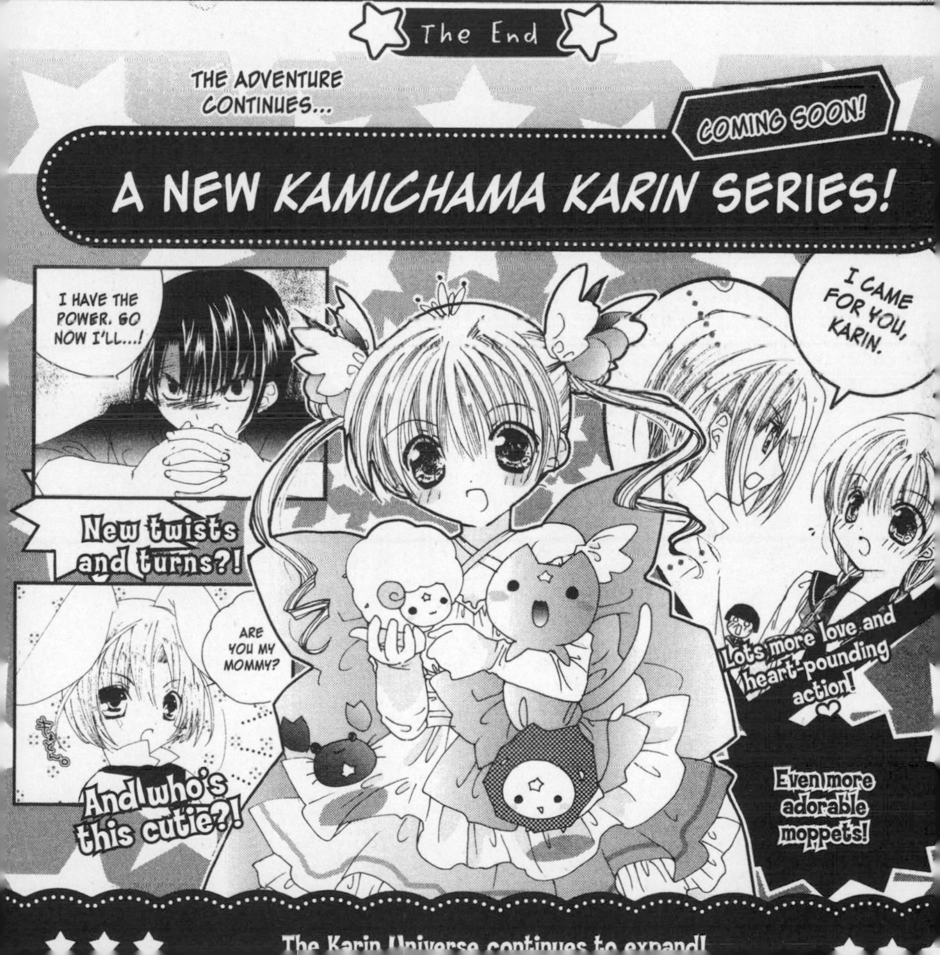
The End
THE ADVENTURE CONTINUES...
COMING SOON!
A NEW KAMICHAMA KARIN SERIES!
I CAME FOR YOU, KARIN.
I HAVE THE POWER. SO NOW I'LL...!
New twists and turns?!
ARE YOU MY MOMMY?
And who's this cutie?!
Lots more love and heart-pounding action!
Even more adorable moppets!
The Karin Universe continues to expand!

- Hey there! Thanks so much for reading through *Kamichama Karin 7*!
- So the series is finally over! Plenty of mysteries have been uncovered, and now the story will continue into the new series. In addition to expanding storylines from these seven books, I'll also be unveiling brand new ones--so sit tight!
- Once again, thank you so much for supporting *Kamichama Karin* through its seven volume run. I'll be starting the new series off fresh and with renewed vigor, so please check it out!

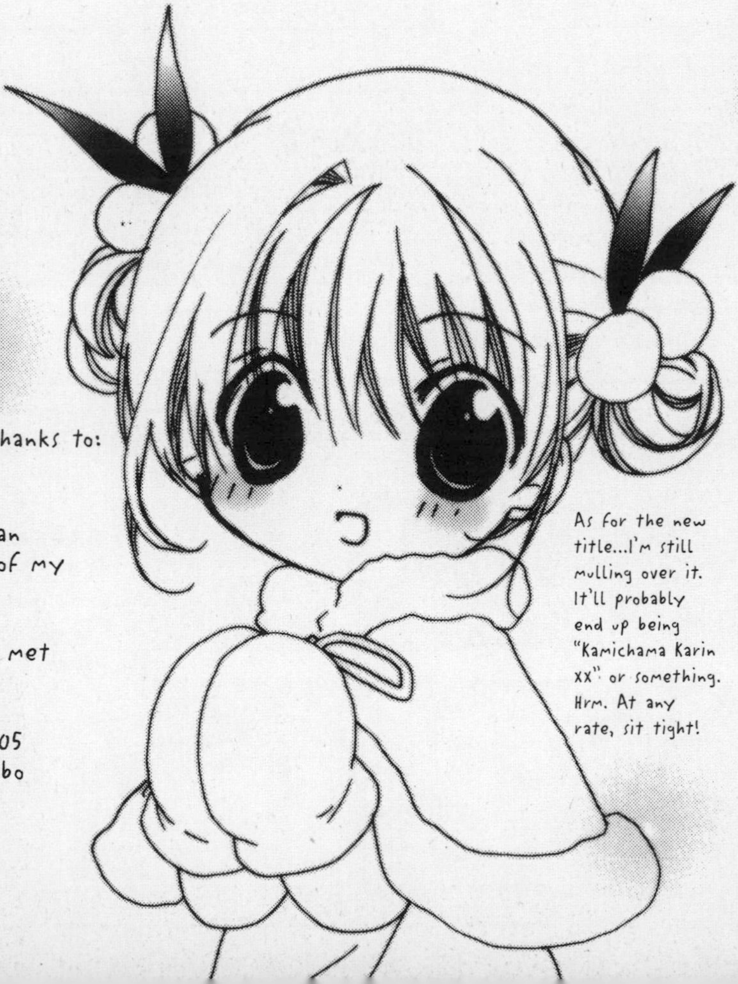

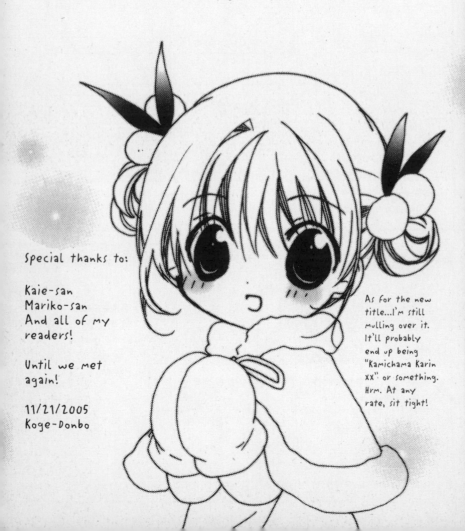

Special thanks to:

Kaie-san
Mariko-san
And all of my readers!

Until we met again!

11/21/2005
Koge-Donbo

As for the new title...I'm still mulling over it. It'll probably end up being "Kamichama Karin XX" or something. Hrm. At any rate, sit tight!

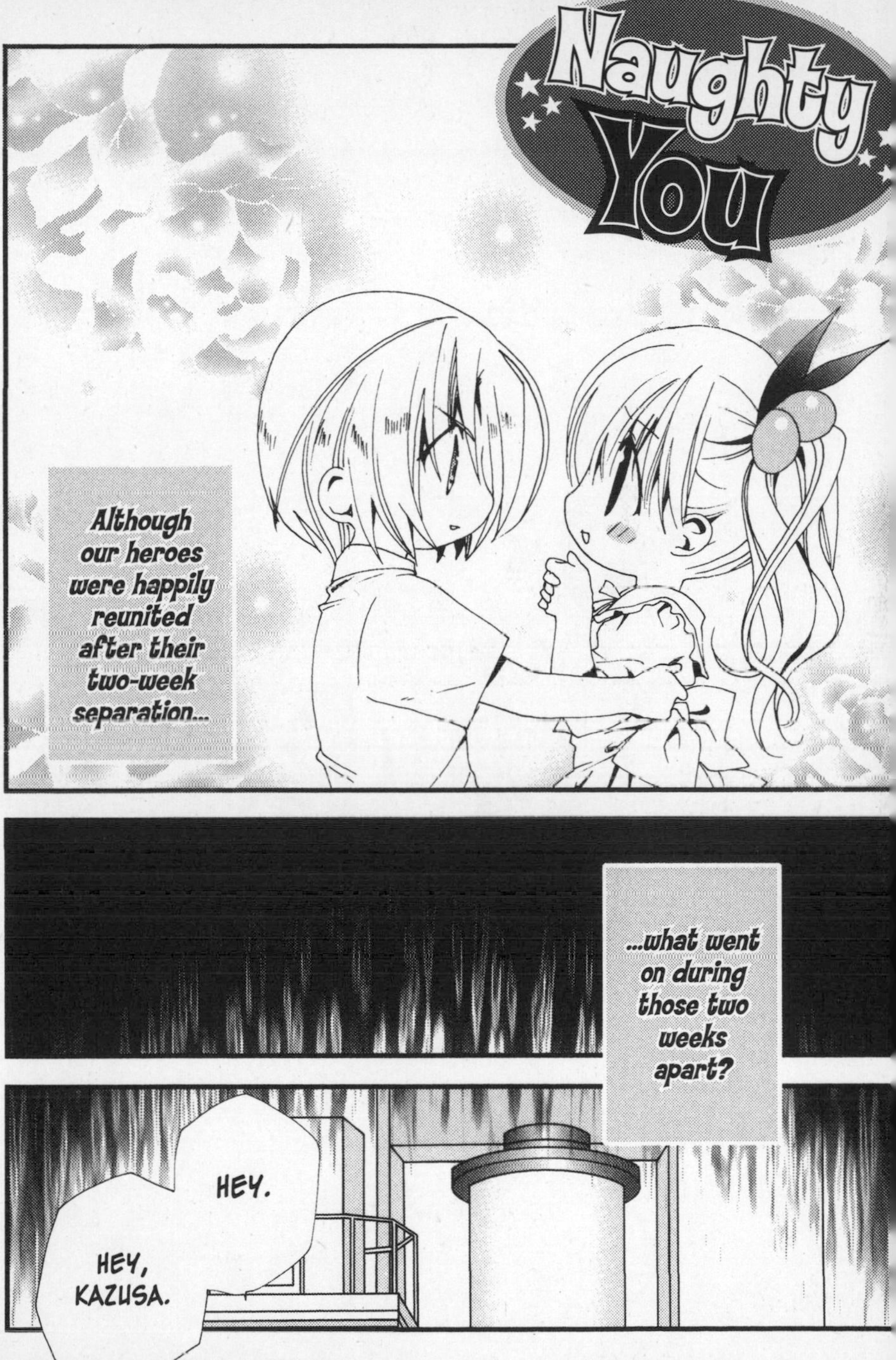
Naughty You
Although our heroes were happily reunited after their two-week separation...
...what went on during those two weeks apart?
HEY.
HEY, KAZUSA.

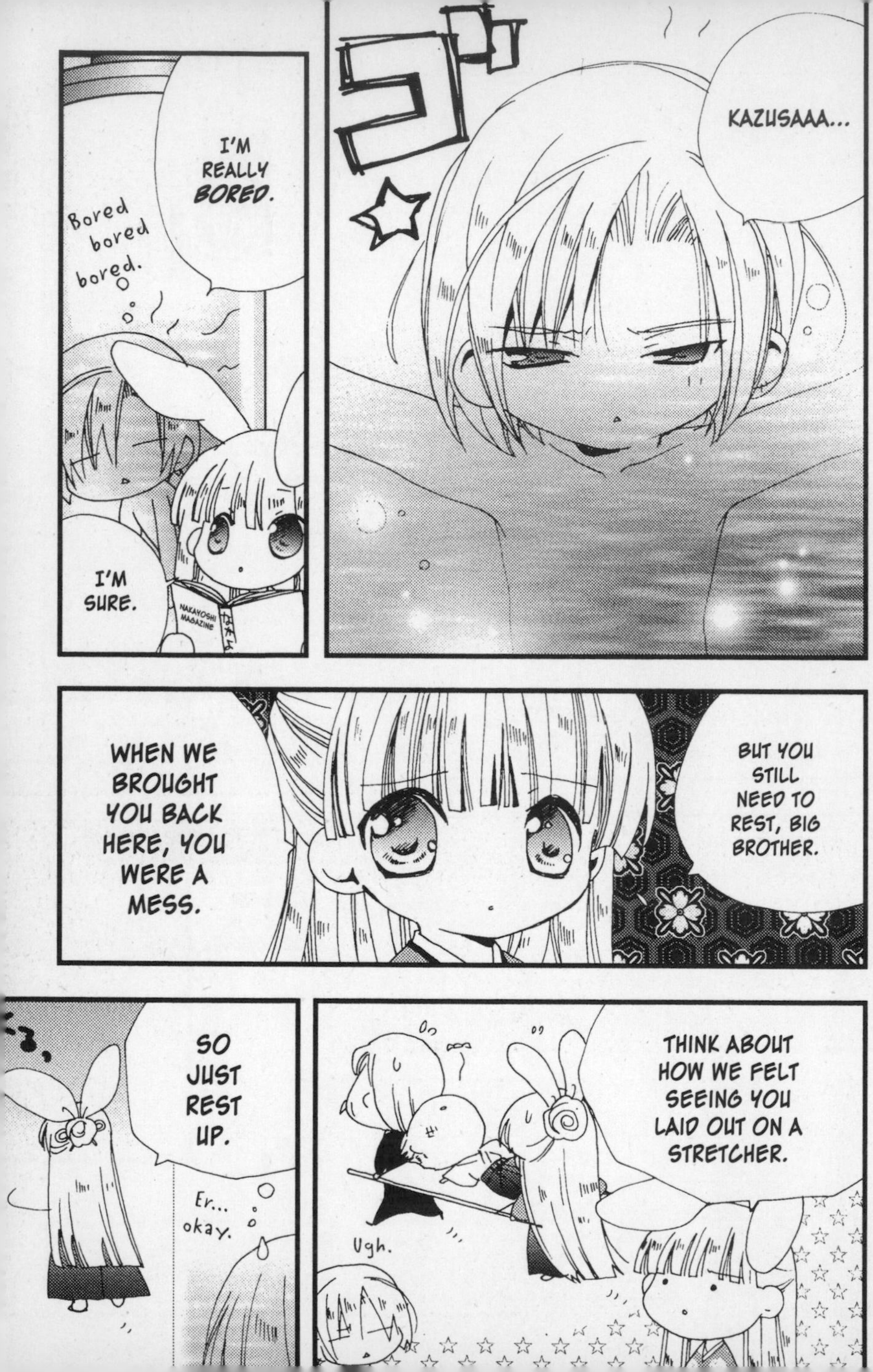
KAZUSAAA...
I'M REALLY BORED.
Bored bored bored.
I'M SURE.
NAKAYOSHI MAGAZINE
BUT YOU STILL NEED TO REST, BIG BROTHER.
WHEN WE BROUGHT YOU BACK HERE, YOU WERE A MESS.
THINK ABOUT HOW WE FELT SEEING YOU LAID OUT ON A STRETCHER.
Ugh.
SO JUST REST UP.
Er... okay.

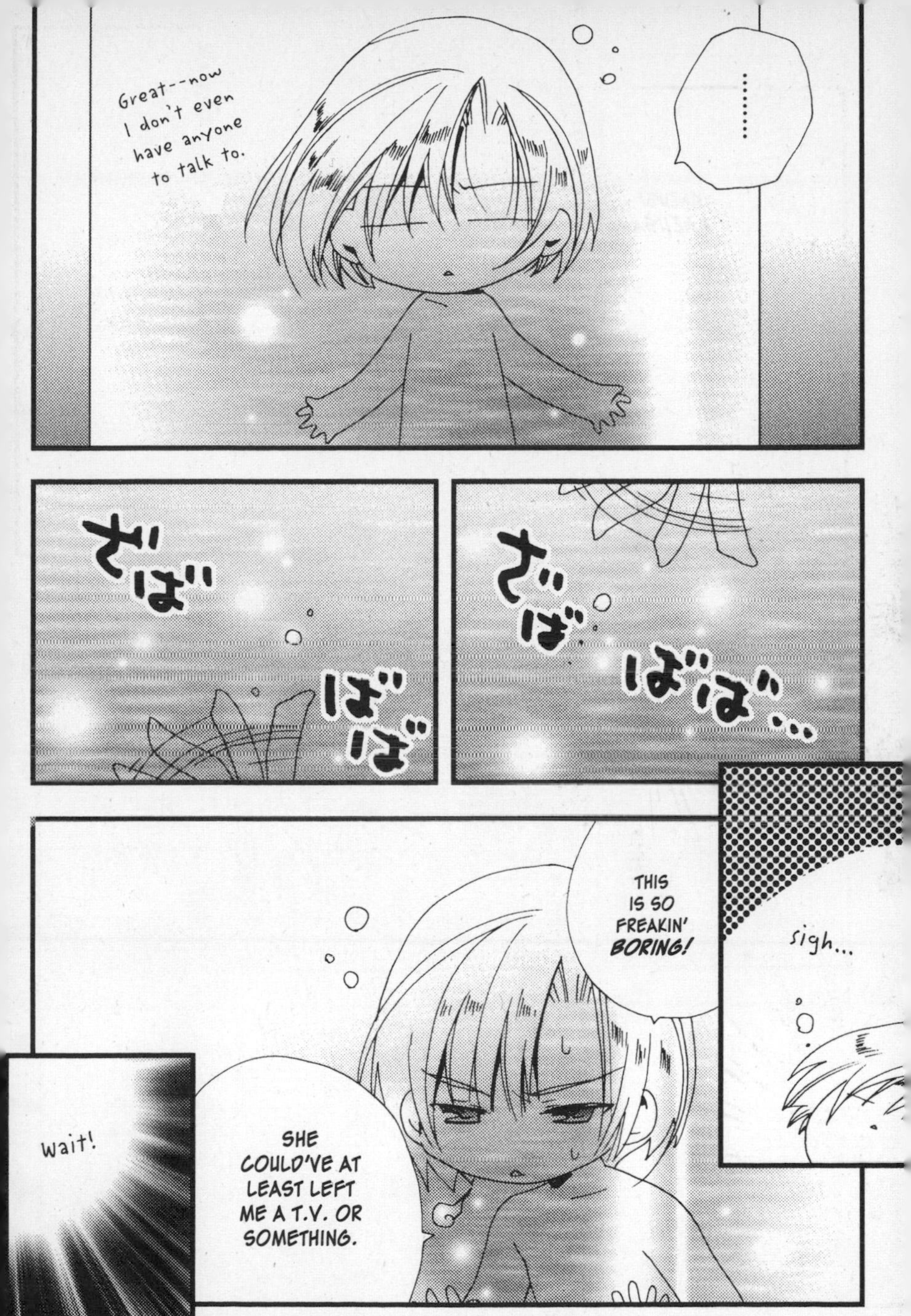

......
Great--now I don't even have anyone to talk to.
ざば ばば...
ざば ばば
sigh...
THIS IS SO FREAKIN' BORING!
SHE COULD'VE AT LEAST LEFT ME A T.V. OR SOMETHING.
Wait!

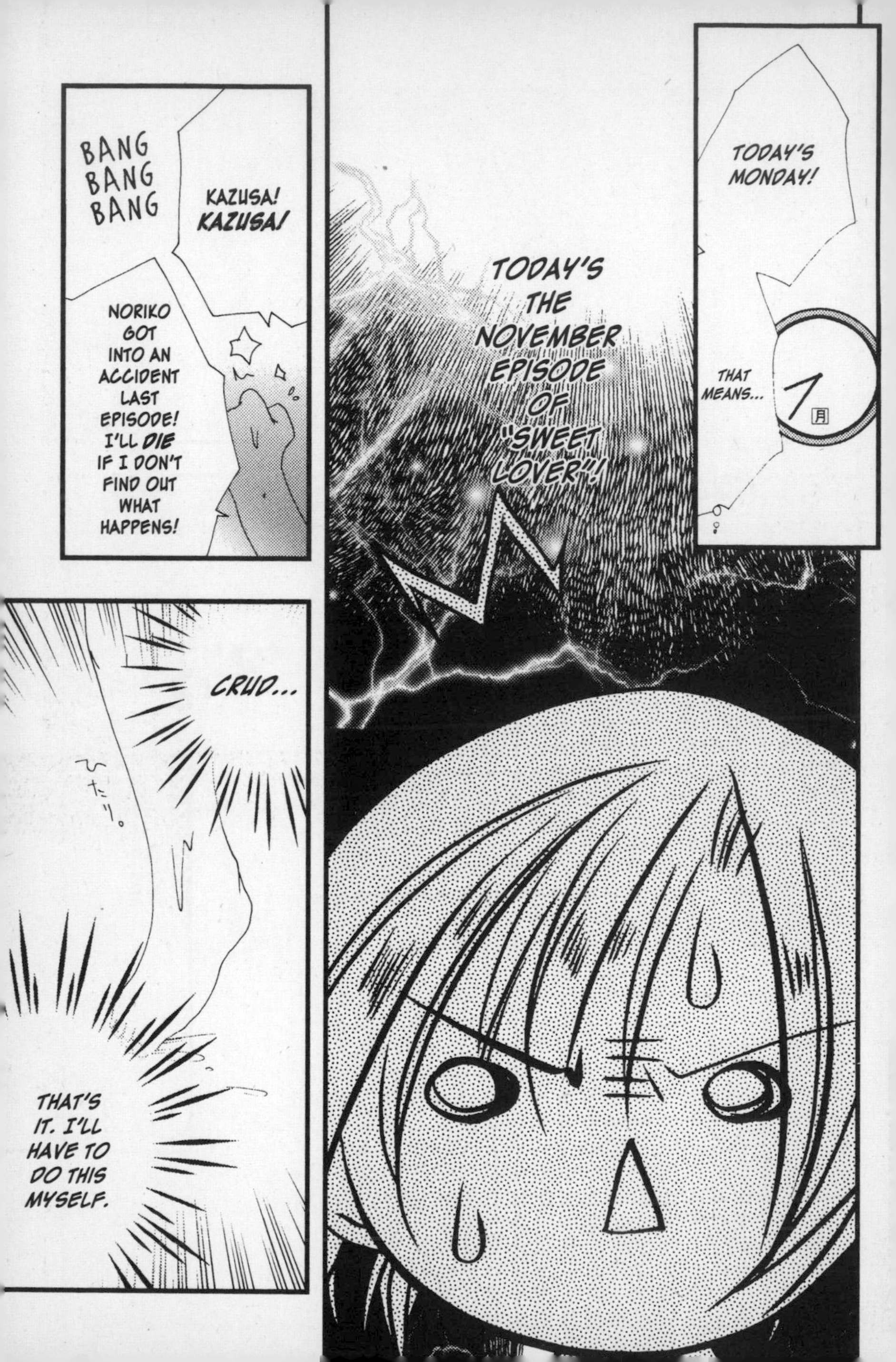
TODAY'S MONDAY!
THAT MEANS...
月
TODAY'S THE NOVEMBER EPISODE OF "SWEET LOVER"!
BANG BANG BANG
KAZUSA! KAZUSA!
NORIKO GOT INTO AN ACCIDENT LAST EPISODE! I'LL DIE IF I DON'T FIND OUT WHAT HAPPENS!
CRUD...
ぴたり。
THAT'S IT. I'LL HAVE TO DO THIS MYSELF.

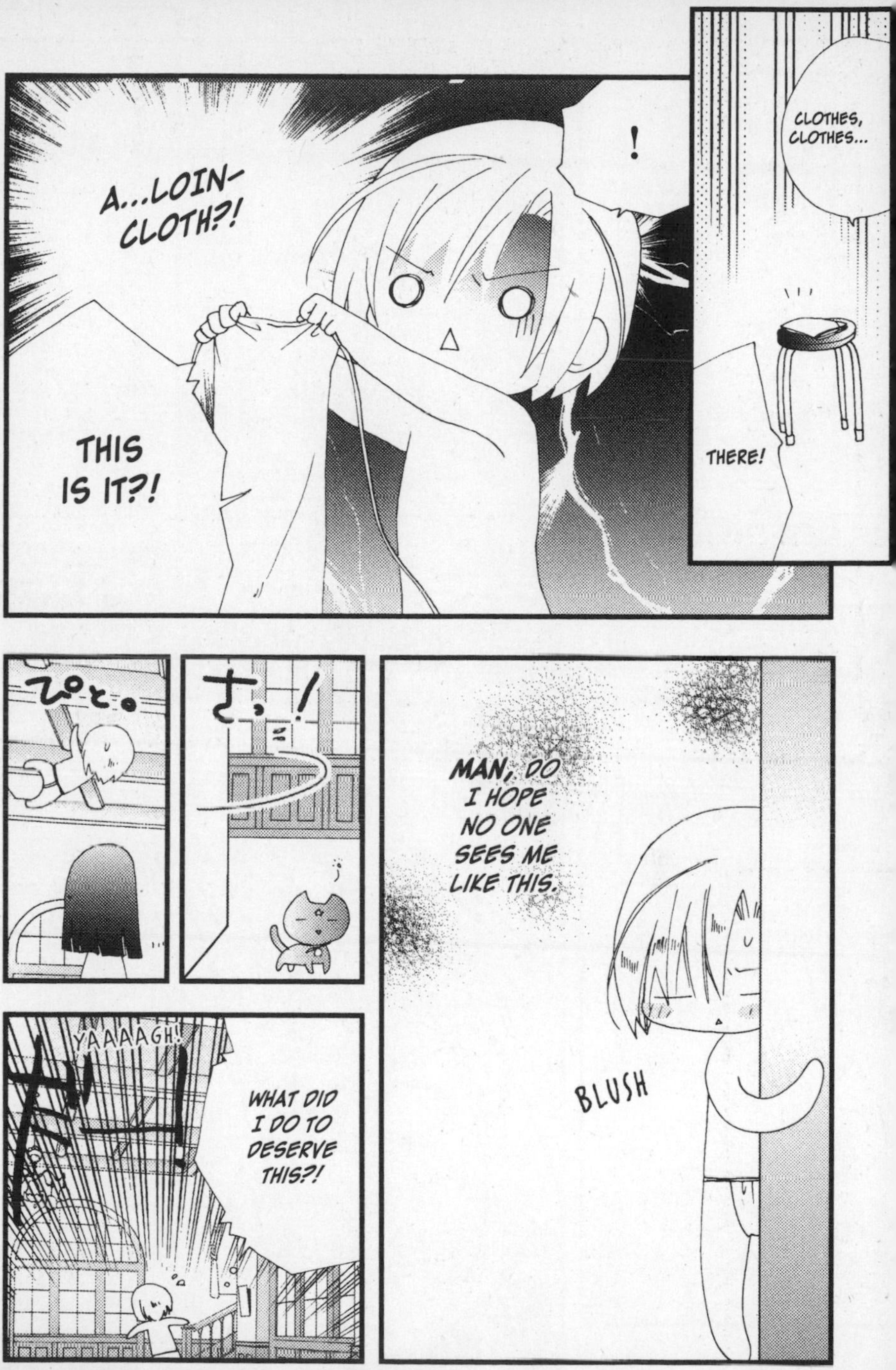
CLOTHES, CLOTHES...
THERE!
!
A...LOIN-CLOTH?!
THIS IS IT?!
MAN, DO I HOPE NO ONE SEES ME LIKE THIS.
BLUSH
さっ!
ぴと。
YAAAAGH!
WHAT DID I DO TO DESERVE THIS?!

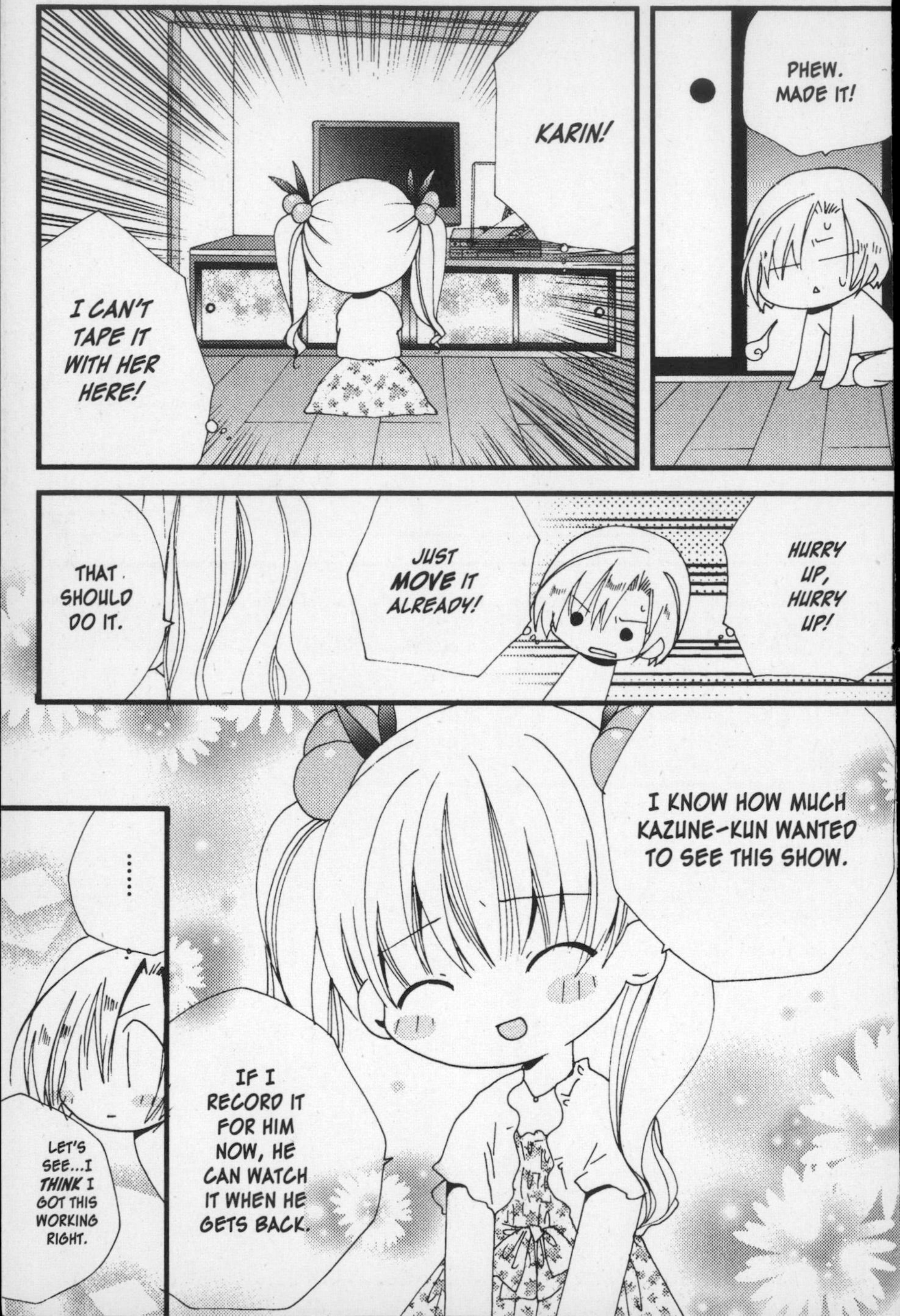
PHEW. MADE IT!
KARIN!
I CAN'T TAPE IT WITH HER HERE!
HURRY UP, HURRY UP!
JUST **MOVE** IT ALREADY!
THAT SHOULD DO IT.
I KNOW HOW MUCH KAZUNE-KUN WANTED TO SEE THIS SHOW.
IF I RECORD IT FOR HIM NOW, HE CAN WATCH IT WHEN HE GETS BACK.
LET'S SEE...I **THINK** I GOT THIS WORKING RIGHT.
......

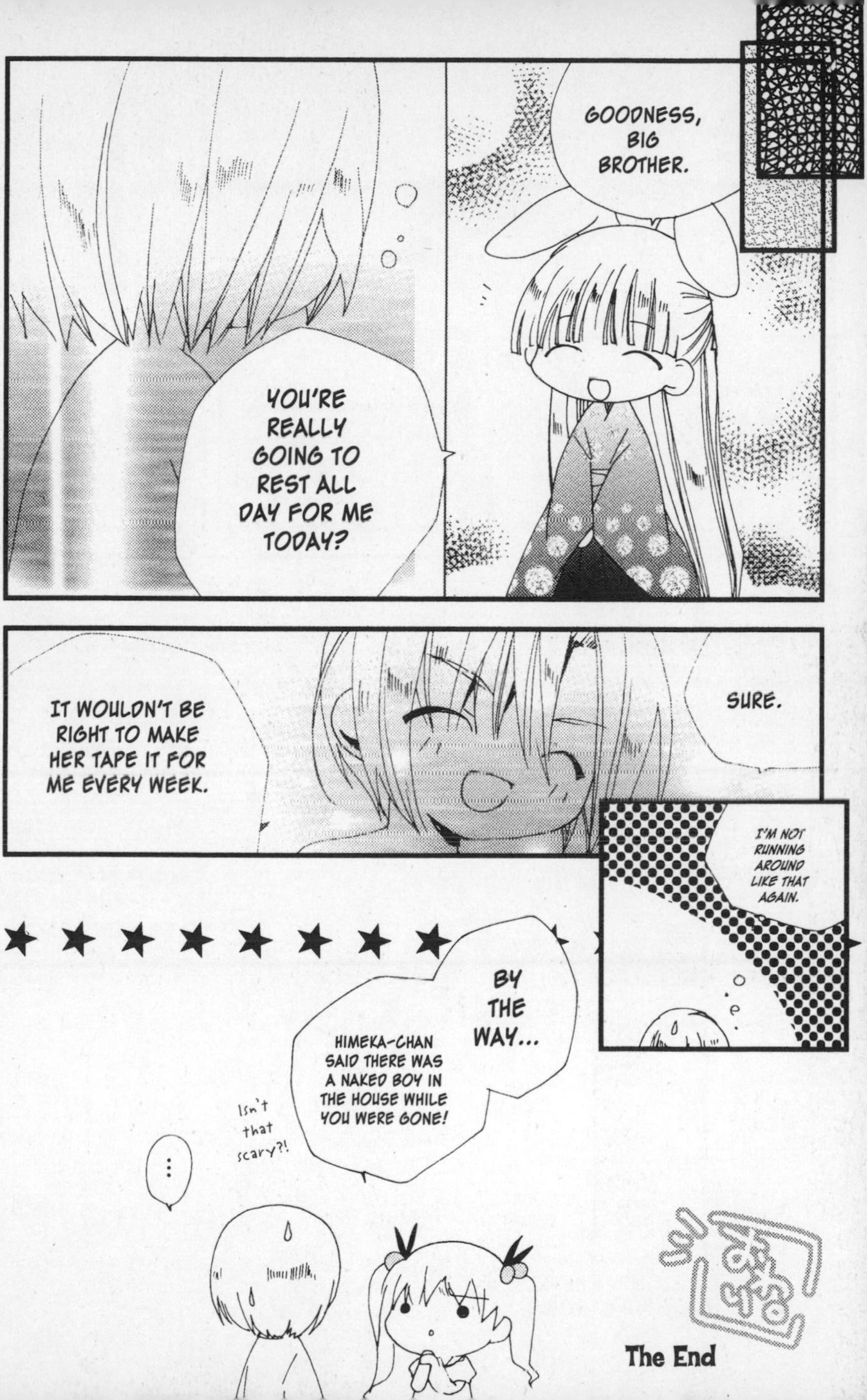
GOODNESS, BIG BROTHER.
YOU'RE REALLY GOING TO REST ALL DAY FOR ME TODAY?
SURE.
IT WOULDN'T BE RIGHT TO MAKE HER TAPE IT FOR ME EVERY WEEK.
I'M NOT RUNNING AROUND LIKE THAT AGAIN.
BY THE WAY...
HIMEKA-CHAN SAID THERE WAS A NAKED BOY IN THE HOUSE WHILE YOU WERE GONE!
Isn't that scary?!
...
The End

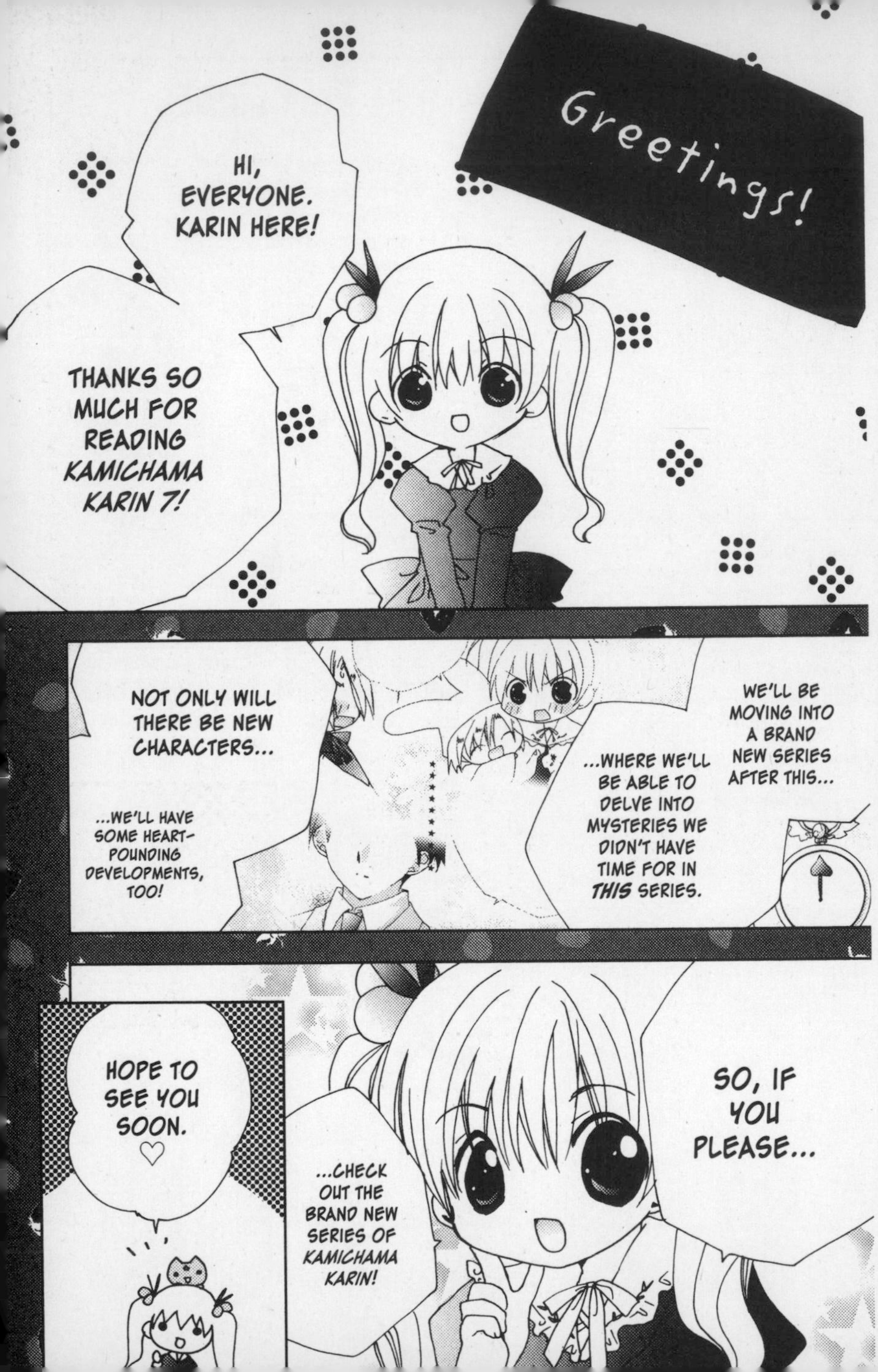
Greetings!
HI, EVERYONE. KARIN HERE!
THANKS SO MUCH FOR READING *KAMICHAMA KARIN 7!*
WE'LL BE MOVING INTO A BRAND NEW SERIES AFTER THIS...
...WHERE WE'LL BE ABLE TO DELVE INTO MYSTERIES WE DIDN'T HAVE TIME FOR IN *THIS* SERIES.
NOT ONLY WILL THERE BE NEW CHARACTERS...
...WE'LL HAVE SOME HEART-POUNDING DEVELOPMENTS, TOO!
SO, IF YOU PLEASE...
...CHECK OUT THE BRAND NEW SERIES OF *KAMICHAMA KARIN!*
HOPE TO SEE YOU SOON. ♡

It's...*sniff*...the very last edition of...
Kamichama Karin Fan Art!

Karin♀+kazune♂ Forever♡

Well...what can I say? It's been quite the ride with our intrepid heroine and her crew of gods, goddesses, cats and boys! I can't tell you how much I've enjoyed your wonderful letters and art, and I am truly sorry I wasn't able to include all of it in the books. -_-' But don't worry! We've kept it all, and are sending it to Koge-Donbo in Japan! Hopefully she'll get a kick out of seeing so many devoted English-speaking fans. Meanwhile, without further ado, I shall turn the stage over to...you guys!

Joy Ortiz
Rio Piedras, PR

WHEN we was LITTLE KAMICHAMA

Anna Wong
Oakland, CA

By:Anna Wong
4-1-06

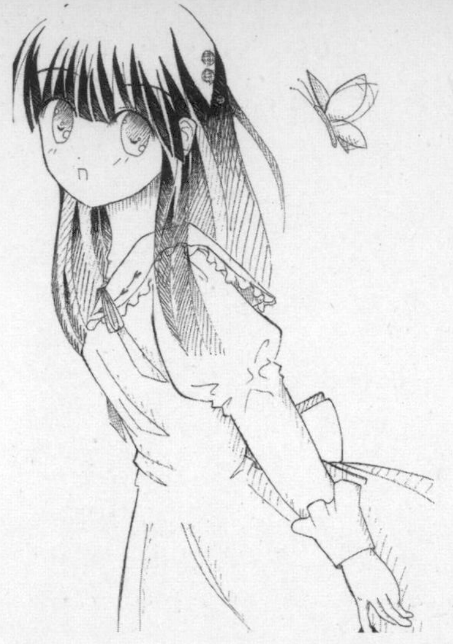

Anna Wong too!
Oakland, CA

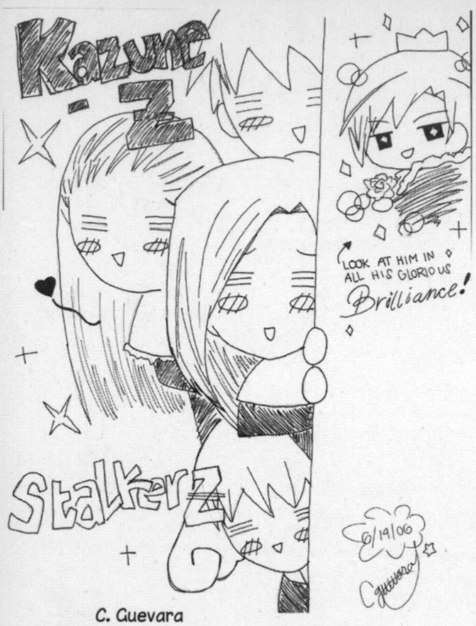
Kazune-Z
Stalkerz
LOOK AT HIM IN ALL HIS GLORIOUS Brilliance!
6/14/06

C. Guevara
Parts unknown, U.S.

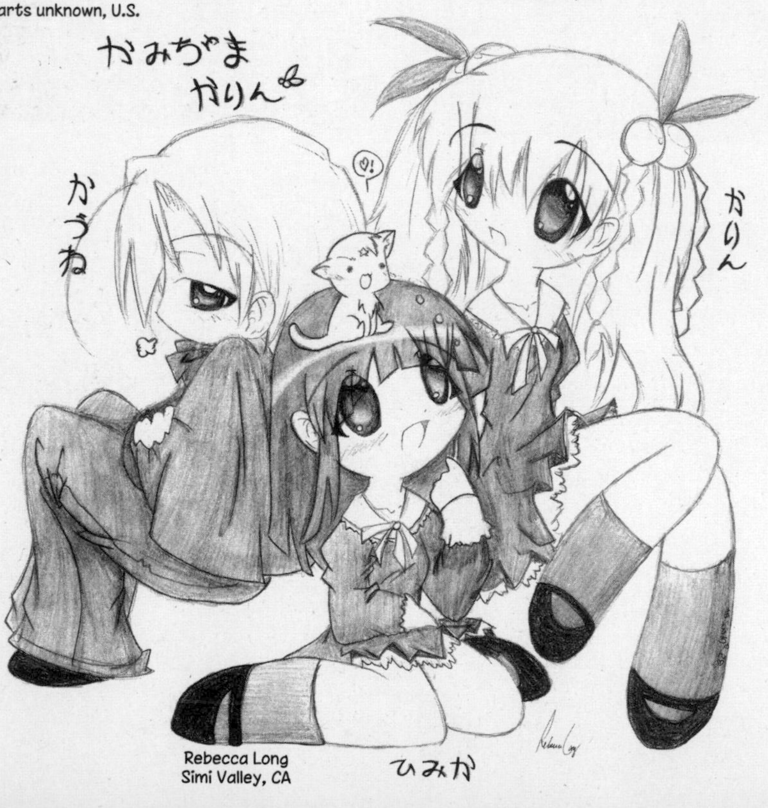
かみちゃま
かりん
かずね
かりん
ひみか

Rebecca Long
Simi Valley, CA

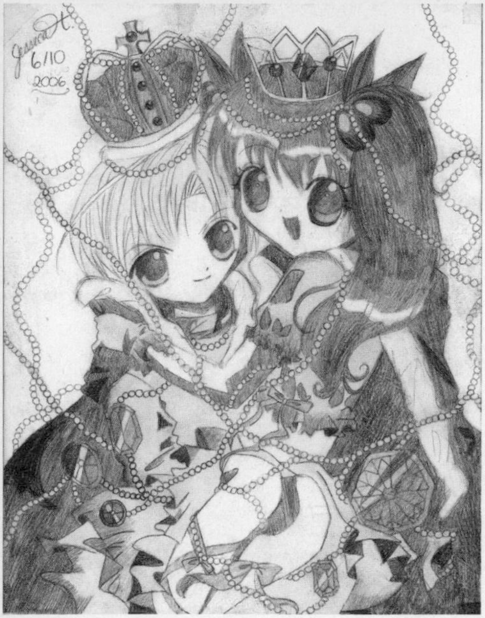
Jessica H.
6/10
2006

Jessica Hannah
Valencia, CA

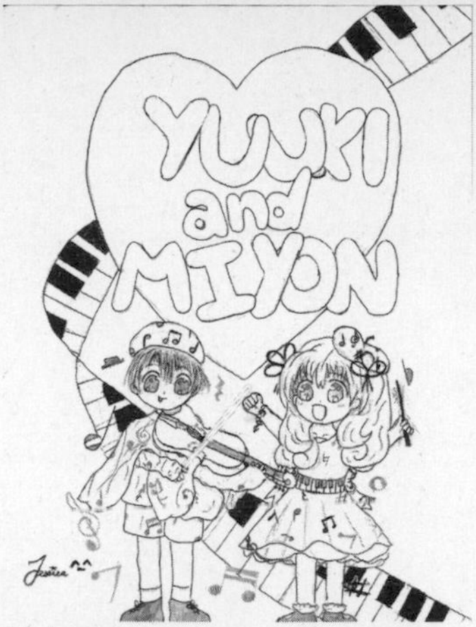
YUUKI
and
MIYON

Jessica Nguyen
London, ON, Canada

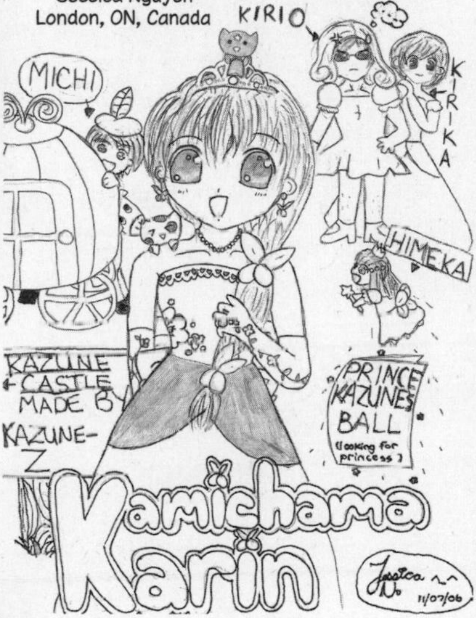
KIRIO
MICHI
KIRIKA
HIMEKA
KAZUNE CASTLE MADE BY KAZUNE-Z
PRINCE KAZUNES BALL
(looking for princess)
Kamichama
Karin
Jessica N. ^^
11/07/06

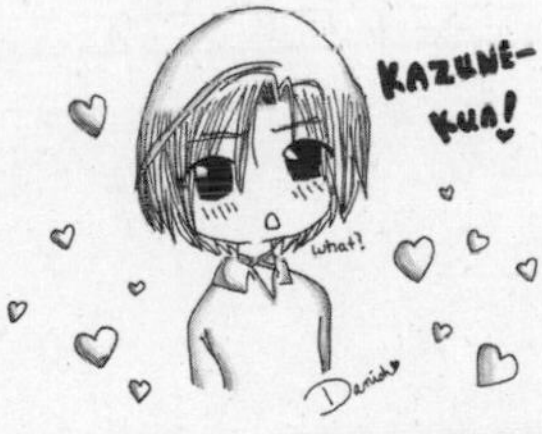
KAZUNE-KUN!
what!

Dana Kalnick
Newtown Square, PA

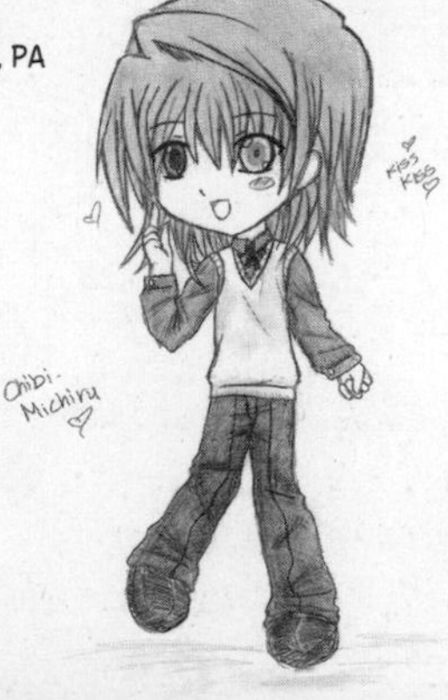
Chibi-Michiru

Ashlyn Yamamoto
Monterey Park, CA

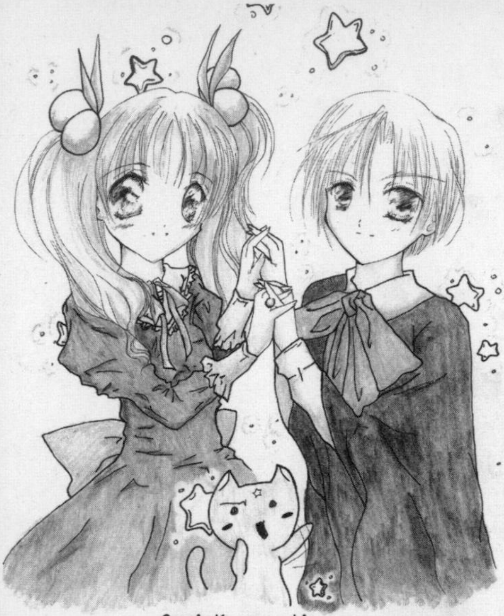

Carrie Kraszewski
New Derry, PA

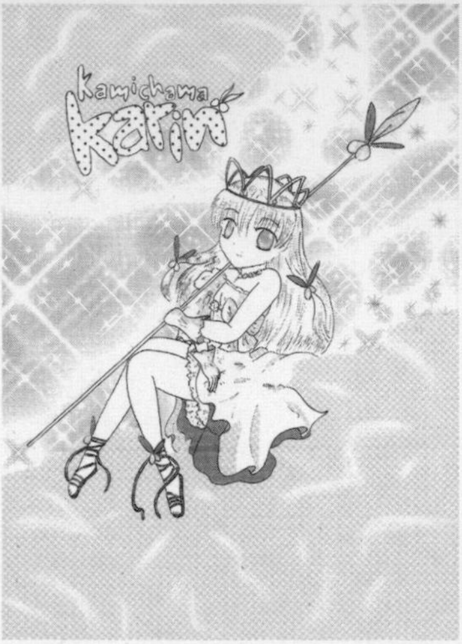
Kamichama Karin

Yvonne Underhill
Barrhead, AB, Canada

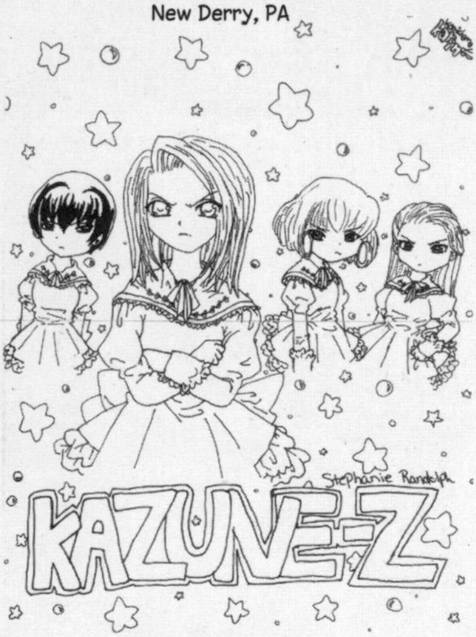
Stephanie Randolph
KAZUNE-Z

Stephanie Randolph
Rockford, IL

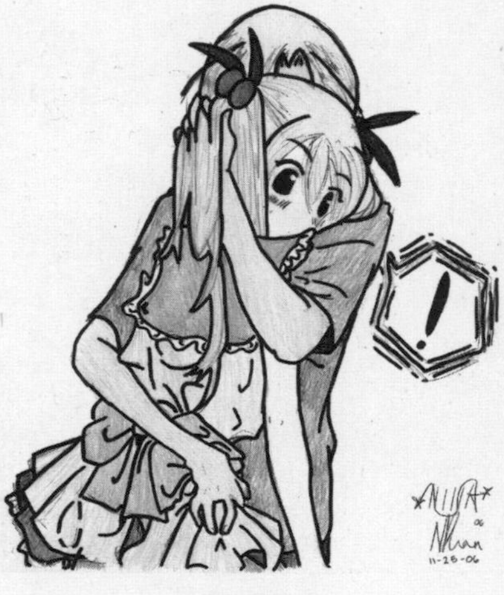
11-28-06

Nina Phan
Jeffersonville, IN

And that's a wrap! Thanks once again for the art and the memories...and most of all, thank you for your support of Kamichama Karin!
–Kamichama Carol, your humble editor alway-Z

AVALON HIGH
CORONATION

VOLUME 1 • THE MERLIN PROPHECY

#1 New York Times bestselling author Meg Cabot's first ever manga!

Avalon High: Coronation continues the story of Meg Cabot's mega-hit novel *Avalon High*. Is Ellie's new boyfriend really the reincarnated King Arthur? Is his step-brother out to kill him? Will good triumph over evil—and will Ellie have to save the day AGAIN?

Don't miss *Avalon High: Coronation #1: The Merlin Prophecy*—in stores July 2007!

MEG CABOT

STOP!

This is the back of the book.
You wouldn't want to spoil a great ending!

This book is printed "manga-style," in the authentic Japanese right-to-left format. Since none of the artwork has been flipped or altered, readers get to experience the story just as the creator intended. You've been asking for it, so TOKYOPOP® delivered: authentic, hot-off-the-press, and far more fun!

DIRECTIONS

1
2
3
4
5
6
7
8
9
10

If this is your first time reading manga-style, here's a quick guide to help you understand how it works.

It's easy... just start in the top right panel and follow the numbers. Have fun, and look for more 100% authentic manga from TOKYOPOP®!

THE MANGA REVOLUTION · LEADING · 漫画革命

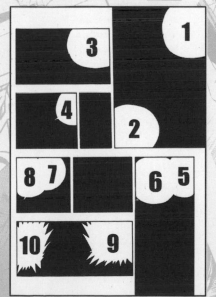

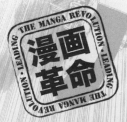